VOLUME 1: Africa

UNDERSTANDING CIVIL WAR

Evidence and Analysis

Edited by
Paul Collier
Nicholas Sambanis

THE WORLD BANK

©2005 The International Bank for Reconstruction and Development / The World Bank
1818 H Street NW
Washington DC 20433
Telephone: 202-473-1000
Internet: www.worldbank.org
E-mail: feedback@worldbank.org

1 2 3 4 08 07 06 05

Cover photo: ©Getty Images/Tyler Hicks

ISBN-10: 0-8213-6047-7
ISBN-13: 978-0-8213-6047-7
eISBN: 0-8213-6048-5
DOI: 10.1596/978-0-8213-6047-7

Library of Congress Cataloging-in-Publication Data

Understanding civil war: evidence and analysis / Paul Collier & Nicholas Sambanis, editors.
   p. cm
   Includes bibliographical references and index.
   Contents: v. 1. Africa – v. 2. Europe, Central Asia, and other regions.
   ISBN 0-8213-6047-7 (v. 1: pbk.) – ISBN 0-8213-6049-3 (v. 2: pbk.)
   1. Civil war-Economic aspects–Case studies. 2. War–Causes–Case studies. I. Collier,
Paul. II. Sambanis, Nicholas, 1967-

HB195.U43 2005
330.9–dc22   2005047813

Contents

FIGURES

TABLES

Foreword

The World Bank's role in addressing the ravages caused by violent conflict is historical—its first loans were made to support the reconstruction of Western European countries devastated by the Second World War. Over the following five decades, as most of the world's conflicts amounted to proxy wars between the superpowers or postcolonial independence struggles, the Bank limited its involvement in conflict-affected countries to providing financial capital and rebuilding infrastructure after conflicts had ended. However, in a post–Cold War era marked by an increase in the number and severity of civil conflicts, the Bank found it had to adapt to different and more complex challenges. Two events in the mid-1990s marked a turning point in the Bank's approach to conflict. The first occurred in 1994, when the Bank was asked to administer the multidonor Holst Fund for the West Bank and Gaza; the second occurred in 1995, when the Bank was asked to take the lead with the European Commission in planning and coordinating international support for postconflict recovery in Bosnia-Herzegovina. The Bosnia-Herzegovina program, in particular, broke the mold and formed the basis for a new postconflict framework that was to become a Bank operational policy within a few years.

Realizing that it faced a far more difficult postconflict environment and growing expectations on the part of the international community, in 1997 the Bank created a small locus of expertise in postconflict reconstruction, the Post-Conflict Unit, and defined the parameters for Bank engagement in countries affected by conflict, firmly focused on the Bank's reconstruction role after the conflict ended. To complement this expertise, in August 1997 the Bank created the Post-Conflict Fund, a grant facility to support countries in transition from conflict to sustainable development and encourage innovation and external partnerships in dealing with conflict-affected countries.

Because poverty has proven to be both a cause and a consequence of conflict, toward the late 1990s the Bank sought to redefine its role more broadly in the context of a more comprehensive approach to development, in line with evolving international initiatives to explore the potential role of development assistance and conflict prevention. The Bank shifted its focus from an approach based on rebuilding infrastructure to one that seeks to understand the root causes and drivers of conflict, to integrate a sensitivity to conflict in Bank activities and to promote development assistance that minimizes the potential causes of conflict. In line with this shift in focus, and following a process of discussion and consultation inside and outside the organization, in January 2001 the Executive Directors of the World Bank approved a new and broader operational policy on Development Cooperation and Conflict. To signal this shift in emphasis toward a broader approach to conflict, the Post-Conflict Unit was renamed the Conflict Prevention and Reconstruction Unit.

At the same time that the Bank sought to redefine its operational role more comprehensively in the conflict and development nexus, findings from the Bank's research arm, headed by Paul Collier, opened up the global debate on the economic causes and consequences of conflict. For an institution well stocked with economists, there had been surprisingly little economic analysis or explanations of conflict in the Bank's research and analytical work. Bank economists were inclined to think of conflict as an exogenous shock, akin to a natural disaster or an adverse swing in the terms of trade—an adverse and unfortunate event that happened from time to time, which was not within the confines of the Bank's analytical arsenal and about which little could be done.

As the Bank broadened its approach to conflict, it also sought to gain a better understanding of the causes of conflict, recognizing, as pointed out in its operational policy on Development Cooperation and Conflict, that important knowledge gaps remained on the links between development assistance and conflict. With stronger intellectual underpinnings, the Bank could more effectively design strategies and programs that were sensitive to conflict and thus begin to realize the objective of viewing development through a conflict lens. To this end, in 1999 Paul Collier and his colleagues in the Development Economics Research Group began a major research effort, partly funded by the Post-Conflict Fund, to study the economics of conflict and violence. The approach, which became known as the Collier-Hoeffler model, confirmed the link between poverty and conflict, but some of its other findings were more controversial and sparked a lively international debate, which came to be known as the "greed versus grievance" debate. The main point of contention centered around whether the Collier-Hoeffler model was too narrowly focused on economic explanations and thus ignored genuine grievances, or other causes of conflict suggested in the political science and international relations literatures. Many critics argued that the statistical and econometric techniques used to try to untangle causality, while perhaps helpful in identifying patterns and risk factors, obscured or disregarded the insights and explanations of conflict that can only emerge from the detailed study of individual conflicts.

Partly in response to these concerns, a second and complementary phase of the research on the economics of conflict and violence sought to adopt a comparative case study approach to refine and expand the economics of conflict model. This second phase, also partly funded by the Post-Conflict Fund, is part of the "Political Economy of Civil Wars" project, a collaborative research undertaking between the World Bank and Yale University. The results of the case studies presented in this volume add considerably to our understanding of conflict. Through these case studies, we gain a more nuanced understanding of conflict and the conditions under which different variables influence the outbreak of violence. In addition, a number of important improvements to the Collier-Hoeffler model have been proposed. An important additional benefit of this research is that it may lay to rest the "greed versus grievance" caricature. The research presented here makes it clear that greed and grievances should not be seen as competing explanations of conflict—they are often shades of the same problem.

Ian Bannon
Manager
Conflict Prevention and Reconstruction Unit
World Bank

Preface

Civil wars around the world since 1945 have killed approximately 20 million people and displaced at least 67 million. Despite this massive scale of human misery associated with civil war, the academic community had not concentrated much attention on the problem of civil war until very recently. A major catalyst for increased academic and policy work aimed at understanding civil war and reducing its prevalence was the World Bank project on the "Economics of Political and Criminal Violence." The World Bank research team conceptualized civil war as a development problem and applied economic models to explain the occurrence, duration, and consequences of civil war. This approach seemed appropriate, given that civil wars occur disproportionately in poor countries and retard economic development in entire regions. If poor economic conditions cause civil wars, then we may be able to design economic policy interventions that reduce their occurrence, mitigating the human suffering that they cause.

The World Bank project made important strides in understanding civil war. Quantitative studies by the project's researchers identified a set of statistically significant correlates of civil war. The project's flagship article, "The Collier-Hoeffler Model of Civil War Onset," has been especially prominent in the literature and has inspired much additional research on the relationship between political conflict and economic development. The project's many empirical findings and theoretical arguments were summarized in a Policy Research Report, *Breaking the Conflict Trap: Civil War and Development Policy,* written by Paul Collier and his research team.

Collier and Hoeffler have put forward an economic model of civil war, arguing convincingly that it is not political and social grievance per se that leads to civil war, but rather, for given levels of grievance, it is the opportunity to organize and finance a rebellion that determines if a civil war will occur or not. The determinants of such opportunity in their model are mainly economic. Their model identifies conditions that make rebellion financially viable. This analysis was based on econometric tests using data that cover all countries for about 40 years (from 1960 to 1999).

Ultimately, the results of the Collier-Hoeffler model should be useful for the design of policy. For the moment, we can only draw very broad policy guidelines from the Collier-Hoeffler model. For example, the model (and related empirical results) demonstrates that by increasing the gross domestic product per capita in developing countries, we will be reducing the risk of civil war. But we clearly need more fine-grained, policy-relevant research on civil war before we can design appropriate interventions. Quantitative studies alone are unlikely to pinpoint specific policies that can reduce war risk in different countries at different stages of a conflict's cycle. To design targeted policy interventions, but also to develop further our theoretical understanding of civil war, we need to understand *how* and *when* the explanatory variables in the Collier-Hoeffler model will lead to civil war. An understanding of the *how* and *when* will improve our ability to identify countries at greater risk of an outbreak of civil war, and the more we understand the process of conflict escalation, the better we will become at designing time-sensitive policy interventions. This two-volume book takes the next step in that direction, by systematically applying the Collier-Hoeffler model to several countries, using a comparative case study design to draw lessons that can help us refine and expand the theory of civil war. The book also makes a methodological contribution as it illustrates a useful way to combine quantitative and qualitative research in political science.

This book is the product of collaborative research involving dozens of scholars, who worked together over a number of years. We thank the authors of the case studies most of all, for their contributions to this book. Ibrahim Elbadawi and Norman Loayza, both of whom had been involved in the World Bank project on the "Economics of Political and Criminal Violence," helped select countries, identify the case study authors, and draft the first set of guidelines that were distributed to authors at the Oslo conference, where the project was launched in June 2001. Ian Bannon and Colin Scott of the World Bank deserve special thanks. Without their help, financial support for this project would not have been available. Both of them made sure that the Bank's research on conflict maintained a clear policy perspective, and they were sources of encouragement and advice throughout the project. We also gratefully acknowledge financial assistance offered by the Yale Center for International and Area Studies. Funds from the Coca-Cola Fund were used to host the April 2002 conference in New Haven, where first drafts of the case studies were presented. We also received useful comments and suggestions from several colleagues, including Anna Grzymala-Busse, Keith Darden, Jennifer Hochschild, Stathis Kalyvas, Jack Snyder, and Sidney Tarrow, most of whom commented on earlier versions of the Introduction and Conclusion (parts of which were camouflaged as an article published in *Perspectives on Politics*). Ian Bannon, Robert Bates, William Foltz, Nils Petter Gleditsch, Anke Hoeffler, Norman Loayza, and Bruce Russett commented on first drafts of the case studies at the Yale conference. Three anonymous referees read through both volumes and offered useful suggestions for revisions. Susan Hennigan did an expert job in helping us organize the Yale Conference in April 2002 and administering the budget for the World Bank grant that financed this project. She and David Hennigan helped edit some of the case studies. The research and administrative staff at the Peace Research Institute, Oslo, helped organize the first conference that launched the project in June 2001.

Paul Collier
Oxford, England

Nicholas Sambanis
New Haven, Connecticut

The Collier-Hoeffler Model of Civil War Onset and the Case Study Project Research Design

1

PAUL COLLIER, ANKE HOEFFLER,
AND NICHOLAS SAMBANIS

In this book, we use a comparative case study design to develop the theory of civil war. We do so by applying a well-known quantitative model of civil war onset—the Collier-Hoeffler (henceforth, CH) model—to several countries, using the model as a guide to conduct systematic case studies of the occurrence or absence of war. Although we apply well-known methods from comparative politics, such as a "most similar systems" design in comparing the cases of Senegal and Mali in volume 1 and civil wars in several states in the Caucasus in volume 2, our book also presents narratives based on a new, innovative design that blends quantitative and qualitative analysis. Our innovation consists of selecting cases based on a formal economic model of civil war and using the cases to develop the theory further and to add context and texture to the basic insights of the CH model. We, therefore, structure a design in which qualitative and quantitative research methods are well integrated, leading to better theory development and, ultimately, to better empirical testing as well.

We draw on 22 case studies of more than 30 civil wars to explore the fit of the CH model to each case.[1] By "fit" we mean several things. We use the cases to see if the empirical measures (often called proxies) in the CH model actually measure the theoretically significant variables. We also use the cases to see if important explanations of civil war are omitted from the CH model. The case studies have several other uses; most important is their ability to track sequences of events leading to civil war. "Thick" (i.e., rich, detailed) descriptions of such sequences help identify the causal mechanisms through which the independent variables in the CH model influence the risk of civil war onset, leading to a deeper understanding of civil war and suggesting possible revisions of the CH model. Some case studies suggest potentially generalizable hypotheses about civil war that the CH model has not considered. These hypotheses could, in another iteration, be incorporated in the model, by adding new measures for all countries and years in the data and by performing new empirical tests of an expanded model. The cases also help us identify similarities or differences across groups of countries and periods, which allows us to evaluate the assumption of unit homogeneity that underlies the empirical tests of the CH model and most quantitative other studies of civil war.

Even if the CH model predicted all cases of civil war onset perfectly, it would still not be able to tell us much about the process through which these outcomes (war or peace) are generated. By contrast, analyzing the process—the sequence of events and the interaction of variables in the CH model over time—is the comparative advantage of case study designs. Quantitative and qualitative research designs are often (mistakenly) considered as substitutes rather than complements in political science. Our book should suggest that there is much to learn by combining the two approaches. Quantitative analysis is the best way to analyze the covariance between civil war and many potentially important determinants of a process leading to war. Qualitative analysis can tell us how these determinants influence war outcomes over time and can help sort out the endogenous from the exogenous variables in the model. Also nontrivially, case studies offer a more textured and nuanced view of civil war and show that the distinction between "greed" and "grievance" in the CH model should be abandoned for a more complex model that considers greed and grievance as inextricably fused motives for civil war.

In this introductory chapter, we offer an abbreviated version of the CH model and empirical results. We omit the most technical parts of the CH article so as to make the chapter accessible to a broader audience. Experts might wish to review the original article for a more technical discussion. We focus here on the April 2000 and October 2001 versions of the CH model, which the case study authors used to structure their analyses. Although there have been slight revisions and improvements to the model since then, we must focus on the earlier versions for the sake of coherence between the theoretical model that guided the case studies and the discussion of the model in the case studies.[2] The published version of the article can be found in Collier and Hoeffler (2004). The data for all quantitative analyses referred to in this book can also be accessed online or by contacting the chapter authors.[3]

Following the presentation of the model in the next section, we turn to the research design for the case study project. We describe the project's aims and guidelines, and discuss important methodological issues in selecting and developing the case studies.[4] The case studies are presented in nine chapters in each volume. The final chapter synthesizes the main findings of the cases and suggests possible revisions and extensions to the CH model, based on the findings of the case study project.

The Collier-Hoeffler Model of Civil War Onset[5]

Civil war is now far more common than international war. Most new outbreaks of large-scale armed conflict occur within the boundaries of sovereign states and pit the government against one or more groups challenging the government's sovereignty.[6]

Our model analyzes civil war and rebellion in terms of both motive and opportunity, but focuses on opportunity as the determining factor of rebellion.[7] In an econometric model of civil war onset, we use measurable variables to test the difference between motive and opportunity in 78 civil wars between 1960 and 1999 (constituting 750 five-year episodes from 1960 to 1999).

Preferences, Perceptions, and Opportunities

In accordance with a small body of economic literature typified by Grossman (1991, 1999), we model rebellion as an industry that generates profits from looting, so that "the insurgents are indistinguishable from bandits or pirates" (Grossman 1999, 269). Such rebellions are motivated by greed, which is presumably sufficiently common that profitable opportunities for rebellion will not be overlooked. Hence, the incidence of rebellion is not explained by motive, but by the atypical circumstances that generate profitable opportunities (Collier 2000). The political science literature focuses on grievance (the demand for rebellion) while economists focus on a different motivation—greed—and explain rebellion as a result of atypical opportunities.

Hirshleifer (1995, 2001) provides an important refinement on the motive-opportunity dichotomy. He classifies the possible causes of conflict into preferences, opportunities, and perceptions. The introduction of perceptions allows for the possibility that both opportunities and grievances might be wrongly perceived. If the perceived opportunity for rebellion is illusory—analogous to the "winners' curse"—unprofitability will cause collapse, perhaps before turning into a civil war. By contrast, when exaggerated grievances trigger rebellion, fighting does not dispel the misperception and indeed may generate genuine grievances.

Misperceptions of grievances may be very common; all societies may have groups with exaggerated grievances. In this case, as with greed-driven rebellion, motive would not explain war. Societies that experienced civil war would be distinguished by the atypical viability of rebellion. In such societies, rebellions would be conducted by viable not-for-profit organizations, pursuing misperceived agendas by violent means. Greed and misperceived grievance provide a common explanation—"opportunity" and "viability" describe the common conditions sufficient for profit-seeking, or not-for-profit, rebel organizations to exist. They can jointly be contrasted with the political account of conflict in which the grievances that both motivate and explain rebellion are assumed to be well-grounded in objective circumstances such as unusually high inequality, or unusually weak political rights. We now turn to the proxies for opportunities and objective grievances.

Proxies for Opportunity

Using and expanding war data from Small and Singer (1982) and Singer and Small (1994), we created a list of civil war occurrence and nonoccurrence for 161 countries covering the period 1960–99 (table 1.1 includes all wars in the data set). Our model tries to explain the initiation of civil war (using the Singer and Small definition).

Table 1.1 Outbreaks of War in the CH Model

Country	Start of the war	End of the war	Previous war	GDP sample	Secondary schooling sample
Afghanistan	04/78	02/92			
	05/92	Ongoing	*		
Algeria	07/62	12/62	*		
	05/91	Ongoing	*	*	*
Angola	02/61	11/75			
	11/75	05/91	*	*	*
	09/92	Ongoing	*	*	*
Azerbaijan	04/91	10/94			
Bosnia	03/92	11/95			
Burma/Myanmar	68	10/80	*	*	*
	02/83	07/95	*	*	*
Burundi	04/72	12/73		*	*
	08/88	08/88	*	*	*
	11/91	Ongoing	*	*	*
Cambodia	03/70	10/91	*		
Chad	03/80	08/88		*	
China	01/67	09/68	*	*	
Colombia	04/84	Ongoing	*	*	*
Congo, Republic of	97	10/97		*	*
Cyprus	07/74	08/74		*	
Dominican Rep.	04/65	09/65		*	*
El Salvador	10/79	01/92		*	*
Ethiopia	07/74	05/91		*	*
Georgia	06/91	12/93			
Guatemala	07/66	07/72	*	*	*
	03/78	03/84	*	*	*
Guinea-Bissau	12/62	12/74			
India	08/65	08/65	*	*	*
	84	94	*	*	*
Indonesia	06/75	09/82	*	*	*
	03/74	03/75		*	*
	09/78	12/79	*	*	*
	06/81	05/82	*	*	*
Iraq	09/61	11/63	*		
	07/74	03/75	*	*	*
	01/85	12/92	*	*	*
Jordan	09/70	09/70		*	
Laos	07/60	02/73	*		
Lebanon	05/75	09/92	*		
Liberia	12/89	11/91		*	
	10/92	11/96	*		
Morocco	10/75	11/89	*	*	*

(Continued)

Table 1.1 Outbreaks of War in the CH Model (*Continued*)

Country	Start of the war	End of the war	Previous war	GDP sample	Secondary schooling sample
Mozambique	10/64	11/75			
	07/76	10/92	*	*	*
Nicaragua	10/78	07/79		*	*
	03/82	04/90			
Nigeria	01/66	01/70		*	*
	12/80	08/84	*	*	*
Pakistan	03/71	12/71		*	*
	01/73	07/77			
Peru	03/82	12/96		*	*
Philippines	09/72	12/96	*	*	*
Romania	12/89	12/89		*	*
Russia	12/94	08/96			
	09/99	Ongoing	*		
Rwanda	11/63	02/64			
	10/90	07/94	*	*	*
Sierra Leone	03/91	11/96		*	*
	05/97	07/99	*	*	
Somalia	04/82	05/88		*	*
	05/88	12/92	*	*	*
Sri Lanka	04/71	05/71		*	*
	07/83	Ongoing	*	*	*
Sudan	10/63	02/72			
	07/83	Ongoing	*	*	*
Tajikistan	04/92	12/94			
Turkey	07/91	Ongoing		*	*
Uganda	05/66	06/66		*	*
	10/80	04/88	*	*	*
Vietnam	01/60	04/75	*		
Yemen, Rep. of	05/90	10/94			
Yemen, Arab Rep. of	11/62	09/69	*		
Yemen, People's Dem. Rep. of	01/86	01/86	*		
Yugoslavia	04/90	01/92			
	10/98	04/99	*		
Zaïre/Congo, Dem. Rep. of	07/60	09/65			
	09/91	12/96	*	*	*
	09/97	09/99	*	*	*
Zimbabwe	12/72	12/79		*	*

Note: The "Previous war" column includes war starts from 1945 to 1994. The "GDP sample" and "Secondary schooling sample" indicate which cases are included in estimations using either of those two explanatory variables. This war list is from the March 2003 version of the CH article. The list included in the draft that was circulated to case study authors might have been slightly different.

The model is tested using quantitative indicators of opportunity and grievance. Financing for the rebels comes from three sources: extortion of natural resources, donations from diasporas, and subventions from hostile governments. Natural resources are proxied by the ratio of primary commodity exports to the gross domestic product (GDP), measured (as all variables are) at intervals of five years, starting in 1960 and ending in 1995. They then consider the subsequent five years as an "episode" and compare those in which a civil war broke out ("conflict episodes") with those that were conflict-free ("peace episodes"). We collected data for all country five-year periods in our data set and present descriptive statistics for all variables in table 1.2.[8]

A second source of rebel finance is from diasporas. We proxy the size of a country's diaspora by its emigrants living in the United States.[9] In our econometric

Table 1.2 Descriptive Statistics: CH Variables

Variable	Sample (*n = 1,167*)	No civil war (*n = 1,089*)	Civil war (*n = 78*)
War starts	0.067	0	1
Primary commodity exports/GDP	0.168	0.169	0.149
GDP per capita (const. US$)	4,061	4,219	1,645
Diaspora (relative to population of country of origin)	0.017	0.018	0.004
Male secondary schooling (% in school)	43.42	44.39	30.3
GDP per capita growth (average for previous 5 years)	1.62	1.74	−0.23
Previous war (% with war since 1945)	20.8	18.5	53.8
Peace duration (months since last conflict)	327	334	221
Forest cover (%)	31.11	31.33	27.81
Mountainous terrain (%)	15.82	15.17	24.93
Geographic dispersion of the population (Gini)	0.571	0.569	0.603
Population density (inhabitants per km^2)	150	156	62
Population in urban areas (%)	45.11	46.00	32.7
Ethnic fractionalization (index, 0–100)	39.57	38.64	52.63
Religious fractionalization (index, 0–100)	36.09	35.98	37.70
Polarization $\alpha = 1.6$ (index, 0–0.165)	0.077	0.077	0.076
Democracy (index, 0–10)	3.91	4.07	1.821
Ethnic dominance (% with main ethnic group 45–90%)	0.465	0.465	0.452
Income inequality (Gini)	0.406	0.406	0.410
Land inequality (Gini)	0.641	0.641	0.631

analysis, we also use predicted values for the diaspora variable, to account for the fact that part of the diaspora is caused by civil war in the country of origin (thus we control for endogeneity).

A third source of rebel finance is from hostile governments. Our proxy for the willingness of foreign governments to finance military opposition to the incumbent government is the Cold War. During the Cold War, each great power supported rebellions in countries allied to the opposing power. There is some support for the opportunity thesis: Only 11 of the 78 wars broke out during the 1990s.

Opportunities for rebellion can also arise from atypically low cost. Recruits must be paid, and their cost may be related to the income foregone by enlisting as a rebel. Rebellions may occur when foregone income is unusually low. We try three proxies for foregone income: mean income per capita, male secondary schooling, and the growth rate of the economy.[10] As shown in table 1.2, the conflict episodes started from less than half the mean income of the peace episodes.[11] The second proxy, male secondary school enrollment, has the advantage of being focused on young males—the group from whom rebels are recruited.[12] The third measure, the growth rate of the economy in the preceding period, is intended to proxy new income opportunities. Conflict episodes were preceded by lower growth rates.

The opportunity for rebellion may be that conflict-specific capital (such as military equipment) is unusually cheap. We proxy the cost of such capital by the time since the most recent previous conflict; the legacy of weapon stocks, skills, and organizational capital will gradually depreciate. Empirically, peace episodes are preceded by far longer periods of peace than conflict episodes (see table 1.2). While this supports the opportunity thesis, it could also be interpreted as reflecting the gradual decay of conflict-induced grievances.

Another dimension of opportunity is an atypically weak government military capability. An unambiguous indicator is whether the terrain is favorable to rebels: Forests and mountains provide rebels with a safe haven. We measured the proportion of a country's terrain that is forested[13] and also created equivalent data on mountainous terrain.[14] Geographic dispersion of the population may also inhibit government capability: Herbst (2000) suggests that Zaire is prone to rebellion because its population lives around the edges of the country. We measure dispersion by calculating a Gini coefficient of population dispersion.[15] Similarly, low population density and low urbanization may inhibit government capability. Before war episodes, both population density and urbanization are low (table 1.2).

A final source of rebel military opportunity may be social cohesion. Ethnic and religious diversity within organizations tends to reduce their ability to function (Alesina Bagir, and Easterly 1999; Collier 2001; Easterly and Levine 1997). A newly formed rebel army may be in particular need of social cohesion, constraining recruitment to a single ethnic or religious group. A diverse society might in this case reduce the opportunity for rebellion by limiting the recruitment pool. The most widely used measure of ethnic diversity is the index of ethnolinguistic fractionalization. This index measures the probability that two randomly drawn people will be from different ethnic groups. We constructed a similar measure of religious fractionalization using data from Barrett (1982) and interacted the two measures to construct a proxy that measures the maximum potential social fractionalization.[16]

Proxying Objective Grievances

We considered four objective measures of grievance: ethnic or religious hatred, political repression, political exclusion, and economic inequality. Ethnic and religious hatreds cannot be easily quantified, but they evidently can only occur in societies that are multiethnic or multireligious, and so our proxies measure various dimensions of diversity. The previously discussed measures of fractionalization are pertinent: intergroup hatreds must be greater in societies that are fractionalized than in those that are homogeneous. However, arguably the source of intergroup tension is not diversity but polarization, which we measured by adapting a measure created by Esteban and Ray (1994). The descriptive data do not suggest that polarization is important; conflict and peace episodes have very similar mean values (table 1.2).

We measure political repression using the Polity III data set (see Jaggers and Gurr 1995). Our index of political rights ranges 0–10 on an ascending ordinal scale. Political rights differ considerably between conflict and peace episodes. We also investigated the Polity III measure of autocracy and a measure of political openness published by Freedom House (the Gastil Index). The quantitative political science literature has already applied these measures to analyze conflict risk. Hegre et al. (2001) find that repression increases conflict except when it is severe.

Even in democracies, a small group may fear permanent exclusion. A potentially important instance is when political allegiance is based on ethnicity and one ethnic group has a majority. The incentive to exploit the minority increases when the minority is larger, since there is more to extract (Collier 2001). Hence, a minority may be most vulnerable if the largest ethnic group constitutes a small majority. We term this "ethnic dominance" and measure it as a binary variable coded "1" if the largest ethnic group in a country constitutes 45 to 90 percent of the population.

Inequality may also drive civil war. The poor may rebel to induce redistribution and rich regions may mount secessionist rebellions to preempt redistribution. We measured income inequality by the Gini coefficient and by the ratio of the top-to-bottom quintiles of income. We also measured asset inequality by the Gini coefficient of land ownership. The data are from Deininger and Squire (1996, 1998).

Finally, we should point out that these measures of opportunity (such as primary commodity exports, income, and school enrollment) are scaled by measures of country size. For given values of these variables, opportunities should be approximately proportional to size. Grievance might also increase with size: public choices diverge more from the preferences of the average individual as heterogeneity increases. We are, however, able to control for three aspects of heterogeneity: ethnic, religious, and income diversity. Empirically, the conflict episodes had markedly larger populations than the peace episodes.

Regression Analysis

The proxies for opportunity and objective grievances are largely distinct and so can be compared as two nonnested econometric models. There is, however, no reason for the accounts to be exclusive, and the aim of our econometric tests is to arrive at an integrated model that gives an account of conflict risk in terms of all those opportunities and grievances that are significant. We use logistic regression to predict the risk that a civil war will start during a five-year episode. We consider only those countries that were at peace at the start of the episode (e.g., January 1965) and predict whether the peace was sustained through to its end (e.g., December 1969).

We start with the opportunity model (see table 1.3). The first regression (column 1) excludes per capita income and diasporas. Because per capita income and enrollment in secondary schooling are highly correlated, they cannot be used in the same regression. The diaspora measure is available only for 29 war episodes, so we explore it as an addendum. The variables included in the first regression permit a sample of 688 episodes, including 46 wars.

Primary commodity exports are highly significant. Although their effect is non-linear, the risk of conflict peaks when they constitute around 32% of GDP, which is a high level of dependence. The other proxy for finance, the end of the Cold War, has the expected sign but is insignificant. The foregone earnings proxies are also both significant with the expected sign: Secondary schooling and growth both reduce conflict risk. Our proxy for the cost of conflict-specific capital is the number of months since any previous conflict (back to 1945), which is highly significant (column 2). The proxies for military advantage also have the expected sign and are marginally significant: mountainous terrain, population dispersion, and social fractionalization. Finally, the coefficient on population is positive and highly significant.

The third column replaces secondary schooling with per capita income. This permits a larger sample—750 episodes including 52 wars. Per capita income is highly significant with the expected negative sign. The change of specification and the expansion of sample make social fractionalization significant and population dispersion nonsignificant.

In the last two columns of table 1.3, we introduce the diaspora variable and retreat to a more parsimonious model to preserve observations (since several of our variables have many missing values). All the included explanatory variables remain significant. The size of the diaspora is not directly significant in the initiation of conflict. However, it is significant when interacted with the number of months since the previous conflict. "Diaspora/peace" divides the size of the diaspora by the time since a previous conflict. The variable is positive and significant; a large diaspora considerably increases the risk of repeat conflict. We control for the potential endogeneity of diasporas in the final column of table 1.3 (see our article for the technical details). Diasporas remain significant and the size of the coefficient is only slightly altered (it is not significantly different from that on the endogenous diaspora measure). This suggests that there is indeed a substantial causal effect of the diaspora on the risk of conflict renewal. The result also guides our interpretation of why the risk of conflict repetition declines as peace is maintained. Recall that in

Table 1.3 Opportunity Model

Variable	1	2	3	4	5
Primary commodity exports/GDP	18.149	18.900	16.476	17.567	17.404
	(6.006)***	(5.948)***	(5.207)***	(6.744)***	(6.750)***
(Primary commodity exports/GDP)^2	−27.445	−29.123	−23.017	−28.81	−28.456
	(11.996)***	(11.905)***	(9.972)**	(15.351)*	(15.366)*
Post-Cold War	−0.326	−0.207	−0.454		
	(0.469)	(0.450)	(0.416)		
Male secondary schooling	−0.025	−0.024			
	(0.010)**	(0.010)**			
Ln GDP per capita			−0.837	−1.237	−1.243
			(0.253)***	(0.283)***	(0.284)***
GDP growth	−0.117	−0.118	−0.105		
	(0.044)***	(0.044)***	(0.042)***		
Peace duration	−0.003	−0.004***	−0.004	−0.00	−0.002
	(0.002)$p = .128$	(0.001)	(0.001)***	(0.001)	(0.001)
Previous war	0.464				
	(0.547)$p = .396$				
Mountainous terrain	0.013	0.014	0.008		
	(0.009)$p = .164$	(0.009)	(0.008)		

	(1)	(2)	(3)	(4)	(5)
Geographic dispersion	-2.211	-2.129	-0.865		
	(1.038)**	(1.032)**	(0.948)		
Social fractionalization	-0.0002	-0.0002	-0.0002		
	(0.0001)p = .109	(0.0001)p = .122	(0.0001)**		
Ln population	0.669	0.686	0.493	0.295	0.296
	(0.163)***	(0.162)***	(0.129)***	(0.141)**	(0.141)**
Diaspora/peace				700.931	
				(363.29)**	
Diaspora corrected/peace					741.168
					(387.635)*
(Diaspora-diaspora corrected)/peace					82.798
					(287.192)
N	688	688	750	595	595
No. of wars	46	46	52	29	29
Pseudo-R^2	0.24	0.24	0.22	0.25	0.25
Log-likelihood	-128.49	-128.85	-146.86	-93.2	-93.23

Note: All regressions include a constant. Standard errors are in parentheses.

***, **, * indicate significance at the 1, 5, and 10 percent level, respectively.

principle this could be either because hatreds gradually fade, or because "rebellion-specific capital" gradually depreciates. How might diasporas slow these processes? Diasporas preserve their own hatreds, which is why they finance rebellion. However, it is unlikely that the diaspora's hatreds significantly influence attitudes among the much larger population in the country of origin. By contrast, the finance provided by the diaspora can offset the depreciation of rebellion-specific capital, thereby sustaining conflict risk.

In table 1.4 we turn to objective grievance as the explanation of rebellion, dropping all the economic measures of opportunity and retaining the number of months since a previous conflict, because this can be interpreted as a proxy of fading hatreds.

Table 1.4 Grievance Model

Variable	1	2	3
Ethnic fractionalization	0.010	0.011	0.012
	(0.006)*	(0.007)*	(0.008)
Religious fractionalization	−0.003	−0.006	−0.004
	(0.007)	(0.008)	(0.009)
Polarization $\alpha = 1.6$	−3.067	−4.682	−6.536
	(7.021)	(8.267)	(8.579)
Ethnic dominance (45–90%)	0.414	0.575	1.084
	(0.496)	(0.586)	(0.629)*
Democracy	−0.109	−0.083	−0.121
	(0.044)***	(0.051)*	(0.053)**
Peace duration	−0.004	−0.003	−0.004
	(0.001)***	(0.001)***	(0.001)***
Mountainous terrain	0.011	0.007	−0.0001
	(0.007)	(0.009)	(0.009)
Geographic dispersion	−0.509	−0.763	−1.293
	(0.856)	(1.053)	(0.102)
Ln population	0.221	0.246	0.300
	(0.096)**	(0.119)**	(1.133)**
Income inequality		0.015	
		(0.018)	
Land inequality			0.461
			(1.305)
N	850	604	603
No. of wars	59	41	38
Pseudo-R^2	0.13	0.11	0.17
Log-likelihood	−185.57	−133.46	−117.12

Note: All regressions include a constant. Standard errors are in parentheses.

***, **, * indicate significance at the 1, 5, and 10 percent level, respectively. In column 1, the two measures of fractionalization and ethnic dominance are not jointly significant.

In the first column, we also exclude the inequality measures because of considerations of sample size. This enables a very large sample of 850 episodes and 59 civil wars.

The four proxies for ethnic and religious tension are surprisingly unimportant. Ethnic fractionalization is significant at 10 percent with the expected sign. Religious fractionalization and polarization are insignificant with the wrong sign, and ethnic dominance is insignificant. These three measures are also not jointly significant.[17] Democracy is highly significant with the expected sign—repression increases conflict risk. The time since the previous conflict is again highly significant, but we have suggested that this is more likely to be proxying rebellion-specific capital than grievance. In the second and third columns, we introduce income inequality and land inequality, respectively. Although the sample size is reduced, it is still substantial—more than 600 episodes with a minimum of 38 wars. Neither variable is close to significance. All three grievance models have very low explanatory power (the pseudo-R^2 is 0.17 or lower).

We now turn to the question of which model—opportunity or grievance—provides a better explanation of the risk of civil war. Because the two models are nonnested (i.e., one model is not a special case of the other), we use the J test as suggested by Davidson and MacKinnon (1981). As shown in the first two columns of table 1.5, we find that we cannot reject one model in favor of the other. Thus, we conclude that while the opportunity model is superior, some elements of the grievance model are likely to add to its explanatory power. We, therefore, investigate a combined model in column 3 of table 1.5.

Since this combined model includes income inequality and a lagged term, our sample size is much reduced (479 observations). In column 4, we drop inequality (which is consistently insignificant). Omitting inequality increases the sample size to 665. In this combined model, neither democracy, ethnic and religious fractionalization, nor the post-Cold War dummy is significant. Other variables are statistically significant or close to significance and the overall fit is reasonable (pseudo-R^2 of 0.26). Since both the grievance and opportunity models are nested in the combined model, we can use a likelihood ratio test to determine whether the combined model is superior. We can reject the validity of the restrictions proposed by the grievance model, but not by the opportunity model.

Although the combined model is superior to the opportunity and grievance models, several variables are completely insignificant and we drop them sequentially. First, we exclude the post-Cold War dummy, then religious fractionalization, then democracy, then polarization, then ethnic fractionalization, and, finally, mountainous terrain, yielding the baseline model of column 5 and its variant with per capita income replacing secondary enrollment in column 6. No further reduction in the model is accepted and no additions of variables included in our previous models are accepted. The baseline model and its variant yield very similar results, although the variant has less explanatory power and two variables lose significance (ethnic dominance and geographic dispersion).

Our baseline model allows us to calculate the change in the probability of war starts for different values of the explanatory variables. This model was used to generate

Table 1.5 Combined Opportunity and Grievance Model

Variable	1	2	3	4	5	6	7
Primary commodity exports/GDP	19.096 (5.993)***		37.072 (10.293)***	23.385 (6.692)***	18.937 (5.865)***	16.773 (5.206)***	50.608 (14.09)***
(Primary commodity exports/GDP)²	−30.423 (12.008)***		−69.267 (21.697)***	−36.33 (12.998)***	−29.443 (11.781)***	−23.800 (10.040)**	−131.00 (42.93)***
Post-Cold War	−0.209 (0.457)		−0.873 (0.644)	−0.281 (0.459)			
Male secondary schooling	−0.021 (0.011)**		−0.029 (0.013)**	−0.022 (0.011)**	−0.031 (0.010)***		−0.034 (0.011)***
Ln GDP per capita						−0.950 (0.245)***	
(GDP growth)$t − 1$	−0.108 (0.044)***		−0.045 (0.062)	−0.108 (0.045)**	−0.115 (0.043)***	−0.098 (0.042)**	−0.113 (0.046)***
Peace duration	−0.0003 (0.002)	0.0005 (0.0014)	−0.0003 (0.0015)	−0.003 (0.001)***	−0.004 (0.001)***	−0.004 (0.001)***	−0.003 (0.001)***
Mountainous terrain	0.005 (0.010)	0.001 (0.008)	0.005 (0.012)	0.015 (0.009) $p = .11$			
Geographic dispersion	−1.978 (1.049)*	0.135 (1.106)	−4.032 (1.490)***	−1.962 (1.149)*	−2.487 (1.005)**	−0.992 (0.909)	−2.871 (1.130)***
Ln population		−0.014 (0.136)	0.927 (0.250)***	0.697 (0.181)***	0.768 (0.166)***	0.510 (0.128)***	1.123 (0.226)***
Social fractionalization	−0.0002 (0.0001)***		−0.0008 (0.0003)**	−0.000 (0.0003) $p = .11$	−0.0002 (0.0001)***	−0.0002 (0.0001)***	−0.0003 (0.0001)***

	(1)	(2)	(3)	(4)	(5)	(6)	(7)
Ethnic fractionalization		0.008 (0.007)	0.041 (0.019)**	0.023 (0.015)			
Religious fractionalization		−0.005 (0.008)	0.015 (0.020)	0.014 (0.019)			
Polarization		−9.358 (8.735)	−25.276 (13.390)*	−15.992 (10.518)			
Ethnic dominance (45–90%)		1.212 (0.648)**	2.020 (0.915)**	1.592 (0.746)**	0.670 (0.354)*	0.480 (0.328)	0.769 (0.369)**
Democracy		−0.036 (0.054)	−0.018 (0.062)	−0.042 (0.054)		$p = .14$	
Income inequality			0.025 (0.024)				
Grievance predicted value	0.767 (0.413)**						
Opportunity predicted value		1.052 (0.212)***					
Primary commodity exports/GDP × oil dummy							−28.275 (9.351)***
(Primary commodity exports/GDP)² × oil dummy							106.459 (38.704)***
N	665	665	479	665	688	750	654
No. of wars	46	46	32	46	46	52	45
Pseudo-R^2	0.24	0.25	0.24	0.26	0.24	0.22	0.30
Log-likelihood	−126.69	−125.29	−89.55	−124.6	−128.21	−146.84	−114.20

Note: All regressions include a constant. Standard errors are in parentheses.
***, **, * indicate significance at the 1, 5, and 10 percent level, respectively.

probability estimates for the case studies and probability estimates for each case are discussed in each chapter. At the mean of all variables the risk of a war start is about 11.5 percent.[18] Our model predicts that a hypothetical country with all the worst characteristics found in our sample would have a near-certain risk of war, whereas one with all the best characteristics would have a negligible risk.

The effect of primary commodity exports on conflict risk is both highly significant and considerable. At peak danger (primary commodity exports being 32 percent of GDP), the risk of civil war is about 22 percent, whereas a country with no such exports has a risk of only 1 percent. The effect is sufficiently important to warrant disaggregation into different types of commodities. We categorized primary commodity exports according to which type of product was dominant: food, nonfood agriculture, oil, other raw materials, and a residual category of "mixed." Of the many potential disaggregations of primary commodity exports permitted by these data, only one was significant when introduced into our baseline regression, namely oil versus nonoil. The results are reported in column 7 of table 1.5. We add variables that interact the primary commodity export share and its square with a dummy variable that takes the value of unity if the exports are predominantly oil. Both variables are significant: Oil exports have a distinct effect on the risk of conflict. However, the effect is modest. At the average value of primary commodity exports, oil has the same effect as other commodities. Low levels of oil dependence are somewhat less risky than other commodities and high levels of dependence are somewhat more risky. The disaggregation slightly reduces the sample size, does not change the significance of any of the other variables, and substantially improves the overall fit of the model.

Recall that the other proxies for financial opportunities, the Cold War and diasporas, are not included in this baseline. The end of the Cold War does not have a significant effect. Diasporas are excluded from the baseline purely for considerations of sample size. In the parsimonious variant in which they are included, their effect on the risk of repeat conflict is substantial. After five years of peace, switching the size of the diaspora from the smallest to the largest found in postconflict episodes increases the risk of conflict sixfold.

The proxies for foregone earnings have substantial effects. If the enrollment rate for secondary schooling is 10 percentage points higher than the average, the risk of war is reduced by about 3 percentage points (a decline in the risk from 11.5 percent to 8.6 percent). An additional percentage point on the growth rate reduces the risk of war by about 1 percentage point (a decline from 11.5 percent to 10.4 percent). Our other proxy for the cost of rebellion is also highly significant and substantial. Directly after a civil war, there is a high probability of a restart, the risk being about 32 percent. This risk declines over time at around 1 percentage point per year.

The only measures of rebel military advantage that survive into the baseline are population dispersion and social fractionalization. Consistent with Herbst's hypothesis, countries with a highly concentrated population have a very low risk of conflict, whereas those with a highly dispersed population have a very high risk (about 37 percent). Consistent with the hypothesis that cohesion is important for rebel effectiveness, social fractionalization makes a society substantially safer. A maximally fractionalized society has a conflict risk only one quarter that of a homogeneous society.

Only one of the proxies for grievance survives into the baseline regression, namely ethnic dominance. If a country is characterized by ethnic dominance, its risk of conflict is nearly doubled. Thus, the net effect of increased social diversity is the sum of its effect on social fractionalization and its effect on ethnic dominance. Starting from homogeneity, as diversity increases, the society is likely to become ethnically dominated, although this will be reversed by further increases in diversity. The risk of conflict would first rise and then fall.

Finally, the coefficient on the scale variable, population, is highly significant and close to unity; risk is approximately proportional to size. We have suggested that proportionality is more likely if conflict is generated by opportunities than by grievances.

These results are generally immune to several tests for robustness. We considered the sensitivity both to data and to method, investigating the effect of outlying observations and of different definitions of the dependent and independent variables. With respect to method, we investigated random effects, fixed effects, and rare events bias. The reader can review the results of these alternative estimations in the original article.

Interpretation and Summary

Using a comprehensive data set of civil wars over the period 1960–99 and estimating logit regressions, we predicted the risk of the outbreak of war in each five-year episode. We find that a model that focuses on the opportunities for rebellion performs well, whereas objective indicators of grievance add little explanatory power. The model is robust to a range of tests for outliers, redefinitions, and alternative specifications.

One factor influencing the opportunity for rebellion is the availability of finance. We have shown that primary commodity exports substantially increase conflict risk. We have interpreted this as being the result of the opportunities for extortion that such commodities provide, making rebellion feasible and perhaps even attractive. Another source of finance is diasporas, which substantially increase the risk of conflict renewal.

A second factor influencing opportunity is the cost of rebellion. Male secondary education enrollment, per capita income, and the growth rate all have statistically significant and substantial effects that reduce conflict risk. We have interpreted them as proxying earnings foregone in rebellion; low foregone earnings facilitate conflict. Even if this is correct, low earnings might matter because they are a source of grievance rather than because they make rebellion cheap. However, if rebellion were a protest against low income, we might expect inequality to have strong effects, which we do not find.

A third aspect of opportunity is military advantage. We have found that a dispersed population increases the risk of conflict and there is weaker evidence that mountainous terrain might also be an advantage to rebels.

Most proxies for grievance were insignificant: inequality, political rights, ethnic polarization, and religious fractionalization. Only ethnic dominance had adverse effects. Even this has to be considered in combination with the benign effects of social fractionalization. Societies characterized by ethnic and religious diversity are safer than homogeneous societies as long as they avoid dominance. We have suggested that diversity makes rebellion harder because it makes rebel cohesion more costly.

Finally, the risk of conflict is proportional to a country's population. Both opportunities and grievances increase with population size, so this result is compatible with both the opportunity and grievance accounts. Grievances increase with population because of rising heterogeneity. Yet those aspects of heterogeneity that we are able to measure are not associated with an increased risk of conflict. Hence, a grievance account of the effect of population would need to explain why unobserved, but not observed, heterogeneity increases conflict risk.

One variable—time since a previous conflict—has substantial effects: Time "heals." Potentially, this can be interpreted either as opportunity or grievance. It may reflect the gradual depreciation of rebellion-specific capital, and hence an increasing cost of rebellion, or the gradual erosion of hatred. However, we have found that a large diaspora slows the "healing" process. The known proclivity of diasporas to finance rebel groups offsets the depreciation of rebellion-specific capital, and so would be predicted to delay "healing." The diaspora effect thus lends support to the opportunity interpretation.

Opportunity as an explanation of conflict risk is consistent with the economic interpretation of rebellion as greed motivated. However, it is also consistent with grievance motivation as long as perceived grievances are sufficiently widespread to be common across societies and time. Opportunity can account for the existence of either for-profit or not-for-profit rebel organizations. Our evidence does not imply, therefore, that rebels are necessarily criminals. But the grievances that motivate rebels may be substantially disconnected from the large social concerns of inequality, political rights, and ethnic or religious identity.

Building on the Collier-Hoeffler Model Using Case Studies[19]

Having presented the core elements of the CH model and all major empirical results, we now turn to the research design for the case study project. We address a number of methodological questions: How were cases selected? Do they represent the population of cases? Can the cases help us develop hypotheses about civil war onset? Do they provide sufficient historical detail to support counterfactual analysis? Do the cases constitute independent, homogeneous observations?[20] We address these and other methodological questions that explain how we use case studies in this project.

Goals of the Case Study Project

The main purpose of the case study project was to supplement the quantitative analysis, develop theory, and improve the causal inferences drawn from the CH model.

Causal theories should explain *how* a particular outcome (in this case, civil war) occurs—*how* and *under what conditions* different explanatory variables lead to that outcome. The CH model suggests a plausible microlevel theory of civil war, but it is tested empirically with macrolevel data that describe conditions under which individual decision making takes place.[21] The empirical findings of the CH model, therefore, do not necessarily test a microlevel theory of civil war.[22] Given that the CH model and the literature on civil war generally suffer from such a "missing link" between microlevel theories and macrolevel data, case studies can be used to improve our understanding of *how* the variables used in the empirical tests influence the probability of civil war. Context-rich narratives of historical processes can provide insight into the causal paths linking independent variables in the CH model to civil war outbreak and can help disentangle complicated multicausal relationships.

To understand better these "how" questions, we asked case study authors to do process tracing[23] and write narratives of individual cases by focusing on a set of common questions.[24] The list of questions structured their research and allowed us to treat their narratives as structured-focused comparisons. Authors were asked to focus on the mechanisms through which the right-hand-side variables (the X's) influence the dependent variable (Y) and were encouraged to explore interrelationships among the X's (interaction effects). The fact that such a large number of case studies systematically addressed the same questions implies that this project was better suited than most other comparative case study projects to test a theoretical model. But, since the CH model had already been tested using large-N statistical methods, we did not need to retest it using case studies. We, therefore, gave the case study project different priorities, such as theory building and exposition of the mechanisms through which the variables in the CH model influenced civil war onset. We also sought to develop alternative explanations of war, given the large amount of variance in civil war outcomes that is left unexplained by the CH model.[25] Moreover, by exploring microlevel processes and tracing their linkages to macrolevel analysis in the CH model, case studies provided us with a better sense of which variables in the CH model are endogenous and which are exogenous.[26] Close attention to country context also allows us to improve the CH model and its empirical tests by refining our empirical proxies and reducing measurement error.

The case study project has value-added because it teaches us about the *process* that leads to war, rather than focusing only on underlying "structural" characteristics of countries that experience civil war (or not). Process matters if different policy interventions can be designed to reduce the risk of war at various stages of conflict. In most cases, quantitative studies that present correlations between X and Y do not demonstrate causality and several competing explanations can be imposed on the same correlation. In other words, statistical methods can perform hypotheses tests, but they cannot necessarily distinguish among rival theories with closely related observable implications.[27] Case studies give us a "feel" for the data that allows us to develop better judgment in discriminating among possible explanations.

Case studies can also help us understand why the model fits some data points well and others poorly. If the statistical analysis identifies outliers (i.e., predictions that are two or more standard deviations from the mean predicted value of Y), case studies can help us understand if this prediction failure is due to systematic variation that is not captured by the model or to idiosyncratic reasons that the model should not try to explain. If several case studies point to a few potentially significant variables that are missing from the model, we could adjust the model and see if these variables can be incorporated in it. Coding these variables for all observations in the CH data set would allow us to test their fit to the data using statistical methods.[28] This approach offers a truly interactive way to blend quantitative and qualitative research and can help us develop better causal theories of civil war.

Our preferred approach of moving back and forth between case study and quantitative research designs reflects the view that case studies alone cannot easily develop generalizable theory and they do not offer the ideal environment for hypothesis testing. For any single case, there is potentially an inordinate amount of historical detail that the analyst must sort through to explain an outcome. Hypotheses about causes of that outcome are generally purely inductive in case studies. No amount of historical detail can be sufficient to recreate past events and the analyst's decision of which events to discuss reflects a prior belief in a plausible explanation for the event in question. Moreover, trying to fit a multivariate explanation of war to a single case runs into the familiar problem of indeterminacy (due to negative degrees of freedom). Our case study project gains degrees of freedom by virtue of the large number of cases (wars and periods of no war) considered and because authors focus on a specified set of variables and do not consider an arbitrarily large number of possible explanations. But even so, the degrees-of-freedom problem is hard to avoid entirely, which is another reason that we use the cases primarily for theory building. We did ask authors to suggest additional explanations for peace or war in their countries, if their narratives would have been incomplete without them. But, ultimately, to see if these explanations can be generalized, we must add them to the CH model and test them using statistical methods.

Case Selection

The fact that case analysis serves a secondary function in this project has implications for case selection. If we had relied primarily on the case studies to test the CH model, then the cases should have been selected so as to provide a representative sample of countries (with and without wars). But the large number of causal relationships implied by the CH model makes it increasingly difficult to use case study methods for empirical tests (Ragin 1987, 49). To avoid problems of identification and multicollinearity, we would have needed many more cases to test the model. With only a few cases, we would have had limited degrees of freedom and high uncertainty surrounding our inferences.

In both qualitative and quantitative research designs, random selection and assignment is typically the best way to reduce the risk of endogeneity, selection, and omitted variable bias. But random selection of countries to include in our study would have resulted in a sample that predominantly included cases of no war, given that civil war occurs relatively rarely. It could also result in a sample with no significant varia-tion in the independent variables (IVs). We could have avoided the first (but not the second) problem by sampling more heavily on cases of war, but nonlinearities that may be present in the data could have complicated the sampling process.[29]

With these constraints in mind, we could select cases from the universe of cases. We selected partly on the dependent variable (DV) and partly on the independent variables.[30] We included mostly countries that had experienced at least one civil war, but also high-risk countries that did not have a war.[31] We can find useful infor-mation both in those cases that the CH model explains well (i.e., cases on the regression line) and in those cases that the model predicts poorly (type I and type II errors). Given that in all cases we knew the values of the DV (i.e., we knew when and where civil wars had taken place), our research design could not legitimately aim to predict values of the DV. By selecting cases with different predicted values of the DV, our project avoids the problem of no variance in the DV, which is some-times encountered in case study research.[32]

The selection of negative cases resembles Mill's "indirect method of difference" in that it "uses negative cases to reinforce conclusions drawn from positive cases. . . . The examination of negative cases presupposes a theory allowing the investigator to identify the set of observations that embraces *possible* instances of the phenome-non of interest" (Ragin 1987, 41).[33] Typically, case studies have difficulty in identi-fying such negative cases "in the absence of strong theoretical or substantive guidelines" (Ragin 1987, 42). Our project makes the application of this method eas-ier, because we identify negative cases on the basis of (theoretically based) predic-tions from the core model.

We did not focus exclusively on the DV in selecting our cases. We also wanted to ensure sufficient variation in some key IVs. Thus, we partly selected cases accord-ing to IVs in the CH model, including a country's history of political violence, level of ethnic fractionalization, degree of dependence on natural resources, type of regime, and so forth. Selection on IVs alone has been described as "the best intentional" research design (King, Keohane, and Verba 1994, 140).[34] We knew the values of the explanatory variables ahead of time, so we could pick countries to ensure that there was sufficient variation.[35] But, since the CH model controlled for these IVs in the regressions, selecting cases to ensure variation in the IVs did not create any inference problems.[36] A matched-case selection might have been a bet-ter research design if we wanted to develop a theory "from scratch." However, the purpose of this project was to build on and refine existing theories of civil war by identifying the causal mechanisms underlying these theories and exploring the fit of the CH model to particular contexts/countries. Case selection proceeded with that purpose in mind.

Case studies of war onset and avoidance in the following countries were finally drafted: Algeria, Azerbaijan, Bosnia, Burundi, Colombia, Georgia, the Democratic Republic of Congo, Jamaica, Indonesia, Côte d'Ivoire, Kenya, Lebanon, Macedonia, Mali, Mozambique, Nigeria, Russia (focusing on Chechnya, Dagestan, and other regions), Senegal, Sierra Leone, Sudan, and the United Kingdom (Northern Ireland).[37]

We include a large subset of these cases in this volume. The geographical distribution of countries roughly corresponds to the prevalence of civil war in different regions of the world, although there is perhaps a greater emphasis on African wars in the selection of cases. Because our selection rules were based on the CH quantitative model, which controls for the variables that might make Africa "special" (such as high ethnic fractionalization, low levels of democracy, and high levels of poverty), we believe that the fact that there is sufficient variation along these dimensions should remove any bias in our case selection.

Authors were asked to focus on the country or the civil war as their unit of observation. Most case studies focus on the country and analyze both periods of peace and war in that country. If a country had recurrent wars, we asked authors to analyze all or most of them and to explore the linkages across episodes of war (see, e.g., the chapters on the Democratic Republic of Congo and Nigeria). If a country had not experienced civil war (Macedonia, Côte d'Ivoire, Jamaica), authors were asked to analyze periods of high risk for war and discuss why war did not occur. In effect, each case study provides us with several observations of peace and war. For example, the Indonesia study focuses on patterns of war and peace in Aceh over eight five-year periods and can, therefore, be considered a study of eight observations (two observations of war and six of no war). The Nigeria study analyzes the politics of several regions over several periods and traces the development of false-positive and false-negative predictions of the CH model in two different regions of the country in the late 1960s and 1980s. This approach actually makes it difficult to establish clearly how many observations we have in each case study and we often end up with many more observations for some countries than for others (some authors made a more conscious effort than others to analyze patterns of war and peace in their country over different periods). The uncertainty about the precise number of observations would have presented more problems if we had wanted to use the case studies to test the CH model rather than as a way to complement, rather than replace, quantitative tests.

Ultimately, it may be impossible for any single case study design to present a compelling and historically accurate test of a theory or to articulate an exhaustive set of hypotheses about the relationship between an antecedent and a consequent. However, we do not rely on the case studies for our theory—at least not all of our theory. Our set of structured, focused comparisons provides rich context against which to evaluate the soundness of the CH economic model and to refine that model.[38] In addition to illuminating the causes of onset of civil war, each chapter in our book offers a perspective on other aspects of civil war, such as the organization of rebel groups, the dynamics of violence during civil war, and the link between intercommunal violence and civil war, or crime and political violence.

Identifying Causal Mechanisms

One of the main contributions of any case study project is that it can explain *how* the antecedent is connected to the consequent. King et al. (1994) argue that many case studies do not achieve this goal because of three frequently encountered methodological problems: endogeneity, selection, and omitted variable bias.[39] These problems, however, are also commonly found in quantitative studies.[40] In fact, rather than being more susceptible to these problems, case study methods can grapple better with endogeneity and selection by constructing a "thick description" of the events leading up to civil war. Reconstructing the chronology of a conflict helps us deal with endogeneity and identifies interactions between pairs of explanatory variables that might have been undertheorized in the original model.

Case studies can also help us distinguish among several competing mechanisms. We probably cannot know all the mechanisms that link the X's to the Y in the CH model, but we can and should identify some central ones. For example, liberal democracy may facilitate conflict resolution in one country by ensuring minority representation and, in another country, by guaranteeing the independence of the judiciary. In a third country, democracy may be a precondition of economic stability, if it ensures property rights. Identifying causal mechanisms shifts the focus of inquiry from the outcome to the process. Some authors would argue that understanding the process is more important than explaining a specific outcome. In their new research project on the "dynamics of contention," McAdam, Tarrow, and Tilly (2001, 4) aim to show "how different forms of contention—social movements, revolutions, strike waves, nationalism, democratization, and more—result from similar mechanisms and processes" . . . and "explore combinations of mechanisms and processes to discover recurring causal sequences of contentious politics." In their work and the work of other political scientists, social processes are understood as sequences and combinations of causal mechanisms. Mechanisms are defined (2001, 24) as a "delimited class of events that alter relations among specified sets of elements in identical or closely similar ways over a variety of situations." So, for example, in explaining resource mobilization in the classic social movement literature, authors would focus on "environmental, cognitive, and relational mechanisms" (p. 25) such as the "significance of organizational bases," "resource accumulation," and the "collective coordination for popular actors" (2001, 17). McAdam et al. point out an important problem, separating mechanisms from correlations, and a more difficult problem, distinguishing between a mechanism and a process (a family of mechanisms).

Ethnic mobilization, for example, can be considered as both a mechanism and a process, and so can political identity formation. Another example of a mechanism is the "sons of the soil" argument that Fearon and Laitin (2003) make to explain political violence as the result of conflict between migrant communities and autochthonous populations in peripheral regions of countries. But how can we be certain that migration is the mechanism through which we get ethnic violence in these cases? If we look "upstream," we can locate an earlier mechanism in the government's decision to reduce the strength of peripheral ethnicities. Migration of other ethnic groups in their areas is one of several possible mechanisms through which violent conflict between peripheral communities and the state can develop. Although we cannot hope to identify all possible mechanisms or establish a hierarchy among them, we can use our case study project to go beyond the statistical analysis in explaining how each X influences Y. The task for the case study authors is to provide a sufficiently detailed process tracing, that is, a narrative of the way in which civil war erupts.

Unit Heterogeneity

Several of our case studies note that ethnic mobilization increases the risk of civil war. A possibility that the CH model does not consider is that wars that are fought by ethnic groups might have different antecedents than wars fought across non-ethnic (or nonracial, nonreligious) cleavages. Most of the literature seems to discard this possibility as it treats civil war as an aggregate category, implicitly assuming that a typology of civil war that distinguishes, for example, secession from revolution would not be meaningful. This assumption of unit homogeneity has not yet been proven in the literature. Is there sufficient evidence in the cases to support a typology of political violence? Can we observe differences between types of civil war and between civil war and other forms of political violence? We say more about this issue in the conclusion, where we review the evidence from the cases.

The data set used to test the CH model assumes unit homogeneity. According to King et al. (1994, 91), "two units are homogeneous when the expected values of the dependent variables from each unit are the same when our explanatory variable takes on a particular value." In the CH model, as in most of the quantitative literature on civil war, "civil war" is considered a homogeneous category. However, if the CH model predicts or explains civil war and other violence (e.g., genocides or criminal homicides) equally well (or equally poorly), then either the model has omitted variables that could help differentiate between the causes of these different forms of violence, or differences across forms of violence are small and the model might be better tested by combining violent events of different forms. For the moment, quantitative studies of civil war are not able to distinguish clearly between civil war and other forms of violence, such as genocide, riots, or coups. The case studies can help us better understand what forms of violence the CH model might be able to explain and can highlight some differences both between civil war and other violence and among different types of civil war.

The assumption of homogeneity implies constant effects across countries and time periods. Most of the influential models of civil war onset (Collier and Hoeffler 2000; Fearon and Laitin 2003; Hegre et al. 2001) assume constant effects. However, if this assumption is wrong, it is likely to bias our causal inferences (King et al. 1994, 94). Case studies allow us to explore the homogeneity of our observations and not to assume that a priori (Ragin 1987, 49). If we suspected substantial unit heterogeneity, an alternative approach would have been to utilize a "most similar systems" design—for example, we could choose only cases from Sub-Saharan Africa or some other region so as to "control" for several explanatory variables and isolate the "treatment" variable, in an effort to create a research design as close as possible to an experimental design (Przeworski and Teune 1970; Ragin 1987, 48). Such an approach, however, would have resulted in exploring only "within-systems relationships" (Przeworski and Teune 1970, 57–59) and might not have allowed us to develop further the CH model, which is not region-specific. Early results from the quantitative literature (Collier and Hoeffler 2002b) also point to no statistically significant differences across regions (e.g., Africa versus the rest of the world) with respect to the fit of the CH model. This suggests that we can forego a most similar systems approach in the case study design.

But other nonlinearities might exist in the data. Recent research suggests that some of the variables in the CH model behave differently in rich and poor countries. For example, democracy is correlated with peace only in highly developed countries (Hegre 2003). This is a question that most studies of civil war have not addressed.[41] Case studies can help us identify the different institutional pathways through which democracy may prevent civil war outbreak in rich countries, but not in poor countries. Other interesting interactive effects are also explored, as between economic growth and democracy, and ethnic heterogeneity and political institutions.

From Statistics to Cases and Back to Statistics

In sum, the case study project has several uses. It helps us establish the internal validity of the logic that underlies the CH model of civil war onset; it identifies problems with data measurement and suggests solutions for it; it helps resolve the endogeneity and selection problems in the statistical analysis of civil war occurrence through detailed historical narratives and a chronological sequence of events; it identifies and selects among causal mechanisms that explain the process of getting to civil war; and it identifies potentially omitted variables that might be usefully incorporated in a model of the causes of civil war.

At the same time, all this is possible because a first attempt at theory building and empirical testing is available through the CH model. Case selection was guided by the statistical analysis and the narratives were structured around questions that referred to the way in which independent variables from the model were connected, or addressed questions that were generated by the statistical analysis. The case studies can then feed back into the statistical analysis, as new candidate variables are identified to expand the theory of civil war onset, and these variables are coded so that they can be integrated in the data set. With the new, refined proxies added to the data set, the new and expanded CH model can be reestimated in another "iteration" of this research. In the conclusion to this volume, we focus much more on the lessons learned from the case studies and on possible expansions of the theory of civil war.

Organization of the Volume

All of the cases that we have chosen to include in this book are rich and engaging accounts of war or, sometimes, of how war was avoided. To help the reader digest the large quantities of facts, conclusions, and conjectures in this book, a synthesis of the cases is presented in the conclusion. We have organized the cases in two volumes. The first volume includes case studies of African civil wars (including Algeria, even though Algeria is often lumped together with the Middle East). The second volume includes cases from all other regions. There is no substantive rationale behind this organization of cases—we do not think that African civil wars are different. This is simply a device to present the material effectively, given the considerable length of the book. The introduction (the model and research design) and the conclusion (the synthesis of the findings of the case studies) are repeated in each volume. The conclusion draws on all cases and relates them back to the CH model. The CH model is not region-specific, so it is appropriate to draw on all cases in the conclusion. This also allows readers who have more geographically defined interests and who will not read both volumes to see how cases from other regions compare to cases from "their" region.

There are some "natural" comparisons across the two volumes. Indonesia and Nigeria are both oil-rich states with much violence throughout their history. Both cases illustrate complex pathways linking oil to violence. Burundi and the Democratic Republic of Congo put in perspective CH's arguments on the impact of resource-dependence and ethnic diversity. Both highlight the importance of the territorial concentration of resources and, in Burundi, the territorial concentration of political power. Bosnia and Indonesia also deal with the issue of regional inequality and ethnic differences across regions. Algeria and Kenya are two cases that force us to think harder about the concept of ethnic war. In both cases the violence took an ethnic hue, but ethnic divisions may not have been the deciding factor underlying that violence. Several cases in both volumes highlight the role of external intervention in inciting and supporting civil war. Civil wars in Lebanon, Mozambique, and Sudan cannot be understood without a close look at the role of external military or economic intervention.

Some of the cases consider the links between political and criminal violence. Not only are there important spatial effects (diffusion and contagion) that explain violence in Russia and Colombia, but there is also a dynamic relationship between the organization of criminal networks and the pursuit of political agendas in civil wars (see the cases on civil wars in the Caucasus as well as Algeria). These cases lead us to consider the effects of state capacity. In Northern Ireland, extreme violence was avoided largely as a result of substantial state capacity. By contrast, in Kenya, war might have been avoided because of substantial state capacity to repress opposition (though the state has caused much intercommunal violence). Those cases push us to think harder about the mechanisms through which state capacity operates to reduce the risk of civil war, because those mechanisms may be different in economically developed and underdeveloped states. In Macedonia, although state capacity was low, a war was averted largely as a result of substantial external assistance and a generally open regime.

Each volume ends with a regional comparison (in chapter 9) between cases that share considerable similarities. Volume 1 includes an analysis of the civil wars in

Mali and Senegal. Volume 2 includes an analysis of civil wars in South Ossetia (Georgia), Abkhazia (Georgia), and Chechnya (Russia), comparing them to cases of war avoidance in Adjaria (Georgia) and Dagestan (Russia). The chapters on Bosnia and Macedonia also offer useful comparisons, as those cases share many of the same underlying conditions and were similarly affected by the collapse of the Yugoslav state.

In chapter 10, the conclusion, we draw out the main lessons from all the cases and suggest ways to use those lessons to modify, refine, or expand the theory of civil war. Now, we turn to the cases.

Notes

1. We do not present all the cases in this book. Drafts of those cases that are mentioned in the introduction or conclusion, but not included in the book, are available from the editors. Some of the chapters/cases cover more than one episode of civil war.
2. See Collier and Hoeffler (2000, 2001, 2002a, 2004).
3. Data, codebooks, and other replication information for the chapters included in this book can be accessed online at: http://pantheon.yale.edu/~ns237/.
4. We offer more details in a supplement posted online (it includes the original set of guidelines given to authors): http://www.yale.edu/unsy/civilwars/guidelines.htm. Our guidelines changed somewhat over time, as we moved away from the idea of using cases to test the theory and toward the idea of using the cases to develop theory and explore other issues, such as mechanisms, sequences, measurement, and unit homogeneity. This shift in focus was communicated to authors during and after the second conference (April 2002 in New Haven), where authors presented first drafts of their case studies.
5. This section draws heavily on Collier and Hoeffler (2001, 2004). Tables with statistical results and excerpts from the article are reproduced with permission from Oxford University Press.
6. Civil war involves such an armed conflict between the government and local rebels with the ability to mount some resistance. The violence must kill a substantial number of people (more than 1,000). See Sambanis (2004b) for a discussion of the definition and measurement of civil war.
7. We use "rebellion," "insurgency," and "civil war" interchangeably.
8. Only brief descriptions of the data and sources are included here. For more details, see Collier and Hoeffler (2001, 2004).
9. The source for the data is the U.S. Bureau of the Census. CH divided these numbers by the total population in the country of origin.
10. *Source:* GDP World Development Indicators.
11. The CH model measures income as real purchasing power parity (PPP)-adjusted GDP per capital. The primary data set is the Penn World Tables 5.6 (Summers and Heston 1991). Because the data are only available from 1960 to 1992 we used the growth rates of real PPP-adjusted GDP per capita data from the World Bank's World Development Indicators 1998 in order to obtain income data for the 1990s. These GDP per capita data were used to calculate the average annual growth rate over the previous five years.

12. We measure male secondary school enrollment rates as gross enrollment ratios, that is, the ratio of total enrollment, regardless of age, to the population of the age group that officially corresponds to the level of education shown. Secondary education completes the provision of basic education that began at the primary level, and aims at laying the foundations for lifelong learning and human development, by offering more subject- or skill-oriented instruction using more specialized teachers. *Source:* World Bank Development Indicators 1998.

13. We used data from the Food and Agriculture Organization to measure the proportion of a country's terrain which is covered in woods and forest. *Source:* http://www. fao.org/forestry.

14. The proportion of a country's terrain that is mountainous was measured by Gerrard (2000), a physical geographer who specializes in mountainous terrain. His measure is based not just on altitude but takes into account plateaus and rugged uplands.

15. We constructed a dispersion index of the population on a country-by-country basis. Based on population data for 400-km^2 cells, we generated a Gini coefficient of population dispersion for each country. A value of 0 indicates that the population is evenly distributed across the country and a value of 1 indicates that the total population is concentrated in one area. Data are available for 1990 and 1995. *Data sources:* Center for International Earth Science Information Network (CIESIN), Columbia University; International Food Policy Research Institute (IFPRI); and World Resources Institute (WRI). 2000. *Gridded Population of the World (GPW), Version 2.* Palisades, NY: IESIN, Columbia University. Available at http://sedac.ciesin.org/plue/gpw.

16. Ethnic fractionalization data are only available for 1960. The source for the data is *Atlas Narodov Mira* (USSR 1964). Using data from Barrett (1982) on religious affiliations, we constructed an analogous religious fractionalization index. The fractionalization indices range from 0 to 100. A value of 0 indicates that the society is completely homogeneous, whereas a value of 100 would characterize a completely heterogeneous society. Social fractionalization is the product of the ethnolinguistic fractionalization and the religious fractionalization index plus the ethnolinguistic or the religious fractionalization index, whichever is the greater. By adding either index, we avoid classifying a country as homogeneous (a value of 0) if the country is ethnically homogeneous but religiously diverse, or vice versa.

17. We measure polarization with $\alpha = 1.6$ and define ethnic dominance as occurring when the largest ethnic group constitutes 45 to 90 percent of the population. For a discussion of religious polarization and its effect on civil war, see Reynal-Querol (2000, 2002).

18. Data and modeling changes were made to the version of the CH analysis that we use here, resulting in different average probability estimates of civil war than the figures reported in several of the case studies. The case studies drew upon an earlier version of the model and data with an average war risk around 6 percent. Probability estimates are slightly dependent on whether GDP or education is used to proxy opportunity cost.

19. This section draws heavily on Sambanis (2004a). Excerpts from that article are reprinted with permission of Cambridge University Press.

20. These are issues that apply equally to qualitative and quantitative studies.

21. In this book, the distinction between micro- and macrolevels is used to reflect the difference between individual-level preferences and actions (the microlevel) and systemwide or country-level opportunity structures and processes (the macrolevel).

22. Green and Seher (2002) identify this as a general problem in the literature on ethnic conflict. The literature clearly suffers from a disjuncture between an abundance of macrohistorical evidence and macropolitical explanations of violence, on the one hand, and a scarcity of individual-level or group-level data and theories of violent conflict on the other hand.

23. Process tracing is a method of making historical arguments about causal processes. It explains the "process by which initial conditions are transformed into outcomes . . . [and] uncovers what stimuli the actors attend to: the decision process that makes use of these stimuli to arrive at decisions; the actual behavior that then occurs; the effect of various institutional arrangements on attention, processing, and behavior; and the effect of other variables of interest on attention, processing, and behavior" (George and McKeown 1985, 35). See, also, George (1979).

24. A set of questions was developed in collaboration with Ibrahim Elbadawi and Norman Loayza. We gave the list to all authors at a conference held in Oslo, Norway, where we launched the project. All authors had read and discussed a set of core papers, including the CH model that they would apply to their cases. Authors were also briefed on the specific targets of the project. Research design refinements were communicated to the authors in a second conference, held in New Haven, CT, where authors presented first drafts of their papers. The editors sent detailed comments and instructions for revisions to all authors after the New Haven conference and, again, after second drafts were submitted. Final drafts were reviewed by the editors and submitted to an external review.

25. In the quantitative literature, the goal of statistical analysis is usually not to maximize the R^2 of a regression, because this can be done by adding nonstatistically significant variables to the model. But if most of the variance is left unexplained, the risk of omitted variable bias should also be greater. If the cases can help develop a model that explains more of the variance while also identifying significant variables, that should also reduce the risk of omitted variable bias.

26. Endogeneity could be caused both by nonrecursiveness in the model (i.e., if a variable such as economic growth influences civil war risk and civil war, in turn, influences economic growth) and by jointly determined explanatory variables (as would be the case, for example, if income level or growth caused the level of democracy and all three variables were included in the model). See Sambanis (2002) for a discussion of problems of endogeneity in quantitative studies of civil war.

27. An example is the interpretation of the statistically significant negative relationship between per capita GDP and civil war onset in Collier and Hoeffler (2000, 2004) and in Fearon and Laitin (2003). Collier and Hoeffler interpret this finding as evidence of their "economic opportunity cost" theory of civil war, whereas Fearon and Laitin argue that GDP measures state capacity and interpret the finding differently. Thus, the same hypothesis test can be used to inform two very different theories with different causal mechanisms leading to civil war.

28. If the model predicts a high risk of civil war for a given country-year and war does not occur, this could be seen as a prediction failure that can be usefully analyzed. Some might say that, even though there was no war, the model is technically still "right" since it only predicts the risk of war, not actual war. Thus, war might have been avoided for random reasons. This is always true with probabilistic models, but the argument can be turned around: War occurrence in countries with a high predicted risk of war might also happen for reasons that are outside the model. The case studies' ability to uncover spurious correlations and detect measurement error helps us improve the model. If we expand the model using theoretical insights derived from the case studies as suggested here and then test the expanded model by taking it back to the quantitative data, we will be able to test formally the significance of the theoretical differences between the old and new versions of the model by formally comparing the models' explanatory power.

29. Nonlinearities imply that the theorized linear relationship between the DV and IV does not apply to the entire data. If ethnic identity matters in different ways in developed and less developed countries (cf. Horowitz 1985), then adding interaction terms is one way to explore conditional effects properly. If such effects are present, then a stratified sampling method should be used, if cases are used for hypotheses testing. Even a case-control design would have resulted in the inclusion of far too many middle-to-high-income countries in our sample. Those countries might well be different from poor countries and they might have less to teach us about civil war.

30. According to King et al. (1994, 141), selecting "observations across a range of values of the dependent variable" is a legitimate "alternative to choosing observations on the explanatory variable." Some of our cases are not included in the CH estimations of civil war risk because of missing data. We select such cases on the basis of IVs and of general interest in the case. Where possible (see Bosnia chapter), we filled in those missing data points and reestimated the CH model, obtaining predictions for those cases. Then we compared those predictions to actual events and to the model's average predictions for the population of cases.

31. In each chapter, authors refer to the estimated civil war risk for each period in their country, according to the CH model. In several cases, authors reestimate that risk after making small changes to the CH model and data, or after filling in missing data. These probability estimates are often different from the CH estimates, if the CH estimates have miscoded some variables or if they have not coded some episodes of civil war.

32. The risk of civil war varies over time. Each case in our project offers several observations, as it includes both periods of war and periods of no war (or, alternatively, periods of both high and low risk of civil war).

33. By contrast, Mill's "method of agreement" identifies necessary conditions that are linked to the observation of a positive outcome.

34. Selecting on the independent variables does not introduce any bias, but may reduce efficiency of parameter estimates. See KKV (1994, 137).

35. We did not use a research design that depended entirely on categories of the explanatory variables because the aim of such a design is to "find out the values of the dependent variable." See King et al. (1994, 139). As mentioned earlier, we already knew where the civil wars had happened.

36. King et al. (1994, 94) write that "If the process by which the values of the explanatory variables are 'assigned' is not independent of the dependent variables, we can still meet the conditional independence assumption if we learn about this process and include a measure of it among our control variables."They also write that, if cases are selected on the basis of values of a given variable, that variable must be controlled for in the model. Thus, we only selected cases on the basis of variables from the CH model.

37. Studies on the following countries were commissioned, but not completed: Afghanistan, El Salvador, Moldova, Somalia, Sri Lanka, Uganda.

38. Thus, we agree with Huber (1996, 141) that case studies illuminate "the logic of the argument rather than the validity of its empirical claims . . . [they] yield a story about *why* . . . variables should be related to each other."

39. Omitted variable bias occurs when a variable is omitted that is correlated with the dependent variable and one or more of the included explanatory variables (King et al. 1994, 169). Endogeneity, in its purest form, refers to simultaneous causation between Y and one or more of the X's. Selection bias refers to the problem of observing an outcome only as a function of an unobserved variable, though there can also be selection on observables.

40. See Elbadawi and Sambanis (2002) and Sambanis (2002) for a discussion of endogeneity and selection problems in the quantitative literature on civil war.

41. Another reason to forego a random sampling rule is that, if there is heterogeneity in the data, random sampling would not result in a representative sample.

References

Alesina, A., R. Baqir, and W. Easterly. 1999. "Public Goods And Ethnic Divisions." *Quarterly Journal of Economics* 114 (4): 1243–84.

Barrett, D. B., ed. 1982. *World Christian Encyclopedia.* Oxford: Oxford University Press.

Collier, Paul. 2000. "Rebellion as a Quasi-Criminal Activity." *Journal of Conflict Resolution* 44: 839–53.

———. 2001. "Ethnic Diversity: An Economic Analysis of its Implications." *Economic Policy* 32: 129–66.

Collier, Paul, and Anke Hoeffler. 2000. "Greed and Grievance in Civil War." Mimeo, DECRG, World Bank, Washington, DC.

———. 2001. "Greed and Grievance in Civil War." Policy Research Working Paper 2355, World Bank, Washington, DC.

———. 2002a. "Greed and Grievance in Civil War." CSAE Working Paper, WPS 2002-01. http://www.economics.ox.ac.uk/CSAEadmin/workingpapers/pdfs/2002-01text.pdf.

———. 2002b. "On the Incidence of Civil War in Africa." *Journal of Conflict Resolution* 46 (1): 13–28.

———. 2004. "Greed and Grievance in Civil War." *Oxford Economic Papers* 56: 563–595.

Davidson, R., and J. G. MacKinnon. 1981. "Several Tests for model specification in the presence of alternative hypotheses." *Econometrica* 49: 781–93.

Deininger, K., and L. Squire. 1996. "A New Data Set Measuring Income Inequality." *World Bank Economic Review* 10: 565–91.

———. 1998. "New Ways of Looking at Old Issues: Inequality and Growth." *Journal of Development Economics* 57: 249–87.

Easterly, W., and R. Levine. 1997. "Africa's Growth Tragedy: Policies and Ethnic Divisions." *Quarterly Journal of Economics* 113: 1203–49.

Elbadawi, Ibrahim A., and Nicholas Sambanis. 2002. "How Much War Will We See? Explaining the Prevalence of Civil War." *Journal of Conflict Resolution* 46 (3): 307–34.

Esteban, J., and D. Ray. 1994. "On the Measurement of Polarization." *Econometrica* 62 (4): 819–51.

Fearon, James D., and David Laitin. 2003. "Ethnicity, Insurgency, and Civil War." *American Political Science Review* 97 (1): 91–106.

George, Alexander L. 1979. "Case Studies and Theory Development: The Method of Structured, Focused Comparison." In *Diplomacy: New Approaches in History, Theory, and Policy*, ed. Paul Gordon Lauren. New York: Free Press.

George, Alexander L., and Timothy J. McKeown. 1985. "Case Studies and Theories of Organizational Decision Making." *Advances in Information Processing in Organizations* 2: 21–58.

Gerrard, A. J. W. 2000. "*What Is a Mountain?*" Mimeo, DECRG, World Bank, Washington, DC.

Green, Donald P., and Rachel L. Seher. 2002. "What Role Does Prejudice Play in Ethnic Conflict?" Unpublished paper, Yale University (September 5 version).

Grossman, Herschel I. 1991. "A General Equilibrium Model of Insurrections." *American Economic Review* 81: 912–21.

———. 1999. "Kleptocracy and Revolutions." *Oxford Economic Papers* 51: 267–83.

Hegre, Håvard. 2003. "Disentangling Democracy and Development as Determinants of Armed Conflict." Paper presented at the Annual Meeting of International Studies Association, Portland, OR, February 27.

Hegre, H., T. Ellingsen, S. Gates, and N.-P. Gleditsch. 2001. "Toward a Democratic Civil Peace? Democracy, Political Change, and Civil War, 1816–1992." *American Political Science Review* 95: 33–48.

Herbst, Jeffrey. 2000. *States and Power in Africa*. Princeton, NJ: Princeton University Press.

Hirshleifer, Jack. 1995. "Theorizing About Conflict." In *Handbook of Defense Economics*, ed. K. Hartley and T. Sandler, Vol. 1, 165–89. Amsterdam: Elsevier Science.

———. 2001. *The Dark Side of the Force: Economic Foundations of Conflict Theory*. Cambridge, UK: Cambridge University Press.

Horowitz, Donald L. 1985. *Ethnic Groups in Conflict*. Berkeley and Los Angeles: University of California Press.

Huber, John D. 1996. *Rationalizing Parliament: Legislative Institutions and Party Politics in France*. New York: Cambridge University Press.

Jaggers, K., and T. R. Gurr. 1995. "Tracking Democracy's Third Wave with the Polity III Data." *Journal of Peace Research* 32: 469–82.

King, Gary, Robert O. Keohane, and Sidney Verba. 1994. *Designing Social Inquiry: Scientific Inference in Qualitative Research*. Princeton, NJ: Princeton University Press.

McAdam, Doug, Sidney Tarrow, and Charles Tilly. 2001. *Dynamics of Contention*. Cambridge: Cambridge University Press.

Przeworski, Adam, and Henry Teune. 1970. *Logic of Comparative Social Inquiry*. Malabar, FL: Krieger Publishing.

Ragin, Charles. 1987. *The Comparative Method: Moving Beyond Qualitative and Quantitative Strategies.* Berkeley: University of California Press.

Reynal-Querol, Marta. 2000. "Religious Conflict and Growth: Theory and Evidence." Ph.D. thesis, London School of Economics and Political Science.

———. 2002. "Ethnicity, Political Systems and Civil War." *Journal of Conflict Resolution* 46 (1): 29–54.

Sambanis, Nicholas. 2002. "A Review of Recent Advances and Future Directions in the Literature on Civil War." *Defense and Peace Economics* 13 (2): 215–43.

———. 2004a. "Expanding Economic Models of Civil War Using Case Studies." *Perspectives on Politics* 2 (2): 259–80.

———. 2004b. "What Is a Civil War? Conceptual and Empirical Complexities of an Operational Definition." *Journal of Conflict Resolution* 48 (6): 814–58.

Singer, D. J., and M. Small. 1994. *Correlates of War Project: International and Civil War Data, 1816–1992.* Ann Arbor, MI: Inter-University Consortium for Political and Social Research.

Small, M., and J. D. Singer. 1982. *Resort to Arms: International and Civil War, 1816–1980.* Beverly Hills, CA: Sage.

Summers, R., and A. Heston. 1991. "The Penn World Table (Mark 5): An Expanded Set of International Comparisons, 1950–1988." *The Quarterly Journal of Economics* 99: 327–68.

USSR. 1964. *Atlas Narodov Mira.* Moscow: Department of Geodesy and Cartography of the State Geological Committee of the USSR.

World Bank. 2000. *World Development Indicators.* Washington, DC: World Bank.

Civil War and Its Duration in Burundi

FLORIBERT NGARUKO
AND JANVIER D. NKURUNZIZA

Burundi has been torn by civil war since the mid-1960s. Since the first outbreak in 1965, the country has experienced four more episodes of civil war in 1972, 1988, 1991, and from 1993 to date. The recurrence of civil war suggests that political elites have failed to create institutions that can promote peace. To the contrary, the political elites who emerged after independence instituted predatory and divisive policies that favored a small group of Tutsis, particularly those from the southern province of Bururi. The exploitation of social divisions by opportunist political elites is at the heart of Burundi's wars and the focus of this chapter.

Independent since 1962, Burundi has an agriculture-dependent economy. The primary sector accounts for 56 percent of the gross domestic product (GDP) and it employs 92 percent of the labor force. The export sector represents about 6.5 percent of GDP; it depends heavily on coffee, which accounts for over 80 percent of total export earnings. Burundians are among the world's poorest people, with a per capita income of about US$200 in 1985 and $113 in 1999. Burundi has a population of 6 million, spread over 27,834 km², giving it the second highest population density in Africa. The population is comprised of two main "ethnic" groups, the Tutsis and the Hutus. However, it is difficult to delineate the boundaries separating the two groups, as they speak the same language, share the same culture, and live intermixed in the same areas.

The history of the settlement of Hutus and Tutsis in the area now known as Burundi is contentious. The currently dominant school of thought—the French school—contends that these groups converged in Burundi from different parts of the continent at different times. In his typology of African civilizations, Maquet (1962) distinguishes five categories. He refers to two of these to describe the patterns of political organization in the Great Lakes region in Africa. The first is that of warrior farmers of the eastern savannahs. The second type is that of herders from the eastern highlands. Maquet argues that when these farmers and herders came to coexist, the result was a hierarchical system founded on the domination of the farmers by the herders in a quasi-feudal regime. To some extent, Chrétien (2000)

35

supports this theory, arguing that, until 2,000 years ago, the area currently known as Burundi was sparsely inhabited by hunter-gatherer Pygmies, the Twas. Since then, waves of Bantu farmers from Central Africa immigrated to this area, while the Tutsi herders from Eastern Africa settled in the area sometime between the 11th and the 15th centuries.

Even if it were true that these people came from different parts of the continent, after hundreds of years of coexistence under a common value system, they should have developed a common identity. It is, therefore, startling to observe how much the difference between the Hutus and the Tutsis has been emphasized in the last several decades as a tool of political entrepreneurship. Historical evidence shows that in contrast to some alleged recurrent conflicts between farmers and herders in places where these groups cohabited, Hutus and Tutsis lived peacefully together, albeit in a hierarchical feudal society. A sophisticated system of social regulation prevented ethnic wars until colonial rule.

We identify three root causes of war in Burundi in the postcolonial period: the Belgian "divide and rule" colonial policy that pitted Tutsis against Hutus; "regionalism" (see below); and Rwanda's 1959 Social Revolution. First, it is the reforms undertaken by the Belgian colonial authority in the 1930s that "racialized" the Hutu versus Tutsi categories (Chrétien 2000). The policy of replacing all Hutu chiefs by Tutsis marginalized the Hutus. What was once a dynamic class system gradually became a rigid system largely characterized by Tutsi domination over Hutus and Twas. Many Burundians from both groups internalized this representation of Burundi society, fueling resentment and conflict.

A second factor, prominent since the 1960s, is what we call "regionalism." The postcolonial Tutsi elite came mostly from the southern province of Bururi and promoted exclusionary politics that resulted in income polarization and tension between the two ethnic groups and, to some extent, between the South and the rest of the country. The combination of these two phenomena has come to define many aspects of Burundians' lives, including politics, education, employment, and social interaction. The Bururi exclusionary political system led to suffering of untold proportions of those excluded, feeding grievances not only from the Hutu group, but also from other entities outside the elite group. The result of these tensions has been a recurrence of political violence.

Given the "cyclical" pattern of violence in Burundi, the underlying conflict may be viewed from two perspectives. One view is that it is a single conflict that has been unfolding over 70 years, since the Belgian administrative reform in the 1930s. The conflict has been punctuated by episodic eruptions of violence. Under this view, to explain war we would have to identify the causes of the turning points in the underlying conflict. Another view is that this is a succession of different conflicts, which have to be analyzed separately. Whichever view one adopts, violence has played a central role in shaping politics and leadership since 1965 and it has provided an easy justification for politicians in both groups to mobilize public support against each other.[1]

The third factor that played a key role in fueling ethnic conflict in the early 1960s was the Social Revolution in Rwanda in 1959. Burundi's northern neighbor experienced a bloody power transfer from the traditional Tutsi monarchy to the Hutu majority. Many Tutsis were killed and thousands were forced into exile, many in Burundi. The similarities between Burundi's and Rwanda's social and institutional structure made this experience very relevant for Burundi. The Hutu elite in Burundi felt that their group's numerical majority should guarantee them de facto control of state institutions. By contrast, Tutsi elites became determined to prevent by all means a similar revolution in Burundi. To achieve this goal they keep their hold on state institutions, especially security institutions. This polarized understanding of the way in which Burundi should be governed creates suspicion and mistrust among politicians from both groups. Tension remains perpetually so high that a simple incident is able to provoke war, as each group is prepared to strike preemptively before the other strikes.

Does the Collier-Hoeffler (CH) model fit this case well? Although many factors highlighted in the CH model are relevant, we argue that the CH model predicts poorly the risk of civil war in Burundi. Both the core and alternative models generate low probabilities of war onset. The highest risk is predicted for 1965 with a probability of 0.29 and 0.36 for the core and alternative models, respectively. The models miss the extremely violent civil war in 1972, with probabilities as low as 0.17 and 0.25 for the core and alternative models, respectively. With respect to the instability in the 1990s, the model's predictions are 0.22 and 0.26 (core and alternative, respectively), even though there had been a civil war in 1988, which should have increased the risk of war recurrence, given the significant impact of the CH variable measuring time at peace since the previous war. Table 2.1 lists all five wars and gives some information on the characteristics of each episode.

Table 2.1 Key Characteristics of Burundi Civil War

Characteristic	1965	1972	1988	1991	1993 . . .
Duration (months)	2	4	2	1	108
Deaths (thousands)	5	200	15	1–3	300
Refugees (thousands)[a]	0	300	50	38	687
Ratio of deaths plus refugees over total population (%)[b]	0.2	14.0	1.3	0.7	17.1
Years from previous war	—	6	16	3	2
Provinces affected	Muramvya	Whole country	Ngozi, Kirundo	Cibitoke, Bubanza, Bujumbura	Whole country

a. Number of Burundi refugees in DRC, Rwanda, and Tanzania due to a specific conflict (UNHCR data). It is the difference between the total number of refugees and the number a year before the crisis. (In 1965, there were displaced people within Burundi, but no refugees outside the country).

b. Population at the beginning of war, except for the 1993 conflict, for which the population of reference is the mean of the 1993–2003 period.

We focus on the episode beginning in 1993, largely because the war is still raging. The current conflict is a continuation of the previous four episodes. It has been the longest and deadliest of all episodes and has claimed the lives of 17 percent of the population.[2] Only the 1972 conflict caused a comparable number of deaths, but it was much shorter.

Background to the 1993 War

Each episode of violence resurfaces the same unresolved issues of poor governance that are related to all previous wars. Governance failure and unresolved prior conflicts explain the recurrence of war. All wars, except for the 1993 episode, have been prompted by Hutu acts of rebellion, in protest against their perceived exclusion. In response, the Bururi Tutsis have used the Tutsi-dominated army to repress the rebels, resulting in even greater exclusion and deeper resentment, which fuels the next episode of violence. In 1993, the war was triggered by members of the army seeking to reinstate the status quo by assassinating Melchior Ndadaye, the newly democratically elected Hutu president.

The total submission of the judiciary to the executive's power is one of the key explanations for the inability to break the cycle of violence. Not only have the conflict's root causes never been addressed, but different governments have never attempted to make credible inquiries to establish responsibilities and bring the culprits to justice. Instead, killing has become the way to silence calls for justice. The Hutus have also adopted killing as the only means of seeking justice and avenging past and present injustices.

Were all these wars predictable? Specifically, how does ethnicity affect the CH model's predictive power and how did the underlying special interests influence the path to the 1993 conflict? We address these questions in three ways: First, we use the CH model to assess the extent to which Burundi's civil wars are predictable. Second, we focus on the pattern of social polarization in Burundi to explain its impact on civil war. Finally, we show how special interests that were based on ethnicity and regionalism were critical determinants of the 1993 war.

Are Burundi's Conflicts Predictable?

Many Burundians view the country's conflicts as idiosyncratic and think the conflicts cannot be understood in the light of similar experiences in Africa and beyond. We discuss the predictability of Burundi's conflicts on the basis of the CH model.

Factors of War Occurrence: Where Does Burundi Stand?

Recent quantitative studies have attempted to estimate the impact of economic, geographical, historical, and social factors on the risk of civil conflict. Collier and Hoeffler show that countries with a substantial share of their income coming from the export of primary commodities are more at risk, and risk is at its highest when primary commodity dependence is around 26 percent of GDP. Education and economic growth are other important variables in the model. A country with a rate of school enrollment ratio of 55 percent, which is 10 percentage points higher than the population average, cuts its risk of conflict from an average 14 percent to around 10 percent. As regards economic growth, each percentage point off the growth of per capita GDP is found to raise the risk of conflict by around 1 percentage point.

These variables and the logic underlying the CH model are relevant to the case of Burundi. The country is dependent on agriculture: Coffee accounts for more than 80 percent of total export income. Education levels are low and poverty levels are high. However, poverty affects Hutus and Tutsis equally, with the exception of a small elite of powerbrokers and their clients (Ngaruko and Nkurunziza 2000).[3] Ndimira (2000) has forcefully made this point by showing that in rural areas, the distribution of land—the main asset of rural populations—is not significantly different between Hutu and Tutsi landowners: The Gini coefficient is between 0.15 and 0.30. To some degree, this is consistent with the CH finding that there is little correlation between land distribution and civil war occurrence.

The CH model highlights the importance of a history of violence. Countries with a recent history of war and those with large diasporas (which may be caused by previous war) face a higher risk of conflict. Burundi has both a high rate of war recurrence and large numbers of refugees in neighboring countries.

What about the role of ethnicity? Collier and Hoeffler found that in countries with a single dominant ethnic group constituting between 45 percent and 90 percent of the population, the risk of conflict doubles. Burundi qualifies as a case of ethnic "dominance." The perception is that a dominant group will seize the opportunity to exploit the minority, pushing the minority to rebellion.[4] But the problem in Burundi is the opposite: It is the minority Tutsi group that dominates the majority Hutu. This is at odds with the theory underlying the CH results on ethnic dominance. Ethnic polarization, combined with authoritarianism, may increase the risk of civil war (Elbadawi and Sambanis 2000). We argue that Burundi's high risk of civil war is partly due to the combined effect of an ethnically polarized society and an ill-governed polity that reifies ethnic differences.

The interaction between demography and geography is also important. In the CH model, the greater the dispersion of the population over the national territory, the more difficult it is for the government to control rebel groups—hence, the higher the risk of conflict. But high dispersion could also make it harder for a rebel group to coordinate collective action in various parts of the country. In Burundi, it is the country's high population density, combined with the hilly terrain, that facilitates rebel insurgency. Rebels blend easily with the civilian population, making counterinsurgency difficult.

Collier-Hoeffler Model Estimates

Collier and Hoeffler (2004) attempt to derive an *ex ante* measure of the probability of a civil war based on a set of country characteristics. In table 2.2, we present

Table 2.2 **Predicted Probability of Civil War in Burundi (1965–95)**

Model	1965	1970	1975	1980	1985	1990
CH core model	0.29	0.17	0.14	0.17	0.20	0.22
CH alternative model	0.36	0.25	0.21	0.22	0.23	0.26
CH modified core model	0.61	0.42	0.20	0.26	0.29	0.32
CH modified alternative model	0.63	0.47	0.25	0.28	0.29	0.32

Note: The "modified" model includes our revised definition of ethnic group and consequent changes in the measurement of ethnic fractionalization, ethnic dominance, and social fractionalization. In the modified model, 1965 is recorded as a year of war (it is not in CH's data).

predicted probabilities of war outbreak in Burundi based on the CH model (rows 1 and 2). The core model uses secondary school enrollment ratio as a proxy of opportunity cost of violence, whereas the alternative model uses GDP per capita.

A number of observations on the results are worth making. First, the average probability of 0.20 and 0.26 for the core and the alternative model are much higher than the averages for the population, which stand at 0.066 and 0.069. This is consistent with the fact that Burundi has seen more war than most countries in the sample. Second, the model generates a relatively high probability estimate of civil war for the 1965 episode.

In general, the model's predictive accuracy is poor. For instance, it fails to predict the 1972 bloody episode even though tension had been rising from 1965 onwards. Instead, the model predicts the lowest probability of conflict for one of the bloodiest periods of Burundi's history (1970–74). Moreover, the facts contradict the model's predictions for the period between 1972 and 1988; the probability of conflict increases in that period, even though that was a period of relative calm.

The poor performance of the model may result partly from measurement error.[5] Consider the index of ethnic fractionalization, which is 4 for Burundi, well below the average of 52.63 for countries with civil wars and 38.64 for countries without war. This measure underestimates the political importance of ethnicity in Burundi, leading the CH model to underpredict the probability of civil war onset. Ethnolinguistic fractionalization (ELF) is defined as the probability that two randomly drawn individuals from a given country speak a different language. In Burundi all three major groups speak the same language, which results in a low ELF score. If Hutu, Tutsi, and Twa spoke different languages, given their respective demographic weights, the ELF index for Burundi would be equal to 26.[6] The new ELF score also affects the estimates of ethnic polarization and dominance. As rows 3 and 4 in table 2.2 demonstrate, measuring these variables properly increases substantially the estimated probability of war in Burundi.

Beyond measurement error, the CH model has a conceptual limitation. The model does not adequately capture the ways in which poor governance increases the risk of violence. An essential feature of Burundi's war—and one outside the purview of the CH model—is that conflict in Burundi is the result of a system of governance based on predation and exclusion of the majority of the population by a tiny minority. To introduce social polarization in their model, Collier and Hoeffler (2004) follow Esteban and Ray (1994), who estimate polarization as a function of the Gini coefficient of inequality and the scale of ethnic diversity. The resulting measure overlooks the most important factor of ethnic polarization: The degree of political instrumentation of ethnicity. Thus, they underestimate ethnic polarization in Burundi, where in reality the degree of political instrumentation of ethnicity is one of the highest in the world, in contrast with a low Gini coefficient among income classes (0.33 in the mid-1990s), and a low degree of ethnic diversity (only three ethnic groups).[7] The following section provides a more thorough discussion of the importance of social polarization with respect to the risk of war in Burundi.

Does Social Polarization Fuel Conflict?

This section argues that polarization of Burundi's society is the result of bad governance. Burundi's political elites use regionalism and ethnicity to secure their political power.

Ethnicity, Regionalism, and Leadership

In the mid1960s, ethnicity was to blame for a particularly volatile political climate. However, politics took an important ethnic dimension well before independence in 1962. Table 2.3 provides insight into this issue. It shows from a set of indicators

Table 2.3 **Long-Term View of Ethnic Distribution of Leadership Positions (Percent of Total Posts)**

Ethnic group	1929	1933	1937	1945	1967	1987	1993	1997	2000a	2000b	End-2001
Tutsis	22	15	18	28	71	72	32	38	89	100	47
Hutus	20	6	2	0	18	28	68	62	11	0	53

Source: Data for 1929–67 are from Lemarchand (1994). Data for the period from 1929 to 1945 refer to the number of chiefs from the different groups. Most chiefs were from the Ganwa princely group not represented in the table because it lost influence after the fall of the monarchy in 1966. Data for 1967 refer to the ethnic distribution of the members of the National Revolutionary Council, the group of Tutsi officers mostly from Bururi who overthrew the monarchy in 1966 under the leadership of President Michel Micombero. Data for 1987 (Ntibazonkiza 1993) refer to government composition at the ministerial level. Data for 1993 (Lemarchand 1994) relate to the composition of the first government after the first democratic elections of June 1993. The 1997 data (FRODEBU 1997) capture the ethnic distribution of senior public office posts.[8] Data for 2000a (ICG, 2001) is on the identity of state firm managers. For 2000b (ICG, 2001), data refer to the composition of the army's high command. Data for end-2001 (Net Press, 2001) are on the composition of the government of transition put in place in November 2001 as a result of the conclusion of the Arusha negotiations in August 2000. One should note that, given that these indicators are "qualitative" and not additive, they have to be considered as capturing different facets of the same phenomenon across time.

that ethnic imbalance in the distribution of leadership positions is not recent in Burundi, and it suggests that ethnicity has been an important dimension of politics since the colonial period. Ethnicity started becoming a political issue in 1929. In that year, the Belgian colonialists imposed administrative reforms that sidelined leaders from the Hutu ethnic group, ignoring the precolonial balance between Hutu and Tutsi in leadership positions (Lemarchand 1994). In addition, table 2.3 demonstrates the inability of Burundians, especially the elites, to overcome this legacy during the postcolonial era. After a slight decrease in ethnic imbalances in the late 1950s and early 1960, as the country was united in the struggle for independence, the data show clearly that the Tutsis dominated leadership, except for the period before 1929, in 1993 and in the period post-November 1, 2001.

In 1966, regionalism and ethnicity began to overlap. All three military presidents who have taken power in coups d'état and ruled the country for more than 90 percent of the time after the demise of the monarchy in 1966 are not only Tutsi, but also from Bururi, one of Burundi's 15 provinces.[9] They have put in place a nondemocratic regime.[10] Using discriminatory appointments to public office and other jobs, excluding Hutus but also to a certain extent Tutsis from other provinces, they have monopolized control over political and economic institutions. The relative importance of regionalism and ethnicity may be gauged from data on the control of political, economic, and military power given in table 2.4. Given their respective demographic weights and compared to Bururi Tutsis, non-Bururi Tutsis have been marginalized by the discriminatory system, even though they have benefited more than Bururi Hutus.

Controlling political power has also led to many economic benefits in the form of rents. Excluding Bujumbura, the capital city, Bururi has benefited the most from the economic policies put in place after independence. Table 2.5 demonstrates this clearly. It shows that Bururi ranks 14th out of 15 provinces in terms of food production per capita, the best indicator of income status in a subsistence agriculture economy, yet Bururi's income per capita is the second highest in the country. Bururi has little cash crop production so its low per capita food production is not

Table 2.4 **Ethnoregional Background of Burundi Leadership (%)**

					Total			
	Tutsis		*Hutus*		*By region*		*By ethnic group*	
Period	*Bururi*	*ROC*	*Bururi*	*ROC*	*Bururi*	*ROC*	*Tutsis*	*Hutus*
1967	50	50	66	33	47	53	71	28
2000a	66	34	25	75	61	39	89	11
2000b	70	30	0	0	70	30	100	0
End-2001	23	77	27	73	25	75	47	53

Sources and definitions: Same as for table 2.3.
Note: ROC = rest of the country.

Table 2.5 Economic Underpinnings of Regionalism

Variable	Bururi province	Average 15 provinces	Standard deviation	Rank of Bururi province
Overall school enrollment ratio	0.39	0.245	0.105	1
Per capita income (1998) in US PPP$	444	328	99	2
Population/hospital ratio (thousands)	107	266	134	2
Teachers per classroom	2	1	0.3	1
Food prod. per capita (tons)	0.41	1	0.15	14
Illiteracy rate	57	64	5	2
Per capita tax (1999)	268	366	90	14

Source: See annex 2.1.

in any way compensated by other agricultural activities. With no other natural resources from which to obtain income, Bururi's high relative income suggests that it benefits from enormous transfers from the central government as well as from remittances from Bujumbura and elsewhere.

Economic transfers to Bururi are confirmed by data on the province's rank in terms of its relative contribution to taxes and its various ranks as a beneficiary of public services funded by the central government. The average values for Bururi systematically fall outside the one standard deviation margin around the mean (see table 2.5). These interprovincial inequalities are magnified by the fact that Bururi Hutus are largely excluded from these benefits except for externalities provided by public infrastructure. Despite its central importance in Burundi politics, the question of regionalism is so sensitive that it is never debated in public. Generating conflict and giving it an ethnic coloration has so far deflected the public's attention from the real culprits: The ruling elites' abysmal record over the last four decades. Playing the ethnic card puts blame on entire groups rather than specific individuals.

Impact of Regionalism on the Risk of Civil War

The system of predation previously described intrinsically incites excluded groups to rebel, consistent with the literature on contentious politics (e.g., McAdam, Tarrow, and Tilly 2001). Azam, Berthélemy, and Calipel (1996) argue that the politico-economic equilibrium of predatory systems depends on the existence of an army-like apparatus, which acts as a militia in the pay of the head of the state. The army's mission consists more in carrying out domestic repression to dissuade opposition than in defending the nation against foreign attackers. In Ngaruko (1998) and Ngaruko and Nkurunziza (2000), the risk of civil war is modeled as an increasing function of shocks that increase predation, weaken the repressive apparatus and effort of the state, and create perceptions that rebellion can be effective. Ngaruko and Nkurunziza argue that these effects have motivated civil war, as has communication and information failure, which has led the parties to develop different expectations about governance and about the results of war (more on this in the next section).

Working under the hypothesis that there may be rational motives for war, it is explicable why "ethnic" violence broke out among people who previously lived together peacefully for many centuries, during the period of rule by Bururi elites. Ethnicity and violence have served both as subgoals and instruments of a wider strategy whose aim has always been to capture and conserve the privileges of ethnoregional and clan entities. Indeed, there is a correlation between the major turning points in the evolution of the distribution of leadership between the two groups and the episodes of war. For example, the 1972 massacres were in part the result of the tension between Muramvya and Bururi Tutsis that had been brewing for a long time. On the other hand, "bashing Hutus" became a potentially important "source of credentials for ambitious Tutsi politicians wishing to enlarge the scope of their influence within the government and the army" (Lemarchand 1994, 84–85). At another level, as Muramvya Tutsis were suspected by extremist Bururi elites of seeking to reestablish the monarchy with Hutu help, Bururi leaders successfully maneuvered to eliminate them from leadership in 1971, while Hutus were simply massacred months later. The dominance of Bururi Tutsis was secured.

Thus, historically, civil wars have been used to secure power, which in turn has underpinned distributive politics in favor of powerful groups. This distributive bias has shaped the conflicts not only through the grievances it has caused, but also because of the generalized use of the state as a tool for personal gain (greed in the CH model). Shocks to any of these three components would impact the system as a whole. Hence, the perception by many observers in the 1990s that the democratic changes enacted on the eve of the June 1993 elections (the restoration of multiparty system, freedom of speech, etc.) were a cause of ethnic tensions was probably engineered by those who stood to lose from the change in leadership. Indeed, such changes threatened to destabilize a system of special interests shaped along regional and ethnic lines.

Such changes were particularly threatening because the system had been enforced for so many years with so much determination; there was much to lose. Indeed, Burundi's history shows that when the change of leadership does not threaten the interests of the dominating group, it is peaceful. Between 1966 and 1987, for instance, three Tutsi military presidents from Rutovu in Bururi province succeeded each other through bloodless palace coups. This contrasts sharply with the bloodbath that resulted from the victory of a non-Bururi Hutu in the June 1993 democratic elections.

In this regard, ethnicity and regionalism are two forces that have profoundly shaped Burundi's society, including the civil society (churches, human rights activists, nongovernment organizations, and other associations). As we argue later, four decades of conflict have created a "learning process," especially among the Hutus. It is the result of this learning process that induced the rebels to adopt new strategies in the 1993 war, which explains the war's particularly long duration.

Belligerents in the 1993 Conflict

To explain the duration and other characteristics of the 1993 war, it is necessary to discuss the various belligerent groups, their strategies and their motives. In this section, we discuss the military strategy to recover power after the June 1993 elections, in which a civilian Hutu won the presidency. Then, we turn to a discussion of the Hutu rebellion.

The October 21 Coup and the Army's Strategy of Tension

The 1993 war has its roots in changes that took place in the late 1980s. Political openness imposed by the international community as a condition for the resumption of aid to the government challenged the political order that had prevailed since the 1960s. This openness resulted in an increasing number of Hutu appointments to key political posts (see tables 2.3 and 2.4). The multiparty system of 1992 and the organization of presidential and legislative elections in June 1993, both of which were largely won by Hutu-dominated parties under the leadership of Melchior Ndadaye, were probably the most important changes brought about by this new system.

Some powerful Tutsi circles viewed the triumph of Ndadaye and his mainly Hutu FRODEBU party as the end of an era during which they had enjoyed every privilege. The strategy that had sustained these privileges since the 1960s included a number of modus operandi to secure the presidency; Ndadaye's triumph was violating those rules. Ndadaye was the first president to be elected in a free and fair election, in a country that had been used to changes of power through the barrel of the gun. The new president was the first Hutu, civilian, and non-Bururi native to lead the country. Hard-liners within the ruling elite could not contemplate the possibility that anyone from outside their group could pretend to the country's highest office, so Tutsi governing elites despised the new democratic regime from its inception.

It must be said that this suspicion was exacerbated by actions taken by Ndadaye soon after his election, such as the replacement of large numbers of Tutsi civil servants with Hutus in response to electoral promises. That action was too much for those who had never imagined that their power could be challenged. As a result, although most observers have only stressed the ethnic identity of the president as the reason he was killed, his actions and the fact that the new leaders were not part of the traditional ruling group could better explain the president's assassination.

No institution felt as threatened as the Bururi-dominated army. On October 21, 1993, paratroopers decapitated FRODEBU leadership by killing president Ndadaye and many FRODEBU public figures. Other ministers and high-ranking party officials escaped death by seeking refuge in the French embassy. If "to rebel is to refuse allegiance to and forcefully oppose an established government or any ruling authority" (Rotberg 1971, xiii), then the army was clearly the first and most important institution to rebel openly against the new leadership.

Not all of the army partook in the assassinations, but there were no serious attempts by the armed forces to defend the president and the new institutions (United Nations 1996). It was in a military barrack that the president was executed on October 21, without resistance from a single army unit. Instead, on the evening of October 21, the commander-in-chief of the armed forces broadcast a communiqué in which he stated that "all army and gendarmerie units" were supporting and streamlining the coup (Reyntjens 1995, 14). However, soon after, the coup started to falter because of several factors.

After the assassinations were known outside the military, violent reprisals targeting Tutsi civilians broke out throughout the country. It has been estimated that as many as 50,000 people, mostly Tutsis, were massacred by Hutus just in the first week following the coup. About 700,000 people, mainly Hutus, fled to neighboring countries (see figure 2.1). Simultaneously, large internal displacements occurred. Tutsis fled to places protected by the army, including cities and administrative centers, while Hutus hid in bushes and swamps. These movements resulted in ethnic cleansing. Tutsis in Hutu-dominated areas were killed by their Hutu neighbors and vice versa.

The international community's swift condemnation of the coup and its ensuing killings and the denunciation of the coup by parts of civil society spread panic among the plotters. On October 22, the United States, France, Belgium, Germany, and the European Community suspended their cooperation with Burundi, a reaction that was unprecedented. As a result, the commander-in-chief of the armed forces read a new communiqué broadcast on the evening of October 23, declaring that the coup had been attempted by "some elements of the armed forces," adding that "the army staff vigorously condemns this ignominious act, and from the beginning has initiated mechanisms for the return to constitutional legality" (Reyntjens 1995).

The coup had failed but war raged on. Despite the announcement about the failure of the coup, the remaining members of the governing party, fearing for their lives, refused to leave the French embassy unless an international military protection force could ensure their safety. Unsurprisingly, both the army and the opposition opposed this intervention. As Reyntjens (1995) points out, they feared that

Figure 2.1 **Refugee Numbers (thousands) and the Geography of Conflict (1985–99)**

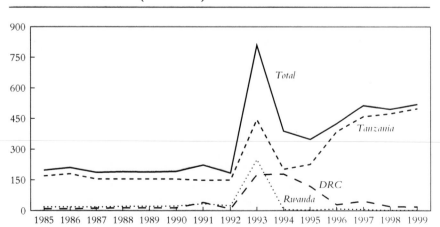

this international force would neutralize them. Eventually, the government left the French embassy on November 8, 1993 to regroup in a hotel at the outskirts of Bujumbura under the guard of 20 French special protection soldiers.

Far from submitting to the legal authority of the government, the army began a long process of sabotaging the government's efforts to bring back peace. The army allied itself with some Tutsi politicians in a subtle strategy to undermine FRODEBU's power and finally take the power back without alienating the goodwill of the international community. This strategy produced even more deaths than the October coup and the ensuing killings. From early 1994 until the July 1996 coup, more than 150,000 people were killed by the army, the Tutsi militia, and Hutu rebels.[11]

Through a series of negotiations with the opposition, FRODEBU lost a substantial part of its prerogatives to the opposition. Under cover of an apparently legitimate request for safety for Tutsis, opposition parties were targeting high-level positions. One of the concessions in September 1994 was the appointment of a prime minister from the opposition, and opposition representation in the intelligence and police services. The opposition was also given 40 percent of positions for provincial governors and municipal administrators and 45 percent of ministerial appointments. The constitution was suspended and replaced by an ad hoc "government convention," which had the prerogative to designate the president of the country and to agree on the appointment of the prime minister. A National Security Council was instituted with the majority of its 10 members coming from the opposition. These concessions eroded FRODEBU's power.

Characteristics of Tutsi Militias

The Tutsi militias were an outgrowth of the military coup that decapitated the country's executive and grew further after the coup. Spearheaded by Tutsi youths who had escaped death at the hands of Hutu militia within Bujumbura and later had been manipulated by a group of Tutsi politicians, a "self-defense" movement resulted in the creation of two militias called "*Sans échec*" (those who never fail) and "*Sans défaite*" (those who never lose). These militias started as gangs of youths without any political agenda. It was only in the aftermath of the October coup and the ensuing civil war that they were manipulated by a few Tutsi politicians to serve the latter's cause.

Although they had only a few hundred members, Tutsi militias were responsible for many revenge killings in Bujumbura, targeting Hutu civilians especially in the first half of 1994. Interethnic violence increased particularly with the organization of "*journées ville morte*" (literally "dead city days"). The militias wreaked havoc in the capital city, killing and looting, making it difficult for the Hutu leadership to exercise any authority. It was not until the return of Buyoya to power in July 1996 that Tutsi militias were neutralized. Some members were imprisoned, while others were integrated into the army.

The army was complicit to this period of terror. Some opposition party leaders supervised these operations. The objective was to force the government to accept political concessions. Strong-handed military interventions in Hutu strongholds such as Kamenge, especially during the disarmament operations beginning in March 1994, contrasted with their laxity in dealing with Tutsi militia.[12]

Hutu Rebel Groups

One striking feature of the 1993 war is that, for the first time in Burundi's history, the army failed to secure a clear and quick victory. What explains the rebels' ability to sustain their insurgency?

Structure of Hutu Rebel Groups and Recruitment Strategy

In June 1994, a number of leading FRODEBU members chose to split from FRODEBU rather than compromise with the opposition. They created the National Council for the Defense of Democracy (CNDD) and its armed branch, the Forces for the Defense of Democracy (FDD). The chairman of these two organizations was Léonard Nyangoma, the interior minister in Ndadaye's government. The FDD started to operate from across the border with the Democratic Republic of Congo (DRC), targeting the neighboring provinces of Cibitoke and Bubanza. Another active rebel group was the Forces Nationales de Libération (FNL), the armed branch of the Parti pour la Libération du Peuple Hutu (PALIPEHUTU), founded in the late 1970s in Tanzanian refugee camps housing Burundians who had fled in 1972. Other minor Hutu groups included the Front pour la Libération Nationale (FROLINA), founded in the 1980s and the Union de Libération Nationale (ULINA), created in 1996.

Hutu rebels (essentially FDD and FNL) and Tutsi forces (the army and the militias) retaliated against each other's killings in a cyclical pattern. The war intensity progressively decreased by mid-1996. On July 26, 1996, the army completed the 1993 coup by placing Major Buyoya back in power. The army changed its strategy by becoming loyal and respectful of the government. Thus, while around 150,000 people were killed between January 1994 and July 1996, "only" 50,000 to 100,000 people have been killed from July 1996 to date. That is, the monthly deaths declined from around 5,000 in 1994–96 to 670–1,350 in the latter period.

The particularly long duration of the 1993 war is attributable to the relative strength of Hutu rebels and their increased effectiveness throughout the conflict. Factors contributing to this result include their recruitment policy, their size, zones of operation, armament, and financing strategies.

Resentment left by decades of army repression and the feeling that the culprits never faced justice have been the driving forces behind the choice of young Hutus to join the rebellion. Rebels are primarily individuals motivated by revenge for the loss of power, relatives, or friends to army repressions. They also want to challenge the army's monopoly on the country's institutions, which have left them alienated. To a lesser extent, other young men and women join rebel groups because they identify with rebel propaganda that manipulates the issue of ethnicity to touch the hearts of their potential recruits. Most of those who voluntarily enroll are uneducated and poor youths with a bleak economic future. Their low opportunity cost induces them to try their luck as rebels (Collier and Hoeffler 1998). Moreover, rebels (as well as government forces) use up to 14,000 child soldiers (IRIN 2002a, 2002b). Most of these children are forcibly recruited or lured into rebel group ranks, both from within and outside Burundi, with promises of jobs and money (East African Standard 2000).

Regarding the identity of rebel leaders, it is relevant to note that what was discussed about government reliance on regional and ethnic ties is also observed in rebel command structures. The founding leader of CNDD, Léonard Nyangoma, is from the southern province of Bururi. Until October 2001, his nephew, Jean-Bosco Ndayikengurukiye, had been commanding CNDD's military wing, the FDD.[13] Moreover, Cossan Kabura, another Hutu from Bururi, was the FNL's commander until February 2001. The problem of regionalism was so deep within rebel groups that bloody in-fights emerged between Bururi fighters and those from other parts of the country. Eventually, Ndayikengurukiye and Kabura were deposed and replaced by Peter Nkurunziza and Agathon Rwasa, respectively, both from the North.

In an interview given on November 8, 2004, Peter Nkurunziza, senior minister in the transitional government, revealed that the Bururi faction within FDD assassinated about 60 non-Bururi officers in a bid to consolidate their control of the movement. He also revealed that FRODEBU, also Hutu dominated, tried to destabilize FDD-CNDD by targeted assassinations. Names of those involved and dates of the events were disclosed, making these revelations believable. This conflict within and among Hutu groups suggests that the conflict cannot be simply termed "ethnic."

Size of Hutu Rebel Groups and Their Zones of Operation

CNDD has an estimated 1,000 combatants, but the bulk of CNDD's fighting force lies in the FDD with about 10,000 combatants. The FNL has between 2,000 and 3,000 combatants. All these groups have some bases within the country but their rear bases are in DRC and Tanzania. Rwandan Hutus from the 1994 disbanded army have actively supported Burundian rebels (Balancie and La Grange 1996; ICG 2000, 2001). The tacit understanding is that Burundian rebels would also help Rwandan rebels to launch attacks against Rwanda. To a large extent, the areas where the rebels strike depend on their capacity to retreat when the army counterattacks (Van Eck 2001; Warigi 2001).

Thus, while many rebel operations took place along the border with the DRC in 1994–96, this area has been relatively safe since Rwanda occupied the eastern region of the DRC in 1996–97. This trend is illustrated by the drop in refugee flows to or from DRC after 1996 shown in figure 2.1. By 1999 and 2000, FDD were more active in the East, particularly in the provinces bordering Tanzania: Makamba, Ruyigi, Cankuzo, and Rutana. Those provinces have been relatively calm since the signature of a ceasefire agreement between FDD and the government in late 2003. FLN forces usually operated in the West of the country (Cibitoke and Bubanza provinces) and around Bujumbura. As fights have resulted in population displacements, one way to determine rebels' operating zones over recent years is to track the flow of displaced people in the different provinces. Table 2.6 presents the data.

We can see (table 2.6) that the provinces bordering Tanzania (Makamba) and the DRC (Bubanza) faced particularly fierce fighting over the period 1997–2000, even though fighting decreased in Bubanza in 2000. It also confirms that the violence in Bujumbura-rural, the province around the capital city, is sporadic because particular effort is made by the army to evict rebels threatening the capital city. However, such fights are particularly fierce as they displaced 75 percent of the population in 1999. The last row suggests that violence decreased in 2000, the year of the signing of the Arusha (Tanzania) Peace Accord,[14] except in Makamba and Bururi provinces (cf. figure 2.1). The increase or decrease of refugees and their destination have largely been determined by the intensity and location of the fighting. Until 1996, there was fierce fighting in the West while the Southeast was relatively calm, although the Southeast became unstable in the late 1990s.

Geography also appears to be an important factor in explaining rebel activity. Rebels prefer regions where terrain offers natural safe havens. For instance, in the East, rebels attack and retreat into the Ruvubu Natural Park, a deep forest that is hard to penetrate. In the West, they launch attacks from their sanctuary in the Kibira national forest (Balancie and La Grange 1996). Bujumbura's proximity to the forest and the hills surrounding the capital have shown the vulnerability of the capital city to rebel attacks.

Table 2.6 **Changes in Regional Distribution of Displaced People (Percent of Population)**

Province	1997	1998	1999	2000
Bubanza	26.18	47.52	61.76	5.23
Bujumbura-Rural	0.00	13.51	74.38	7.24
Bururi	13.54	19.97	19.98	20.40
Cankuzo	1.94	0.00	0.00	3.28
Cibitoke	13.41	3.67	0.20	0.00
Gitega	3.40	2.96	3.41	0.83
Karuzi	38.92	9.94	3.50	0.59
Kayanza	14.86	6.12	5.56	1.60
Kirundo	4.12	5.72	1.21	1.03
Makamba	13.39	10.85	25.32	35.86
Muramvya	8.52	5.70	4.74	5.74
Muyinga	4.88	6.85	3.52	1.91
Ngozi	3.29	4.41	3.51	0.75
Rutana	1.54	1.08	6.83	0.89
Ruyigi	2.15	0.72	0.24	0.36
Average	**10.01**	**9.27**	**14.28**	**5.71**

Source: Computed from data in Nkurunziza (2000).

Duration and Consequences of the 1993 War

The dynamics and duration of the war are partly attributable to factors related to the war's onset and partly to different factors. We discuss both internal and external factors; assess whether this case is consistent with cross-country results; and offer some statistics on the economic, social, and psychological consequences of the 1993 war.

Internal Factors of War Duration: Learning and Errors of Anticipation

One important fact that has emerged from cross-country studies of war duration is that if a conflict has not ended in the first year, the probability that it becomes a protracted war increases dramatically (Collier, Hoeffler, and Soderböm 2004). In Burundi, the cyclical pattern of war resulted in a learning process. Even before the 1993 war, the army's brutalities and mass killings of Hutus sought to send the message that anyone who attempts to challenge the Bururi political order would trigger a merciless repression not only against himself, but also against his whole ethnic group. Revolts by Hutus have always focused on Tutsi civilians, seen as soft targets. Rather than pursuing the Hutu culprits, the army represses the Hutus as a group to avenge the killing of their fellow Tutsis (see annex 2.2). This strategy was employed successfully by the army in the first four episodes in which the conflicts ended with a clear victory by the army. The army's repressive methods reinforce the conviction among the Hutus that once hostilities have broken out, they should not expect mercy from the army whether they are guilty or innocent.[15] The decapitation of a democratically elected Hutu government convinced many Hutus that they could never expect justice, prompting many of them to seek revenge rather than justice. Viewing the army as a permanent threat, many Hutus saw themselves as having a choice between preparing to fight for survival or doing nothing and getting killed. As a result, there are many Hutus who believe they are fighting for survival, which explains their unprecedented determination to fight on, prolonging the current war. Moreover, the rebels' realization that the army could not crush them as it had in the past boosted their morale and their urge to keep fighting.

The duration of the 1993 war is also attributable to the relative weakening of the Burundian army or, alternatively, the relative strength of the rebellion. Factors that weakened the army include their dramatic errors of anticipation. One such error was the failure to anticipate the violent reaction of the population to the killing of the president. The army was overconfident and could not envisage any situation that they would be unable to control. Even a warning from the captured and humiliated president before he was killed did not deter them from committing this ignominious act (see United Nations 1996, 45). The army was surprised by the scale and rapidity of reprisals in rural areas, causing it to lose control.

The long duration of the war has also been attributable to a failure of communication between the belligerents. The army simply could not envisage any compromise with the rebels, given the embattled history between the two groups, and this situation led to a stalemate. Moreover, the relative weakness of the army, both diplomatically and financially, and the assistance to rebels from different sources induced the rebels to believe in the possibility of a military victory. Furthermore, the fact that government commitments to settlement lacked credibility may explain the rebels' reticence to engage in negotiations with the government in spite of pressure from different external actors (Collier et al. 2004). In part, this is a result of the learning process we mentioned. In the past, wars ended through military victory, not negotiation, and Hutus learned not to trust the army. Many peace accords have been concluded between the government and the rebels since 1993, but it took 10 years to see some noticeable change on the ground, when the FDD and the government signed an agreement in 2003.

In addition, the factional splits within rebel groups and within opposition parties have complicated communication. These factional splits had their roots in tactical or strategic considerations rather than political ideology. This was illustrated in Arusha, where surprising but ephemeral alliances were concluded, such as the agreement between FRODEBU and the rather extremist Tutsi Parti pour le Redressement National (PARENA—literally, party for national revitalization). These splits and cross-party alliances lengthened the negotiation process and hence the war.

The most striking illustration of such tactics was collusion between President Buyoya and Cossan Kabura, the leader of the Hutu hard-liner FNL. The latter was accused of having made secret deals with President Buyoya. It was reported that in February 2001, Buyoya offered Kabura a "gift" of 100 million Burundi francs (over US$100,000) through Augustin Nzojibwami, the Speaker of Parliament (ICG 2001). Many Burundians interpreted this as a "Bururi deal," because Kabura, Nzojibwami, and Buyoya are all from there, although the latter two are Hutus. Kabura's non-Bururi followers saw him as an accomplice of the regime and as having sold out to Bururi regionalist policies. He was deposed in the aftermath of this scandal and replaced by Agathon Rwasa, an even more hard-line non-Bururi Hutu leader.

External Factors Explaining War Duration

In comparison with all the previous episodes of the conflict, external factors have had a major impact on the duration of the last episode.

DIPLOMACY.   External intervention significantly influences war duration. Elbadawi and Sambanis (2000) found that external intervention prolongs civil wars if the wars equalize power among the factions. In the case of Burundi, most intervention was indirect and the duration of the 1993 war (10 years) is equal to the average for all civil wars in which there was external intervention.

Some members of ex-Forces Armées Rwandaises (FAR) who fled Rwanda in 1994 returned to fight in the Hutu rebellion in Burundi, but this does not constitute external intervention as it is usually defined. More in conformity with standard notions of intervention was the assistance offered by Rwandan government forces (around 3,000 troops) to Burundi's army since 2001 (ICG 2002). However, it is not clear if this intervention was decisive in preventing the defeat of the government. Also, the posting of a military detachment from South Africa in Burundi cannot be considered as a full-blown intervention force since its role is to provide protection to opposition figures returning from exile. Nevertheless, the presence of a foreign force on Burundian soil, irrespective of its size, was a diplomatic victory for the opposition and a moral boost for the rebellion.

A number of factors mentioned by Elbadawi and Sambanis (2000) as disincentives for external intervention might explain the absence of a full-blown external military intervention in Burundi. One of the belligerents, the army, is considered strong and has discouraged attempts to intervene by threatening to attack foreign troops. The call for an external force remained a bone of contention between the army and the embattled FRODEBU government until 1996 when the latter was deposed.

Other external factors that prolonged war in Burundi include the attitude of the international community toward the belligerents. Access to bilateral and multilateral resources is a crucial source of military funding in Burundi. Unlike countries in which internal resources can finance a sustained war, combatants in Burundi largely rely on foreign aid, which can be appropriated to fund the war effort. In this respect, control of the state confers a decisive advantage. The fact that the Hutu had access to such means explains partly how they were able to resist the army by arming Hutu militias.

Another error of judgment was the army's expectation of international support. Within hours of the 1993 coup attempt, Burundi donors had unreservedly condemned it. However, external aid was maintained during the years of war when the survivors of the democratic government were still in office (table 2.7). The drop in external aid became more severe after July 1996 when Buyoya overthrew the remnants of FRODEBU. Neighboring countries imposed a total economic embargo,

Table 2.7 Economic Indicators During the Period of Conflict

	Average for the 1980s	1991	1993	1995	1997	1999
Aid per capita (US$)	33	46	37	47	9	11
Military expenditures (% of government expenditures)	7.2	8.7	7.8	12.5	20.6	—
Government expenditure (% of GDP)	—	28.7	31.2	30.6	24	—
GDP per capita (at 1995 $)[16]	194	211	191	163	143	110
Tax revenue (% of GDP)	—	16.3	15.7	17.9	12.7	—
Taxes on international trade (% of total revenue)	30.5	23.7	21.1	28.9	19.2	—

Source: World Bank (2000).

Note: The decline in aid per capita, military expenditures, and taxes on international trade resulted from the July 1996 coup, the final blow to a shaky Hutu-led government elected in 1993.

while the few remaining aid agencies closed their doors. This not only weakened the government diplomatically and financially, but also gave a moral boost to the rebels.

ECONOMIC AND FINANCIAL FACTORS. The drastic reduction in external aid after 1996 and the loss of governmental income as a result of the breakdown of the economy impeded military operations. This was especially the case in the aftermath of the economic embargo imposed in the summer of 1996. Thus, neither the decision to reestablish military service for high school graduates before entering university, nor the establishment of a special contribution to the war effort in 1997, nor the expansion of the army from 20,000 to around 60,000 troops could allow the army to defeat the rebellion.

With respect to the rebels' armament, it improved remarkably over time, helping them sustain the war. As reported by Reyntjens (1995), Hutu rebels were armed by FRODEBU when it was in power in the early days of their rebellion. Balancie and La Grange (1996) point out that at the beginning of the war about three to four rebels shared one assault rifle. This ratio changed over time as the rebels diversified their sources of armament. One such source has been the thriving black market for arms within the region (ICG 2001; IRIN 2001b).

What about funding? It is clear that the government army uses the country's budget and other extra budgetary taxes to fund the war. Similarly, rebels have been levying taxes on the population. They have also engaged in looting on a large scale—stealing food, cattle, money, and even clothing. As for external funding of the war, the belligerents do not in any significant way depend on funding from the diasporas who overwhelmingly reside in poor neighboring countries. However, it is no secret that the rebels have recruited their fighters heavily from the Burundian refugee camps in Tanzania. Moreover, the involvement of the parties, especially FDD, in the Congolese war provided an opportunity to finance their war effort with sales of Congolese natural resources. Zimbabwe and the Democratic Republic of Congo also assisted the rebels with training and logistics (Human Rights Watch 2000; ICG 2001), while Sudan might have provided financial assistance to Nyangoma (Balancie and La Grange 1996).

Finally, one of the unintended results of the international community's financial support of the Arusha negotiations might have contributed to prolonging the war. The daily allowance of US$100 to the negotiators is equivalent to two-thirds of the annual per capita GDP and may have induced some of the negotiators to delay the conclusion of the peace accord (Sindayigaya 2002).

Socioeconomic Consequences of the War

Not surprisingly, this long war has had a devastating impact on the economy. Collapse in infrastructure and the inability of the rural population to farm their land have led to a decline in agricultural production, both in cash and food crops. The resulting rate of malnutrition and undernutrition increased from 6 to 20 percent of the population (Nkurunziza 2002; World Bank 1999). More than 14 percent of the population was displaced in 1999, making it impossible for them to engage in economic activity. Infant mortality rates in 1997 had increased to their 1982 level (almost 12 per thousand), while this index had decreased from 9.7 to 4.4 for Sub-Saharan Africa, on average, during the same period. Life expectancy at birth had dropped to 42 years in 1997 compared with 47 years in 1982.

Military spending increased by more than 60 percent between 1992 and 1998, crowding out resources that had been previously invested in social sectors. The international community reduced economic aid to Burundi, which had a profound impact on the economy. The ratio of aid to GDP dwindled to a mere 4 percent in 1998 from 29 percent in 1992. Per capita aid dropped from its record high of US$54 in 1992 to its record low of US$9 in 1997 (an 83 percent decline). Government revenue declined from 20 to 12.6 percent of GDP in just five years between 1992 and 1997. Macroeconomic instability increased as illustrated by the high level of inflation (31 percent in 1997) and the depreciation of the rate of exchange (the rate of the Burundi franc to the dollar more than doubled between 1992 and 1999). The purchasing power of urban populations dwindled, following job losses in the private sector and a two-thirds decline of real wages, both in the public and private sectors.

Although these figures are illustrative, they cannot convey the level of distress and the long-term psychological impact of the war. Rural households have suffered frequent raids by pillaging rebels. Seventy-seven percent of households interviewed in 1998 had been affected by the war and 16 percent of them had lost all their money and household durable goods (ISTEEBU 2001). The psychological impact has been even more devastating. Every Burundian has probably lost a friend, relative, neighbor, or at least an acquaintance. In a survey carried in several parts of the country, 22.5 percent of household heads have been widowed by the war. Seventy-seven percent of household heads admit to have been directly affected by the crisis, of whom 57 percent have been strongly affected. Twenty-eight percent have lost close relatives, while another 23 percent have been displaced as a result of the fighting (ISTEEBU 2001). Therefore, in addition to the more direct economic impact of the crisis on households, its psychological impact may be the most important long-term factor that will have to be overcome to rebuild Burundi's society and its economy.

Conclusion

The purpose of this chapter is twofold. First, it explains civil war occurrence in Burundi by applying the CH model and discusses the model's fit to the case. The model showed that, depending on the variable used to proxy for the opportunity cost of joining a rebellion, the predicted probability of war for Burundi is three to four times as high as the average for the countries included in the CH data set.

Qualitatively, the CH model captures the fact that Burundi has had a higher incidence of civil war than the average country. However, quantitatively, the probability of civil war in Burundi is underestimated in the CH model. Moreover, this chapter shows that the model does not distinguish clearly between periods of particularly high and particularly low risk of war. As a result, the model fails to predict with reasonable accuracy some of the episodes of war, while showing high probabilities of war onset for periods that were calm. This inaccuracy may have been partly due to errors in the coding and measurement of some variables used for Burundi, such as the definitions of ethnicity based on linguistic fractionalization and the definition of social polarization in the context of Burundi. The use of a recomputed index of fractionalization improved the predictions.

Second, we focus on the 1993 war to explain its long duration relative to previous wars. We discuss the number and types of actors, their motives and strategies, and regional and international influences on the war. We argue that the main difference between the 1993 war and previous wars is that Hutu rebels acquired the diplomatic support, financing, arms, and skills that they lacked previously. Some of these factors are consistent with Collier et al. (2004), especially with their finding that when a conflict is not resolved during its first year, the probability that it will drag on for many years becomes very high.

While pressure from both the international community in general and the regional leaders in particular succeeded in pushing the government to compromise with the opposition, it is clear that the negotiations have overwhelmingly emphasized the distribution of political posts to the detriment of more fundamental issues, such as justice and governance. To a large extent, the prospects for a peaceful future rest with the political elites, both those in the traditional ruling class and rebel or former rebel leaders, who are holding the population hostage for the pursuit of their personal interests.

In this respect, our argument is that, despite popular beliefs, these wars are not fundamentally ethnic. The motivations of the different combatants go beyond ethnicity. Ethnicity is used by elites from the Hutu and Tutsi groups to achieve political goals. There is no doubt that there have been numerous instances of selective killings, where the Hutus targeted Tutsis and vice versa. But there have also been tens of thousands of Hutus killed by fellow Hutus and cases of Tutsis killed by other Tutsis, as long as the victims were perceived as standing in the way of their killers.

The "ethnic hatred" explanation becomes even weaker in light of the behavior of political leaders in both groups. If the Hutus and Tutsis were viscerally opposed to each other, how would one explain the documented complicity of President Buyoya, a Tutsi from Bururi, with some of the key Bururi Hutu rebel leaders who are supposedly at war against all Tutsis? How would one explain the short-lived alliance between PARENA, arguably the most radical of all Tutsi parties, and FRODEBU, a Hutu-dominated party, during the Arusha negotiations? If the war were just an ethnic contest between the Hutus and the Tutsis, there would not have been bloody fights within FDD in which 60 non-Bururi Hutu officers were eliminated by their Bururi Hutu commanders to consolidate the latter's power within the armed movement. The bottom line is that the conflict in Burundi is complex. It has a strong regionalist component and is not simply an ethnic contest.

The chapter also highlights the link between the conflicts in Burundi and Rwanda. As the two countries have a similar ethnic and social structure, conflicts in one country have loud echoes in the other. Rwandan rebels have fought alongside Burundi rebels, while government armies in both countries have collaborated closely in their strategies to deal with their respective rebellions. For decades until the overthrow of the Hutu government in 1994 in Rwanda, many Hutu leaders in Burundi identified more easily with the Hutu regimes in Rwanda. Most Hutus who fled the killings in Burundi in 1965, 1972, and 1988 sought refuge in Rwanda, where they felt that the regime was friendlier. Similarly, hundreds of Rwandan Tutsis who fled in 1959 and throughout the 1960s and 1970s came to Burundi where a Tutsi regime was expected to be friendlier. Harboring hundreds of thousands of refugees opposed to the neighboring regime tested relations between Burundi and Rwanda on several occasions.

There is an important lesson to be learned from the wars in Burundi and Rwanda. As noted earlier, many Hutus in Burundi interpret democracy in terms of numbers: They believe that their numerical majority should give them de facto right to govern the country, a move that they argue would make the society more democratic and peaceful. The recent history in Rwanda has shown that having incumbent leaders from the majority group does not necessarily result in a democratic system. It is known that the power in Rwanda was controlled by a tiny group of individuals constituting what was termed "Akazu" (a small house). Similarly, power in Burundi was controlled by a "kitchen cabinet" (Ajello 2000) dominated by Bururi Tutsis. As a result, most Tutsis in Burundi and most Hutus in Rwanda did not identify with their leaders.

These experiences suggest that the Burundi elites' claim that they are fighting for an ethnic cause is pure demagogy. They use ethnicity, a highly charged issue, to mobilize the masses for private gain. Those who organized the 1994 genocide in Rwanda were Hutu politicians who opposed sharing power with ethnic Tutsis who were reaching a compromise with the government. In Burundi, many of those who incite Tutsis and Hutus to violence are unscrupulous politicians interested in private gain. Once in power, they quickly forget their coethnics who fought for them. Burundians often give the example of Joseph Nzeyimana, a vocal opposition party leader. When he joined the government as a minister, his attitude changed. Asked to explain this change, he used an old Burundian proverb: "A well raised child does not talk when his mouth is full."

Annex 2.1 Inequality Across Provinces

Province	Overall school enrollment ratio (%)	Per capita income[a] (1998)	Population/ hospital ratio (thousands)	Teachers per classroom	Food production per capita (tons)	Illiteracy rate	Per capita tax (1999)
Bubanza	9	326	275	1.3	0.66	68.7	305
Buja Rural	32	410	427	1.4	0.46	64	347
Bururi	39	444	107	2.0	0.41	57	268
Cankuzo	38	344	84	1.0	0.63	52	431
Cibitoke	13	401	370	0.9	0.51	58	558
Gitega	33	290	154	1.0	0.75	62	294
Karuzi	13	162	346	0.8	0.47	69	265
Kayanza	23	220	236	1.0	0.79	67	364
Kirundo	15	379	487	0.9	0.71	70	530
Makamba	25	514	338	1.0	0.31	59	320
Muramvya	42	231	237	1.0	0.6	61	365
Muyinga	15	405	469	0.9	0.75	68	375
Ngozi	24	339	194	1.0	0.78	67	341
Rutana	27	230	119	1.0	0.54	70	282
Ruyigi	2	229	147	0.8	0.51	65	448

a. In US PPP$.
Source: Data on the first six variables are from Ministère de la Planification du Développement et de la Reconstruction and UNDP (1999). Data on per capita tax are from Ministère de l'Administration du Territoire et du Développement Communal (2001).

Annex 2.2 Phases of Different Episodes of War

Event	1965	1972	1988	1991	1993
Exclusion of Hutus in political leadership, education, and the economy	A	A	A	A	
Provocations, imprisonment, humiliations, and harassment of Hutus			B	B	
Assassination of Hutu leaders	C	D			A
Coup attempt by Hutus	B	B			
Coup attempt by Tutsis					B
Massacre of Tutsis by Hutus	D	C	C		C
Hutu rebellion versus Tutsi-controlled army confrontation	E	E	D	C	E
Massacre of Hutus by the army and Tutsi militias	F	F	E	D	D

Note: The table should be read vertically, episode by episode. Letters represent the succession of events or phases, ordered alphabetically from A to F.

Notes

Funding from the Yale/World Bank Project on the Economics of Civil War and Criminal Violence is gratefully acknowledged. We thank Nicholas Sambanis and Benjamin Shirlaw for detailed comments on an earlier draft. All remaining errors are ours.

1. In Ngaruko and Nkurunziza (2000), we discuss all five civil war events in detail.
2. We use here as a benchmark the population's mean value for 1993–2003.
3. Ajello (2000) writes that Burundi is controlled by a group of no more than 100 families represented by a "kitchen cabinet."
4. The next subsection discusses in detail how to interpret the "dominance" result in the CH model and also discusses measurement error in the data used in CH.
5. For example, the variable measuring time at peace since the previous war overlooks the 1965 conflict and this would affect the predictions for the 1970–74 period.
6. This is computed as ELF= $100*\{1-[(0.85*0.85)+(0.14*0.14)+(0.01*0.01)]\}$.
7. In the CH regression, the coefficient of ethnic polarization is very low, but the relevance of this coefficient is weakened by the inconsistency in how it is defined.
8. FRODEBU (1997) notes, however, that even though the Hutus headed most ministries in 1997, Hutu incumbents held only 11 percent of the most influential positions. With this in mind, it should also be acknowledged that some of the data covering the years 1987, 1997, 2000a, and 2000b may overemphasize the marginalization of the Hutus as the data may have selected the sectors in which discrimination is most acute. Nevertheless, the reality is unaltered: Evidence of Tutsi domination is overwhelming.
9. More precisely, they all come from Rutovu, one of the nine communes in Bururi province.
10. According to the index of democracy published by World Audit (2001), Burundi ranks 136th out of 149 countries, near the bottom of the index.
11. The coup was completed in July 1996 when the army brought back Major Pierre Buyoya, the Bururi Tutsi who had lost the 1993 elections to Ndadaye.
12. Observers have remarked that the Hutu militias had been armed by the then Hutu government (Reyntjens 1995).
13. The speaker of parliament, Augustin Nzojibwami, is Ndayikengurukiye's elder brother (PANA 2001).
14. The Peace Accord is a framework of power sharing among the different political parties in the country, except the FDD and FNL, which opted to continue fighting.
15. Many examples illustrate this strategy. During Burundi's wars, the army rarely holds prisoners of war: those captured are simply executed. In 1972, for example, common criminal Hutu prisoners who were already in custody for various reasons before the conflict broke out could hardly be suspected of participating in the Hutu rebellion. However, they were among the first to be executed by the Tutsi army and other security services. Also, the manner in which President Ndadaye was killed in October 1993 was a way of sending a similar message. Prior to his execution, the president was savagely mutilated at the hands of the army. A similar message was also sent to the Tutsis who were collaborating with FRODEBU. Gilles Bimazubute, a Bururi Tutsi member of FRODEBU's political bureau and then vice-president of the National Assembly, was among the first persons to be executed by the army.

16. In order to have an idea of the cost of the repetitive civil wars in terms of economic wealth, Nkurunziza and Ngaruko (2002) assumed that the country would have had the mean growth rate of African countries. It turns out that by 1997, purchasing power parity (PPP) GDP per capita would have been $667, an amount that is 68 percent higher than the actual figure of $397. Including the mean growth rate of countries that have experienced no war would increase the figure even further. This simple figure gives an idea of the cost of Burundi policies over the years since 1960.

References

Ajello, Aldo. 2000. *Aldo ajello cavalier de la paix: pour une politique Européenne en Afrique.* Paris: Editions Complexe.

Azam, J. P., J. C. Berthélemy, and S. Calipel. 1996. "Risque Politique et Croissance en Afrique." *Revue Economique* 3: 819–29.

Balancie, Jean-Marc, and Arnaud de La Grange. 1996. *Mondes rebelles: Acteurs, conflits et violences politiques.* Paris: Editions Michalon.

Chrétien, Jean-Pierre. 2000. *L'Afrique des grands-lacs. Deux mille ans d'histoire.* Paris: Aubier.

Collier, Paul, and Anke Hoeffler. 1998. "On Economic Causes of Civil Wars." *Oxford Economic Papers* 50: 563–73.

———. 2004. "Greed and Grievance in Civil War." *Oxford Economic Papers* 56: 563–95.

Collier, Paul, Anke Hoeffler, and Mans Söderbom. 2004. "On the Duration of Civil Wars." *Journal of Peace Research* 41: 253–73.

East African Standard. 2000. "Burundi Bishop in Child Soldier Saga." March 20.

Elbadawi, Ibrahim, and Nicholas Sambanis. 2000. "External Interventions and the Duration of Civil Wars." Paper presented at the World Bank Conference on the Economics and Politics of Civil Conflicts, Princeton University, Princeton, NJ, March 18–19.

Esteban, J. G., and D. Ray. 1994. "On the Measurement of Polarization." *Econometrica* 62 (4): 819–51.

FRODEBU. 1997. *Burundi: Un apartheid qui ne dit pas son nom.* Enquête Réalisée par le FRODEBU, Bujumbura, Août.

Human Rights Watch. 2000. "Burundi: La justice doit faire partie du processus de paix." *World Report,* March 23.

ICG (International Crisis Group). 2000. *Scramble for the Congo: Anatomy of an Ugly War.* Africa Report 26, Nairobi/Brussels (December).

———. 2001. *Burundi: Breaking the Deadlock: The Urgent Need for a New Negotiating Framework.* Africa Report 29, Brussels/Nairobi (May).

———. 2002. *Après six mois de transition au Burundi: Poursuivre la guerre ou gagner la paix?* Africa Report 46, Nairobi/Brussels.

IRIN (Integrated Regional Information Networks). 2002a. "L'UNICEF lance un projet pour les enfants-soldats." February 28.

———. 2002b. "Government Forces Accused of Involvement in Arms Trade." February 18.

ISTEEBU. 2001. *Enquête prioritaire 1998: Etude nationale sur les conditions de vie des populations,* Bujumbura, Burundi.

Lemarchand, René. 1994. *Burundi: Ethnic Conflict and Genocide.* Cambridge, UK: Cambridge University Press.

Maquet, Jacques. 1962. *Les civilisations noires.* Paris: Marabout Université.

McAdam, Doug, Sidney Tarrow, and Charles Tilly. 2001. *Dynamics of Contention.* Cambridge, MA: Cambridge University Press.

Ministère de la Planification du Développement et de la Reconstruction and UNDP. 1999. *Rapport sur le développement humain au burundi. La pauvreté au Burundi,* Bujumbura, September.

Ministère de l'Administration du Territoire et du Développement Communal. 2001. *Recettes fiscales communales,* Bujumbura, Burundi.

Ndimira, Pascal-Firmin. 2000. "Dimension economique de la resolution du conflit Burundais." Paper presented at the Forum sur la Dimension Economique de la Résolution du Conflit Burundais, Bujumbura, Burundi.

Ngaruko, Floribert. 1998. *Essai d'analyse institutionaliste du financement de la croissance economique en Afrique Sub-Saharienne,* Ph.D. Dissertation, University of Nice, France.

Ngaruko, Floribert, and Janvier Nkurunziza. 2000. "An Economic Interpretation of Conflict in Burundi." *Journal of African Economies* 9 (3): 370–409.

Nkurunziza, Janvier. 2002. *Policy, War and Food Security in Burundi.* Manuscript prepared for FAO. CSAE, Oxford University.

Nkurunziza, Janvier, and Floribert Ngaruko. 2002. "Explaining Economic Growth in Burundi: 1960–2000." Working Paper WPS2002/03, CSAE, Oxford University.

Nkurunziza, Pascal. 2000. "Organisation du rapatriement des Réfugiés Burundais." Paper presented at the Conférence de la Paix à l'Intention de la Diaspora Burundaise Séjournant en Europe Organisée par l'Assemblée Nationale de Transition de la République du Burundi et l'AWEPA, Brussels, December 9–10.

Ntibazonkiza, Raphael. 1993. *De l'indépendence à nos jours (1962–1992). Vol. 2: Au royaume des seigneurs de la lance. Une approche historique de la question ethnique au Burundi.* La Louvière: Centre d'Animation en Langues.

PANA (Panafrican News Agency). 2001. "Un proche de Jean Bosco Ndayikengurukiye dresse son portrait." February 8.

Reyntjens, Filip. 1995. *Burundi: Breaking the Cycle of Violence.* London: Minority Rights Group International.

Rotberg, Robert. 1971. *Rebellion in Black Africa.* Oxford, UK: Oxford University Press.

Sindayigaya, Jean-Marie. 2002. *La saga d'Arusha.* Bruxelles: Editions ARIB.

United Nations. (1996). "Rapport de la Commission d'Enquête Internationale chargée d'etablir les faits concernant l'assassinat du président du Burundi, le 21 Octobre 1993, ainsi que les massacres qui ont suivi." Document S/1996/682, New York, August.

Van Eck, J. 2001. "Polarisation of Parties Into "Win Power" and "Keep Power" Camps Threatens the Collapse of Peace Process." Burundi Report 2001/1 (April), Centre for Conflict Resolution, Cape Town, South Africa.

Warigi, Gitau. 2001. "A Beautiful Country is Bleeding to Death." *The Nation (Nairobi),* Opinion, posted to the Web on April 28, http://allafrica.com/stories/200104280051.html.

World Audit. 2001. *Democracy Table.* http://www.worldaudit.org/democracyaudit.htm.

World Bank. 1999. "Burundi. Poverty Note. Prospects for Social Protection in a Crisis Economy." Report 17909-Bu, Washington, DC, February 23.

——. 2000. *Africa Data Base 2000.* Washington, DC: World Bank.

The Economics of Civil War

The Case of the Democratic Republic of Congo

3

LÉONCE NDIKUMANA
AND KISANGANI F. EMIZET

The Democratic Republic of Congo (DRC) has experienced many civil wars since its independence in 1960. These wars share common features, but also differences, with regard to their causes. The purpose of this chapter is to analyze the causes of eight wars in the DRC and investigate how the DRC case fits in the context of the Collier-Hoeffler (CH) model of civil war (Collier and Hoeffler 1998, 2001, 2002).[1]

We make five arguments in this chapter. First, the low-level income and low growth rate reduced the cost of organizing rebellions and also reduced the government's ability to fight a counterinsurgency. Second, although regional ethnic dominance served as a basis for mobilizing rebels, ethnic antagonism was also an obstacle to expanding these wars to different regions of the country. Third, although natural resource dependence, as predicted by CH, was a significant determinant of civil wars in the DRC, it is not dependence per se that motivated the conflicts, but rather the geographic concentration of natural resources and their unequal distribution among ethnic groups. Fourth, the government's ability to fight a counterinsurgency depended more on external support than on the government's own capacity. Fifth, discriminatory nationality laws and shocks to the ethnic balance of the eastern region as a result of an influx of Rwandan Hutu refugees in 1994, and intervention by neighboring regimes on behalf of their coethnics—all variables omitted from the CH model—were significant causes of war in the 1990s.

The chapter is organized as follows. The first section analyzes the civil wars that occurred in the DRC since 1960. The second section examines the CH model's ability to predict the wars in the DRC and distinguishes good from poor predictions.[2] The final section draws conclusions. Overall, we find that some elements of the CH model are important in explaining wars in the DRC, while a number of other critical determinants of the timing and location of rebellion are missing from the model.

Table 3.1 Characteristics of DRC's Wars

Conflict & dates	Prominent leaders	Ideology & objectives	Ethnic base of parties	Areas affected/ controlled	Financing sources	Foreign support		Death toll
						Support to rebels	Support to government	
Katanga secession: 7/1960–1/1963	Moise Tshombe	Secessionist	Lunda–Yeke; Luba; Bemba	Katanga region	Minerals; Belgium	Belgium, South Africa	UN forces	80,000–110,000
Kasai secession: 8/1960–2/1962	Albert Kalonji	Anti-Lumumba	Luba–Kasai; Kuba	Kasai region	Diamonds; agricultural resources	None	None	2,000–5,000
Kwilu rebellion: 1/1964–12/1965	Pierre Mulele (Mumbunda); Louis Kafungu (Mumbunda)	Pro-Marxist; against foreign control of the economy	Bambunda and Bapenda	Kwilu region	Supported by villagers	None	None	3,000–6,500
Eastern rebellion: 4/1964–7/1966	Gaston Soumialot; Christophe Gbenye; Nicholas Olenga; Laurent Kabila (section commander)	Against US–Belgian military invasion/economic exploitation	Diverse ethnic base; predominance of Bakusu and Batetela	South Kivu and North Katanga	Own production of grenades/land mines; smuggling of minerals	Burundi (refuge for rebels); Algeria, Sudan, Egypt	USA, Belgium	46,000
Shaba I: 3/1977–5/1977	FLNC	Anti-Mobutu; anti-imperial	Lunda–Yeke; Luba; Bemba	Shaba region	Mineral resources	Angola	Morocco, France	850–1,200
Shaba II: 7/1978–6/1978	FLNC	Anti-Mobutu; anti-imperial	Lunda–Yeke, Luba; Bemba	Shaba region	Mineral resources	Angola	France, Belgium, USA	1,000–3,500
Anti-Mobutu: 10/1996–5/1997	Laurent Kabila (with AFDL)	Opposition to Mobutu	Banyamulenge Mai Mai	Countrywide control	Mineral resources; Rwanda, Uganda	Rwanda, Uganda, Angola	None	234,000–237,000[a]
Anti-Kabila rebellion: 8/1998–ongoing	E. W. D. Wamba; J. P. Ondekane; J. P. Bemba	Anti-Kabila	Several groups	Kivu; Equateur; Katanga; Kasai	Mineral and agricultural resources	Rwanda, Uganda	Angola, Namibia, Zimbabwe	450,000–700,000

a. Includes 232,000 Hutu refugees (see Emizet 2000b, 178).

Wars in the DRC Since 1960

The DRC experienced eight civil wars since 1960. Table 3.1 lists the wars and describes some of their characteristics. We discuss the causes of these wars next.

Katanga's War of Secession: July 11, 1960–January 14, 1963

The Katangan secessionist movement dates from the colonial era. Under the Congo Free State, Katanga was administered by the privately owned Comité Spécial du Katanga until 1910, when its administration was transferred to a vice governor general (Meditz and Merrill 1994). In 1933, administrative reorganization brought Katanga in accordance with the other provinces under the central colonial administration, despite strong resentment by Katanga's European residents. Because of the diversity and abundance of its natural riches, Katanga attracted a large number of Europeans and accounted for more than 30 percent of the total non-African population in the Congo in 1955 (Gérard-Libois 1966; Meriam 1961). However, only 7 percent of these (2,310 out of 31,847) could be regarded as genuine settlers, the rest consisted of temporarily employed civil servants, industrialists, technicians, and missionaries (Lemarchand 1964, 233–234). The province is the sole producer of copper (70 percent of national production) and cobalt. At independence, Katanga accounted for 75 percent of the Congo's mineral output, about 50 percent of total national resources, and roughly 20 percent of the government's total budgetary expenditures. It is the home of the dominant ethnic groups—the Lunda, Baluba of Katanga, and Bayeke—who historically have claimed to be unrepresented in the central government. Another important feature of the province is the rapid growth of a large urban (nonagricultural) wage-earning population (36 percent in 1959). This was a base for political mobilization by leaders of the secessionist movement.

The Katangan secession war was influenced by the ethnic character of the political parties that developed in the period leading to independence. The main parties that contested power at independence were polarized along ethnic lines, except for Lumumba's Mouvement National Congolais (Congolese National Movement, MNC), which advocated national unity and transcended ethnic affiliation (Young 1965). In Katanga, the leading political force was the Confédération des Associations Tribales du Katanga (CONAKAT), created on October 4, 1958, to defend the interests of "authentic Katangans" (mainly the Lunda, Baluba of Katanga, and Bayeke) against the threat of "strangers," mostly from Kasai (Lulua and Baluba from Kasai) recruited by the Union Minière du Haut Katanga (UMHK) to work in the mines. CONAKAT was motivated by the outcome of the communal elections of December 1957, where no "authentic Katangans" were elected. The xenophobia of native Katangans was promoted by urban mining workers seeking to protect their employment as well as by the political elite (led by Tshombe) seeking to advance their political agenda.

DISPUTES OVER CONSTITUTIONAL ORIENTATION: UNITARISM, FEDERALISM, AND SECESSIONISM. Disputes about the constitutional orientation of the country were a central factor in the Katangan secessionist movement and generated antagonism within the national political elite and between nationalists and Belgium. The *Loi Fondamentale,* the transitional constitution at independence, provided for a parliamentary democracy that ceded substantial autonomy to the provinces. But the constitution was too ambiguous about the division of power between the president and prime minister and the degree of central control of the provinces.

Prime Minister Lumumba and his party advocated a unitary and centralized Congo state as the expression of true national independence. Lumumba's opponents, led by CONAKAT president Tshombe, wanted secession or at least broad independence of the provinces from the central government. Tshombe believed that provincial sovereignty was a means of achieving a fair distribution of resources based on each province's needs and contribution to national wealth (Gérard-Libois 1966, 47). Kasavubu, president of the country and of the Alliance of the Bankongo (Alliance de Bakongo, ABAKO), also shared Tshombe's views, supported the organization of the Congo into a federal system, and at times threatened secession.

RELATIONS WITH BELGIUM AND THE WEST. Lumumba favored a truly independent Congo, while maintaining cooperative relations with Belgium and other Western countries. In contrast, Tshombe wanted to maintain a patrimonial relationship with Belgium (Gérard-Libois 1966, 33). Tshombe served Belgium's neocolonial interests in the Congo. Lumumba's nationalist views were met with hostility from Belgium and his socialist views caused suspicion and antagonism from the United States and even the United Nations. Lumumba was seen as an obstacle to Belgian neocolonialism and a threat to Western anticommunism in Africa, and this ultimately cost him his life.

TRIGGER FACTORS OF THE SECESSIONIST WAR. Congolese soldiers had expected that, following independence, they would replace Belgians in leadership positions, a change that Belgians were not ready to accept. On July 4, 1960, elements of the armed forces in the capital revolted against their Belgian officers. Adding fuel to fire, on July 5, 1960, Gérard Jansens, commander-in-chief of the Congolese army, declared that there was no question of Africanizing the command of the army: "Before independence = after independence" (De Witte 2001, 6). Following a special meeting of the Council of Ministers on July 8, Lumumba took steps to Africanize the officer corps, naming Kasaian Victor Lundula as commander-in-chief of the army (named Armée Nationale Congolaise, ANC), Colonel Joseph Désiré Mobutu as chief of staff, and the Belgian Colonel Henniquian as chief adviser of the ANC.

Starting from July 9, 1960, the mutiny of the armed forces spread to other parts of the country (Young 1965, 316). The following day, Congolese civilians in Kabolo tried to stop the departure of a train evacuating Belgians. Panic among Europeans still in the Congo led to Belgium's decision to deploy forces to evacuate Belgian nationals.

Tshombe seized the moment to declare the autonomy of Katanga. He argued that he needed to restore order to prevent the political chaos in the central government from disrupting Katanga's economic and administrative system. On July 11, despite attempts by some Belgian officials to dissuade him, Tshombe proclaimed the total independence of Katanga, but kept in place economic ties with Belgium. Although the Belgian government did not officially recognize the Katangan secession, it nonetheless strongly supported Tshombe's government militarily, financially, and diplomatically (Gibbs 1991). Belgian troops prevented attacks by the ANC against Katanga, and Belgium established consular relations with Tshombe's government.

Lumumba appealed for assistance to the United Nations (UN), but the UN, some say in collaboration with Belgium and the United States, undermined Lumumba's regime. Lumumba threatened to call for help from the Socialist bloc, which invited a negative reaction from the West. It seemed unlikely that any pro-Western government could come to power in the Congo while Lumumba remained active. It was then decided that Lumumba had to be eliminated physically. He was assassinated on January 17, 1961 in a plot orchestrated by Belgians.[3]

After Lumumba's death, the Belgian attitude toward Katangan secession changed significantly. The Belgian government held the position that the integrity of the Congolese territory had to be preserved in a federal system. However, Tshombe refused to participate in the post-Lumumba government led by Ileo. Tshombe's insistence on separation caused the diplomatic isolation of his Katangan government.

In addition to diplomatic isolation, the Katangan secession was handicapped by the antagonism between the "authentic Katangese" and other groups, especially the Baluba from northern Katanga. In January 1961, the Association of the Luba People of Katanga (BALUBAKAT) proclaimed the secession of Northern Katanga. On February 21, 1961, the UN passed a resolution calling for measures to stop the war in the Congo by authorizing the use of force if necessary. United Nations forces eventually defeated Tshombe's rebels in January 1963.

The Kasai Secession War: August 8, 1960–February 2, 1962

The secessionist movement in the Kasai was driven by three interrelated factors: the Lulua-Baluba (Kasai) conflict, ideological divergence between Lumumba and Kalonji (a Muluba) over the constitutional orientation of the country (unitary vs. separatism), and the struggle for the control of diamonds in the Kasai region.

Known as the "diamond state," southern Kasai has large reserves of both gem quality and industrial diamonds. Until the mid-1970s, the Congo was the single largest producer of industrial diamonds, averaging about one-third of world total output (Kaplan 1978, 224). However, unlike Katanga, the Kasai region did not have long-standing backing from a Belgian settler community, so it received no support from the West.

The Kasai secession was led by Albert Kalonji, one of the prominent founders of the MNC. The MNC split in two factions in July 1959 over political differences between, on the one hand, Lumumba and, on the other hand, moderate leaders

Ileo and Ngalula and trade union leader Cyrille Adoula. They accused Lumumba of being an autocrat and tried to replace him with Albert Kalonji, but failed. These dissidents then formed a separate wing of the MNC led by Kalonji (and known as MNC-Kalonji), which opposed MNC-Lumumba. Kalonji espoused Tshombe's opposition to a centralized system.

The Kasai secession can be traced to the territorial expansion of the Baluba beyond southern Kasai to the Lulua area in the late 19th century, which created animosities between the Baluba and the Lulua. Because of scarcity of cultivable land, the Baluba moved to Luluabourg (in Lulua land) in the early 1920s and eventually dominated most clerical colonial jobs. The fear of domination by the Baluba prompted the creation of the Association of Lulua-Frères in 1951 by a Lulua chief, Sylvain Mangole Kalamba.

The antagonism between the Lulua and Baluba was exacerbated in December 1957 when the Baluba won the municipal elections in Luluabourg (today's Kananga). In 1959, the Lulua regrouped and won the legislative elections, thus securing the majority in the provincial parliament. The relationship between Baluba and Lulua reached a crisis when the local administration proposed to resettle Baluba farmers from Lulua land (an economically booming center province) back to their impoverished homeland in southern Kasai. This provoked a reaction from the Baluba that escalated into the first deadly conflict on October 11, 1959. The government sent an investigative team to the area and organized a conference between government representatives and leaders of the two ethnic groups. At the conference it was suggested that 100,000 Baluba should return from Lulua land to their homeland in southern Kasai to avoid further conflict. Although a large number of Baluba moved to southern Kasai, tension continued to escalate.

Kalonji was disappointed by MNC-Lumumba's support of the Lulua in Kasai. Until the latter part of 1959, the MNC-Lumumba had kept a neutral stand in the conflict between Lulua and Baluba. However, in a bid to secure majority seats in the Kasai legislative assembly, the MNC-Lumumba entered into an alliance with the Lulua and defeated the MNC-Kalonji (Lemarchand 1964, 209; CRISP 1962). Kalonji exploited these local tensions and the chaos in the central government to declare the secession of southern Kasai. The secessionist war was eventually put down in February 1962 by government forces after 3,000 to 7,000 people were killed. These figures include combat deaths as well as ethnic massacres.

The Kwilu Rebellion: January 22, 1964–December 31, 1965

In the post-Lumumba period, the UN invested diplomatic efforts for the national reconciliation and unification of the Congo (CRISP 1962). The UN organized a conference including parliamentarians and leaders of the provincial governments of Katanga, South Kasai, Haut Congo, and Kinshasa in a neutral venue at Lovanium University. From the conference, a new central government was formed led by Adoula, who had unanimous approval from parliament. Adoula formed a diverse government, including such key pro-Lumumbists as Gigenza and Gbenye (CRISP

1963). To appease regionalist demands, the Adoula government submitted to parliament an amendment to the *Loi Fondamentale* aimed at restructuring the country into 21 autonomous provinces (up from the six provinces initially created by the *Loi Fondamentale*). The amendment was promulgated on April 27, 1962. While the Adoula government tried to find a constitutional solution to the political crisis in the Congo, the opposition organized itself with the aim of a revolutionary overthrow of the regime.[4] Pierre Mulele led the Kwilu rebellion while the Conseil National de Libération (National Liberation Council, CNL) organized the eastern rebellion (Verhaegen 1969).

Mulele was a dedicated Lumumbist, influenced by Maoist ideology and served as Secretary General of the radical wing of the Parti Solidaire Africain (PSA) of Gizenga in 1959–60 and Minister of Education in the Lumumba government. He also served as a representative of Gizenga's Stanleyville provincial government in Egypt and socialist countries. In August 1961, Mulele refused national reconciliation and chose exile, during which he perfected his revolutionary ideology and tried to organize a peasant guerilla force. Mulele accused the central government of having sold out to the interests of the West and advocated a second "liberation," which attracted support from the rural population.

Mulele was from the Mbunda ethnic group, whereas Gizenga was an ethnic Mpende. Both groups were from the Kwilu province and claimed to be marginalized by the central government. The ethnic orientation of the Mulelist rebellion facilitated recruitment of combatants but also prevented the rebellion from gaining ground beyond the Mbunda-Mpende territory. Unlike the Katangan and Kasai rebellions, the Kwilu rebellion was not motivated by the control of provincial mineral resources. Thus, the rebellion could not count on external economic support and was entirely supported by the local population.

There are no easily identifiable factors that triggered the Kwilu rebellion. On his return from exile in July 1963, Mulele mobilized and trained his combatants who were subjected to a rigid code of discipline. The Mulelist rebels posed stiff resistance to government troops despite the rudimentary nature of their military equipment. The rebellion was eventually defeated in December 1965, leaving only pockets of isolated resistance in the rural area.

The Eastern Rebellion: April 15, 1964–July 1, 1966

The Adoula government failed in its mission of national unification and instead became a vehicle of indirect Belgian recolonization of the Congo. Antagonism between the parliament and the government—this time with the president and the prime minister on the same side—led President Kasavubu to suspend the parliament on September 29, 1963. The same day, opposition nationalist parties opened an extraordinary conference that ended on October 3 with the creation of the CNL, whose objective was to overthrow the Adoula government and to achieve "total and effective decolonization of the Congo thus far dominated by a coalition of foreign powers" (Vanderlinden et al. 1980, 124).

The leaders of the CNL fled to Brazzaville and formed a cartel of Lumumbist-nationalist parties, the most important ones being MNC-Lumumba led by Gbenye and PSA led by Gizenga (Vanderlinden et al. 1980). The CNL had a socialist orientation, which proved useful in mobilizing support from the left-leaning public by accusing the central government of selling out to capitalist interests. However, CNL's pro-Soviet leanings also kept it from receiving economic assistance from the West.

In January 1964, the CNL sent Gaston Soumialot and Laurent Kabila to Burundi with the mission of preparing the rebellion in the east (Kabila in north Katanga and Soumialot in Kivu). On April 15, 1964, the rebellion started in the Ruzizi plain south of Bukavu and, a month later, Uvira was under the control of the *simba* (which means lions), the rebel forces of the Armée Populaire de Libération (Popular Liberation Army, APL) of the CNL. The rebellion drew its forces from the large population of young, uneducated, and unemployed Congolese. The APL advanced quickly with little resistance from the government forces. The *simba* were believed to possess magical powers acquired from taking a traditional potion that was purported to transform enemy bullets into water (Verhaegen 1969).

In two months, the rebels conquered northern Katanga, Maniema, Sankuru, and the Orientale province. On September 5, 1964, the "people's government" of Stanleyville was installed in Haut Congo, headed by President Gbenye of the MNC-Lumumba who was also president of the CNL. By the end of September, about half of the country was under control of the APL.

The rich endowment in mineral resources of the eastern provinces was a major motivation and source of financing for the rebellion. In this respect, the eastern rebellion has similarities with the secessionist wars of Katanga and southern Kasai. Furthermore, like the Katangan, southern Kasai, and Kwilu rebellions, the eastern rebellion was also supported by a large ethnic base dominated by the Bakusu and Batetela.

The Adoula government continued to experience instability and its army was unable to contain the rebellion. The government turned to Tshombe (in exile in Spain) who still had some influence in the Katanga region and was backed by Belgian officials. More important, he had contacts with both the CNL and the Adoula government. Tshombe was believed to be the man who could achieve national reconciliation and control the rebellion (Gibbs 1991). He returned on June 26, 1964 and President Kasavubu assigned to him the task of forming a transitional government. Tshombe angered many when his government did not include representatives from key opposition groups, most notably the CNL. He rallied his former Katangan gendarmes with the assistance of Belgian mercenaries and advisers and with backing from the United States and Belgium. The rebels unsuccessfully tried to use white hostages to stop the advance of Tshombe's forces. Stanleyville was captured on November 24, 1964, but as many as 200 Europeans and 46,000 Congolese were killed.[5] The leaders of CNL retreated from the provincial capitals but continued to fight in rural areas. It was only in 1967 that the Orientale and Maniema provinces were fully controlled by government forces. The APL retained limited control over some rural areas in southern Kivu (Fizi and Baraka) under the command of Kabila. The rebellion was completely defeated by 1968.

Although Tshombe was instrumental in defeating the rebellions in the east and in Kwilu, his mission to stabilize the country was compromised by his personal quest for power and his conflict with Kasavubu, as well as by antagonisms between Kasavubu and Mobutu. According to the 1964 Constitution, Tshombe's transitional government was required to organize national legislative elections by April 30, 1965, at which point its authority would end. The elected parliament would form an electoral college to elect the head of state. The elections took place from February to August 1965. As Tshombe sought to support his bid for the presidency, he formed an alliance of 49 tribal-based parties under the heading of the Convention Nationale Congolaise (CONACO, Congolese National Convention) (CRISP 1967). Although the CONACO coalition remained fragile because of factional conflict, it won the elections with 122 out of a total of 167 parliamentary seats. However, many of the electoral results were contested because of irregularities and the Kinshasa Court of Appeals declared ballots from several precincts in Kivu, Cuvette Centrale, and Kwilu null and void. Nonetheless, the Tshombe coalition won a commanding majority in parliament, securing the presidency and vice-presidency of the lower house and the vice-presidency of the upper house of the parliament.

According to the 1964 Constitution, these election results meant that Tshombe had a high chance of being elected prime minister by the parliament or head of state by the electoral college. To Tshombe's dismay, during the first meeting of the new parliament on October 13, 1965, President Kasavubu announced the nomination of Evariste Kimba from the anti-Tshombe coalition as the new prime minister. The CONACO-dominated parliament blocked this nomination and Kasavubu's further attempts to renominate the same candidate were defeated as well.

This conflict between Kasavubu and Tshombe created a constitutional deadlock, which threatened to paralyze the government. Taking advantage of the situation, Mobutu staged a military coup and assumed the office of head of state, while Colonel Leonard Mulamba was nominated as prime minister of the new government of national unity. Mobutu's takeover received wide approval in the West, especially the United States. Mobutu became a key strategic ally for the West in the struggle against communism, which earned him financial and military support that helped to consolidate his power.

Shaba I (March 8–May 8, 1977) and Shaba II (May 13–June 3, 1978)

The Shaba wars were the first major challenges to Mobutu's rule. Four features of Mobutu's rule were particularly important in explaining civil wars under his regime. First, Mobutu sought to build a sense of national identity as a way of consolidating national unity. In 1971, he initiated a radical program known as "authenticity," which aimed at promoting the traditional culture and eliminating Western cultural influence. The name of the country was changed to Zaire and the names of provinces (Katanga becoming Shaba) as well as major cities were changed to Zairian names.

In the mid-1970s, "authenticity" turned into "Mobutuism," which promoted a cult of personality aimed at legitimizing Mobutu's absolutism. To consolidate power, Mobutu fused the party and state institutions and placed members of his ethnic group in key governmental positions and in the parastatal sector. This further alienated the political elite and antagonized interregional and interethnic relations.

Second, Mobutu managed to cultivate strong international support for his regime by manipulating the country's strategic position during the Cold War, mainly by controlling the country's vast natural resources. He became a vital Western ally against communism in Africa. Not only did Mobutu's strategy earn him economic and military assistance, it also allowed him to get away with repression and human rights violations.

Third, starting in 1974, Mobutu took measures to eliminate the political influence of the army (see Emizet 2000a and Metz 1996 for details). He replaced the general chief of staff with four chiefs of staff heading four autonomous branches of the security forces (land forces, air force, coast guard, and the gendarmerie). He expanded the web of competing and overlapping military units, trying to balance their power, while encouraging them to oversee each other so as to repress potential opposition.[6] The national army (Forces Armées Zairoises, FAZ) was underpaid or irregularly paid, and ill-equipped. This reduced the risk of a military threat to Mobutu's power, but also made the country militarily weak.

Fourth, Mobutu intimidated or co-opted influential officers. In 1974, he nominated the chiefs of the armed forces as members of his party's political bureau and the army became a partner in Mobutu's kleptocracy.

THE ECONOMIC CONTEXT: POST-ZAIRIANIZATION CRISIS. The Shaba wars broke out during the post-Zairianization crisis which was characterized by the systematic decline of economic activity. The economy of the Congo underwent four distinct phases following independence: the postindependence growth (1960–74) that continued the preindependence growth,[7] the post-Zairianization crisis of 1974–78, the period of failed adjustment of 1978–88, and collapse since 1988 (see figure 3.1 and table 3.2). In the period following independence, the Congo continued to experience moderate growth as in the preindependence era. The economic activity was boosted by high copper prices, expansion of mineral production, and the introduction of the first International Monetary Fund (IMF)-funded economic stabilization program in July 1967.

Starting in November 1973, Mobutu initiated "Zairianization" whereby foreign-owned small and medium-size businesses were either nationalized or simply distributed to private individuals. In 1974, Mobutu announced "radicalization," a program allegedly aimed at redressing major economic problems, including unemployment, inflation, social injustice, and individualism. However, radicalization resulted in the nationalization of the remaining large Belgian-owned companies. Mobutu took a further step to control the country's resource wealth by creating the Société Zairoise pour la Commercialisation des Minerais (SOZACOM), which was put in charge of marketing all mineral resources.

Figure 3.1 **Real GDP per Capita (1996 PPP $) and Value Added by Sector (1995 $)**

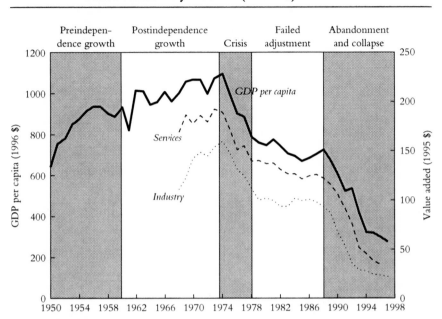

Source: Penn World Tables (GDP using chain rule); World Bank Database (value added).

The effects of Zairianization and radicalization were devastating (see Emizet 1997; Young and Turner 1985). Zairianization damaged private sector confidence, undermining international credit worthiness and resulting in a sharp decline in private lending. As private lending declined, Mobutu resorted to bilateral lenders, using his position as a strategic ally of the West. While the government accumulated debt, only a fraction of the debt was actually used to finance economic development as Mobutu and his entourage channeled borrowed funds abroad in the form of capital flight.[8]

In the second half of the 1970s, the Mobutu government undertook several adjustment programs sponsored by the IMF and the World Bank that aimed at reversing the effects of the post-Zairianization crisis and the repercussions of trade shocks. However, the effects of these programs were minimal. Real per capita gross domestic product (GDP) declined at an annual rate of 1.2 percent from 1978 to 1988 and inflation continued at an average rate of 56 percent per annum (see table 3.2).

THE 1977 INVASION IN SHABA. A large number of the Katangan gendarmes who had fought in Katanga and in the Eastern rebellion fled to Angola where they worked for the Portuguese in the fight against liberation movements in that country. With the victory of the Movimento Popular de Liberação de Angola (MPLA)

Table 3.2 **GDP Growth, Value Added by Sector, Inflation, and Budget Deficits, 1960–98**

Period	Per capita GDP (% annual growth)	Value added in agriculture (% annual growth)	Value added in industry (% annual growth)	Value added in services (% annual growth)	Inflation (CPI, % annual growth)	Budget deficit (% of GDP)
1960–1967	-0.3	NA	NA	NA	NA	NA
1967–1974	1.5	-3.3	6.2	1.9	21.4	-3.9 (1971–74)
1974–1978	-6.5	-2.7	-8.5	-7.3	51.2	-5.6
1978–1988	-1.2	-0.6	-1.7	-1.3	55.9	-2.1
1988–1998	-7.8	-0.6	-15.8	-14.7	3,367.6	-6.1
			(1988–96)	(1988–96)	(1988–97)	(1988–97)

Source: Authors' computation using data from *World Development Indicators* (2001) and *World Bank Africa Data Base* (2000). The growth rates are computed as the annual compounded growth rates between the beginning and the ending year of each subperiod. The figures for inflation and the fiscal deficit are simple averages of annual values.

Note: NA = data not available.

in Angola, the Katangan gendarmes were unemployed and sought to return to the Congo and reclaim their region (now named Shaba) under the banner of the Front for the National Liberation of Congo (Front pour la Libération Nationale, FLNC). Initially, the rebels encountered little resistance from the disorganized, under-equipped, and demoralized government forces. However, before the rebels could capture the mining town of Kolwezi, Mobutu was rescued by Moroccan troops which were airlifted by French aircraft in May 1977.

After the first Shaba war, Mobutu embarked on a fierce repression mission in which dozens of military officers were hastily tried and handed various sentences ranging from several years in prison to execution. These decisions caused high political tension. The FLNC took advantage of this context of political tension and economic distress to launch the second invasion in Shaba. This time the FLNC declared that its aim was less to conquer Katanga than to remove Mobutu from power. Instead of launching an outright invasion as in Shaba I, the rebels infiltrated the country to prepare the ground for the FLNC battalions, which entered the country in early May. The rebels launched their attack at dawn on May 13, 1978 and captured the strategic mining town of Kolwezi the same day. The United States accused the Soviet Union and Cuba of sponsoring the rebellion, but found no evidence (Young and Turner 1985). The rest of the country remained relatively calm during the second Shaba war. Mobutu was rescued by a contingent of 700 French troops and 1,700 Belgian soldiers with logistical support from the American Air Force (Young and Turner 1985).

The Kabila-Led Rebellion: October 17, 1996–May 17, 1997

In the second half of the 1970s, the Congolese economy continued to deteriorate following the post-Zairianization crisis. In an attempt to avert total economic chaos, the IMF came to the rescue and concluded a new agreement with Mobutu. The IMF forced him to settle the country's debt arrears to the IMF and to bring the IMF-backed Kengo Wa Dondo into the government as prime minister with a mandate to resume structural adjustment. In a concerted effort to give Mobutu another chance, the United States, Belgium, France, and Germany decided to write off portions of the debts owed by Zaire.

In addition to economic crisis, the Mobutu regime also faced mounting challenges from domestic political opposition. Mobutu's reaction to the opposition's demand for reform was intransigent and violent. In May 1990, when students in Lubumbashi protested against Mobutu's decision to rescind the political reforms announced a month earlier, government troops responded by killing 294 students (Emizet 1997, 44). This action further alienated Mobutu in the eyes of his Western allies. In the same year, both the United States Congress and the French government announced that further aid would be conditional upon progress toward democratization. When Mobutu failed to cooperate, the West abandoned him and suspended foreign aid. It is in this context of economic crisis and political chaos that the Kabila-led rebellion broke out in October 1996 and eventually toppled

Mobutu's 32-year-long regime in May 1997.

One of the main factors that triggered the rebellion was the influx of more than 1.2 million Rwandan Hutu refugees in June 1994, following the victory by the Tutsi-led Rwandan Patriotic Front (RPF). The refugees included thousands of former Rwandan soldiers and the *Interahamwe* militiamen who committed the Rwandan genocide. The influx of Rwandan Hutu refugees had major consequences for the political and security situation in the Congo (Emizet 2000b). First, the arrival of refugees altered the ethnic balance in the Kivu region by increasing the marginalization of Banyamulenge traditionally associated with Tutsi origin. By colluding with the *Interahamwe,* rival "native" ethnic groups took advantage of this opportunity to settle old antagonisms with the Banyamulenge. Second, the presence of armed Hutu refugees in eastern Congo posed a major security threat to the new government of Rwanda.

In an attempt to gather support from "native" Congolese, the Mobutu regime adopted drastic measures against all Kinyarwanda-speaking ethnic groups, the Banyamulenge (comprising only Congolese of Tutsi origin) and the Banyarwanda (comprising both Hutu and Tutsi).[9] On April 28, 1995, the transitional parliament adopted a resolution that stripped the Banyarwanda and Banyamulenge of their Congolese nationality. Then in early October 1996, the deputy governor of South Kivu ordered the Banyamulenge and Banyarwanda to leave the Congo in accordance with the 1995 parliamentary resolution, but they refused to leave and turned to Rwanda for help. The Rwandan government took advantage of this call for help and intervened to resolve the security issue by dismantling the refugee camps, which resulted in the massacre of thousands of Hutu refugees (Emizet 2000b).[10]

This chaotic political situation led to the Alliance des Forces Démocratiques de la Libération (Alliance of Democratic Liberation Forces, AFDL), led by Laurent Kabila, staging a rebellion in eastern Congo in October 1996 with military support from Rwanda, Uganda, and Angola. The AFDL combatants included Banyamulenge and other groups who were opposed to the Mobutu regime, such as the Mai Mai. For the Banyamulenge, the main motivation was to defend their rights to nationality. For local "native Congolese," the rebellion was a means of overthrowing the Mobutu regime that had marginalized and repressed them. Social tensions among ethnic groups as a result of land disputes also contributed to igniting the rebellion. The rebel forces encountered little resistance from Mobutu's army and were met by cheering crowds as they captured towns en route to Kinshasa. The rebels entered the capital city of Kinshasa on May 17, 1997, and, 12 days later, Laurent Kabila was sworn in as the new president of the DRC.

The Anti-Kabila Rebellion: August 2, 1998–Ongoing

After he took office, Kabila reinforced the ethnic base of the political system by favoring people from his native province of Katanga and Congolese of Rwandan descent. The visibility of Banyamulenge in key government positions created resentment and Kabila was seen as promoting the strategic interests of Rwanda and Uganda.

In late July 1998, Kabila announced the end of military cooperation with Rwanda and Uganda and ordered all foreign troops to leave the country. The Tutsi members of the government felt threatened by this move and left the country immediately. On August 2, 1998, with the help of Rwanda and Uganda, an anti-Kabila revolt broke out, and Kabila's regime was rescued by Angola, Namibia, and Zimbabwe. The anti-Kabila rebellion was strongly opposed by many ethnic groups in Kivu. Many found that whereas the 1996–97 rebellion liberated them from Mobutu, the 1998 rebellion only served the interests of Rwanda and Uganda (International Crisis Group, 2003).

On January 16, 2001, Laurent Kabila was assassinated and his son Joseph Kabila took over the leadership of a country that was partly occupied by rebel troops and foreign forces and suffered from an economy in total chaos. Rwanda and Uganda played a major role in the conflict, directly by the presence of troops on the ground (until they were forced to pull out in 2002) and indirectly by sponsoring specific rebel groups.

The two wars of the 1990s in the DRC, especially the anti-Kabila rebellion, illustrate the intricate relationships between conflict and mineral resources, and the convergence of domestic and international financial interests in perpetuating conflict. (Table 3.3 gives details on the main rebel groups.) Natural resources provided incentives to fight to capture the resources and helped finance the war. Once conflict started, various parties lived off the "war economy." Exploitation of mineral resources blurred the distinction between economic and political-military interests and forged unlikely political alliances. As a result of economic gains that accrued to parties during the war, ending the war was not a concern of the major parties.

There are many channels through which rebel organizations have been able to sustain the rebellions. The first mode of financing the war was taxation of natural resources by both armies and rebel forces. For example, between January and October 2000, coltan exports through *comptoirs* controlled by the Rassemblement Congolais pour la Démocratie (RCD-Goma) totaled $6.7 million (International Peace Information Service [IPIS] 2002, 12). There was both in-kind and direct taxation in rebel-controlled territories. For example, the RCD collected a tax of about 8 percent of total mineral exports by the *comptoirs* in addition to a $15,000 annual license fee per *comptoir* (IPIS 2002). A fraction of the taxes collected by the RCD was remitted to Kigali and Kampala as payments for military assistance.

The war has also been financed through looting, expropriation, and confiscation of mineral resources and other forms of wealth. Rwandan and Ugandan troops established a monopoly over the exploitation and commercialization of mineral resources by forcing local entrepreneurs out of business, while flooding the region with products imported from Rwanda, Uganda, and Burundi (UN Security Council 2001). Rwanda and Uganda have gained financially from the war by trading natural resources acquired in the DRC. Rwanda's receipts in taxes on international trade for 1997–99 averaged 15.1 billion Rwandan francs, a 31 percent increase from 1996 (IMF 2001). The official data from these countries reveal important discrepancies between exports and production (table 3.4). Rwanda's coltan exports increased from

Table 3.3 Characteristics of Main Rebel Movements Involved in the Anti-Kabila War

Name and date of creation	Prominent leaders	Ideology and objectives	Ethnic base	Size of group and areas controlled	Financing sources	Foreign support	
						Support to rebels	Support to government
RCD, 1998	Ernest Wamba Dia Wamba; Jean Pierre Ondekane	Unpaid soldiers in the East; Ethnic representation in government; Ugandan and Rwandan interests	Banyamulenge; former AFDL fighters	Large part of eastern region; 11,000 members in 2002	Mineral resources	Rwanda, Uganda	Angola, Namibia, Zimbabwe
MLC, 1998	Jean-Pierre Bemba	Anti-Kabila[a]; Ugandan security and strategic interests	Former Mobutu presidential guard and members of Equateur's ethnic groups	Equateur region; 5,000–10,000 members in 2002	Diamonds, gold, timber; Taxes on diamond trade	Uganda	Angola, Namibia, Zimbabwe
RCD-Kisangani, 1999	E. W. D Wamba[a]	Anti-Kabila[a]; Uganda and Rwanda security and interests	Several groups	Kisangani, central-eastern region; 15,000 members in 2002	Mineral resources; Foreign financial support	Uganda	Angola, Namibia, Zimbabwe
RCD-Goma, 1999	Emile Ilunga; Déo Bugera; Adolphe Onusumba	Anti-Kabila[a]; Ugandan and Rwandan interests	Several groups	North and South Kivu, parts of North Katanga; 17,000 members in 2002	Mineral resources; Foreign financial support	Rwanda	Angola, Namibia, Zimbabwe

Note: AFDL = Alliance des Forces Démocratiques pour la Libération du Congo-Zaire; RCD = Rassemblement Congolais pour la Démocratie; MLC = Mouvement pour la Libération du Congo.

Since 2002, RCD-Goma split into three factions: RCD-Originel, RCD-Authentique, RCD-Congo.

a. The opposition accuses Kabila of monopolization of power while Uganda and Rwanda accuse him of reneging on his promises to resolve their border security concerns.

Table 3.4 Mineral Exports by Rwanda and Uganda, 1994–2000

	Gold			Coltan		Rough diamonds	
	Uganda		Rwanda	Uganda	Rwanda	Uganda	Rwanda
Year	Production (tons)	Exports (tons)	production (kg)	exports (tons)	exports (tons)	exports (000$)	exports (000$)
1994	0.002	0.22	—	NA	NA	NA	NA
1995	0.002	3.09	1	NA	54	NA	NA
1996	0.002	5.07	1	NA	97	NA	NA
1997	0.006	6.82	10	2.57	224	198	720
1998	0.008	5.03	17	18.57	224	1,440	17
1999	0.005	11.45	10	69.5	122	1,813	439
2000	0.004	10.83	10	NA	83	1,263	1,788

Source: United Nations Security Council (2001), *Report of the Panel of Experts on the Illegal Exploitation of Natural Resources and Other Forms of Wealth of the Democratic Republic of the Congo* (April 12, 2001).
Note: NA = not applicable.

$11.4 million in 2000 to $44.5 million in 2001, becoming the largest export for the country (Economic Intelligence Unit 2002).

The DRC government, in turn, has financed its war effort through a scheme referred to as *taxe parafiscale,* in which state companies were required to hand over a fraction of their profits to the government. The UN Security Council (2001) reported that the Société Minière de Bakwanga (MIBA) turned over 40 percent of its earnings to the government, while the Générale des Carrières et des Mines (GECAMINES) transferred about one-third of its profits to the government.

The war was also supported by a network of financial institutions based in Rwanda, Uganda, and developed countries (UN Security Council 2001). Rwandan banks have served as the primary suppliers of the cash dollars used to purchase minerals by local *comptoirs* and international traders.[11] The trade of natural resources involves Western banks as well. For example, Banque Bruxelles Lambert of Belgium has handled the financial operations of Aziza Kulsum (alias Madame Gulamali), a notorious arms and minerals trader and one-time general manager of RCD-Goma's Société Minière des Grands Lacs (SOMIGL). Citibank of New York also had important indirect financial dealings with rebel groups via their suppliers (UN Security Council 2001, paragraph 132).

The DRC and the Collier-Hoeffler Model

Main Findings from the Model

Using the data and the core and alternative CH model of war onset, in figure 3.2 we graph the predicted probabilities of war for the DRC. Each year on the horizontal

Figure 3.2 Risk of War: Prediction from Collier and Hoeffler (2002)

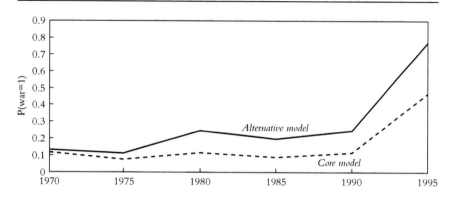

axis is the beginning year of a five-year period (which is the frequency of observations used in the CH data). The probability of civil war in the DRC is much higher than the population average: It ranges from 8 percent during 1975–79 to 77 percent during 1995–99, as compared to an average risk of war of 7 percent for all country-periods in the data.

Table 3.5 presents summary statistics for the variables used in the CH model for the DRC and all other countries.[12] Except for ethnic dominance, the factors included in the model make the DRC more prone to civil war than the typical country in the sample. The DRC has lower values for per capita income, income growth (except for 1970–74), and peace duration, whereas it has higher values for the share of primary commodities in total exports, ethnic fractionalization, population, and geographic dispersion of the population, implying a higher risk of civil war.

Among the factors included in the model, income, its growth rate, and dependence on primary commodities play a central role in causing conflict in the Congo. Low income and low expected economic growth reduce employment and profit expectations, which not only decrease the opportunity cost of joining a rebellion, but also weaken the government's ability to counteract the rebellion.

The dependence on mineral exports makes the DRC prone to conflict, according to the CH model. The DRC is on the ascending part of the mineral resource dependence curve, below the 26 percent level that is associated with the highest risk of war (Collier and Hoeffler 2002, 17). However, the CH model does not account for regional distribution of mineral resources as a mechanism through which mineral resources cause conflict. As discussed in the previous section, it is regional concentration of mineral resources more than resource dependence per se that has made the DRC particularly prone to conflict.

The CH model predicts an increase in the probability of civil war in the 1990–99 period compared to the previous periods, and an even larger increase from 1990–94

Table 3.5 Means of Variables in the Collier-Hoeffler Model for DRC and Sample

Year	pgdp sample	pgdp DRC	gdpcap sample (weighted)	gdpcap DRC	Gy1 sample	gy1 DRC	sxp sample (weighted)	sxp sample (simple)	sxp DRC	geogia sample	geogia DRC
1960	—	—	2163	489	—	—	0.044	0.158	0.076	0.57	0.61
1965	0.094	—	2518	548	2.71	2.28	0.046	0.162	0.076	0.57	0.61
1970	0.067	0.131	2968	686	3.19	4.49	0.047	0.165	0.140	0.57	0.61
1975	0.070	0.111	3236	637	2.42	-1.48	0.057	0.183	0.078	0.57	0.61
1980	0.070	0.247	3630	476	2.22	-5.82	0.073	0.201	0.112	0.57	0.61
1985	0.061	0.197	3799	442	-0.43	-1.48	0.056	0.154	0.131	0.57	0.61
1990	0.058	0.248	3836	375	0.81	-3.29	0.049	0.146	0.141	0.57	0.61
1995	0.064	0.772	4188	222	0.37	-10.48	0.048	0.142	0.141	0.58	0.63

Year	frac sample	frac DRC	etdo4590 sample	etdo4590 DRC	peace sample	peace DRC	lnpop sample	lnpop DRC
1960	1,777	5,940	0.47	0	157	172	14.98	16.54
1965	1,777	5,940	0.47	0	213	—	15.09	16.68
1970	1,777	5,940	0.47	0	263	51	15.21	16.82
1975	1,783	5,850	0.47	0	301	111	15.32	16.96
1980	1,788	5,850	0.47	0	354	171	15.41	17.11
1985	1,788	5,850	0.47	0	415	231	15.51	17.27
1990	1,788	5,850	0.47	0	454	291	15.61	17.44
1995	1,788	5,850	0.47	0	468	9	15.70	17.59

Source: Authors' computations are from data obtained from Anke Hoeffler.

Variables: pgdp = predicted probability; gdpcap = per capita GDP; gy1 = lagged GDP growth rate; sxp = share of primary commodities in exports; frac = ethnolinguistic fractionalization; etdo4590 = ethnic dominance; peace = peace duration before war; lnpop = log of population; geogia = geographic dispersion of the population.

to 1995–99. The probability of war jumps from 0.11 to 0.47 in the core model, and from 0.25 to 0.77 in the alternative model between 1990–94 and 1995–99. Thus, the CH model fits quite well the 1995–99 civil wars in the DRC.

Two variables in the model may explain the increased risk of civil war in the 1990–99 period: per capita GDP and its growth rate. As discussed earlier, the economy of the Congo began to collapse in 1988. This would explain the higher risk of war in 1990–94 compared to 1985–89. Income and its growth rate further deteriorated in 1995–99. Per capita GDP dropped from $442 to $375 (a 15 percent decline), while its growth rate worsened from an average of −3.28 percent to −10.48 percent per annum. As table 3.5 shows, average per capita GDP in the sample was increasing during that period. None of the other explanatory factors in the CH model experienced large changes that could have caused a significant change in the predicted probability of war in the 1990s.

Even though the CH model correctly predicts a large increase in the risk of war in the 1990s, it leaves out risk factors that according to our case study are critical to understand civil war in the DRC. The most important ones are the trigger factors, especially the influx of Rwandan Hutu refugees that disrupted the ethnic balance and exacerbated land disputes in eastern Congo, the military activity of Rwandan militias that induced Rwanda to take an aggressive stand, and the nationality laws that targeted Congolese of Rwandan origin. While economic crisis (captured in the CH model by per capita income and its growth rate) created an environment that facilitated the formation of the rebellions, these trigger factors were essential in determining the timing of these rebellions. The role of mineral resources in attracting Ugandan and Rwandan military invasion also explains the higher risk of war in the 1990s. This factor is also not captured in the CH model because this is not reflected in the ratio of mineral exports to total exports.

CH Predictions and Remaining Puzzles

We do not have war probability estimates for the period of the 1960s because of the lack of data, so we start with the wars of the 1970s. The CH model predicts a higher risk of war for the DRC than for the average country. The fact that the DRC has had several wars seems in agreement with the model's predictions. The deterioration of economic activity, especially following Zairianization, which is captured by the CH model, was a key factor in igniting the rebellions. The struggle for regional control of mineral resources, which is not included in the CH model, also played a key role in motivating secessionist movements. A puzzle in this period is that the period 1975–79 has the lowest probability of war in the entire sample period, even though this period had two wars (the Shaba wars) and was marked by severe economic crisis. The data used to test the CH model show a large decrease in the share of primary exports in total exports from 0.140 to 0.078, which would explain the drop in the estimated risk of war. But we find no historical explanation for this decrease.

The higher probability of war in 1980–85 compared to 1975–79 may be explained by the large decline in income (–5.8 percent per annum compared to –1.5 percent in the 1975–79 period; see table 3.5) as well as the higher share of primary commodities compared to 1975–79. However, we do not have a good explanation for the increase in the share of primary commodities in this period. Furthermore, there were no wars in the 1980s. The model's predictions for 1980–85 do not seem to be consistent with history.

By contrast, the model's predictions for the 1990s are consistent with history. What drives these predictions is the decline in real per capita income (both level and rate of growth). The contest to control natural resources by domestic and foreign agents, the nationality laws, and the influx of refugees are all relevant factors that are not included in the CH model. But, on balance, the CH model predicts quite well the wars in the 1990s.

Conclusion

This chapter examines the factors that motivated several civil wars in the Congo since independence. We discuss the predictive power of the CH model with reference to these civil wars and find that the model performs well, although it omits several variables that could help improve its predictions of the timing and location of rebellion.

Declines in the level and growth of income increased the risk of war by reducing the cost of organizing rebellion, as hypothesized by CH. These declines also weakened the government's ability to counteract the rebellions. But the government's ability to fight the rebels depended more on external support than its own economic capacity.

Natural resource abundance also increased the risk of conflict in the Congo. Although the geographic concentration of resources and unequal distribution of wealth provided incentives for secession, these variables are outside the CH model. Consistent with the model, the struggle to control mineral resources contributed to higher risk of war in the 1990s. However, foreign agents also claimed these resources and the model does not account for such external intervention.

Three important factors that are omitted from the model are worth emphasizing. First, the identity and nationality laws that targeted Congolese of Rwandan descent helped fuel interethnic tensions in eastern Congo and provided incentives (or a pretext) for the Rwandan and Ugandan regimes to support the rebellions. Second, the influx of Rwandan Hutu refugees in eastern Congo in 1994 disrupted the ethnic balance by marginalizing the Congolese of Rwandan Tutsi affiliation. Third, Tutsi-dominated regimes in Burundi and Rwanda and the pro-Tutsi orientation of the Ugandan regime made those regimes sensitive to the discrimination against Congolese of Tutsi descent and partially explained their readiness to intervene in the Congo. This might also explain the opposition to Tutsi members of Kabila's first government, as people learned about the dangers of ethnic dominance from nearby Burundi and Rwanda.

External interests were also critical and there was external support on both sides of the conflict. External intervention had been the norm in Congolese politics in the Cold War, given the country's strategic importance and mineral wealth. As Mobutu lost his allies in the early 1990s, his capacity to counter rebellion was severely diminished. Consequently, the rebellions of the 1990s received stronger support from abroad compared to those of the 1960s and 1970s. This explains why the wars of the 1990s ended either in the victory of the rebellion (in 1996–97) or in a military stalemate, whereas in earlier wars the government was victorious.

Notes

We are grateful for helpful comments and suggestions from Paul Collier, Frank Holmquist, Janvier Désiré Nkurunziza, Nils Petter Gleditsch, and Nicholas Sambanis. We also thank Anke Hoeffler, who supplied cross-country data.

1. See Emizet (2001) for further details on these eight wars and other smaller rebellions that are not covered in this study. See Sambanis (2002) for a survey of the theory and empirical evidence on the causes of civil wars. Also see De Soysa (2002) for a discussion of the Collier-Hoeffler model and its predictions.
2. We do not have probability estimates for the 1960s because of missing data.
3. In January 2002, 41 years after Lumumba's assassination, Belgium officially acknowledged and apologized for its responsibility in the assassination of Lumumba. Needless to say, most Congolese regard the apology as a tardy, meaningless diplomatic act. Nevertheless, Lumumba and his ideology remain a galvanizing force among opposition movements that seek to project a nationalistic image.
4. On January 10, 1964, a Constitutional Commission held meetings under the leadership of Ileo and adopted a law to be submitted to a referendum. The project proposed a change of the name of the country to Democratic Republic of Congo, officially established the 21 provinces as autonomous entities, made the president the head of the executive branch, and limited control by the Parliament over the government in that cabinet members, once confirmed by the Parliament, were answerable only to the president.
5. De Witte (2001, 164) provides a figure of 200,000 deaths. This number seems quite incorrect because most people in the Kwilu and eastern Congo welcomed the rebels as they were praising Lumumba. The rebels mostly targeted bureaucrats whom they accused of taxing them. The rebellion itself was against the establishment.
6. The main security units were the Forces Armées Zairoises (FAZ, the regular army), the French-trained 31st Parachute Brigade, and the Israeli-trained Special Presidential Division (DSP). The DSP was regularly paid and was dominated by Mobutu's Ngbandi ethnic group.
7. The literature often refers to the "growth years" as the period starting with the first IMF adjustment program in 1967 and ending with Zairianization and radicalization in 1974 (Kaplan 1978; World Bank 1980). However, the choice of 1967 as a starting point is not supported by the historical data.
8. From 1970 to 1996, the estimated cumulative stock of capital flight from the country amounted to $19 billion (see Boyce and Ndikumana 2001; Ndikumana and Boyce

2003). Also see Ndikumana and Boyce (1998), Askin and Collins (1993), Blumenthal (1982), and Gould (1980) for further discussion of capital flight, corruption, and embezzlement of national wealth under the Mobutu regime.

9. The Banyamulenge are Congolese of Tutsi origin who were separated from Rwanda in 1910, when boundaries of the Belgian Congo were redrawn by the colonial powers (Emizet 2000b). The Banyarwanda include natives of North Kivu (Banyabwisha) separated from Rwanda in 1910, Rwandan Hutu and Tutsi immigrants who arrived in the Congo during the colonial period, and some Tutsi refugees who fled from Rwanda during the 1959 ethnic conflict (Willame 1997).

10. Estimates of the number of Hutu refugees killed in eastern Congo vary by source. Some sources estimate that over 200,000 Hutu refugees were killed in the 1996–97 war (Emizet 2000b).

11. One of the important financial institutions involved in the trade of natural resources from the DRC is the Banque de Commerce, du Dévelopment et d'Industrie (BCDI) in Kigali. Created in November 1996, BCDI handled most of the financial transactions of the AFDL during the 1996–97 war.

12. Per capita GDP values in table 3.4 are slightly different from those in figure 3.1. Figure 3.1 reports GDP figures (constant PPP 1996 dollars) from updated Penn World Tables (for the period 1950–97), whereas table 3.4 reports data used in the Collier-Hoeffler analysis, that are in 1985 prices from the earlier Penn World Tables (extrapolated for 1989–99). The growth rates of per capita GDP in the two series are very close.

References

Askin, Steve, and Carole Collins. 1993. "External Collusion With Kleptocracy: Can Zaire Recapture Its Stolen Wealth?" *Review of African Political Economy* 57: 72–85.

Blumenthal, Erwin M. 1982. "Zaire: Rapport sur la credibilite financiere internationale." In *Mobutu et l'argent du Zaire: les revelations d'un diplomate ex-agent des Services Secrets (annexe 2),* ed. Emmanuel Dungia, 136–55 (April 7). Paris: L'Harmattan.

Boyce, James K., and Léonce Ndikumana. 2001. "Is Africa a Net Creditor? New Estimates of Capital Flight From Severely Indebted Sub-Saharan African Countries, 1970–96." *Journal of Development Studies* 38 (2): 27–56.

Collier, Paul, and Anke Hoeffler. 1998. "On the Economic Incidence of Civil War." *Oxford Economic Papers* 50: 563–573.

———. 2001. "Greed and Grievance in Civil War." Policy Research Working Paper 2355, World Bank, Washington, DC.

———. 2002. "On the Incidence of Civil War in Africa." *Journal of Conflict Resolution* 46 (1): 13–28.

CRISP. 1962. *Congo 1961.* Brussels: CRISP.

———. 1963. *Congo 1962.* Brussels: CRISP.

———. 1967. *Congo 1965.* Princeton: Princeton University Press.

De Soysa, Indra. 2002. "Paradize Is a Bazaar? Greed, Greed, and Governance in Civil War, 1989–99." *Journal of Peace Research* 39 (4): 395–16.

De Witte, Ludo. 2001. *The Assassination of Lumumba.* New York: Verso.

Economic Intelligence Unit. 2002. *Rwanda Country Report.* London (February).

Emizet, Kisangani. 1997. "Zaire After Mobutu. A Case of a Humanitarian Emergency." UNU/WIDER, Research for Action 32.

——. 2000a. "Explaining the Rise and Fall of Military Regimes: Civil-Military Relations in the Congo." *Armed Forces and Society.* 26 (2): 203–27.

——. 2000b. "The Massacre of Refugees in Congo: A Case of UN Peacekeeping Failure and International Law." *Journal of Modern African Studies* 38 (2): 163–202.

——. 2001. "Domestic and International Roots of the Congo Conflict: Prospects for Peace and Implications for Post-War Reconstruction." Mimeo, July 30, Kansas State University.

Gérard-Libois, Jules. 1966. *Katanga Secession.* Madison: University of Wisconsin Press.

Gibbs, David N. 1991. *The Political Economy of Third World Intervention.* Chicago: University of Chicago Press.

Gould, David J. 1980. *Bureaucracy, Corruption, and Underdevelopment in the Third World: The Case of Zaire.* New York: Pergamon Press.

IMF (International Monetary Fund). 2001. *Rwanda: Statistical Annex.* IMF Country Report (January).

International Crisis Group. 2003. *The Kivus: The Forgotten Crucible of the Congo Conflict.* ICG Africa Report 56 (January).

International Peace Information Service. 2002. *Supporting the War Economy in the DRC: European Companies and the Coltan Trade.* IPIS Report (January).

Kaplan, Irving (ed.). 1978. *Zaïre: A Country Study.* Washington, DC: The American University.

Lemarchand, R. 1964. *Political Awakening in the Congo.* Berkeley: University of California Press.

Meditz, Sandra W., and Tim Merrill (eds.). 1994. *Zaïre: A Country Study.* Washington, DC: The American University.

Meriam, Alan P. 1961. *Congo: Background of Conflict.* Evanston, IL: Northwestern University Press.

Metz, Steven. 1996. "Reform, Conflict, and Security in Zaire." Mimeo, U.S. Army War College.

Ndikumana, Léonce, and James K. Boyce. 1998. "Congo's Odious Debt: External Borrowing and Capital Flight in Zaïre." *Development and Change 29:* 195–17.

——. 2003. "Public Debts and Private Assets: Explaining Capital Flight From Sub-Saharan African Countries." *World Development* 31 (1): 107–30.

Sambanis, Nicholas. 2002. "A Review of Recent Advances and Future Directions in the Quantitative Literature on Civil War." *Defence and Peace Economics* 13 (3): 215–43.

United Nations Security Council. 2001. "Report of the Panel of Experts on the Illegal Exploitation of Natural Resources and Other Forms of Wealth of the Democratic Republic of the Congo." United Nations.

Vanderlinden, J., A. Huybrechts, V. Y. Mudimbe, L. Peeters, D. Van der Steen, and B. Verhaegen. 1980. *Du Congo au Zaïre 1960–1980: Essai de Bilan.* Bruxelles: Centre de Recherche et d'Information Socio-Politiques.

Verhaegen, B. 1969. *Rebellions au Congo.* Brussels and Kinshasa: CRISP and IRES.

Willame, J. C. 1997. *Banyamulenge et Banyarwanda: Viloences ethniques et gestion de l'identitaire au Kivu.* Brussels and Paris: Institut African-Cédaf L'Harmattan.

World Bank. 1980. *Zaïre: Current Economic Situation and Constraints.* Washington, DC: World Bank.

——. 2000. *World Bank Africa Data Base.* CD ROM. Washington, DC: World Bank.

——. 2001. *World Development Indicators.* CD ROM. Washington, DC: World Bank.

Young, Crawford. 1965. *Politics in the Congo.* Princeton, NJ: Princeton University Press.

Young, Crawford, and Thomas Turner. 1985. *The Rise and Decline of the Zairian State.* Madison: The University of Wisconsin Press.

Theory Versus Reality

Civil War Onset and Avoidance in Nigeria Since 1960

4

ANNALISA ZINN

Nigeria is fraught with political and economic contradictions. Although it was considered a "beacon of hope for democracy" at independence in 1960, military governments have ruled Nigeria for a total of 29 years. Despite being the world's sixth largest petroleum exporter, it ranks among the world's 20 poorest countries. Comprised of at least 250 ethnic groups, Nigerian society is highly fractionalized, and yet a single ethnoregional political cleavage has polarized the country. And although Nigeria is a federation of 36 states, fiscally its political system is highly centralized with oil revenue accruing directly to the federal government.

There is also a discrepancy between Nigeria's predicted risk of civil war onset and its actual conflict history. The Collier-Hoeffler (CH) model of civil war onset considers a country to be "at risk" for civil war if the country is predicted to have around 20 percent or greater chance of a civil war in the given five-year period. This means that, on one hand, Nigeria is a false negative. Although the CH model predicts an insignificant chance of war in 1965–69 (12.5 percent), in 1967 the Biafran war of independence began. On the other hand, Nigeria is a false positive. According to the CH model, Nigeria was at high risk for civil war onset from 1985 to 1999[1] and, although 60 conflicts resulting in at least 8,804 deaths started during that period (see table 4.1), this violence does not meet the conventional definition of civil war. Only for 1980–84, with a predicted risk of war equal to 25.3 percent, does the model correctly predict the outbreak of a civil war. But even then, the mechanisms suggested by the CH model do not seem to fit the reality of that civil war.

This chapter investigates three episodes of armed conflict in Nigeria—the Biafran War (1967–70), Maitatsine War (1980–85), and violence since 1986—in an attempt to determine why there appears to be an incongruity between the predictions of the CH model and Nigeria's actual conflict history. The benefits of analyzing these diverse cases of violent conflict within the context of a single study are twofold. First, I am able to analyze intracountry temporal variation to explain why violence

(text continues on page 96)

Table 4.1 **Summary of Violent Conflicts in Nigeria, 1986–99**

	Dates (mo/yr)	Locations [city (state)]	Nonstate combatants	GOV	ORG	Deaths	Incompatibility
1	5/86	Zaria (Kaduna)	University students	Yes	No	20	Government authority
2	3/87	Kafanchan (Kano)	Christians vs. Muslims	No	No	9	Religion
3	3/87	Kaduna (Kaduna)	Christians vs. Muslims	No	No	11	Religion
4	11/88	Sokoto (Sokoto)	Muslims	Yes	No	10	Control of tribal government
5	5–6/89	Benin City (Bendel) Lagos[a]	Students	Yes	No	100	Economic reforms
6	4/90	Lagos	Mutineers	Yes	Yes	10	Control of central government
7	4/91, 1/92, 9/96, 1/98, 9/98	Katsina (Katsina), Kaduna (Kaduna), Kano (Kano)	Muslim Brotherhood	Yes	Yes	275	*Government authority, Religion; Implementation of *shari'a*
8	4/91	Tefawa Belawa (Bauchi)	Christians vs. Muslims	No	No	500	Religion
9	10/91	Kano (Kano)	Christians vs. Muslims	No	No	300	Religion
11	12/91	Anambra and Enugu States	Adani vs. Omasi	No	No	6	State boundary
12	2/92, 5/92	Zangon Kataf (Kaduna)	Christian Katafs vs. Muslim Hausa	No	No	830	*Economic power, Religion
13	10/91–3/92	Taraba State	Jukun vs. Tiv	No	Yes	2,210	Land
14	3/92	Taraba State	Christians vs. Muslims	No	No	200	Land
15	5/92	Kaduna (Kaduna)	Christian Katafs vs. Muslim Hausa	No	No	300	*Retaliation for previous violence, Religion
16	8/92	Anioma (Anambra)	Local traders	Yes	No	2	State boundary

#	Date	Location	Parties				Issue
17	12/92	Port Harcourt (Rivers)	Odtikas vs. Ogoni	No	No	60	Economic power
18	1/93	Funtua (Katsina)	Almajiri vs. Kalakato sects (Muslim)	No	Yes	60	Religion
19	2/93	Uyo (Akwa Ibom)	University students	Yes	No	1	Economic goods
20	6/93	Lagos, Osun & Oyo States	Students, Hausa vs. Yoruba	Yes	No	100	Annulment of elections
21	7–9/93	Rivers State	Andoni vs. Ogoni	No	Yes[b]	1,085	Unclear
22	7/93, 7–8/94	Lagos (Lagos)	Nupeng, Pengassan, Campaign for Democracy[c]	Yes	No	98	*Annulment of elections Regime type
23	12/93	Ovwian (Delta)	Ovwian community	Yes	No	3	Government authority
24	12/93	Port Harcourt (Rivers)	Ogoni vs. Okrika	No	Yes	90	Land
25	4/94	Rivers State	Ogoni vs. Okoloma	No	Yes	30	Land
26	4/94	Jos (Plateau)	Muslim Hausa–Fulani vs. Christian Jerom	No	No	5	Control of local government
27	5/95	Kano (Kano)	Christian Ibos vs. Muslim Hausa	No	No	5	Economic goods
28	6/95	Kano (Kano)	Christians vs. Muslims	No	No	30	Religion
29	6/96	Kaduna State	Muslim student groups	Yes	No	10	Government authority
30	9/96	Kafachan (Kaduna)	Christians vs. Muslims	No	No	2	Religion

(Continued)

Table 4.1 Summary of Violent Conflicts in Nigeria, 1986–99 (Continued)

	Dates (mo/yr)	Locations [city (state)]	Nonstate combatants	GOV	ORG	Deaths	Incompatibility
31	3–4/97 6/97, 10/97, 7/98, 10/98, 6/99, 11/99	Warri (Delta) Orgubo (Delta)	Ijaw vs. Isekiri. Note: The Urhobo were at times allied with the Ijaw.	No	Yes	454	Control of local government
32	3/97, 9/97, 12/98, 1/99, 9/99, 11/99	Yenagoa & Odi (Bayelsa)	Ijaw	Yes	Yes	234	*Government authority Distribution of oil resources
33	4/97	Jos (Plateau)	Christian Birom vs. Muslim Hausa	No	No	3	Economic goods
34	4/97	Jos (Plateau)	Panyam vs. Gindiri	No	No	8	Control of tribal government
35	8–9/97, 11–12/97, 1/98, 8/98	Osun State	Ife vs. Modakeke	No	Yes	186	Control of local government
36	10/97, 1/98, 8/99	Taraba State	Chamba vs. Kuteb	No	Yes	208	Control of local government
37	11/97	Nassarawa State	Bassa vs. Ebira	No	No	24	Control of tribal government
38	1/98	Arinkinkin (Oyo)	Fulani herdsmen vs. Yoruba farmers	No	No	20	Land
39	1/98	Gombe State	Settled farmers vs. migrant herdsmen	No	No	30	Land

40	3/98	Bayelsa State	Ijaw vs. Urhobo	No	Yes	31	Control of local government
41	5/98	Ibadan (Oyo)	Prodemocracy activists	Yes	No	7	Regime type
42	5/98	Lagos (Lagos)	Muslim extremists	Yes	No	8	*Government authority, Religion
43	7/98	Lagos, Lagos State	Hausa–Fulani vs. Yoruba	No	No	55	Annulment of elections
44	7/98	Ibadan, Oyo State	Hausa–Fulani vs. Yoruba	No	No	5	Retaliation for previous violence
45	10/98, 7/99, 9/99	Akpata (Ondo), Ajegunle (Lagos), Akure (Ondo)	Ijaw vs. Ilaje	No	Yes	225	Land
46	10/98	Isanyawa (Kano), Warri (Delta)	All People's Party vs. People's Democratic Party	No	No	14	Electoral results
47	10/98	Gboko (Benue)	Ibo vs. Tiv	No	No	3	Retaliation for previous violence
48	2/99	Taraba State	Fulani herdsmen vs. Wurukum farmers	No	No	100	Land
49	3/99	Lagos (Lagos)	Oodua People's Congress	Yes	Yes	12	Electoral results
50	4/99, 7/99	Anambra State	Aguleri vs. Umuleri (Ibo)	No	Yes	420	Land
51	5/99	Kafanchan (Kaduna)	Hausa vs. Ninzam	No	No	100	Control of tribal government
52	6/99	Ibadan (Oyo)	Hausa cattle dealers vs. Yoruba traders	No	No	7	Economic goods
53	7/99	Sagamu (Ogun)	Hausa–Fulani vs. Yoruba	No	No	66	Tribal practices
54	7/99	Kano (Kano)	Hausa–Fulani vs. Yoruba	No	No	70	Retaliation for previous violence
55	9/99	Lagos (Lagos)	Nigerian Dock Workers Union factions	No	No	16	Union leadership
56	9/99	Kaduna (Kaduna)	Maitatsine vs. Sunni sects	No	Yes	4	Religion

(Continued)

Table 4.1 Summary of Violent Conflicts in Nigeria, 1986–99 *(Continued)*

	Dates (mo/yr)	Locations [city (state)]	Nonstate combatants	GOV	ORG	Deaths	Incompatibility
57	10/99	Port Harcourt (Rivers)	Elemes vs. Odrikas	No	No	30	Land
58	11/99	Lagos (Lagos)	Ijaw vs. Yoruba & Oodua People's Congress	No	Yes	15	Unclear
59	10/99	Olomoro (Delta)	Isoko vs. Oleh communities	No	No	50	Economic goods
60	11/99	Lagos (Lagos)	Hausa traders vs. Oodua People's Congress & Yoruba traders	No	Yes	100	Economic power

Notes: All the conflicts in this table began sometime between 1986 and 1999 (the last episode of the Maitatsine war, which occurred in April 1985, has been therefore excluded) and meet the following definition of collective violence: (1) the loss of human life occurs as a result of the event; (2) the violence is reciprocal, meaning that all parties to the conflict are both perpetrators and victims of the violence; and (3) both the perpetrators and the victims are defined by a specific noncriminal group identity (e.g., as members of an ethnic or religious group, a labor union, a political party, the police forces, an ideological organization, etc.). The purpose of this last criterion is to differentiate between organized criminal violence and violence which is either civil or intercommunal in nature.

This list of conflicts was compiled from a general survey of the following news sources: Amnesty International Annual Reports; Economist Intelligence Unit Country Reports; Human Rights Watch Reports; Integrated Regional Information Network; Keesing's Record of World Events; Lexis–Nexis Universe (which includes many Nigerian newspapers); Minorities at Risk Project Group Assessments.

In cases where there were discrepancies among the different sources, the death count that has been reported is that for which there was the most agreement (i.e., reported by at least two sources). It is important to note that the death counts refers only to those specific incidents in a conflict that were reported in one or more of the sources (i.e., vague, unsubstantiated estimates of the death count are not considered). Although this method may mean that the death count often is underreported, especially because several of these conflicts occurred in remote areas of Nigeria that are not readily accessible to journalists or humanitarian workers, and the Nigerian press was controlled by the government in various degrees throughout the majority of this period, this study contends that this method was the most straightforward and consistent method available for determining the death count in these conflicts.

The GOV variable indicates whether or not the government (defined as the police, military, government personnel and establishments) was a principal combatant in the conflict (i.e., a target of the violence rather than a third-party peacekeeping force).

The ORG variable indicates whether or not the nonstate combatants were militarily organized (i.e., the group had a hierarchy which oversaw the combat training of recruits). This variable essentially differentiates between riots and sustained armed campaigns.

The parties to communal conflicts are listed alphabetically.

"Incompatibility" refers to the issue over which the main parties to the conflict were in disagreement. Twenty such issues have been identified: *annulment of elections* (includes all violence connected to the annulment of Abiola's win in 1993 presidential election, including violence that erupted in 1998 after Abiola's death); *control of local government* (includes conflicts over the location of local government as in those cases that are directly tied to control of local government); *control of state government*; *control of tribal government*; *control of central government*; *distribution of oil resources*; *economic goods* (e.g., disputes over products, money, and other goods such as the provision of water); *economic power* (refers to conflicts whose focus was the destruction of markets or whose main disagreement was the location of a marketplace); *economic reforms* (refers to protests over the austerity measures in the late 1980s imposed by the IMF's structural adjustment program); *electoral results*; *government authority* (e.g., responses to government repression or regulations, such as constraints on the freedom of assembly); *implementation of shari'a* (includes protests either for or against); *land* (includes disputes over grazing rights); *religion* (refers to disputes over religious beliefs, practices, and/or rights); *retaliation for previous violence*; *regime type* (e.g., protests by prodemocracy groups); *state boundary* (includes disputes over proposed changes to state boundaries); *tribal practices*; *unclear* (e.g., conflicts that were reported to be due to ethnic hatred and nothing else); *union leadership*.

Several conflicts involved more than one incompatibility; an asterisk (*) has been used to indicate the incompatibility which appears to have fueled the conflict to the largest degree (i.e., was the issue over which most of the combatants fought or was the issue that fueled the violence for the longest period of the conflict).

a. In 1991 Bendel State was divided into Delta and Edo States. Benin City is the capital of Edo State. Lagos was the Federal Capital Territory until 1991.

b. The Andoni, the key perpetrators of the violence, were backed by men in Nigerian army uniforms (but there is no evidence of the Ogoni attacking the military men). The Ogoni were organized under MOSOP, in particular its militant youth wing, NYCOP.

c. Nupeng = National Union of Petroleum & National Gas Workers; Pengassan = Natural Gas Senior Staff Association of Nigeria.

escalates to the level of civil war even when many of the structural risk factors in the Collier-Hoeffler model remain fairly constant. Second, I am able to identify a recurring determinant of civil war onset and avoidance: government actions in response to nascent or impending violence.

An Unexpected War? Biafra's Attempted Secession, 1967–70

Favorable prospects for growth and stability marked Nigeria's dawn of independence in 1960.[2] With a gross national product (GNP) growth rate of 4 percent per year, 1.5 points higher than the population growth rate, poverty did not seem to be an inescapable curse. Exports had more than doubled since 1949 and were forecasted to grow exponentially as oil production, begun in 1958, swelled to 1.5 million tons in 1960 and was expected to expand to 5 million tons by 1964. With Africa's best-trained and largest civil service, Nigeria was becoming a magnet for foreign investment.

Nigeria emerged as a British-style parliamentary democracy, pledged to respect human rights in a federal constitution that provided for three semiautonomous regions—Northern, Western, and Eastern—dominated, respectively, by the Hausa-Fulani, Yoruba, and Ibo. In response to minority ethnic group complaints of domination, a fourth region, the Mid-Western, was added in 1963. The first federal government was a civilian coalition, led by the Northern People's Congress (NPC) with the Eastern-based National Council for Nigeria and the Cameroons (NCNC) as the minority partner. Nevertheless, by mid-1967 Nigeria was embroiled in a full-scale civil war as the federal government sought to block the secession of the Eastern region, renamed by the separatists as the Republic of Biafra. Given the positive nature of Nigeria's first years of independence, and in particular the power-sharing arrangement between the Ibo and the Hausa-Fulani, consistent with the CH model, the Biafran war may seem to have been unexpected. In reality the ethnoregional struggle for political power and economic resources that characterized Nigerian politics since colonial times had never subsided.

A History of Ethnoregional Competition

Although the Northern and Southern Protectorates of Nigeria were joined in 1914, British colonial policy continued to differ significantly across the two regions.[3] In the Muslim North, the British minimized their presence: Traditional rulers were the primary agents of colonial policy, Christian missionaries were barred, and education was harmonized with Islamic institutions. By contrast, in the South, Western-style education and the spread of Christianity became the norm.

This difference in colony policy was the genesis of the ranked cleavage between the Muslim North and the Christian South, which is the most politically salient of the multiple rifts present in Nigerian society.[4] As a by-product of Western education, the South became the most developed region and Southerners acquired positions in the colonial administration. These developments led Northerners in the 1940s to champion federalism, which would allow them to escape Southern domination. Because Nigerian nationalism at that time was concentrated in the South, the British sought to maintain the loyalty of the North and, hence, promulgated in 1946 the Richards Constitution, which provided for the establishment of three regions (North, East, and West). By splitting the South, the British exacerbated competition between the Ibo and Yoruba and in so doing facilitated Northern domination of Nigerian politics.

Although the Richards Constitution laid the foundation for the federation of Nigeria, the colony's federal structure was not made explicit until the Lyttleton Constitution of 1954. This constitution gave the regions responsibility for everything besides foreign relations, defense, police, transportation, communications, finance, and trade policy, all of which remained under control of the central government. Because these functions necessitated only a portion of federal revenue, excess funds were to be divided among the regions according to two principles: the principle of derivation, which allocated to each region a percentage of the revenue generated in that region, and the principle of even progress in development, which allocated on the basis of each region's need for developmental assistance.

Although these principles sought to strike a fair balance between returning revenues to their region of origin and allowing poorer regions the opportunity to catch up with the rest of the country, each region worked to shift the allocation formula in its favor. The more populous North argued for the distribution of revenues on a per capita basis, while the West, the richest and most developed region, called for strict adoption of the principle of derivation. The East, which prior to the 1956 discovery of oil lacked industrial development, favored the principle of even progress.

As the British withdrew in the late 1950s, access to the national resources increased and ethnoregional rivalry intensified. As the better-educated Yoruba, and in particular Ibo, occupied government posts left behind, patronage—whereby government officials favor their home regions in granting inter alia access to government jobs, funds for local development, and government contracts—became widespread. The ambition to control the federal government also grew, especially after the advent of oil production in 1958 and the 1959 decree that all mineral resources were federal property. Unsurprisingly, therefore, each of the three main political parties—the NPC, the NCNC, and the Western-based Action Group (AG)—campaigned aggressively in the December 1959 national legislative elections. In the end, the majoritarian system permitted the NPC, which represented the more populous North, to secure victory.

Mounting Tension and the Outbreak of War

By May 1962, the new Nigerian state was already in crisis as violent intraparty clashes forced the AG out of power in the Western region. The new Western party, the Nigerian National Democratic Party (NNDP), was not freestanding as the AG had been, but rather allied itself with the NPC. This realignment in the West, the widespread appointment of Northerners to key civil service posts, and bitter disputes over the 1962 and 1963 censuses weakened the federal coalition. The Ibo, who had dominated the civil service in colonial times, became increasingly wary of Northern domination, especially because it seemed inescapable with the system's reliance on population figures for the allocation of both parliamentary seats and government revenue.

Following NCNC electoral losses in 1964–65 and allegations of fraudulent practices by the Northern party and its Western allies, a group of officers—many of whom were Ibo—staged a coup in January 1966 in which the prime minister (a Northerner), the premier of the Northern region, the highest ranking Northern army officers, and the premier of the Western region (who was closely allied with the NPC) were killed, along with only one Ibo officer. Following the coup, the Ibo commander-in-chief of the army, General Ironsi, emerged as head of state.

Although individuals from all the regions held top-level positions in this regime, as Ironsi appointed Ibos to several key government positions, Northerners perceived political dominance to be shifting to the Eastern region. These perceptions deepened in May 1966 when Ironsi promulgated Decree No. 34, which replaced the Nigerian federation with a unitary government and made merit the sole criterion for appointment and promotion in the civil service—an advantage to the better-educated Ibo. In protest, some Northerners massacred thousands of Ibos living in the North and in July 1966 a countercoup installed General Gowon—a Christian from the Middle Belt, though still a Northerner—as head of state. His first act was to reverse the unification decree.

Following the massacres of May 1966 and the countercoup, talk of secession became official in the Eastern region. In a radio broadcast on August 1, 1966, Governor Ojukwu declared that "the brutal and planned annihilation of officers of Eastern Nigerian origin in the last few days has again cast serious doubts as to whether the people of Nigeria, after these cruel and bloody atrocities, can ever sincerely live together as members of the same nation" (Ojukwu 1969, 35). These statements were in stark contrast to Ojukwu's speech of June 27, 1966, in which he declared that Nigeria's "very survival is through unity; without it we will perish" (Ojukwu 1969, 28).

At this point, however, the Eastern region was not unique in its aspirations for more autonomy. At the Ad Hoc Constitutional Conference convened in September 1966, the Northern, Eastern, and Western delegations all demanded a loose confederation of the regions with the constitutional right to secede. However, before any agreement could be reached, the conference was interrupted by the massacre of at least 30,000 Ibos and other Easterners by Northern troops and civilians in early October and the subsequent friction between the Eastern region and the federal government. These massacres also led to the exodus of about 1 million Easterners from the Northern region back home to the East.

In response to the mounting tension, in January 1967 regional and federal leaders signed the Aburi Agreement, which regionalized the national army and mandated unanimous approval by the regional military governors for any new federal legislation. A follow-up conference in February granted the federal government the right to take over any regional government during a "period of emergency" and to employ "appropriate measures" against attempted secession. Ojukwu rejected this provision.

Ojukwu's denunciation of federal authority intensified in late March as he decreed that all revenues derived from the East must be paid directly to the regional treasury. Gowon responded with economic sanctions, but this prompted Ojukwu to order the confiscation of all federal property in the region. On May 1, 1967, Western leaders announced that if the East were allowed to secede, either by commission or omission, their region would follow suit. These statements worried Northern leaders because their region, being the most economically backward, was critically dependent on its share of the revenue from the other regions, particularly the oil-rich East. Gowon, therefore, in mid-May issued a decree implementing the Aburi Agreement and he offered to lift the economic embargo against the Eastern region in exchange for the repeal of the antifederal decrees that it had passed. Ojukwu refused this olive branch and on May 26, 1967 the Eastern Region Consultative Assembly mandated Ojukwu "to declare at the earliest practicable date Eastern Nigeria a free, sovereign and independent state by the name and title of the REPUBLIC OF BIAFRA" (Ojukwu 1969, 193).

On May 28, 1967, Gowon proclaimed a state of emergency and unveiled plans for the redivision of the country into 12 states, which purportedly undermined the possibility of continuing Northern domination and thus offered a major concession to the East, even though these plans violated the Aburi Agreement. But at the same time the Ibo heartland would be deprived of control over the Niger Delta's oil fields, the East's major industrial city (Port Harcourt), Nigeria's only oil refinery, as well as access to the sea. The "practicable date" had arrived and Ojukwu declared Biafra's independence on May 30, 1967. On July 6, 1967, federal troops invaded the breakaway region.

Ojukwu's Declaration of the Republic of Biafra contained three statements that explain why the "people of Eastern Nigeria" wanted independence:

> AWARE that you can no longer be protected in your lives and in your property by any government outside Eastern Nigeria; BELIEVING that you are born free and have certain unalienable rights which can best be preserved by yourselves; UNWILLING to be unfree partners in any association of political or economic nature. (Ojukwu 1969, 193–94)

The first statement, which points to the federal government's alleged inability to protect the lives of Easterners and its complicity in the massacres of the previous year, asserts the motivation for secession that was most emphasized in propaganda and political statements at the time and has been most cited in scholarly works since then. But the other statements, which propose that secession is necessary to preserve certain rights and freedoms, cannot be ignored as they seem to signify more than just rhetoric.

Key documents of Biafran propaganda during the civil war insinuate that control over the oil resources in the Eastern region was one of the rights and freedoms sought by the Biafran secession. After declaring that the "Biafran revolution" is an attempt to "recover the originality of the people," a pamphlet by the Biafra Students' Association in the Americas makes a clear bid for the region's natural resources:

> The masses of Africa must rise and recover that which belongs to them. They must assume control of all the products of their own soil because whatever is contained in a piece of land is a part of it, and if a country belongs to a people, the people and not foreign oil companies should be the masters of their land. (Anyaogu 1967, 4, 13).

The connection is clear: Biafra's sovereignty is the main objective and a key element of this sovereignty is control over Biafra's resources, of which the most important is oil.

Another pamphlet printed by Biafrans in the United States concurs with this view:

> The Biafran struggle represents more than an "attempt to seize oil." It is a revolutionary struggle committed to the building of a progressive state, in which the "wealth of the land will belong to the people." (Nwankwo 1969, 11).

Even a pamphlet by the Britain-Biafran Association aimed at convincing the British government, which along with British oil companies had been supporting Nigeria financially and militarily, to become neutral in the war admits, albeit carefully, that control over its oil revenue was part of the rationale for secession:

> There is no evidence to suggest that secession was affected from motives of greed, e.g. so as to enable Biafrans to enjoy exclusively the profits to be derived from the old Eastern Region's oil resources. Unlike Katanga, East Nigeria had a tradition of willingness to enjoy its resources with the other members of the Federation. *Indeed it was the refusal of the Federal Government to grant Eastern Nigeria its due share of Federal revenues that was an immediate factor in bringing the divorce to a head.* (Birch and St. George 1968, 28, italics mine).

Because the success of Biafra's secession hinged largely on international support, Biafran apologists were clearly motivated to deny having economic motives and instead emphasized their grievances. The fact that these pamphlets nevertheless mention control over the region's oil as an objective of the secession suggests that this was a significant contributing factor. The timing of the declaration of independence also reinforces this view, for had the Biafran secession been successful, the region would have controlled over 67 percent of Nigeria's total oil revenue, as opposed to 43 percent under the prewar arrangements and 14 percent under Gowon's proposed redivision of the country (Forrest 1995, 32). At the least, the East's oil wealth would permit the economic viability of an independent Biafran state (cf. Oyeweso 1992, 107).

Explaining the Puzzle: Data Measurement and Theory Refinement

As evident in the previous narrative of the Biafran war, two of the CH model's significant predictors of civil war onset—ethnic dominance and natural resource dependence—figure prominently in accounting for the outbreak of the war. Why, then, is this war not predicted by the CH model? The proposed explanation is twofold: (1) the CH model does not include variables that mattered significantly in the mounting of tension, namely abrogation of regional autonomy agreements and large-scale massacres; and (2) the CH model measures ethnic dominance and natural resource dependence in ways that are not relevant to the Biafran war.

CH operationalize ethnic dominance as a binary variable indicating whether the most populous ethnic group in the given country constitutes 45–90 percent of the country's total population. Since Nigeria's largest ethnic group, the Hausa-Fulani, comprises only 29 percent of the population (CIA World Factbook 2002), the CH model codes Nigeria as free of ethnic dominance, whereas in reality ethnic dominance has been a key feature of Nigerian politics since colonial times and especially in the first years of independence.

This discrepancy suggests that a better measure of ethnic dominance is necessary, for although a numerically dominant ethnic group may exclude minority ethnic groups from the political system and thus increase the risk for civil war (Collier and Hoeffler 2002), this does not have to occur. Ethnicity could be politically irrelevant since ethnopolitical cleavages could be colonial constructions, as in Nigeria. Minority groups could also control the system, as occurred after the January 1966 coup, or there could be institutionalized power sharing, akin to Nigeria's coalition government of the early 1960s. Furthermore, it could be a regional coalition of ethnic groups, who perhaps share a common religion, that dominates the political sphere, as in the case of Northern political dominance in Nigeria. All this suggests that a better measure of ethnic dominance would be an indicator for ethnoregional *political* dominance.

As with the ethnic dominance variable, the CH model's proxy of natural resource dependence—the ratio of primary commodity exports to gross domestic product (GDP)—does not capture the effect of natural resources, namely oil, on the onset of the Biafran war. For although the value of this variable for Nigeria in 1965–69 was, at 12.3 percent, significantly lower than highest risk ratio (32 percent), the presence of oil in the Eastern region is likely to have been a motivating factor for both the secession and the federal government's determination to keep the country together (Nafziger and Richter 1976, 15).

This discrepancy between theory and reality does not necessarily mean that the CH model's measure of resource dependence is flawed. Rather, it suggests that there may be more than one mechanism that relates natural resources to civil war onset, so more than one natural resource measure may be needed to predict more accurately the onset of civil war. Although natural resources may increase the risk of civil war by being a source of rebel finance as the CH model predicts, they may also (1) stimulate and/or facilitate the demand for secession and (2) motivate the central government to respond more forcefully to declarations of independence by

oil-rich regions. A binary variable for the presence or absence of regionally concentrated oil reserves should therefore be a significant predictor of secessionist civil
war. The absence of this variable in the CH model may explain why Nigeria is a
false negative for 1965–69, even though natural resource dependence was a major
factor in the Biafran war (cf. Nafziger and Richter 1976; Post 1968).

Nigeria Battles the Maitatsine Sect, 1980–85

Biafra's unconditional cease-fire in January 1970 and Gowon's subsequent declaration that there would be "no victor and no vanquished" ushered in an era of reconciliation, reconstruction, and prosperity. Amnesty was offered to all secessionists,
rebels were reintegrated into the military, economic development was a government
priority, oil revenue increased 350 percent between 1973 and 1979, and plans for
returning to civilian rule came to fruition with the 1979 inauguration of Shehu
Shagari as president of the Second Republic (Metz 1992, 72). But not all was rosy.
Unemployment increased from an already high rate of 13.5 percent in 1970 to
18.7 percent in 1979, with a peak of 20.5 percent in 1974 (International Labor
Office 1979). Lack of work was especially acute in urban centers where farm workers lingered even after they failed to find higher-paying jobs and refugees flocked
to escape the severe regional drought of 1972–74. In this atmosphere of high unemployment and reduced repression, Alhaji Muhammadu Marwa, founder of the
Maitatsine sect, was able not only to attract more followers to his maverick religious
beliefs, but also to build a "state within a state" in the Yah Awaki district of Kano.
He organized his followers into a cohesive group, which at its height in December
1980 numbered between 8,000 and 12,000 members (Falola 1998, 143).

Origins and Prewar Operations of the Maitatsine Sect[5]

The Maitatsine sect can be traced back to the 1950s when Marwa, a minimally educated convert to Islam, posed as a Koranic teacher in Kano and in that capacity began
challenging the basic tenets of Islam, particularly the legitimacy of Mohammed as
the final prophet of Allah. Such ideas naturally brought Marwa in conflict with the
Islamic authorities and in 1962 the Emir of Kano repatriated him to Cameroon.
There, Marwa continued his provocative preaching, much to the annoyance of the
local authorities, who in early 1963 exiled him to Gongola State, Nigeria.

When, in late 1963, the Emir of Kano abdicated his position, no regulatory power
against maverick preaching remained in the city. So Marwa returned to Kano and
posed once again as a teacher in Nigeria's *almajiri* system, which provided for the
apprenticeship of boys aged 10–14 to a Koranic scholar who would serve as a spiritual guide and father figure. Since this system allowed for indoctrination into particular beliefs and lifetime loyalty to a leader, posing as a Koranic teacher provided
Marwa with the opportunity to form a rebel force.

These early recruitment efforts were interrupted in 1973 when, as part of Gowon's
campaign to incarcerate all dangerous sectarian leaders, Marwa was imprisoned for

brainwashing young boys, many of whom had reportedly been abducted. With the end of the Gowon regime in 1976, Marwa was released and he returned to Kano with what appears to have been a renewed determination to fight the mainstream Muslim sects based there. To facilitate recruitment he divided the city into three zones, each headed by one of his lieutenants, who searched for new members at railway stations, parking lots, and other public places where homeless and unemployed migrants congregated. Most of Marwa's followers were, therefore, young, poverty-stricken male peasants who had flocked to Kano seeking employment and religious instruction, but there were also refugees from Cameroon, Chad, and Niger who had only to gain—including such basic commodities as shelter—by joining such a sect.[6]

New recruits were brought to Marwa, who forced them to drink hypnotizing potions before indoctrination sessions and to pledge life-long allegiance. Initiated recruits took part in morale-boosting sessions, during which they received magic charms to "preserve them from bullets" and were taught to trivialize death. They also underwent military training, given by sect members who had served in the Nigerian security forces. Despite rumors that the Maitatsine rebels used "sophisticated weapons" obtained from Libya or Israel, a government tribunal set up to investigate the causes of the war found that they were largely armed with primitive weapons such as machetes, arrows, spears, and a few rifles. Such weapons were most likely all that could be afforded, given that the major sources of the sect's finances were daily begging (a typical activity for *almajiri* students), occasional looting from their neighbors' properties, and the profits from Marwa's sale of charms and medicines.[7]

In addition to overseeing recruitment efforts and brewing magic charms, after 1976 Marwa became a familiar sight in Kano as he publicly demanded to be revered as the final prophet of Allah. He condemned many as infidels, including mainstream Muslims, Christians, government authorities, and all persons seemingly accepting of Western culture, such as those wearing wrist watches, riding bicycles, or driving cars. Such use of abusive language earned Marwa the name *Maitatsine,* which signifies "he who swears." Marwa's followers frequently attacked government officials and those unreceptive to Marwa's preaching, which prompted Marwa's arrest in April 1978. After a year of hard labor he was released, but no longer made public appearances. His followers, by contrast, became increasingly visible and violent.

With the return to civilian democratic rule in October 1979, the Nigerian government at all levels became less repressive. In this more relaxed atmosphere the Maitatsines extended their enclave by confiscating neighboring property and erecting illegal structures on it. Their enclave, which housed approximately 6,000 persons in 1980, became a "state within a state"; it included a kangaroo court that executed all those brought to it, including Maitatsines who were suspected of being disloyal and "infidels" who were kidnapped by sect members.

A Riot-like War

As the Maitatsines' violence and defiance of the law increased, the people of Kano pressured their government to suppress the sect. In early 1980, a bill was introduced in the Kano House of Assembly to curb abusive religious preaching. It did not pass, however, reportedly for fear of losing patronage from mainstream religious preachers. In October and November 1980, the Kano police commissioner asked for reinforcements and permission to use force against Marwa, but neither request was granted. Finally, on November 26, 1980, Mohammed Rimi, the Governor of Kano State, wrote to Marwa asking that the Maitatsines demolish all their illegal buildings and vacate the enclave, or else face the government's "appropriate action."

Although Rimi also secretly told Marwa that he could disregard the letter if he was open to dialogue, Marwa nevertheless concluded that war had been declared against him and he summoned all of his followers to come to his defense. Convinced that fighting against the infidels would gain holy martyrdom for them, scores of Maitatsines joined Marwa's well-trained army already in Kano, and on December 18, 1980 they unleashed terror on the city as they battled civilians, policemen, and federal troops. After 11 days of fighting at least 4,000 people had been killed, including Marwa.[8]

Despite the deaths of its founder and many members, as well as repression in the form of arrests, the Maitatsine sect continued to exist. In October 1982, violence in Maiduguri (Borno State) broke out as police attempted to arrest sect members. At least 452 persons were killed in the fighting, which then spread to Kaduna, where an additional 44 persons were killed. Clashes occurred once again in February 1984 when sect members escaped from jail in Jimeta (Gongola State) and rampaged through the city killing indiscriminately, which led to the deaths of more than 1,000 persons. The Maitatsines rebelled one last time in April 1985, when police tried to arrest Marwa's successor. About 150 persons were killed, bringing the war's total death toll to at least 5,646 lives.[9] Given this death count and the government's direct involvement in the conflict, the Maitatsine War does qualify as a civil war, although some data sets do not include it.

Insights from the Maitatsine War

The case of the Maitatsine War is consistent with the CH model's insight that low opportunity cost for rebel labor is the mechanism that explains the correlation between poverty and civil war onset. Most of Marwa's recruits were homeless, unemployed urban migrants and refugees. But the reason they joined the Maitatsine sect was not to protest their poverty. On the contrary, sect members were forced to live in strict austerity, on the grounds that material possessions would detract from their spiritual lives and ultimate ends. Why, then, did so many unemployed and homeless persons join the sect? A likely answer is that they had only to gain from a sect that both provided for basic needs such as shelter and gave transcendent meaning to their poverty.

This case further demonstrates that civil war can erupt in the absence of significant opportunities to obtain rebel finance. As mentioned, the Maitatsine rebels did not receive funding from a diaspora or foreign governments, nor were they involved in looting natural resources. Their weapons were largely primitive. Although these constraints may explain why the war was not longer or more intense in terms of casualties, the onset of war despite these constraints suggests that modern military technology and the resources needed to obtain it may not be necessary conditions for civil war. On the contrary, "fearless fighting," as was observed by Nigerian security forces during the war (cf. Zahradeen 1988), may mitigate the disadvantages of low technology.

An insight from this case is that the government responses to nascent violent conflict are affected by the political context, which sometimes limits the government's ability to respond effectively. Rimi's letter to Marwa was the event that triggered the outbreak of the war, and had Rimi not been a democratic governor, it is possible that he would have dealt with Marwa's defiance of the law just as military governors had dealt with dissidents and offenders in the past: using detention without trial, physical assault, torture, and executions.[10] But in light of the 1979 constitution, which guaranteed a wide range of human rights, Rimi faced constraints on the legitimate use of coercion, and given the power rivalries that marred the Second Republic, also in the city of Kano, he may have realized the political costs of overstepping these constraints.

Perhaps for this reason, until the onset of war, Rimi opted for what Tarrow (1998) refers to as "partial repression." This is repression that is unfocused, inconsistent, and arbitrary or limited by domestic or international pressures and it may stimulate the radicalization of a nonviolent or minimally violent opposition group by inspiring fear for the group's safety (cf. Petersen 2002), while leaving open the possibility of violent rebellion. When the Maitatsine uprising began on December 18, 1980, the state's response was quite sharp with both ground and aerial bombardments and this further suggests that the Kano government's response to the Maitatsines' prewar breaches of peace was conditioned by lack of political will, rather than by inadequate capabilities.

At High Risk for a Civil War, 1985–99

Between 1985 and 1999 Nigeria was ripe for the outbreak of yet another civil war. Ethnic dominance combined with deteriorating economic conditions and growing opportunities for natural resource predation, all of which are significant determinants of civil war in the CH model, combined to produce a high-risk situation.

Incentives and Favorable Conditions for Rebellion

Northern political dominance, a principal source of Southern grievance, persisted throughout this period until May 29, 1999, when Olsegun Obasanjo, a Christian Yoruba and former military head of state, became not only Nigeria's first democratic president after 15 years of military rule, but also the only Southerner to hold onto central power since he voluntarily relinquished power in 1979. With the exception of Ernest Shonekan, who chaired an interim government for less than three months in 1993, the four other military heads of state between January 1985 and May 1999 were both Northerners and Muslim.[11] Such dominance, however, was not limited to the position of head of state, but had ripple effects throughout the entire political system as positions tended to be assigned with deference to patron-client ties determined by ethnoregional origin.[12] For example, in the Council of Ministers, Northerners held the preponderance of seats for 84 percent of the 1985–99 period, even after controlling for the North's larger population share.[13] The significance of the North's preponderance of seats is that it granted that ethnoregional group advantages in terms of access to political appointments and, most importantly, government wealth (cf. Umoren 1996, 135–37; Uwujaren 1998).

Poor economic conditions marked the 1985–99 period as negative growth rates in the early 1980s, due to declining oil production and prices, combined with population increases to produce a GDP per capita which by 1986 was 35 percent lower than its peak in 1977, and even 19 percent below its level in 1970 at the end of the Biafran war. Although there was modest economic recovery in 1988–91, it was short-lived. With oil production facing restraints imposed by the Organization of the Petroleum Exporting Countries (OPEC), economic policy drifting as the government lost interest in structural adjustment, and increasing political unrest as elections were first delayed and then annulled, real GDP growth slowed steadily from 1991 to 1994. It fell to only 0.1 percent in 1994. Despite a small pickup in economic growth in 1995–96, these periods of small growth contributed to a marked increase in the percentage of the Nigerian population living in poverty. Most (66 percent) of the population lived below the poverty line in 1996, compared to 43 percent in 1992 and only 28 percent in 1980. The situation worsened in 1997–99, as falling oil prices caused growth to decrease from a 1996 high of 4.3 percent to 1.1 percent in 1999.[14]

Such poor economic conditions decreased the opportunity cost of rebel labor, which in turn increased the risk of civil war by facilitating the formation of rebel organizations. The CH model posits that natural resource predation can help finance a rebel organization and, based on this dimension, Nigeria was also at high risk for civil war. As its network of oil pipelines expanded to meet the growing domestic demand for oil, and pipelines built during the 1960s and 1970s aged, there were increasing opportunities to obtain rebel financing by black market sales of oil obtained by pipeline sabotage and/or leaks. It appears that these opportunities were indeed exploited. The Nigerian National Petroleum Corporation reports, for example, that incidents of pipeline sabotage jumped from 57 in 1998 to 497 in 1999 (EIU Country Report 2nd Quarter 2000, 27).

Predictions Versus Reality

Given these incentives and favorable conditions for rebellion, it is no surprise that the CH model places Nigeria in 1985–99 at high risk for civil war. Likewise, it is no surprise that during this period there was widespread internal violence in Nigeria, with the onset of 60 violent conflicts culminating in a total of at least 8,804 deaths.[15] Yet none of these conflicts qualify as civil war under the conventional definition that classifies an internal conflict as a civil war if it involves an identifiable rebel organization that challenges the government militarily and the resulting violence results in more than 1,000 combat-related deaths, with at least 5 percent on each side (Collier et al. 2003, 11). Specifically, of the conflicts that erupted in Nigeria in 1985–99, the government was a principal combatant in only 12 (20 percent) and of these, only four involved an organized opposition group and none seem to have resulted in at least 1,000 battle-related deaths, even as of October 2004.[16] Given that Nigeria was at high risk for civil war from 1985 to 1999, how did these conflicts fail to escalate to the level of civil war?

To analyze this question, I look into the Ijaw and Muslim Brotherhood rebellions, both of which occurred within the time period covered by the CH data set, but do not qualify as civil wars because of low deaths.[17] I also consider why there was only one attack on Northern political hegemony (the April 1990 mutiny) and why it failed. In March 1999 there was some antigovernment violence by the Oodua People's Congress (OPC), a Yoruba separatist organization, because this violence was an isolated incident and not yet part of a larger antigovernment violent campaign, it is not a case of civil war avoidance for this time period covered by the CH model.

Explaining the Puzzle of War Avoidance, 1985–99

Ethnic Competition: An Obstacle to Southern Rebellion

Drawing on their repertoire of previous contentious politics, Southerners could have rebelled against Northern political hegemony through either a secessionist revolt or a coup d'état. Although there was no attempt at the former, the attempt at the latter failed. One possible explanation is that ethnic competition among the Southern groups was an impediment to the formation of a cohesive Southern rebel force, while the North's dominance of top-level military positions prevented the realization of a successful coup d'état by Southern officers.

Competition among Southern ethnic groups can be observed on many levels, with the most visible being the rivalry between the two major groups, the Ibo and the Yoruba. Each of those groups seems so opposed to the political power of the other that both prefer to uphold Northern hegemony rather than support a presidential candidate belonging to the rival Southern group. For instance, in the 1979 presidential elections, Shehu Shagari and the other three Northern candidates each won more votes in the Ibo states than the Yoruba candidate, while Shagari won more Yoruba votes than the Ibo candidate (Okeke 1992, 105–106). This pattern repeated itself in the June 1993 and December 1998 presidential elections (MAR and EIU Country Report 1st Quarter 1999, 13).

Another level of ethnic competition is between minority ethnic groups and their dominant counterparts. This competition has been manifest in the decades-long agitation by minority groups for the creation of new states—agitation that has been fueled by perceptions that minorities are being cheated in the distribution of resources by the majority-dominated regional and state governments

(Amuwu et al. 1998, 281). Finally, there has also been competition between minority groups themselves; this was made evident in the incidence of 10 communal conflicts among Southern ethnic groups in the 1985–99 period (see table 4.1).

Because such competition among Southern ethnic groups was facilitated by ethnic fractionalization, the absence of a Southern rebellion in 1985–99 suggests that ethnic dominance may increase the risk of war only when ethnic fractionalization is low. But this is not the only lesson that can be gained from this case of war avoidance. Rather, it seems that government policy has the potential to avert violent conflict.

Recall that Nigeria has a hybrid federal/unitary political structure, which means that although states and local government areas are responsible for nearly all governmental functions except for defense, the police, external relations, and customs, they are also fiscally dependent on the central government and, by the 1999 Constitution, are not permitted to have their own constitutions or to pass legislation that contradicts national legislation. This tension between federalism and fiscal centralization has been a source of ethnoregional competition since colonial times and was a cause of the Biafran war. However, the government's policy to allow for the formation of new states, particularly in the late 1980s and 1990s when one-half of Nigeria's 36 states were created—2 in 1987, 10 in 1991, and 6 in 1996—seems to have contributed to the avoidance of civil war in two ways. First, it enabled both majority and minority ethnic groups to gain a larger share of the national pie without the costly resort to war, and second, it provoked competition among ethnic groups, which rendered difficult the formation of a Southern rebel force. This competition was at times violent, as seen in the Ijaw versus Itsekiri disputes over the imposed relocation of local government headquarters in Warri (Delta State), but federalism could still be an effective conflict prevention strategy, provided that it is crafted carefully with respect for traditional ethnic boundaries.

Why Did the April 1990 Coup Fail?

With claims to be acting on behalf of the "oppressed and enslaved people" of the Christian Middle Belt and South, middle-ranking Army officers tried to depose President Babangida on April 22, 1990.[18] The attempt began at 2 a.m. with an assault on the headquarters of the military government. Soon after 6 a.m., the rebels took control of Radio Nigeria and announced both their political objectives and that Babangida had been deposed. At noon, however, after 10 hours of fighting that claimed 10 lives (the bloodiest coup attempt in Nigerian history), it was broadcasted that the coup had failed. Soon after 1 p.m., as sporadic gunfire continued to be heard in the capital, General Sani Abacha, the Chairman of the Joint Chiefs of Staff and Chief of Army Staff, declared that the Chiefs of Staff had pledged their loyalty to the president, and that the plotters had already been arrested.

Since the only successful coups in Nigerian history have been those carried out by or with the backing of a top military official, it is no surprise that the April 1990 mutiny—the only Southern attempt in the 1985–99 period to overthrow a Northern government—failed. For in order for the coup attempt to have been successful, it seems that the mutineers would have to have been top officials rather than middle-ranking officers so that the army would have been forced to support the coup, rather than fight it. But there were no Southerners among the senior officers in the military government nor in the infantry, the artery of Nigerian military power,[19] which suggests that the relative weakness of the South in terms of its representation in the military was another reason why there was no successful Southern rebellion against Northern political dominance. Such weakness, however, may only have been a short-term deterrent to rebellion because in the long-term it may spark more resentment by reinforcing feelings of exclusion.

The Ijaw Rebellion: Balancing Cost and Effectiveness

The Ijaw, Nigeria's fourth largest ethnic group, inhabit the oil-rich Niger Delta region. Their current political activity in pursuit of greater autonomy began in 1992 when the Movement for the Survival of the Ijaw Ethnic Nationality adopted its charter and began to lobby for an Ijaw state, a demand that came to fruition in 1996 with the creation of Bayelsa State.[20] Antigovernment and ethnic violence, as well as militant actions against oil multinationals, began in March 1997 after the relocation of the Warri Southwest local government headquarters—and the corresponding access to municipal patronage, oil royalties, and government funds—from an Ijaw to an Itsekiri town.

According to newspaper[21] and human rights reports, the Ijaw rebellion seems to be a low-intensity conflict. Therefore, the civil war literature would suggest that war was avoided by the presence of factors that inhibit the outbreak of civil war, for example, harsh government repression (Hegre et al. 2001), accommodation of the organization's demands (Gurr 2000), decreases in the opportunity cost for rebel labor (Collier and Hoeffler 2002), and insufficient rebel finance (Collier and Hoeffler 2002). However, empirical evidence suggests that none of these factors was present. The Ijaw continued to be active even after the worst cases of repression, such as the massacres in January and November 1999 (see tables 4.2 and 4.3). And they have denounced the accommodation they were offered, most significantly the Niger Delta Development Commission Act of 2000.

Furthermore, poverty levels in the Ijaw's Niger Delta region remained among the country's highest, and its education rates among the country's lowest. Approximately 75 percent of Nigerian children are deemed to attend primary school, and national adult illiteracy is estimated at 43 percent, but in parts of the Delta attendance at primary school drops to less than a third and illiteracy is presumably correspondingly higher. The poverty level is exacerbated by the high cost of living. The influx of people employed in the well-paid energy sector has made Port Harcourt and the other urban areas of the region among the most expensive in Nigeria, but the oil sector employs only a small percentage of the indigenous workforce (Human Rights Watch 1999). Finally, the Ijaw are well armed with a large stock of sophisticated

(text continues on page 114)

Table 4.2 Reported Antigovernment Violence in the Ijaw Rebellion

Date (mo/yr)	Description of event	Loss in oil revenue?	Rebel deaths	Gov't deaths	Government response to that specific event (excludes general repression measures)
3/97	Set fire to market in Warri (Delta State) & to residence of former gov't minister	No	2	1	Gun battle with police followed; police reinforcements sent to area; military governor called Ijaw & Itsekiri chiefs to negotiations.
9/97	Kidnapped 4 soldiers, killed 1 of them	No	0	1	Security forces raided Ijaw villages & arrested dozens.
7/98	Rampaged through Government House in Yenagoa, the Bayelsa state capital, & released detained leader	No	0	2	*Not reported*
12/'98–1/99	Attacked soldiers in Yenagoa on Dec. 31 to avenge shooting of unarmed protesters on Dec. 30; clashes followed during army raids of Ijaw communities	Yes	125 *(# dead on each side not reported)*		Declared state of emergency; imposed curfew; sent troops to oil installations; raided several Ijaw communities (with aid of Chevron boats & helicopters), & carried out mass rapes, torture, and killings.
1/99	Attacked army barracks near Shell Forcados terminal	Yes	15	4	Soldiers opened fire on the protesters.
9/99	Clashes following police intervention in gunfight between Ijaw youth & motorcycle operators	No	19 *(# dead on each side not reported)*		*Not reported*
11/99	Kidnapped and killed 12 policemen in the area of Odi, Bayelsa State	No	53[a]	12	Soldiers destroyed Odi & occupied Choba for 2 weeks. Widespread rape, torture, & destruction of property. Obasanjo condemned Ijaw violence as "sheer criminality" that will be brought to justice.

Sources: Amnesty International; EIU Country Reports; Human Rights Watch; Keesing's Record of World Events; Lexis-Nexis Universe; MAR Group Assessments.

a. While this is the maximum number of rebel deaths reported in the press, Human Rights Watch World Report 2001 says that information collected from community leaders a year later indicates that as many as 2,000 civilians were killed in revenge attacks by the military. Because it seems that these deaths were the result of one-sided violence, it is not clear that they merit inclusion in the death count for the conflict (i.e., it is not clear that they are battle-related deaths).

Table 4.3 Reported Anti-Oil Company Activity in the Ijaw Rebellion

Date (m/yr)	Description of event	Loss in oil revenue?	Rebel deaths	Oil company response	Government response to that specific event (excludes general repression measures)
3/97	Occupied 6 Shell flow stations & held 127 local staff hostage	Yes	0	Negotiations & ransom payments	Troops deployed to Warri
4/97	Attacked service boat & kidnapped its captain	No	0	Not reported	Navy ship deployed to allow boat to complete passage
10/97	Stormed Shell flow station at Odema Creek	No	0	Not reported	Not reported
10/97	Closed down Shell flow station & 12 wells	Yes	0	Negotiations[a]	Not reported
2/98	Barricaded Mobil operational base	No	0	Negotiations	300 protesters were arrested
2/98	Closed down Agip Tebidaba flow station	Yes	0	Negotiations	Community Relations Committee established in area
5/98	Closed down 5 Shell flow stations	Yes	0	Negotiations	Not reported
5/98	Occupied Chevron platform for 3 days	Yes	2	Transported troops	Soldiers killed 2 unarmed protesters
5/98	Held 200 Chevron workers hostage	No	0	Ransom payments[b]	Not reported
5/98	Vandalized property belonging to Agip	No	0	Not reported	Dusk-to-dawn curfew on Brass
6/98	Attacked Shell flow stations	Yes	0	Not reported	Not reported
6/98	Vandalized Agip's terminal	No	0	Not reported	Not reported
6/98	Stopped operations at Agip flow station	No	0	Negotiations	Not reported
7/98	Held 9 Texaco workers hostage	No	0	Ransom payments	Not reported

(Continued)

Table 4.3 Reported Anti-Oil Company Activity in the Ijaw Rebellion (*Continued*)

Date (m/yr)	Description of event	Loss in oil revenue?	Rebel deaths	Oil company response	Government response to that specific event (excludes general repression measures)
8/98	Blew up a Shell trunk line	No	0	*Not reported*	*Not reported*
8/98	Damaged Agip's Brass terminal	Yes	0	*Not reported*	*Not reported*
8/98	Damaged Shell's Forcados & Brass terminals	Yes	0	*Not reported*	*Not reported*
8/98	Seized 2 Texaco boats & kidnapped workers	No	0	Ransom payments	*Not reported*
10/98	Occupied 15 Shell & 6 Chevron flow stations	Yes	0	Negotiations	After weeks, armed troops flown into area
10/98	Forced Agip's pipeline to suspend loading	Yes	0	Negotiations	*Not reported*
10/98	Held 4 Chevron workers hostage	Yes	0	Ransom payments	*Not reported*
10/98	Seized 2 Shell helicopters & 1 oil rig	No	0	Negotiations	*Not reported*
11/98	Hijacked Texaco helicopter	No	0	Negotiations	*Not reported*
11/98	Kidnapped 8 foreign Texaco workers	No	0	Negotiations	Arrested kidnappers & released hostages
12/98	Occupied Shell site in Delta State	Yes	0	Urged gov't to use dialogue, not force	Delta State administrator issued severe warning to Ijaw activists, asking them to withdraw immediately
2/99	Kidnapped expatriate Shell worker	No	0	Ransom payments	*Not reported*

Date	Event			Response	Notes
4/99	Took over 7 Shell flow stations and 6 Agip flow stations; seized barges & tugboats	Yes	0	Negotiations	*Not reported*
7/99	Caused closure of Elf oil well in Rivers State	Yes	0	Negotiations	*Not reported*
7/99	Held 64 Shell employees hostage for 2 days & seized a drilling rig	Yes	0	Ransom payments	Arranged meeting between Ijaw youths & oil company officials
8/99	Held 5 Britons hostage	No	0	Ransom payments	*Not reported*
8/99	Attacked off-shore Texaco platform	Yes	0	*Not reported*	*Not reported*
9/99	Blockaded newly completed liquefied natural gas plant at Bonny Island	Yes	0	Negotiations	Obasanjo said government should have retrained workers who built the plant but were now unemployed
10/99	Held 6 Shell employees hostage	No	0	Ransom payments	*Not reported*
12/99	Occupied 3 Shell flow stations & seized work boats belonging to Daiwoo, Saipem, & Wilbros	No	0	Negotiations	State crisis mediator requested an end to such militancy & greater sensitivity of the part of the oil companies

Sources: EIU Nigeria Country Reports (1997–99); Keesing's Record of World Events; Lexis-Nexis Universe; MAR Group Assessments.

a. While the oil company's response is not always reported, the general trend for dealing with occupations of oil facilities appears to have been negotiations, sometimes complemented by promises of employment or development. So "negotiations" has been indicated as the oil company response in every case that an occupation occurred.

b. The main reason the Ijaw kidnapped and held hostage oil workers was to obtain ransom payments. These payments are not always reported in the press, but they are assumed to have been the oil company's response to the kidnapping/hostage taking *unless* otherwise noted in the press.

weapons, either looted from government armories or obtained via sea smuggler's routes and purchased with ransom payments and the proceeds of black market oil sales (Human Rights Watch 1999, Lexis-Nexis).

So why did the Ijaw rebellion not become a civil war? It may be that a less stringent definition of civil war is needed. Or, the answer lies in the determinants of conflict escalation. Most civil war models do not explain escalation, but rather focus on the underlying structure of violence. Between March 1997 and December 1999, the Ijaw were involved in three main types of conflict: intercommunal warfare with the Itsekiri, Urhobo, and Ilaje; antigovernment violence (i.e., an event that caused the death of at least one government personnel); and militant actions against oil multinationals (MNCs). Of these three activities, militant actions were the most frequent, followed by intercommunal warfare.[22] This suggests two, perhaps complementary, hypotheses to explain why the Ijaw rebellion has not become a civil war: (1) intercommunal warfare was diversionary, as in detracting resources from fighting the state; and (2) the Ijaw preferred militant actions against oil multinationals to antigovernment violence.

For the first hypothesis to be valid, the first condition to be met would be temporal distance and spatial concurrence between incidents of intercommunal violence and incidents of antigovernment violence, as this would suggest that the same fighters were involved in both conflicts. But this did not occur between March 1997 and December 1999. Fifty-seven percent of the reported incidents of antigovernment violence occurred within the same month as intercommunal warfare, and while the intercommunal warfare took place primarily in Delta and Ondo States, the antigovernment violence occurred in Bayelsa State. The prevalence of intercommunal warfare therefore does not seem to explain why the Ijaw rebellion did not rise to the level of civil war.

Turning to the second hypothesis, its validity depends on whether there are sound theoretically driven and empirically substantiated reasons for why the Ijaw chose to concentrate their human and physical resources on militant actions against oil multinationals (e.g., occupation of oil production facilities, hostage taking) as opposed to violence directly against the government. At first glance, this choice of conflict activities is puzzling because, although the Ijaw did have some demands for the oil MNCs (e.g., more employment opportunities and community development, immediate compensation for oil spillage), ultimately their rebellion was against the government, as demonstrated by the Kaima Declaration of December 11, 1998.

This declaration, written by youth representatives of 500 Ijaw communities, contained five resolutions, three of which were directed to the federal government. These included demands for the control of natural resources in Ijaw territory; military withdrawal from that territory; rejection of antidemocratic legislation such as the Land Use Decree of 1978, which requires certificates of occupancy from the government for land held under customary and statutory rights and the payment of rent to the government; and revocation of the Petroleum Decree of 1969, which states that all oil found under Nigeria or offshore belongs to the government. Only one resolution placed demands on the oil MNCs—withdrawal from Ijaw territory by December 30—and this ultimatum was conditional upon the government's failure to meet the mandates that it had received (Olojede et al. 2000, 41–43).[23]

However, once the decision-making process governing an opposition group's choice of tactics is taken into consideration, the picture becomes clearer. Lichbach (1987) argues that opposition groups decide which tactics to employ on the basis of both availability and relative cost and efficacy. He defines the cost of a given tactic as the resources necessary for the execution of the tactic *plus* the amount of government repression, as seen in the number of opposition group members who are killed by the government, that the group incurs in response to its use of that tactic. By these terms, militant actions against oil MNCs were clearly less costly than antigovernment violence because they were often successful without a display of arms[24] and they incurred rebel deaths in only 2 percent of the reported events, as opposed to 72 percent of the cases of reported antigovernment violence (see tables 4.2 and 4.3).

In terms of the relative effectiveness of available tactics (i.e., which tactic is capable of or has the greatest potential for achieving government accommodation), militant actions against oil MNCs also seem to have been preferable to antigovernment violence. Tables 4.2 and 4.3 demonstrate that the government was more amenable to granting concessions following militant actions, as opposed to incidents of antigovernment violence. In the former case, the government promised accommodation on three occasions, which constitutes 25 percent of the cases in which there was a direct government response, whereas in the latter case, the government only responded with violence.

Why would the government be more likely to repress antigovernment violence compared to militant actions against oil MNCs? A likely explanation is that governments are more likely to repress and less likely to accommodate groups that threaten their authority (Tilly 1978, 111–13). All this suggests that there is reason to believe that the Ijaw rebellion failed to become a civil war because the Ijaw focused their resources on militant actions, which, being less threatening to the security of the regime, were both less costly and potentially more effective than antigovernment violence.

The Muslim Brotherhood: Trying to Reclaim Its Leader

The Nigerian Muslim Brotherhood, a militant group of Shiite fundamentalists, was formed in the 1980s by Mallam Ibrahim El-Zak-Zaky, a former Muslim student leader, who after leading pro-*shar'ia* (Islamic law) student demonstrations in 1970 and 1980 spent some time in Iran attending conferences, rallies, and various training events relevant to Islamic rhetoric and revolution, along with several close associates (Best 1999). Based in Zaria (Kaduna State) with branches in other Northern cities, including a few breakaway factions, the Muslim Brotherhood recruited primarily well-educated young men (i.e., with at least a secondary education). Citing a list of antigovernment grievances—social injustices, economic marginalization of the common man, corruption of the judiciary, political recklessness on the part of Nigeria's leaders—its main goal was the violent overthrow of the current regime and the establishment of an Iranian-style Islamic state under the leadership of El-Zak-Zaky (Uwazie, Albert, and Uzoigwe 1999, 82–83).

The Muslim Brotherhood's first recorded public activity was in April 1991, when it led several weeks of rioting in Katsina State, both in protest of an allegedly blasphemous newspaper article published in December 1990 and to demand the implementation of *shar'ia*. At least 246 people were killed in these clashes.[25] Even though Shiites are only a small minority even in the predominantly Muslim North, the Nigerian government seemed to recognize immediately that the Muslim Brotherhood could, nevertheless, pose a significant security threat, perhaps because its leaders had been trained in Iran and there were rumors that it was receiving financial support from Iran and possibly also Sudan and Libya (Best 1999). In September 1991, a sect leader and 65 members were sentenced to jail for six to nine months. In addition, a multiyear police hunt for Shiite fundamentalists began in late 1991 with the arrest of 263 sect members.

These arrests, which to the Muslim Brotherhood symbolized the corruption of the police and judiciary and hence the need for the implementation of *shar'ia*, provoked another riot in January 1992 in which 10 persons were killed. Years of quiet followed, until January 1995, when nonlethal clashes were reported in Kano between students and members of the Brotherhood. In September 1996, anti-government violence erupted once again as police tried to disperse sect members protesting the arrest of El-Zak-Zaky and 20 followers, who were detained for questioning about their organization's activities.

From then on, the Muslim Brotherhood's antigovernment violence would no longer be aimed toward the creation of an Islamic state. Rather, as demonstrated in the January, May, and September 1998 riots, which became violent only after the police tried to disperse the demonstrators and led to the cumulative deaths of at least 20 persons (mostly sect members), the Brotherhood's focus was to obtain the release of its leader. This end was realized in December 1998 when, as part of the government's campaign to release political prisoners prior to the return to civilian rule, El-Zak-Zaky and three other leading members of the Muslim Brotherhood were released after charges of inciting public disaffection and sedition were withdrawn.

In sum, although the Muslim Brotherhood, with a clear violent antigovernment ideology and backing from Iran, had the potential of becoming a significant security threat, the arrest of its leader prevented any attempts at an Islamic revolution and shifted the group's conflict activities toward obtaining the release of their leader. In fact, some of these activities may have been completely nonviolent had the police not tried to break up the nonviolent demonstrations in 1998. This case suggests that selective repression, such as the detainment of a rebel group's leader, can effectively prevent conflict escalation, particularly in cases in which the goal of the violence would be the leader's ascent to power. Such repression should, of course, conform to human rights standards, not just to respect these rights, but also to prevent further violence.

Conclusion

Compared to the theory (the CH model), the reality of Nigeria's conflicts is often puzzling, but it is precisely for this reason that this case offers several insights that may further our understanding of civil war. One insight is that certain variables in the CH model, such as ethnic dominance and natural resource dependence, have to be re-operationalized. Another is that the way in which the government responds to protest matters in the process of conflict escalation and can trigger or prevent a civil war.

Abrogation of autonomy agreements, as occurred prior to the Biafra secession, and partial repression, as occurred prior to the Maitatsine rebellion, can trigger the outbreak of violence, particularly when they threaten a rebel group's key interests. By contrast, federalism, attempts at accommodation, and selective repression may prevent the escalation of a conflict, even when, as in the case of Nigeria 1985–99, the predicted risk of civil war onset is high. For example, the arrest of the Muslim Brotherhood's leader halted the group's revolutionary designs, thus containing its violent activity, and the Ijaw rebellion did not escalate because militant actions against oil MNCs were both less costly and more effective at gaining government concessions than antigovernment violence. Such centrality of government actions to the onset and avoidance of civil war suggests the need for studying civil war as a dynamic phenomenon.

Notes

I thank Nicholas Sambanis and two anonymous reviewers for helpful comments and gratefully acknowledge support from the World Bank-Yale Project on the Political Economy of Civil Wars.

1. The model predicts a 46.2 percent chance of civil war in 1985–89, a 54 percent chance of war in 1990–94, and a 50 percent chance of war in 1995–99.
2. See Wergeles (1960) and EIU Nigeria Country Profiles.
3. This account of the background to the Biafran war has been drawn from multiple sources: Balogun (1973), Banks and Muller (1999), Bartkus (1999), EIU Nigeria Country Profiles, Forrest (1995), Metz (1992), Nafziger and Richter (1976), Nixon (1972), Nnoli (1978), Osemwota (1994), Oyeweso (1992), and Post (1968). I used cross-checking and the primary documents contained in these sources to resolve any inconsistencies.
4. See Nnoli (1978) and Okeke (1992). Other rifts include rivalry among the three major groups and between minorities in major group areas and the major group (e.g., Christian groups of the Middle-Belt vs. the Hausa-Fulani).
5. Narrative compiled from Falola (1998); Hackett (1987), Metz (1992), Uwazie et al. (1999), Zahradeen (1988), and various newspaper articles obtained from Lexis-Nexis Universe, an online world news archive.
6. Women could also be found at Marwa's enclave, though only very few of them seemed to have joined the sect voluntarily; most were tricked or forcibly coerced into providing a variety of services to the men.

7. Another interpretation of the Maitatsines' reliance on primitive weapons could be that it stemmed from Marwa's rejection of materialism and technology. This interpretation is doubtful because when technology served his aims, Marwa did employ it, as evidenced by the fact that he traveled around in cars despite his accusation that those who used cars were infidels.

8. Metz (1992); various newspaper articles obtained from Lexis-Nexis Universe.

9. Death count from various newspaper articles obtained from Lexis-Nexis Universe.

10. See Metz (1992). Human rights violations were especially frequent after the creation of the Nigerian Security Organization (NSO) in 1976. The return of democratic rule in 1979 reduced the violations, though there was still room for improvement in the human rights record.

11. See Fatula (2000) and Osso (1990).

12. See Reno (1999) and Forrest (1995) for a discussion of the prevalence of patron-client ties in Nigerian politics.

13. Statistic compiled from various sources: EIU Country Profiles (1986–99), EIU Country Reports (1986–99), Federal Office of Statistics (1999), Keesing's Record of World Events, MAR Group Assessments, Okeke (1992), Omonijo (1999), Osso (1990), and Uwechue (1991). "Controlling for larger population share" means that if Northerners held 53 percent of the seats in a given council, that council is not considered to have been an instance of Northern dominance because the combined population of states forming the original Northern region is 53 percent of the total Nigerian population. Without controlling for the North's larger population share, Northerners held the preponderance of seats in the Council for 96 percent of the 1985–99 period.

14. The statistics in this paragraph are from these sources: EIU Country Data, EIU Country Profile (1987–88, 12) and EIU Country Report (3rd Quarter 1999, 22).

15. This statistic is derived from table 4.1, which charts media-reported conflicts that began sometime between 1985 and 1999. Events were grouped together into conflicts on the basis of identical actors and issues.

16. The Muslim Brotherhood does not appear to have been violent after September 1998. The reported death count for the Ijaw versus government conflict is 373 for January 2000 to October 2004, which amounts to a total reported death count of 607. Data are from Keesing's Record of World Events, Lexis-Nexis Universe, and Human Rights Watch.

17. The well-known Movement for the Survival of the Ogoni People is not included in this list of antigovernment rebellions because up to 1999 (the end point of this study) it appears to have used nonviolent means (see table 4.1).

18. This narrative comes from Keesing's Record of World Events.

19. Uwujaren (1998). Southerners did dominate the navy, but the army was superior in power and importance.

20. MAR Group Assessments and Ejobowah (2000). A precursor to the Ijaw rebellion occurred in 1966 when Ijaw youth declared their homeland the Niger Delta People's Republic. This rebellion was crushed.

21. Since the press was highly influenced by the government during this period, it is possible that civilian deaths have been underreported (cf. Davenport and Ball 2002).

22. It is likely that the militant actions reported in the press are only a fraction of those that actually occurred. Since other ethnic groups also carried out such actions, they were

rather commonplace. For example, Shell reports that between December 1998 and May 1999, 50 of its workers or contractors were kidnapped and 150 of its installations were occupied, closed down, or halted (Lexis-Nexis Universe). The press, however, is likely to underreport such "commonplace" events (cf. Davenport and Ball 2002, 431).

23. The other resolution called on all Ijaws to join in the fight.

24. News reports point out that the protestors were often unarmed (Lexis-Nexis Universe).

25. Keesing's Record of World Events. The statistics in this section of the chapter are all from Keesing's.

References

Amnesty International. *Annual Reports: 1997–2001.* http://www.amnesty.org. Accessed July 12, 2002.

Amuwu, 'Kunle, Adigun Agbaje, Rotimi Suberu, and Georges Herault. 1998. *Federalism and Political Restructuring in Nigeria.* Ibadan: Spectrum Books Limited.

Anyaogu, Godwin Nnamdi. 1967. *The Philosophy of the Biafran Revolution: A Call for African Originality.* New York: Africa House.

Balogun, Ola. 1973. *The Tragic Years: Nigeria In Crisis 1966–1970.* Benin City: Ethiope Publishing Corporation.

Banks, Arthur S., and Thomas C. Muller, eds. 1999. "Nigeria." In *Political Handbook of the World: 1999.* Binghamton, NY: CSA Publications.

Bartkus, Viva Ona. 1999. *The Dynamic of Secession.* Cambridge: Cambridge University Press.

Best, Shedrack. 1999. "The Islamist Challenge: The Nigerian 'Shiite' Movement." In *Searching for Peace in Africa: An Overview of Conflict Prevention and Management Activities,* ed. Monique Mekenkamp, Paul van Tongeren, and Hans van de Veen. Utrecht: European Platform for Conflict Prevention and Transformation.

Birch, Geoffrey, and Dominic St. George. 1968. *Biafra: The Case for Independence.* London: Britain-Biafra Association.

CIA World Factbook 2002. http://www.cia.gov/cia/publications/factbook/. Accessed June 13, 2003.

Collier, Paul, and Anke Hoeffler. 2002. "Greed and Grievance in Civil War." DERG Working Paper, World Bank, Washington, DC.

Collier, Paul, V. L. Elliott, Håvard Hegre, Anke Hoeffler, Marta Reynal-Querol, and Nicholas Sambanis. 2003. *Breaking the Conflict Trap: Civil War and Development Policy.* Washington, DC: World Bank and Oxford University Press.

Davenport, Christian, and Patrick Ball. 2002. "Views to a Kill: Exploring the Implications of Source Selection in the Case of Guatemalan State Terror, 1977–1995." *Journal of Conflict Resolution* 46 (3): 427–50.

EIU (Economist Intelligence Unit). *Nigeria Country Profiles.* 1986–2002. London: Economist Intelligence Unit Limited.

———. *Nigeria Country Reports.* 1986–2002. London: Economist Intelligence Unit Limited.

Ejobowah, John Boye. 2000. "Who Owns the Oil? The Politics of Ethnicity in the Niger Delta of Nigeria." *Africa Today* 47 (1): 28–47.

Falola, Toyin. 1998. *Violence in Nigeria: The Crisis of Religious Politics and Secular Ideologies.* Rochester, NY: University of Rochester Press.

Fatula, Olugbemi. 2000. *2000 Foremost Nigerians. Vol. 1: 200 Profiles.* Ibadan: Caltop Publications Limited.

Federal Office of Statistics. 1999. *Annual Abstract of Statistics.* Lagos: Federation of Nigeria.

Forrest, Tom. 1995. *Politics and Economic Development in Nigeria.* Boulder, CO: Westview Press.

Gurr, Ted Robert. 2000. *Peoples Versus States.* Washington, DC: U.S. Institute of Peace.

Hackett, Rosalind I. J. 1987. *New Religious Movements in Nigeria.* Lewiston, NY: Mellen Press.

Hegre, Håvard, Tanja Ellingsen, Nils Petter Gleditsch, and Scott Gates. 2001. "Toward a Democratic Civil Peace? Democracy, Political Change and Civil War 1816–1992." *American Political Science Review* 95 (1): 33–48.

Human Rights Watch. 1999. *The Price of Oil: Corporate Responsibility and Human Rights Violations in Nigeria's Oil Producing Communities.* Available at: http://www.hrg.org/reports/1999/nigeria/Nigew991-01.htm. Accessed July 2, 2002.

———. *World Reports: 1998–2001.* http://www.hrw.org. Accessed May 18, 2002.

Keesing's Record of World Events. http://www.keesings.com. Accessed March 9, 2002; April 21, 2002.

International Labor Office. 1979. *Yearbook of Labor Statistics.* Geneva: ILO.

Lexis-Nexis Universe. Reports from various news services including Africa News Service, Associated Press, BBC, Facts on File World News Digest, Reuters, Inter Press Service, UN Integrated Regional Information Network, Xinhua News Service. Available at: http://web.lexis-nexis.com/universe/. Accessed July–October 2002.

Lichbach, Mark Irving. 1987. "Deterrence or Escalation? The Puzzle of Aggregate Studies of Repression and Dissent." *Journal of Conflict Resolution* 31 (2): 266–97.

Metz, Helen Chapin. 1992. *Nigeria: A Country Study.* Washington, DC: Department of the Army.

Minorities at Risk (MAR) Group Assessments. Available at: http://www.cidcm.umd.edu/inscr/mar. Accessed June 2002.

Nafziger, E. Wayne, and William L. Richter. 1976. "Biafra and Bangladesh: The Political Economy of Secessionist Conflict." *Journal of Peace Research* 13 (2): 91–109.

Nixon, Charles R. 1972. "Self-Determination: The Nigeria/Biafra Case." *World Politics* 24 (4): 473–97.

Nnoli, Okwudiba. 1978. *Ethnic Politics in Nigeria.* Enugu, Nigeria: Fourth Dimension Publishers.

Nwankwo, Nehe. 1969. *The Truth About Biafra and Nigeria.* New York: Author.

Okeke, Okechukwu. 1992. *Hausa-Fulani Hegemony: The Dominance of the Muslim North in Contemporary Nigerian Politics.* Enugu, Nigeria: Acena Publishers.

Olojede, Iyabo, et al. 2000. *Nigeria: Oil Pollution, Community Dissatisfaction and Threat to National Peace and Security.* Harare: African Association of Political Science.

Ojukwu, C. Odumegwu. 1969. *Biafra: Selected Speeches and Random Thoughts of C. Odumegwu Ojukwu, With Diaries of Events.* New York: Harper & Row.

Omonijo, Mobolade. 1999. *Political Factbook and Who's Who in Nigeria.* Ikeja: Winngam Communications Ltd.

Osemwota, Osa. 1994. *Regional Economic Disparity and Conflict in Nigeria.* Benin City: Omega Publishers Ltd.

Osso, Nyaknno, Ed. 1990. *Who's Who in Nigeria.* Lagos: Newswatch Communications, Limited.

Oyeweso, Siyan, Editor. 1992. *Perspectives on the Nigerian Civil War.* Ojokoro, Lagos: OAP Publications.

Petersen, Roger D. 2002. *Understanding Ethnic Violence: Fear, Hatred, and Resentment in Twentieth-Century Eastern Europe.* Cambridge: Cambridge University Press.

Post, K. W. J. 1968. "Is There a Case for Biafra?" *International Affairs* 44 (1): 26–39.

Reno, William. 1999. "Crisis and (No) Reform in Nigeria's Politics." *African Studies Review* 42 (1): 105–24.

"Shell Gives Up on Ijaw Youths." P.M. News (Lagos), October 26, 1998. Available at: http://web.lexis-nexis.com/universe/form/academic. Accessed October 17, 2002.

Tarrow, Sidney. 1998. *Power in Movement: Social Movements and Contentious Politics.* 2nd ed. Cambridge: Cambridge University Press.

Tilly, Charles. 1978. *From Mobilization to Revolution.* Reading, MA: Addison-Wesley.

Umoren, Joseph A. 1996. *Democracy and Ethnic Diversity in Nigeria.* Lanham, MD: University Press of America.

Uwazie, Ernest E., Isaac O. Albert, and Godfrey N. Uzoigwe, eds. 1999. *Inter-Ethnic and Religious Conflict Resolution in Nigeria.* Lanham, MD: Lexington Books.

Uwechue, Raph, ed. 1991. *Africa Who's Who.* London: Africa Books Limited.

Uwujaren, Wilson. 1998. "Nigeria: Masters and Slaves." *Tempo,* September 30.

Wergeles, Ed. 1960. "A Free Nigeria Emerges in Churning Africa . . . Are Its Soaring Hopes Within Reach?" *Newsweek,* October 3, 34–35.

Zahradeen, Nasir B. 1988. *The Maitatsine Saga.* Zaria: Hudahuda Publishing Co.

Sporadic Ethnic Violence

Why Has Kenya Not Experienced a Full-Blown Civil War?

5

MWANGI S. KIMENYI
AND NJUGUNA S. NDUNG'U

Extreme poverty and the collapse of law and order can become mutually reinforcing, producing a conflict trap (Blomberg et al. 2000; Elbadawi, Ndung'u, and Njuguna 2001). In Sub-Saharan Africa, many countries are caught in such a conflict trap and one out of every five people is directly affected by civil wars (Elbadawi et al. 2001). In Kenya, poverty levels almost doubled in the 1990s, a decade marred by ethnic violence, but the country has avoided the conflict trap. This chapter analyzes civil conflict in Kenya and asks why the cycles of ethnic conflict have not escalated into a full-blown civil war.

A civil war can be said to occur when a trigger factor, or a combination of factors, results in what may be referred to as a "tipping point," when factions in a society engage in an all-out armed conflict. Before that tipping point is reached, a country may be characterized by tensions but not by widespread conflict. For many countries, the triggers for a civil war are not strong enough to result in a tipping point; hence such countries are characterized by relative peace, although there may be tensions within the society among different factions. In a number of studies, Paul Collier and his colleagues have sought to explain the determinants of civil wars. They provide a systematic analysis of the causal factors of civil war initiation, duration, and recurrence. Collier and Hoeffler (1998, 2001; henceforth CH) find strong empirical support for their "opportunity cost" explanation of civil war onset. In this chapter, we refer to the CH model and discuss why the availability of significant opportunity for war in Kenya did not reach the tipping point that would turn ethnic violence into civil war.

Postindependence Kenya has been marked by a state of relative political stability and peace. In many respects, Kenya resembles other countries in Africa that have had prolonged civil wars. However, unlike most of the countries in Sub-Saharan Africa, Kenya has neither been under military dictatorship nor experienced any major internal strife that could be classified as a civil war. In fact, before the early 1990s, internal conflict was virtually nonexistent, except for banditry in the Northeastern province and near the Somali border. However, during the 1990s, Kenya experienced a number of "ethnic clashes." These clashes neither translated into civil wars nor lasted long. To a large extent, ethnic clashes have been localized in limited geographical areas and have not affected life in other parts of the country. Furthermore, the clashes have not involved rebel groups fighting to dislodge the government and therefore did not result in casualties on the government side. By all measures then, Kenya has not had a civil war during the postindependence era.

Kenya is often cited as an example of peace and stability in a chaotic region. Peace and stability have often been attributed to the quality of leadership or the "peace-loving" nature of Kenyans. Another argument is that the presence of the middle class is strong, and that class would stand to lose a lot in a civil war, so it supports the peace. But the fact that Kenya has not had a civil war may be consistent with the predictions of the CH model and may have little to do with either Kenyan leadership or the nature of Kenyan people. The CH model does not place Kenya in the high-risk cluster of countries during the period we study (the risk of civil war in 1990 was around 1 percent). We explain why sporadic ethnic violence has not resulted in widespread civil war and argue that this case supports the CH model. Some of the key civil war "triggers" have not been strong enough in Kenya to cause a tipping point to civil war.

This chapter discusses some of the relevant literature on the causes of civil wars to place the CH model in a broader context, focuses on ethnic conflicts in Kenya and provides some general explanations of their causes, and explains why the sporadic ethnic violence in Kenya has not resulted in large-scale civil war.

Explaining Civil Wars

In addition to the CH model (see chapter 1), earlier contributions to the literature by public choice scholars had advanced theories of conflict that are worth considering here briefly. Gordon Tullock (1974) offered a model that was quite similar to the CH framework. Focusing on rebellions and revolutions, Tullock suggested that the decision by an individual to engage in such activities was the outcome of a rational choice whereby the individual evaluates the costs and benefits of getting involved in armed conflict. A central contribution by Tullock, which underlies the distinction between civil wars and criminal violence, is that the participation by an individual in civil wars generates a public good while participation in crime generates a private good. That is, an individual who engages in armed conflict incurs high private costs (including the risk of death), but the result of a civil war is often a change in government that benefits many. The "public good" nature of civil wars explains why individuals are reluctant to participate in them (because of the well-known collective action problems associated with the production of public goods). Another important factor in the Tullock model is that the cost of organizing violence limits the formation of viable rebel groups. For example, rural communities may incur much higher transaction costs for organizing a political action than urban communities. In a related perspective, Kimenyi (1989) analyzed ethnicity and its impact on institution building in Africa. He treated ethnic groups as "permanent interest groups" that compete in the market for wealth transfers and seek to maximize "group welfare" through the transfer of resources from other groups. The most efficient way to accomplish this is to control the instrument of wealth transfers—the government. Ethnic groups will use violence to take control of the government to redistribute benefits to their members. Civil war may be the result of such efforts.

Along the same lines, Kimenyi and Mbaku (1993) argued that institutional instability is the result of coups and civil wars that disrupt corrupt and "rent-seeking" interest groups that compete for transfers of wealth. They showed that the availability of easily extractable resources from poorly organized groups (farmers) and growth in income help maintain stability. By contrast, economic reforms that limit the government's ability to broker wealth transfers can trigger instability. Likewise, the presence of many ethno-religious groups complicates the rent-seeking competition. Ethnic identity is essential for the formation of a special interest group that has the size and capacity to compete politically in Africa. The number and size of ethnic groups affect political competition in Africa. Kenya is ethnically diverse and the various groups compete for political control, which could raise the risk of civil war in Kenya.

Ethnic Violence in Kenya

As previously noted, conflicts are a recent phenomenon in Kenya, which is considered one of the few stable and peaceful African nations. Nevertheless, during the last decade, and coinciding with the introduction of competitive politics, sporadic incidences of violence have been experienced that have targeted certain ethnic groups. Starting in September 1991, organized bands of arsonists calling themselves "Kalenjin warriors" unleashed terror on Luo, Luhyia, Kikuyu, and Kisii in the Rift Valley region. They targeted farms populated by these ethnic communities, looted and destroyed homes, drove away the occupants, and killed indiscriminately. The attackers were often dressed in informal uniforms, their faces marked with clay in the manner of initiation candidates, and were armed with traditional bows, arrows, and machetes (even though the arrows were reportedly imported from Korea). The violence resulted in displacement of thousands of people from their farms.

Similar incidents erupted in Mombasa and Kwale districts in the Coastal region in August 1997. In these clashes, the Digo, who are one of the local Mijikenda tribes, targeted members of tribes from outside the Coast province, mainly the Kikuyus and Luos. By the time the clashes subsided after about two weeks, 65 people—including 13 police officers—had been killed, property worth millions of shillings destroyed, and more than 10,000 people displaced. The tourism industry, which is the lifeline of the coastal area, bore the brunt of the "collateral damage," suffering a fall of nearly 70 percent and a loss of more than 5,000 jobs (Mazrui 1997).

In 2001, 62 people died and scores were injured in clashes pitting the Kisii and Maasai along the Gucha Transmara border; more than 50 people died in a single week of fighting between the Pokomo and Wardei tribes in Tana River district; and in Nairobi's Kibera slums, three days of clashes left 12 people dead and more than 50 houses razed to the ground in fights between tenants and landlords. Although the Kibera clashes were basically over rent, some observers have linked them to ethnic factions because the majority of the landlords are Nubians and Kikuyus, whereas the tenants are mainly Luos. In February 2002, another new form of political violence emerged in Nairobi where different political "private armies" aligned to individuals in different political parties clashed and killed more than 20 people in one night.

The violence in the Rift Valley and Coastal region is of particular significance because it was widely viewed as constituting a serious threat to the existence of a united Kenyan nation, the rule of law, and the institutions of private property, contract, and the market economy. The violence appeared senseless. People who had lived together for decades were suddenly killing each other. The true objectives of the attackers largely remain a matter of speculation. Even the identity of the attackers is puzzling. The label "ethnic clashes" is itself somewhat paradoxical because the clashes did not involve significant numbers of any ethnic community up in arms against another ethnic community. Instead, most reports give the numbers of raiders in the hundreds, sometimes in the dozens. While the victims are from specific ethnic communities, the aggressors hardly qualify as an ethnic group. In many ways, the raids resemble Mueller's description of opportunistic depredation waged by small bands of criminals and thugs, often scarcely differentiable from ordinary crime (Mueller 2001).

Table 5.1 provides a detailed analysis of ethnic conflicts in Kenya. The table lists the locations where conflict took place, their time and duration, the groups involved, the causes given for the conflicts, the resulting damage, and the manner in which they were resolved. Notable is the fact that most ethnic clashes occurred around the first and second multiparty elections in 1992 and 1997. Also, most of the conflicts were in the Rift Valley province. Finally, the majority of the clashes relate to party politics and land ownership. In the following section, we focus on some of the credible explanations for the causes of the clashes.

Causes of the Violence

Three main factors have been associated with ethnic violence in Kenya: deep ethnic cleavages, conflict over land distribution, and political competition.

Ethnicity

The most commonly cited cause of the violence in Kenya is ethnic cleavage. The country is ethnically diverse, with at least 42 distinct tribal groups, and it has been established that ethnic identification in Africa is very strong (Kimenyi 1997). Collier (2001), for example, observes that the tribe and kin groups are the most powerful levels of social identity. Tribal identification has been shown to be an important way of solving collective action problems (Kimenyi 1998), but it can also have negative implications for nonmembers. Because violence has been organized along ethnic lines, the inference is that ethnic clashes in Kenya have been purely the result of "ethnic hatred." But this hatred must be qualified. It is linked to electoral politics and competition among new arrivals in a region, groups with large land ownership, and native groups who feel threatened by the others.

At one extreme, there is the view that ethnic violence was the resurgence of precolonial barbarism. But it is hard to explain how the relationship between tribes can suddenly turn from cordial to unreasoned hostility and violence. Another view is that democratic transition in 1991 inflamed latent tribal hatreds. Murungi (1995), for example, argues that there has been a reservoir of resentment and mistrust of the Kikuyu (the ethnic group most affected by violence) arising from the Kikuyu's expansionism.

Some aspects of the violence have a historical dimension. Bates (1989) argues that the Kikuyu were forced to migrate out of their traditional areas as a result of displacement by the white settlers and settled in the Rift Valley. After independence, the Kikuyus remained in the Rift Valley settling there permanently. Of Kenya's tribes, the Kikuyu were the first to embrace capitalism and were able to exploit the opportunities created by the independence government. They were, for example, the leading beneficiaries of small holder credit schemes and held the majority of senior civil service jobs as a result of their education opportunities (Leys 1975). Tribal animosities were heightened by the policy of returning land to Africans after independence, when the Kikuyu are said to have benefited disproportionately. Thus, a government minister is reported to have justified the recent bloody eviction of the Kikuyu from Maasai land as a correction of historical wrongs.

This pattern of ethnic conflict in Kenya seems to agree with some large-N empirical studies that have found evidence of a positive correlation between ethnic diversity and the incidence of civil war (Ellingsen 2000; Hegre et al. 2001; Sambanis 2001). This contrasts with the CH model.

We will now look more closely at the relationship between violence and ethnic heterogeneity in the various regions of Kenya. As of 1991, Kenya was subdivided into 8 provinces and 41 districts. We measure the ethnic heterogeneity of each district by $(1 - s^2)$, where s is the share of the population that belongs to the largest ethnic group. We then rank districts in descending order of ethnic heterogeneity as shown in table 5.2 (on p. 140). The results show that of the 13 most ethnically diverse districts in Kenya, 12 (or 92 percent) have had violent conflicts of one type or another. Additionally, of the 8 most ethnically homogeneous districts, only one (Kisii) has experienced violent conflicts. Moreover, the violence in Kisii is confined to its border with Transmara. From this we can infer that conflicts do have an ethnic dimension.

Land

Conflict over land rights is often seen as being at the center of ethnic conflict in Kenya. In fact, violence was directed at members of minority ethnic groups in

(text continues on page 138)

Table 5.1 **Ethnic Violence in Kenya**

Province	Location	Duration (estimate)	Date	Tribes
Rift Valley				
Elgeyo Marakwet	Various (e.g., Kapsawar, Chebyego Hills, Kamalakon, Kapcherop)	>10 years		Pokot vs. Marakwet
Kericho	Belgut division/ Muhoroni border, Sondu	2 months or less	March 6, 1992	Kalenjin vs. Kisii, Luo
	Ainamoi division, Buru farm/ Thessalia Holdings ground	5 months	Nov. 5, 1992	Kipsigis vs. Luo
	Chilchila division, Kiptenden farm, Kunyak scheme	4 months	Nov. 3, 1991– March 1992	Kalenjin vs. Luo, Kikuyu, Kisii, Luhya, Teso, Turkana
	Londiani		1992	
	Thesalia	1 month	Jan. 1996	
	Kericho	1 day	March 1999	Luo vs. Kalenji
Laikipia	Ol-Moran division and Ng'arua	3 weeks	Jan. 12, 1998	Kikuyu, Samburu, Pokot

Cause	Damage	Resolution
Cattle rustling	Theft of livestock, deaths	NA
The Kalenjin burned down homes of Luos, triggering retaliatory attacks. Political dimension because Luos were associated with FORD, an opposition party while Kipsigis were KANU supporters.	People injured, food stores burned down, 24 people died	The clashes were stopped after the attackers achieved their objective of forcing Luos out of the region.
An attempt by Kipsigis and the provincial administration to evict Luos from Buru farm. Luos were alleged to be supporters of opposition parties.	Destruction of 150 houses and property, people injured and 250 families displaced	Calm returned after Luos were displaced from the area. Attack also succeeded in bringing in confusion to voters as they were threatened to vote in a predetermined manner.
Political incitement	People displaced	
	6 killed, 40 houses burned	
	One dead, 200 evicted	
Burning down of Kikuyu houses by Pokots and Samburus. Theft of livestock of Kikuyus by armed gangs. Political differences as the Kikuyu largely supported opposition parties while Pokots and Samburu supported KANU. Kikuyus were either to support KANU or face expulsion from the area. Illegal occupation of Kikuyu-owned land by pastoralists.	Injuries, deaths and destruction of property. At least 3 people dead, 50 houses burned.	

(continued)

Table 5.1 **Ethnic Violence in Kenya (*Continued*)**

Province	Location	Duration (estimate)	Date	Tribes
Nakuru	Highlands-Molo, Njoro Olenguruone	About 3 years (not continuous)	1991, 1992, 1996, 1997	Kalenjin community vs. immigrants mainly Kikuyu, Luo, and Kisii
Nandi	Songor location, Tinderet division, Cheboigony and Kapenguria farms	3 months	Oct. 1991, Nov. 1991, March 1992	Nandis attacked non-Kalenjin tribes, mainly Kisiis
	Kamasia subloca-tion, Kipkelion division, Cheplaskei village	1 month	Dec. 12, 1991	Nandis vs. Luhya and Teso
	Mitetei location, Tinderet division (Mitetei farm, scene of first arsonist attack)	5 months	Oct. 29, 1991	Nandi warriors attacken non-Nandi's (Luhya, Kikuyu, Kisii) living on Mitetei farm
Narok	Gucha/Trans-mara district along Kisii-Maasai-Kikuyu borderlands	3 months	1991, 1993, Oct. 14, 1997 Feb., May, and June 2001	Maasai vs. Kisii

Cause	Damage	Resolution
Politically instigated as Rift Valley politicians wanted to create a KANU zone (opposition-free area). Cattle rustling, land dispute, differences over pasture.	More than 1,500 people killed. More than 300,000 displaced. Collapse of agricultural sector heightened by the violence.	
Politically instigated after cabinet ministers, 34 councillors and top KANU officials vowed to expel non-KAMATUSA[a] tribes from Rift Valley Province.	20 farms were attacked.	The government did not do much to resolve the conflict. Calm was restored after non-Kalenjins were ejected from the area.
Political incitement following inflammatory statements by KANU leaders to kick out tribes associated with opposition politics.	Deaths, displacement	Peace was restored after raiders, all strangers, stopped their arson attacks.
Differences over ownership of Mitetei farm in Tinderet division. The Kalenjins wanted to expel other tribes (Kikuyu, Luhya, Kisii) from the farm. Politicians exploited the land dispute to wage war against non-Kalenjin for political reasons. Inflammatory statements by politicians during political rallies held in the province in Sept. 1991.	Destruction of property, people injured and displaced	The clashes ended after non-Kalenjin tribes were driven out, and the government legalized the subdivision of the land among the Kalenjin shareholders.
Political instigation as Kisiis are believed to have ditched KANU for the opposition. Cattle rustling as Maasai raid Kisii homes for livestock. Land dispute as Maasai alleged that their land had been taken over by Kisii. Likewise, the Kisii alleged that their crops were being illegally harvested by Maasai.	24 people killed, hundreds displaced	Clashes eased after elections (1992, 1997) as they were intended to influence the voting pattern in favor of either KANU or the opposition. The current clashes can be linked to the forthcoming election and are likely to be on and off until after the general elections.

(continued)

Table 5.1 **Ethnic Violence in Kenya (*Continued*)**

Province	Location	Duration (estimate)	Date	Tribes
	Narok district, Mau–Narok division, Enoosupukia Hills	1 year	Dec. 9–29, 1992, Oct.–Dec. 1993	Maasai vs. Kikuyu
	Naivasha		Early 1994	Maasai vs. Kikuyu
Trans Nzoia	Trans Nzoia, Endebbess division, Endebess location	~3½ months	Dec. 16, 1991– March 1992	Sabaots vs. Bukusu
	Mount Elgon district, Kapsakwony location/Kaptam location, Border between Luhya and Kalenjin areas	6 months	Nov. 26, 1991	Kalenjins vs. Bukusu and Kikuyu Sabaots vs. Bukusu and Teso
Uasin Gishu	Ainabkoi division, Burnt Forest	2 months	Dec. 3, 1992	Kalenjin vs. Kikuyu
	Burnt Forest	1 week	April 1994	Kalenjin vs. Kikuyu

Cause	Damage	Resolution
A land quarrel led to the burning of Kikuyu houses by Maasai. Politically motivated following the introduction of multiparty politics. Maasai supported KANU, Kikuyu predominantly in opposition. Environmental concerns—Maasai claimed the area inhabited by the Kikuyu was a water catchment area.	More than 30 people killed and more than 30,000 displaced. Destruction of houses, crops.	The attacks stopped after the elections in 1992 and a government attempt to resettle displaced families at the Maela refugee camp. The attacks were aimed at influencing the election in KANU's favor.
	10,000 displaced	
Differences over ownership of Sabaots Cooperative Farm in Endebbes location as Sabaots attempted to evict Bukusu. Political differences between Sabaots who were in KANU and Bukusu who supported FORD.	Injuries and displacement	There was calm after Sabaot attackers succeeded to force the Bukusu out of the farm. The Sabaot were better organized, trained, and armed than Bukusu.
The Sabaot attacked Kikuyus, Teso, and Bukusu tribes by burning down houses for political reasons. Bukusu supported KANU while Sabaots supported FORD-Kenya.	About 30 houses of Bukusu burned down at Kapsokwony location	
The Kalenjin burned down Kikuyu houses in all major farms in the area. The aim was to expel Kikuyus who were associated with the opposition. Differences over grazing land.	Destruction/burning of houses; 15,000 displaced	
	12 killed; 65 houses burned	

(continued)

Table 5.1 **Ethnic Violence in Kenya (*Continued*)**

Province	Location	Duration (estimate)	Date	Tribes
West Pokot		Many years—sporadic	1976 and before to present	Pokot vs. Marakwet, Turkana, Samburu
			May 1998	Pokot vs. Marakwet
Western Province Bungoma	Chemichimi, Chwele	4 months	March–July 1992	Kalenjin vs. Luhya
Coast Province Kwale	Matuga, Ngombeni location, Msambweni, Shonda, Mtongwe	3 months	August 1997–Nov. 1997	The local KANU politicians supported Majimbo/ federalism, hence planned to attack upcountry tribes. The politicians mainly targeted Kikuyu and Luo who were believed to be allied to the opposition.
Mombasa	Likoni, Kisumu Ndogo, Maweni, Shauri Yako	3 months	August 13–Sept. 1997	Digo vs. Kikuyu, Luo, Luyha, Kamba
Tana River	Tana River	Sporadic	1991, 1992, 1995	Oromo, Pokomo

Cause	Damage	Resolution
Cattle rustling—raids a rite of passage for young men. Land—taken away by colonial government later allocated to influential people from other communities.		
	2,000 displaced; 60 killed	
Clashes erupted after well-trained raiders attacked residents of the area, targeting noncoastal (upcountry) tribes, mainly the Luo and Kikuyus. Fight over resources, Business rivalry. Politically motivated as the local politicians rallied their tribes to support federalism/Majimbo and kick out tribes opposed to federalism. Upcountry tribes had to be ejected from the area to prevent them from voting for opposition candidates.	Thousands displaced About 65 people killed including 13 police officers. Destruction of property, including a police station. Collapse of tourism industry. Loss of jobs for displaced people.	The violence ended after the 1997 general election as the aim was to influence results of this election in a way that favored coastal tribes. The government deployed police to stop the clashes, albeit too late, and arrested some people involved in the attacks.
	62 killed, including 10 police officers; 30 automatic weapons stolen; 100,000 displaced	
Cattle rustling	More than 2,000 cows and goats stolen	Ended after government troops intervened

(continued)

Table 5.1 **Ethnic Violence in Kenya (*Continued*)**

Province	Location	Duration (estimate)	Date	Tribes
Eastern Province Isiolo	Isiolo	2 weeks	May 1, 2000	Borana and Samburu vs. Somalis of Degodia clan
				Somali vs. Borana
		Jan., Feb., March 2000	Jan., Feb., March 2000	Borana, Meru, Somali, Turkana, Samburu, Sekuye, Gabra
Kitui	Mwingi district	1 month	1991, 1992	Kamba vs. Shifta
Meru	Tharaka, Meru	1 month	—	Interclan war over land
Nyanza	South Nyanza, Maasai Kisii border	3 months	Nov. 1997	Maasai vs. Kisii
Northeastern Province	Marsabit Moyale–Sololo division		Traced to pre-colonial times Examples, July 1996 throughout 1980s	Somalis (Shiftas) Boran vs. REGABU (Rendille, Gabbra Burji)
			June 1996	1996—Samburu vs. Boran Somali
	Marsabit and Moyale			

Cause	Damage	Resolution
Fighting over pasture land, cattle rustling. Politics—Somalis came to graze, settled, registered as voters and influenced voting patterns. Local leaders demanded sacking/ expulsion of migrant Somali pastoralists from Wajir and Mandera. These tribes had lived peacefully for many years. The problem started with multiparty politics. The local politicians want to expel the Merus who are associated with the opposition.	40 people killed; 2,000 cattle, 500 goats stolen	
Cattle rustling		
Land dispute	Property destroyed, people killed	
	30+ killed	
Began as struggle for land and other economic resources. Cattle rustling. Somalis wanted to secede (1963–68). 68—Somali relinquished its claim. Sporadic acts of banditry.		
	13 killed	
Ethiopian army makes incursions into Kenya, accuses Boran of harboring OLF[b] rebels	Torture, abduction, murders, livestock theft (e.g., March 1996 to May), 61 people killed	
Politically instigated		

(continued)

Table 5.1 **Ethnic Violence in Kenya (*Continued*)**

Province	Location	Duration (estimate)	Date	Tribes
Nairobi	Kibera slums	1 week	Oct. 1995	Luos vs. Nubians
		3 days	Nov./Dec. 2001	Landlord vs. tenants
	Mukuru slums, South B	3 days		Muslims vs. Christians

Sources: Law Society of Kenya: *Report of the Law Society of Kenya on the Judicial Commission of Inquiry into Ethnic Clashes in Kenya* (unpublished); Nation newspapers (various) ICE Case Studies: *Ethnic Cleansing and the environment in Kenya:* The PEOPLE Newspaper (various); KHRC: *The Forgotten People: Human Rights Violations in Moyale and Marsabit Districts.*

specific regions of the country with the intent of expelling them from those areas. The primary result of these conflicts has been the displacement of people who had settled in parts of the country other than their ancestral land. There is a consensus that Kenya's "land question" is the primary source of the ethnic clashes. Kanyinga (2000) observes that violence resulted from the elite's appropriation of the land issue to fight those opposed to them by reactivating demands for territorial land claims in the Rift Valley and on the Coast.

In precolonial times, land was communally owned and traditional rights and obligations ensured direct access to all. Colonialism disrupted these relationships. Colonial authorities assumed that all land to which private ownership could not be established by documentary evidence was ownerless (Okoth Ogendo 1999). The colonial government parceled out more than 7 million acres of land, including some of the most fertile land in Kenya, and earmarked them for cultivation by Europeans. These areas came to be known as the white highlands. Indigenous ethnic communities who had occupied these areas were relegated to marginal reserves and all land not in their occupation was declared crown land. This resulted in overpopulation in the reserves and, as a result, significant numbers of Luo, Kisii, Luhya, and Kikuyu migrated to the Rift Valley province as squatters and to provide labor on settler farms.

The colonial powers, while creating white highlands, limited access to land rights, but indirectly increased access to land. The outcome was to promote migration to the white highlands, radically expanding the range of Kikuyu settlement. Thus the Kikuyu settled outside the Central province. White settlers restricted the possibility of establishing land rights. So, when independence was won, and power was seized by a conservative fraction of Kenya's rural society, the first order of business was to settle issues of investment and private property, including land rights. Sharp disagreements arose as to who would get reversionary interest in the highlands.

	Cause	*Damage*	*Resolution*
	Political differences, luo support Ford Kenya, Nubians support KANU	5 killed 12 killed, 50 houses razed	
	Rent		
			Church, mosque, and other property burned

Note: We have no data on violence for a number of regions, so they have been excluded from this table. These regions are: Samburu, Turkana, Kilifi, Lamu, Taita Taveta, Machakos, and Marsabit.

a. Acronym for Kalenjin, Maasai Turkana and Samburu ethnic groups.

b. OLF = Oromo Liberation Front—a guerrilla movement in Southern Ethiopia fighting against the Ethiopian government.

The contest was quickly ethnicized: The Kalenjin, Maasai, Turkana, and Samburu (KAMATUSA) of the Rift Valley regarded the settler farms as their ancestral land and favored a federal system that would provide guarantees against "land hungry" squatters and migrants. The squatter and migrant communities naturally were keen to protect their territorial gains outside their ancestral land. There were also sharp divisions over land reforms, with a radical faction that advocated seizure of land arguing that the land the settlers held was stolen by the crown and at independence should be returned and freely distributed to the indigenous people. Liberal groups, on the other hand, supported a system that would be less antagonistic to settlers and foreign investors. This broader group also was concerned with land productivity because agriculture was the main economic activity. This emerging class of a national economic development-conscious group may help to explain the pattern of land acquisition in Kenya after independence. It also supports Bates's (1989) argument that the government of postindependent Kenya favored rural, landed interests at the expense of the country's urban, industrial interests.

These issues threatened to delay the speedy transfer of political power. In the end, political independence was negotiated without resolving the land issue. At the second 1962 constitutional conference, all Kenyan tribes renounced their claims to the land that had belonged to them in precolonial Kenya but had been alienated to Europeans. It was agreed that the Europeans could part with the land on a willing seller–willing buyer basis. The validity of colonial expropriation was accepted and guaranteed by the independence constitution. Many of the migrants, individually or collectively, subsequently bought land from white settlers and settled in areas outside their ancestral homes, principally in the Rift Valley province.

The land issue was never fully addressed. British settlers' interests were safeguarded, and no effort was made to sort out the competing claims of those pastoral ethnic groups who had been ousted from the Rift Valley by the British and by squatters.

Table 5.2 **Ethnic Composition and Heterogeneity by District**

Rank	District	Percent of largest ethnic group	$1 - s^2$
1	Mombasa	27.91	0.922
2	Marsabit	28.2	0.92
3	Nairobi	32	0.898
4	Isiolo	34.16	0.883
5	Tana River	36.95	0.863
6	Lamu	40.35	0.837
7	Narok	47.28	0.776
8	Mandera	48.94	0.76
9	Wajir	51.66	0.733
10	Trans Nzoia	52.03	0.729
11	Uasin Gishu	52.63	0.723
12	Kajiado	56.55	0.68
13	Nakuru	59.65	0.644
14	Embu	60.5	0.634
15	Busia	61.4	0.623
16	Laikipia	67.75	0.541
17	Taita Taveta	71.5	0.489
18	Nandi	73.64	0.458
19	Samburu	74.65	0.443
20	South Nyanza	76.49	0.415
21	Kwale	82.56	0.318
22	Kericho	82.66	0.317
23	Bungoma	82.79	0.315
24	Baringo	83.79	0.298
25	Garissa	84.17	0.292
26	West Pokot	85.15	0.275
27	Kiambu	87.98	0.226
28	Meru	88.96	0.209
29	Kisumu	89.24	0.204
30	Kilifi	90.27	0.185
31	Elgeyo Marakwet	91.32	0.166
32	Turkana	94.5	0.107
33	Kakamega	94.52	0.107
34	Nyandarua	95.66	0.085
35	Siaya	95.77	0.083
36	Muranga	95.86	0.081
37	Nyeri	96.57	0.067
38	Kitui	96.97	0.06
39	Machakos	97.01	0.059
40	Kirinyaga	97.4	0.051
41	Kisii	98.23	0.035

There was further migration into the Rift Valley and Coast provinces from Central, Western, and Eastern provinces in the period immediately after independence. The high net inflows of people in the Rift Valley were attributed to settlement schemes that were initiated by the government soon after independence. In the Coast province, the largest number of immigrants came mainly from Machakos, Kitui, Kisumu, Kakamega, and Siaya. Immigrants in the Rift Valley came mainly from Central province, Kakamega, Bungoma, and all districts in Nyanza (Mbithi and Barnes 1975).

The settlement schemes formed the focal point of much of the violence while the "settlers" formed the bulk of the victims. Starting with the schemes initiated by the colonial government in areas such as Makueni, Gedi, Shimba Hills, and Olenguruone, little attempt was made to deal with claims of indigenous groups to lands earmarked for settlement. The case of Olenguruone division of Nakuru district illustrates this. From 1932 to 1933, the Kenya Land Commission established that the Kikuyu needed more land than they had access to; and around 1941, the colonial government purchased 34,700 acres in Olenguruone division to settle more than 4,000 Kikuyu squatters from Central Kenya who had been displaced by white settlers. This area was originally part of Maasai land, and the Kikuyu settlement created deep animosity. Olenguruone witnessed some of the worst atrocities in the 1991 violence and most of the displaced have been unable to return.

The postindependence settlement schemes designed to transfer land from settlers to Africans were similarly controversial. In a program known as the million-acre settlement scheme, the government bought some European farms ostensibly to settle the landless. There is evidence that the Kikuyu ended up being the main beneficiaries of the scheme. As Kanyinga (2000) observes, they were the most land-hungry and, being the ethnic group best placed to raise capital, led the way in land purchase cooperatives. Leys (1975) reports that, in a survey of 162 cooperatives, 120 were exclusively Kikuyu and an additional 38 consisted of Kikuyu with members of other tribes. The Kikuyu could be found participating in faraway schemes in places such as Lamu, Kilifi, Trans Nzoia, and Uasin Gishu, whose intended beneficiaries were from other ethnic communities. The resettlement schemes thus provided fertile ground for ethnic animosities.

Land reform policies in Kenya have been based on free-market models emphasizing individual freeholder rights over customary tenure in the belief that this would encourage investments in farm productivity, and that land markets would emerge that would transfer land to more efficient farmers and provide farmers with collateral for raising credit. There is mounting evidence that the economic and social benefits of such programs are questionable and that they may, in fact, cause conflict. As Toulmin and Quan (2000) observe, latent conflict is awakened by the irrevocable nature of land transfers. Recent conflicts in the Tana River district offer an example. This feud pits the Pokomo against Orma and Wardei neighbors and centers on land and grazing rights. The Orma and Wardei pastoralists accuse the Pokomo farmers of restricting their access to water points and grazing fields, while the Pokomo accuse pastoralists of grazing on their farms and destroying their crops.

An important issue that has not been given adequate attention is the impact of an ongoing land adjudication process. The pastoralists are opposed to the process; however, the government has insisted that it will go on.

To elaborate further on the dynamics of land ownership in Kenya, we investigate a theory of conflict based on grievance arising from land alienation. Kenya's land is categorized as government land, freehold land, or trust land. Government land refers to all land that was vested in the crown during the colonial period. On independence, the land became vested in the government of Kenya. The Government of Kenya Land Act Cap 280 (Cap refers to chapter) empowers the president to make grants of unalienated government land to any person. The act spells out how the government can dispose of this land. One of the three ways to do so is to offer land for agricultural purposes. The act says that the commissioner of lands may, on direction of the president, divide land into farms and that the leases on such farms can be auctioned. Local communities are often disadvantaged by such sales because most cannot afford the lease or purchase price. This process therefore dispossesses some communities of land that was previously under their use.

Trust lands (called reserves before June 1, 1963) constitute the single largest category of land. The Northeastern province is an exception: It was classified as crown land before independence, but it is now classified as trust land. All trust land vests in the county council of the area in which it is situated. The land tenure system in trust lands is communal and the council holds the land in trust for the benefit of the persons ordinarily resident on that land. County councils have wide-ranging powers in regard to trust land and may, through an act of parliament, set apart an area of trust land for use and occupation by individuals. There are reports of councils having irregularly alienated such land. Additionally, the provisions of the trust land act vests the management of trust lands in the commissioner of lands. Again, reports exist in which the commissioner allocated trust land to individuals for whom it was not meant, thereby causing resentment among the local communities (Wanjala 2001). In the 1990s, this pattern of land allocation accelerated and focused on all urban land especially set aside for public utilities and forests.

We would expect a positive correlation between violence and the amount of government and trust land that has been alienated. We investigate this relationship by comparing alienated land to total land area in each district in table 5.3. The data indicate a higher than average percentage of alienated land in all of the districts affected by political violence except Mombasa. The districts with the highest percentage of alienated land are Kajiado, Laikipia, Trans Nzoia, Uasin Gishu, and Nakuru. All are in the Rift Valley and all have been affected by the violence. Most of the ethnic violence during or before the general elections took place in these districts. This would seem to be consistent with the "grievance" component of the CH model.

We also investigate the "greed" perspective. The Rift Valley province is an expansive area covering about 40 percent of Kenya's land mass, including some of Kenya's most productive land (see table 5.4). Land can be considered a "lootable resource." However, the problem is that there are no quick gains associated with

Table 5.3 Alienated Land by District

District	Land area (km²)	Alienated land (govt. & trust) (km²)	Percent of total
Laikipia	9,718	8,343	85.85
Kajiado	20,963	15,460	73.75
Trans Nzoia	2,468	1,754	71.07
Uasin Gishu	3,784	2,535	66.99
Nakuru	7,024	4,145	59.01
Kwale	8,257	3,303	40
Kilifi	12,414	4,955	39.91
Narok	18,513	7,227	39.04
Nairobi	684	225	32.89
West Pokot	5,076	1,236	24.35
Nandi	2,745	656	23.9
Taita Taveta	16,959	3,868	22.81
Lamu	6,506	1,472	22.63
Samburu	20,809	4,613	22.17
Muranga	2,476	534	21.57
Machakos	14,178	2,745	19.36
Kiambu	2,448	438	17.89
Kericho	4,890	771	15.77
Tana River	38,694	5,485	14.18
Nyeri	3,284	313	9.53
Kirinyaga	1,437	100	6.96
Nyandarua	3,528	222	6.29
Kisumu	2,093	128	6.12
Meru	9,922	533	5.37
South Nyanza	5,714	121	2.12
Kitui	29,389	499	1.7
Siaya	2,523	41	1.63
Mandera	26,470	202	0.76
Embu	2,714	18	0.66
Bungoma	3,074	1	0.03
Busia	1,629	0	0
Kakamega	3,520	0	0
Kisii	2,196	0	0
Isiolo	25,605	0	0
Marsabit	73,952	0	0
Baringo	10,627	0	0
Elgeyo Marakwet	2,722	0	0
Turkana	61,769	0	0
Garissa	43,931	0	0
Wajir	56,501	0	0
Mombasa	210	0	0
Average			18.4

taking control of that land; profit requires time, effort, and the investment of resources. Nonetheless, one of the objectives of the violence was to redistribute agricultural land by expropriating one ethnic group's land and giving it to another. There is considerable anecdotal evidence to support this conclusion. It was common, in political rallies that preceded the clashes, to hear the calls for the eviction of "outsiders" from the Rift Valley.

Studies conducted after the initial incidences of violence support the view that land appropriation was indeed a motivating factor behind the clashes. Many found widespread occupation of abandoned farms by the Kalenjin. For example, the Sabaots were reported to have occupied the farms and houses of victims who fled from some of the settlement schemes. After its entire population relocated to Central province as a result of the violence, Rironi farm in Burnt Forest was reported to have been taken over by Kalenjin farmers who proceeded to rename it Kaplalech. Other reports in Molo indicate similar occupation of abandoned farms by Kalenjins; for example, a large-scale farm that borders one of President Moi's farms is now occupied by Kalenjin teachers from the Kericho district. At Mitetei farm, the scene of the first attacks thought to be a land dispute between Kalenjin and Luo shareholders, land was subdivided and title deeds conferred exclusively to Kalenjin shareholders after the others were evicted. Evidence given to a judicial commission of inquiry into the clashes indicated that a cabinet minister from the Kalenjin ethnic group occupies and grows sugarcane on land in Buru farm from which the Luo were evicted (Law Society of Kenya 1998).

Areas with high proportions of high- and medium-potential land can be found in both conflict and nonconflict zones (see table 5.4). However, if we focus on the Rift Valley, we find that, except for the Laikipia district, all the regions that are well endowed agriculturally experienced political violence. The districts that were least affected by violence—Samburu, Turkana, Baringo, and West Pokot—all have low-potential land. This is consistent with the CH "greed" theory.

Could land have been the primary motivation behind the violence? There are several arguments that considerably weaken the case for land hunger and related grievance as the root cause of conflict. First, there exist large tracts of prime land in the violence-torn areas owned by individuals and corporations. Rational land predators would be expected to have targeted these farms. Surprisingly, the raiders targeted none of them. Instead the violence occurred in settlement schemes with small-scale farms but large populations, suggesting an objective of displacing large numbers of people.

Second, grievances related to the alienation of land date back to colonial times and are not confined either to the Kalenjin or Coastal ethnic groups. For example, under the colonial government, the Kikuyu lost much of their land to the white settlers. European settlement began in the southern districts of Kikuyu land. By 1933, 109.5 square miles of valuable Kikuyu land had been alienated for European settlement. In the Kiambu–Limuru area alone, about 60,000 acres of land were alienated between 1903 and 1906 and thousands of people were rendered homeless (Kanogo 1987). Subsequent land reform programs, such as the Swynerton Plan, are credited

Table 5.4 Land Potential in Kenya

Province / District	High potential[a]	Medium potential[a]	Total [a]	Percent of total land area
Central Province				
Kiambu & Muranga	386	5	391	48
Kirinyaga	98	10	108	75
Nyandarua	265	0	265	75
Nyeri	160	0	160	49
Western Province				
Bungoma	253	0	253	92
Busia	163	0	163	100
Kakamega	325	0	325	92
Nyanza Province				
Kisii	220	0	220	100
Kisumu and Siaya	432	29	461	100
South Nyanza	566	5	571	99
Eastern Province				
Embu	66	186	252	93
Isiolo	0	0		0
Kitui	67	1,137	1,204	41
Machakos	125	771	896	63
Marsabit	4	0	4	0.05
Meru	241	95	336	34
Rift Valley Province				
Baringo	166	84	250	24
Elgeyo Marakwet	104	0	104	
Kajiado	22	0	22	85
Kericho	380	0	380	78
Laikipia	130	0	130	13
Nakuru	291	39	330	47
Nandi	234	0	234	85
Narok	908	0	908	49
Samburu	140	0	140	7
Trans Nzoia	208	0	208	84
Turkana	12	0	12	1
Uasin Gishu	327	0	327	87
West Pokot	103	0	103	20
Northeastern Province				
Garissa	0	0	0	0
Mandera	0	0	0	0
Wajir	0	0	0	0

(continued)

Table 5.4 Land Potential in Kenya (*Continued*)

Province/District	High potential[a]	Medium potential[a]	Total[a]	Percent of total land area
Coast Province				
Kilifi	104	247	351	28
Kwale	126	162	288	35
Lamu	7	319	326	50
Mombasa	21	0	21	0
Taita Taveta	42	10	52	3
Tana River	73	58	131	3

a. Numbers are in thousands of hectares.

with generating more disputes than they resolved. The resulting land distribution in Central province was skewed in favor of chiefs, loyalists, and the wealthy. The reforms were undertaken at a time when many who participated in the freedom struggle were in detention and thus lost their rights in former communal land.

One, therefore, has to look elsewhere for the primary trigger factor. Given the importance and depth of land grievances, a widely held view is that they were used by political entrepreneurs for political mobilization. We turn to political contest as a cause for the conflicts in the next section.

Politics: The Control of the State

It is doubtful that land and interethnic hostilities, singularly or together, could have led to the kind of atrocities in the Rift Valley. The central rationale of the violence appears to have been to maintain the political and economic status quo in the region during the run up to the general elections in 1992 and 1997. The main motivation behind the violence was to influence voting in favor of the incumbent.

Public choice scholars have attributed ethnic conflicts in Africa to the failure of political institutions to accommodate diverse interests. They argue that the lack of political models to deal effectively with diversity in centralized states where competition for resources and power is prevalent leads to conflicts. Until 1991, postindependence Kenya was characterized by one-party rule and excessive centralization of power. In such a scenario, the leader and group who capture the state have control of an enormous amount of resources and thus can reward supporters, provide for group members, and create barriers to entry into political and economic markets. Violence in the Rift Valley was part of such a strategy.

At the onset of the violence, Kenya was on the verge of a political transition to a multiparty system. Kenyans had long sought the abolition of the one-party state because the ruling party, Kenya Africa National Union (KANU), had been responsible for widespread repression and corruption. By mid-1991, scores of people had died in violent confrontations between reformists and state security. International pressure was also intense. It became clear that the government could only resist the pressure for change at the cost of massive bloodshed. In December 1991, the KANU government reluctantly repealed section 2A (which allowed only for a one-political-party system) of the constitution, paving the way for the formation of other political parties. With the introduction of multiple parties, the ruling elite faced its biggest real challenge to monolithic power and access to state resources since the failed coup in August 1982.

This perspective of the violence in Kenya is therefore consistent with the research findings of an inverted U-shaped curve defining the relationship between democracy and domestic violence (Hegre et al. 2001; Sambanis 2001). The research found that semidemocracies exhibit a higher propensity for conflict than either autocratic regimes or established democracies. Additionally, the research found a high correlation between domestic violence and political change. That is, states in political transition experience more violence. Consistent with this view is Mueller's argument that political entrepreneurs take advantage of the opportunity provided by the weakening of state authority that is occasioned by political transition (Mueller 2001, 22).

The elite's response was to target for violence ethnic groups associated with the opposition. The government capitalized on unresolved land ownership issues and ethnic mistrusts to provoke the displacement and expulsion of certain ethnic groups en masse from their longtime homes for political and economic gain. The government secretly employed surrogate agencies, such as ethnic or religious militias, to attack supporters of opposition political parties or government critics. Evidence suggests that in the areas where violence occurred, constraints on violence were typically weak. The reports of various committees investigating the clashes are replete with incidences pointing to state complicity (National Council of Churches of Kenya [NCCK] 1992, 2001; National Elections Monitoring Unit [NEMU] 1993a, 1993b).

It took the government eight years to launch any sort of inquiry into the root causes of the violence and even when the inquiry was completed, no action was taken to dispense justice. Skeptics wonder whether the stakes in the struggle for the control of the state were so high as to call for such radical measures. As some political economists have argued, in Kenya, as in many Sub-Saharan African countries, the state control over the economy is so entrenched and the premium for controlling political power is so high that political parties and ethnic groups are willing to pay whatever it costs to acquire or have meaningful access to the state (ICJ 2000).

Those in the ruling coalition clearly had comparative advantage in the competition for resources. This advantage was threatened by the introduction of democracy. In addition, defeat would have an impact on their financial fortunes. Press reports also indicate that opposition activists and lawyers are keen on prosecuting members of the Moi government for crimes ranging from murder and crimes against humanity to corruption (see *People Daily,* September 3, 2001, for example). A report by the Law Society of Kenya on the clashes recommended that a number of people, among them senior politicians, several ministers in the current cabinet, senior civil servants, and members of the judiciary (including the attorney general), be investigated and, if adequate evidence is found, prosecuted for conspiracy to commit mass murder; inciting the public to commit mass murder, arson, and rape; and other offenses related to clashes.

Given such expectations, it would appear rational for political entrepreneurs to resort to extreme measures to maintain the status quo. The question is, faced with the prospect of loss of political power, was violence a viable strategy for the government?

Some studies have found that KANU acquired a political advantage through the physical displacement of a hostile community vote and that the progovernment elite emerged as the ultimate beneficiaries of the violence (see Kenya Human Rights Commission 1997 on the coastal violence, for example). Analysis also supports the view that the pre-election violence was aimed at altering the political demography and thus at predetermining the pattern and outcome of the elections. The fears of the incumbent losing power were real. As table 5.5 demonstrates, a coalition of tribes perceived to be opposed to the ruling regime would win in an electoral contest.

This electoral outcome assumes that voting would proceed along ethnic lines. The empirical work of public choice scholars argues that ethnic identification in politics is alive and well in Africa (Kimenyi 1997), which results in ethnicity being perhaps the single most effective predictor of political preferences (ICJ 2000). This has been demonstrated by the limited Kenyan experience with political party competition. Political parties are by and large tribal factions—they display a clear ethnic character, with the ruling KANU being the party of the Kalenjins and the minority tribes, the National Development Party (NDP) being the party for the Luo, and the Democratic Party (DP) and FORD Asili Party being largely Kikuyu parties.

Table 5.5 Tribes Perceived to Be in the Opposition

Tribe name	Population (1989)	Percent of total
Kamba	2,448,302	11.4
Kikuyu	4,455,865	20.8
Kisii	1,318,409	6.2
Luhya	3,083,273	14.4
Luo	2,653,932	12.4
Total	13,959,781	65.1
Kamatusa tribes (ruling coalition)		
Kalenjin	2,458,123	11.5
Maasai	377,089	1.8
Samburu	106,897	0.5
Turkana	283,750	1.3
Total	3,225,859	15.0

Violence was aimed at disrupting the registration of voters before the elections, preventing thousands of those opposed to the ruling elite in the conflict areas from voting and thus ensuring a favorable outcome for KANU. We suggest that the violence was designed to instill such anxiety as to cause a sufficient number of people to abandon their homes, thereby giving the ruling elite a head start in elections.

Analysis of 1989 census and 1992 election data suggests this to be a plausible strategy. First, the Rift Valley province accounts for the largest number of seats in parliament with a total of 44 out of 188 constituencies in 1992 (or about 23 percent). The president further had the power to nominate 12 members of parliament. Taken together, this implies that evicting opposition sympathizers from the province would assure KANU victory in close to 30 percent of the parliamentary seats even before the elections began. Table 5.6 provides an indication of the likely impact of evicting the tribes targeted by the violence from the Rift Valley. It can be seen from this table that the intensity of the conflict was also in places where the KAMATUSA coalition was outnumbered. For example, in the Nakuru district about 60 percent were Kikuyus with about 16 percent of the KAMATUSA. The fear of numbers in politics was thus terrifying for the KAMATUSA.

Clearly, the non-Kalenjin vote in Laikipia, Nakuru, and Trans Nzoia was and would have been decisive. In Kajiado, Nandi, Kericho, Nandi, Narok, and Uasin Gishu the proportions of the non-Kalenjins, although not constituting a majority, are significant. In an election with narrow margins of victory, for example, these ethnic groups could determine the outcome of an election. In sum, the diaspora's support had the potential to affect electoral outcomes in 9 of the 12 districts in the

Table 5.6 **Ethnic Composition in the Rift Valley, 1989 (Percent of Total Population)**

District	Kamba	Kikuyu	Meru	Kisii	Luhya	Luo	Subtotal	KAMATUSA tribes
Baringo	0.21	7.2	0.05	0.59	1.46	1.41	10.92	83.88
E. Marakwet	0.21	2.98	0.04	0.34	2.42	0.74	6.73	91.41
Kajiado	8.02	23.76	0.41	0.7	2.09	3.13	38.11	57.07
Kericho	0.19	3.6	0.03	4.62	1.82	5.96	16.22	82.7
Laikipia	1	67.75	3.93	0.56	1.13	1.04	75.41	12.71
Nakuru	1.34	59.65	0.29	3.5	7.42	7.26	79.46	15.72
Nandi	0.1	1.67	0.01	0.02	17.52	3.89	23.21	73.7
Narok	0.42	11.32	0.12	5.05	0.99	1.56	19.46	77.69
Samburu	0.18	2.82	0.54	0.17	0.51	0.45	4.67	76.59
Trans Nzoia	0.53	9.58	0.1	2.77	52.03	2.53	67.54	22.42
Turkana	0.12	0.72	0.24	0.14	1.49	0.62	3.33	95.05
Uasin Gishu	0.66	16.90	0.13	1.35	18.46	5.02	42.52	52.94
West Pokot	0.31	2.72	0.07	0.53	5.05	1.34	10.02	85.22

Source: Adapted from Government of Kenya Population Census 1989.

province. Table 5.7 provides estimates of the numbers of voters from the ethnic groups targeted for eviction in the two areas affected by the clashes. The numbers suggest that disenfranchising the diaspora results in a definite advantage to the ruling elite in the presidential election. In the 1992 presidential election, the difference between president Moi and his closest rival was 392,516 votes, less than half of the estimated votes from the diaspora.

In addition, the constitution was amended in August 1992 to the effect that the winning presidential candidate needed to garner at least 25 percent of the votes cast in the presidential election in at least five of the eight provinces. The rule, widely viewed as diluting the one-person one-vote principle, ensured that a presidential candidate supported by the major tribes could still be stopped from ascending to the presidency, even after gaining a majority of the votes, if more than three provinces controlled by the minority tribes did not support such a candidate. The data show that the majority tribes in the Rift Valley consisted of 36 percent of the population. An opposition candidate backed by the major tribes would have easily met the requirement. There was, therefore, an incentive on the part of the KANU regime to reduce this population to below the 25 percent requirement. Thus political competition is a credible explanation of ethnic violence.

Why Has Kenya Not Experienced Civil War?

We have argued that civil wars occur when a combination of factors result in a tipping point. The fact that the clashes in Kenya did not escalate to civil war suggests that the underlying factors have not been strong enough. There are several factors that could raise the probability of civil war in Kenya. Kenya is a low-income country with relatively high dependence on primary commodity production. During the

Table 5.7 **Estimated Voter Population of Selected Tribes in Clash Areas**

Tribe name	Total population by province		Total
	Rift Valley	Coast	
Kamba	45,877	126,949	172,826
Kikuyu	962,341	58,456	1,020,797
Kisii	123,692	6,748	130,440
Luhya	484,547	55,498	540,045
Luo	193,862	83,128	276,990
Total	1,810,319	330,779	2,141,098
Estimated voters[a]	778,437	142,235	920,672

a. 43% of the total being the percentage of the national population over 19 years as per census data.

1990s, the larger ethnic groups were excluded from the government, a situation that could have triggered an uprising. The country has been governed poorly by one of the most corrupt regimes in the world. Since the mid-1990s, economic conditions have declined, recording negative growth rate for the first time since independence. Poverty has also increased and recent estimates show that by 2002, 56 percent of the population was below the poverty line.

Yet, Kenya is not another African nightmare. The limited scope of violent conflict in Kenya should not be surprising. First, as far as ethnic heterogeneity is concerned, it is true that conflicts have been between different ethnic groups. But the idea that the violence was motivated by ethnic hatred lacks support. Most of these groups live side by side in urban areas with no ethnic violence. Ethnic divides are not large enough to trigger an all-out war. Second, whereas most regions of Kenya are relatively ethnically homogeneous with a few being polarized, Kenya as a nation is highly fractionalized (table 5.8). It should be noted that most ethnic groups are not culturally homogeneous. The Luhya, for example, are a collection of several smaller groups, including Bukusu, Dakho, Kabras, Khayo, Kisa, Marachi, Maragoli, Marama, Nyala, Nyole, Samia, Tachoni, Tiriki, Tsotso, and Wanga. The existence of such subtribes implies that the country is in fact much more ethnically fractionalized than the data available indicate. This ethnic diversity contributes to relative stability. As discussed earlier, there is safety in societies that are highly fractionalized arising from the high transaction costs of collective action. None of the ethnic communities

Table 5.8 **Population of the Largest Tribes in Kenya (1989)**

Tribe name	Total	Percent of total
1. Kikuyu	4,455,865	20.78
2. Luhya	3,083,273	14.38
3. Luo	2,653,932	12.38
4. Kalenjin	2,458,123	11.46
5. Kamba	2,448,302	11.42
6. Kisii	1,318,409	6.15
7. Meru	1,087,778	5.07
8. Mijikenda	1,007,371	4.70
9. Masai	377,089	1.76
10. Turkana	283,750	1.32
11. Embu	256,623	1.20
12. Taita	203,389	0.95
13. Teso	178,455	0.83
14. Ogaden	139,597	0.65
15. Kuria	112,236	0.52

Source: Adapted from Kenya Population Census 1989.

is large enough or even homogeneous enough to have a realistic probability of victory and the coordination costs across ethnic communities may be too high.

The land issue is certainly a source of grievance and intensifies ethnic conflict. Nevertheless, only a small part of the country and a few ethnic groups are affected by these grievances. Thus, it is unlikely that intergroup conflicts over land will spread. In essence, involvement of other communities outside the affected regions would have no significant payoff. In this regard, grievance directed to people on settlements outside their ancestral lands can be expected to result only in isolated conflicts. Furthermore, the grievance has not been directed at government. We therefore tend to hold the view that if all the victims of land clashes had organized themselves to retaliate, this retaliation would have been directed at the government and its administrative centers in those areas and could have given rise to a full-blown civil strife. The inability to organize a counter to these ethnic clashes may be an important factor that explains their duration and their sporadic nature. Thus, ethnic clashes have not taken the form of a rebellion.

Probably a key factor explaining the limited scope of the ethnic clashes has to do with the uncertainty about the expected economic gains. While it is the case that successful displacement of outsiders would make land available to members of the ethnic group initiating the conflict, there are no guarantees that those involved in the conflict would benefit themselves. Thus, the clashes involve serious collective action problems. One of the lessons learned painfully by those who fought for independence in Kenya is that those who do the fighting incur the costs, but the benefits are spread widely among members of the group. Moreover, there are no assurances that the property rights of the original owners would be revoked by the government following displacements. Thus, it does appear that individuals who engaged in violence did so for short-term gains and were directly incited and supported by the government, as suggested by several reports (Human Rights Watch 1997).

The most compelling argument for the ethnic clashes is political expediency. The ruling party sought to create instability in some regions primarily to win the presidency. But once this goal was achieved, it was in the best interest of the government to restore law and order. Continued instability would have had negative implications on production, therefore potentially harming the same people who instigated the crisis. We are therefore compelled to conclude that the same government that played a role in initiating the violence also had the means to stop the violence after elections, which explains the short duration of the conflicts.

The literature on civil wars also identifies several other trigger factors, including the role of the diasporas. Diasporas can have an impact on civil war by providing financial and materials support. The presence of large diasporas, outside the country or in the same country but outside the conflict area, could therefore influence the direction of the civil war. It appears that the role of the diasporas from Nairobi and Central province who were willing to help those who were being evicted was a factor in explaining the short durations. In 1997, for example, Nairobi and Central province residents who are Kikuyus started championing the idea that the groups had a right to defend themselves. They are also said to have provided massive financial support. The retaliation that followed in Nakuru, Baringo, and Laikipia quickly led to the end of the ethnic conflict in 1997. This suggests that once the diasapora support strength was feasible and plausible, the organizers feared a broadened agenda of a civil war—and this was not their original agenda. This may partly explain the sporadic nature of this ethnic conflict.

Another factor that explains the sporadic nature of clashes in Kenya is the absence of lootable resources. Most clashes were associated with competition for land, and, even though land is lootable, it does not provide quick and continuous income to support a rebel group. Thus, clashes could not be sustained for long periods. Hence the clashes served only to displace some people.

Some of the recent literature on civil war suggests a generalized increase in war aversion in developed countries. Mueller (2001, 5) writes that war "has increasingly become discredited and has progressively fallen from fashion." Similar sentiments have been reported among some communities in Kenya. The Kikuyu, for example, are reported to dread the prospect of war primarily because they are not strangers to war. During the Mau Mau uprising against colonial rule, it is estimated that 13,000 of their tribesmen were killed and more than 100,000 relocated. Thousands were tortured and detained. Faced with the possibility of another war, the elders are reported to have counseled restraint (Finance Magazine 1996). This attitude perhaps explains why the ethnic conflict did not spread to other regions and also why localized retaliation was restrained. In addition to this, the political establishment took advantage of the fact that the Kikuyus would be the biggest losers since they are the most resourceful accumulators. Thus, restraint from within and a reminder by the ruling elite perhaps explain why violence did not spread to other regions.

It should also be noted that, besides being at the forefront of the independence struggle, the ethnic communities targeted in the violence were the ones most involved in the market economy. The opportunity cost of a rebellion would therefore have been higher for them.

Empirical studies have found a positive relationship between risk of civil war and regime change in the short run. Perhaps another major reason why Kenya has not disintegrated is the fact that there was no regime change in over two decades between 1978 and 2002, during which time President Moi ruled Kenya. In the 1992 elections, his party KANU emerged victorious, with a majority of 82 parliamentary seats. The victory was repeated in the 1997 elections, but this time the majority was much slimmer. Incidences of violence abated after 1993. Observers have attributed the abatement not just to the election victories but also to the fact that the ruling elite succeeded in achieving what it set out to do. Thousands remain displaced and dispossessed. One report estimates that in the Uasin Gishu, Nandi, Trans Nzoia, Kericho, and Nakuru districts, 20 percent of the displaced people would probably never return to their land without "circumspect and realistic political intervention" (Kenya Human Rights Commission 1996).

Others attribute the stability to the international community, pointing to lulls in the violence at times when international observers were present in the country.

A lull in March 1993, for example, was attributed to the presence of officials from the International Monetary Fund (IMF) and the World Bank who were in the country to assess the implementation of political and economic reforms on which western donors insisted when they suspended quick disbursement aid in November 1991. Thus, the donor community coordinated by the IMF and the World Bank may have pushed for restraint. If this view were correct, it would seem to consolidate the foregoing arguments that the sporadic ethnic violence was primarily being engineered by the incumbent government to influence the voting patterns in key and strategic areas. Once the government achieved its goals, the conflict was no longer necessary.

Conclusion

Kenya possesses many of the risk factors that can lead to civil war, but the CH model does not place Kenya in the high-risk category. Thus, the fact that Kenya has not experienced a full-blown civil war is not totally unexpected and is consistent with the CH model. Nevertheless, the country has had sporadic ethnic clashes, particularly during the 1990s. The fact that these clashes have not escalated into civil war cannot be fully explained by the CH model. We have reviewed some plausible explanations, going beyond the CH model and exploring both grievance factors (such as land disputes) and electoral politics, which are outside the scope of the CH model.

Our analysis reveals that ethnic clashes have been caused by a number of factors, including political expediency. Most ethnic violence has occurred in areas into which the dominant tribes moved to acquire land and engage in commerce. Violence was aimed at displacing members of tribes that were perceived to be opposed to the regime. Displacements were intended to secure a favorable electoral outcome during the country's transition to multiparty rule in the early 1990s. This motive explains why the conflicts were sporadic and of short duration.

The limited scope of the conflicts can also be explained by the organizational structure of the groups involved. In civil wars, citizens identify themselves with the rebel groups or the state such that strong identities are formed and groups have well-defined goals. In Kenya, those involved in the clashes have had neither a well-defined group identity nor well-defined long-term goals. The multiethnic ruling elite did not break ranks, so we did not see a strong elite movement to forge an ethnically based rebel group. If this had happened, the ethnic conflict would have been more persistent and would have spread to other areas of the country. Finally, diasporas here served to contain the conflict by offering support to those being evicted, and the lack of easily lootable resources (such as minerals) also limited the scope of the conflicts.

This chapter examines the CH model and discusses why, contrary to the common expectation that Kenya should be characterized by civil war like other countries in that region of Africa, there has been no civil war. The occurrence of ethnic clashes during the 1990s, however, proves that the country is not completely immune to a civil war and such clashes could escalate into a full-blown war should some of the factors reach critical levels resulting in a tipping point.

References

Bates, R. 1989. *Beyond the Miracle of Markets: The Polictical Economy of Agrarian Development in Kenya.* New York: Cambridge University Press.

Blomberg, S. B., G. D. Hess, and S. Thacker. 2000. "Is There Evidence of a Poverty-Conflict Trap?" Working Paper 2000–96, Department of Economics, Wellesley College, Wellesley, MA.

Collier, P. 2001. "Ethnic Diversity: An Economic Analysis of Its Implication." *Economic Policy* 32: 129–66.

Collier, P., and A. Hoeffler. 1998. "On Economic Causes of Civil War." *Oxford Economic Papers* 50: 563–73.

———. 2001. "Greed and Grievance in Civil War." World Bank Working Paper 2355, World Bank, Washington, DC.

Elbadawi, Ibrahim A., N. S. Ndung'u, and S. Njuguna. 2001. "The Economics of Civil Wars and Post-Conflict Recovery." Working Paper, Development Research Group, Africa Region, World Bank, Washington D.C.

Ellingsen, Tanja. 2000. "'Ethnic Witches' Brew: Linguistic, Religious and Ethnic Fragmentation, 1945–94." *Journal of Conflict Resolution* 44 (2): 228–49.

Finance Magazine. March 1996. "Whither Kenya? Why There Is No Chaos Yet." Nairobi, Kenya.

Hegre, H., E. Tanja, S. Gates, and N. P. Gleditsch. 2001. "Toward a Civil Peace? Democracy, Political Change and Civil War, 1816–1992." *American Political Science Review* 95 (1): 33–48.

Human Rights Watch. 1997. *Failing the Internally Displaced. The UNDP Displaced Persons Program in Kenya.* New York.

ICJ (International Commission for Jurists). 2000. *The Political Economy of Ethnic Clashes in Kenya.* Nairobi, Kenya: ICJ.

Kanogo, T. 1987. *Squatters and the Roots of Mau Mau 1905–63.* Nairobi: East African Educational Publishers.

Kanyinga, K. 2000. *Re-distribution From Above. The Politics of Land Rights and Squatting in Coastal Kenya.* Nordiska Afrikainstitutet, Research Report 115, Uppsala.

Kenya Human Rights Commission. 1996. *Ours by Right, Theirs by Might. A Study on the Land Clashes.* Nairobi, Kenya: Kenya Human Rights Commission.

———. 1997. Kayas of Deprivation, Kayas of Blood: Violence, Ethnicity and the State in Coastal Kenya. Nairobi, Kenya: Kenya Human Rights Commission.

Kimenyi, M. S. 1989. "Interest Groups, Transfer-Seeking and Democratization: Competition for Benefits of Governmant Power May Explain African Political Instability." *American Journal of Economics and Sociology* 48: 339–49.

———. 1997. Ethnic Diversity, Liberty and the State. Cheltenham, UK: Edward Elgar.

———. 1998. "Harmonizing Ethnic Claims in Africa: A Proposal for Ethnic-Based Federalism." *Cato Journal* 18 (1): 43–63.

Kimenyi, M. S., and J. M. Mbaku. 1993. "Rent Seeking and Institutional Stability in Developing Societies." *Public Choice* 77 (2): 385–05.

Law Society of Kenya. 1998. *Impunity.* Report of the LSK on the Judicial Commission of Inquiry Into Ethnic Clashes in Kenya. Nairobi, Kenya: Law Society of Kenya.

Leys, C. 1975. *Underdevelopment in Kenya. The Political Economy of Neo-colonialism.* Berkeley and Los Angeles: University of California Press.

Mazrui, A. 1997. *Violence, Ethnicity and the State in Coastal Kenya.* Kenya Human Rights Commission. Nairobi, Kenya: Kenya Human Rights Commission.

Mbithi, P., and C. Barnes. 1975. *Spontaneous Settlement Problem in Kenya.* Nairobi: East African Literature Bureau.

Mueller, J. 2001. "The Remnants of War: Thugs as Residual Combatants." Working Paper, Department of Political Science, Ohio State University, Columbus, OH.

Murungi, K. 1995. *Ethnicity and Multi-Partism in Kenya.* Nairobi, Kenya: Kenya Human Rights Commission.

National Council of Churches of Kenya. 1992. *The Cursed Arrow: Contemporary Report on the Politicized Land Clashes in Rift Valley, Nyanza and Western Provinces.* National Council of Churches of Kenya.

——. 2001. *National Agenda for Peace Survey Report.* National Council of Churches of Kenya.

National Elections Monitoring Unit. 1993a. *Multi-party General Elections in Kenya.* Nairobi, Kenya: National Elections Monitoring Unit.

——. 1993b. *Courting Disaster: A Report on the Continuing Terror, Violence and Destruction in the Rift Valley, Nyanza and Western Provinces of Kenya.* Nairobi, Kenya: National Elections Monitoring Unit.

Okoth Ogendo. 1999. *The Land Question in Kenya: Critical Issues on the Eve of the 21st Century.* DFID East Africa, Nairobi, Kenya.

Sambanis, Nicholas. 2001. "Do Ethnic and Nonethnic Civil Wars Have the Same Causes? A Theoretical and Empirical Inquiry (Part 1)." *Journal of Conflict Resolution* 45 (3): 259–82.

Toulmin, C., and J. Quan. 2000. *Evolving Land Rights Policy and Tenure in Africa.* London: International Institute for Environment and Development, and Chatham, UK: Natural Resources Institute.

Tullock, G. 1974. *The Social Dilemma: The Economics of War and Revolutions.* Blacksburg, VA: Center for the Study of Public Choice.

Wanjala, S. 2001. "The Land Question: Critical Issues in Constitutional Reform Debate." Mimeo, Nairobi, Kenya.

The Civil War in
Mozambique
The Balance Between Internal and External Influences

6

JEREMY M. WEINSTEIN
AND LAUDEMIRO FRANCISCO

I n the 1980s and 1990s, it was fashionable to think of the civil war in Mozambique as a war that never should have happened. To many observers of the political scene in South Africa, the campaign of the Mozambican National Resistance (Resistência Nacional Moçambicana, RENAMO) against Mozambique's Front for the Liberation of Mozambique (Frente de Libertação de Moçambique, FRELIMO) government was nothing more than external aggression. From its roots in Rhodesian counterintelligence to the ongoing financial and military support provided by South Africa through the 1980s, RENAMO was considered an external puppet without an internal social base (Minter 1995). Propaganda emerging from the government and its newspapers and radio in Maputo, as well as much "social-scientific" analysis at the time, echoed this line of reasoning.

A small but concerted group of scholars began in the late 1980s to criticize this approach to understanding Mozambique's war. Focusing on the failures of FRELIMO's socialist agricultural policies, the political repression at the national and local levels, and the perceived "southern" dominance in the political establishment, these analysts drew attention to the grievances that might help explain how an external puppet evolved into an organization with approximately 20,000 troops, operating in every province throughout Mozambique (Geffray and Pedersen 1986).

This gulf between advocates of "external" and "internal" explanations exists up until the present. Scholars are still reluctant to explore the interaction between external and internal influences, feeling that it somehow detracts from their capacity to paint as "evil" either the South African apartheid regime or FRELIMO's Marxist government.

In this chapter, we address four fundamental questions. Why did a civil war break out in Mozambique in 1976, so soon after independence? What type of rebel organization emerged to wage the insurgency? Why did the war last for 16 years? What determined the intensity of the violence? In answering these questions, we take a step back from the polarizing debates about external and internal causes and focus centrally on their interactions. We argue that the combination of immediate and continued financial viability for an insurgency (provided externally) with a growing base of internal discontent was an explosive mix. We look at the relative importance of "preferences" (grievance) and "constraints" (opportunity) and their interaction, in explaining the course of the conflict.

We present an analytic narrative, testing hypotheses about the factors that might explain the war's initiation and evolution. We draw on a range of sources, including evidence gathered in interviews with former combatants and civilians who lived in war-affected areas, a new data set on the incidence and intensity of the war, and primary-source literature on the local dynamics of the conflict.[1]

A new examination of the Mozambican case demonstrates three fundamental points. First, we highlight the causal importance of external actors in understanding war initiation, duration, and intensity. At every point in Mozambique's conflict, foreign intervention played a crucial role: It provided the means to mobilize domestic grievances, the resources to wage a protracted war, and the financial incentives to end the war. Although the presence of "lootable" commodities was not a proximate cause of the war, external forces demonstrated their capacity to ensure the financial viability of armed conflict. In this sense, the Mozambican conflict illustrates the central insight of the Collier-Hoeffler (CH) model: To successfully challenge a state, a rebel group must be able to finance itself.

Second, we discuss the relative influence of grievances in an analysis of the onset, duration, and termination of Mozambique's civil war. While RENAMO proved adept at raising an army—with external support and amidst Mozambique's crushing poverty—its structure and strategy were intricately linked to the nature of political grievances developing within the country and across the region. RENAMO's initial recruits came from privileged classes subject to punishment at the hands of the FRELIMO government, its external backers took interest in the nascent insurgency because of their hostility toward FRELIMO's support for African liberation struggles, and RENAMO grew in strength in the countryside as the government's policies dealt serious blows to the political and social livelihood of Mozambican peasants.

Third, we show that coercion played a critical role in how the war was fought from the earliest stages. RENAMO used force at every point for almost every purpose, including conscription, the collection of resources, "political" mobilization, and control. Even in regions where the insurgency could realistically expect civilian support, RENAMO employed coercive tactics in its relations with noncombatant populations. In looking inside RENAMO's organization, we explore this puzzle in greater detail. We find that grievances did not drive individual participation in RENAMO. Instead, the organization was held together by material incentives from the beginning. Attracted by the promise of salaries and protection, RENAMO's emerging leadership joined up with the Rhodesians in 1976, sidestepping a process of group formation that could have laid the groundwork for massive political mobilization in Mozambique. Lacking a coherent political framework after Rhodesia's collapse, RENAMO turned to coercion to recruit new

members, and looting and pillaging to keep them engaged. Thus, the financial viability of insurgency in Mozambique contributed, in part, to the corruption of the
rebel movement, attracting opportunists rather than activists to the insurgency.
More broadly, we argue that scholars should not focus solely on the factors that
affect *cohesion* in rebel organizations. Understanding how and why *coercion* emerges
as a key strategy in the course of conflict deserves more serious attention.

Preconditions for Conflict

A Macro Story

Was Mozambique destined in 1975 to have a civil war the following year? According
to the CH model, Mozambique faced a relatively high risk of civil war. The model
predicts a 39.6 percent probability of civil war in Mozambique in 1975, far exceed-
ing the mean prediction of 6.7 percent.

Collier and Hoeffler propose a set of hypotheses about the risk factors for conflict that we can apply explicitly to Mozambique. Their key variables are economic.
Civil conflict is more likely in poor countries, with slow growth, and an economy
structured around the export of primary products. Mozambique's economic situation in 1975—characterized by low secondary school enrollment and negative
growth rates over the previous five years—thus contributed to a significant risk of
civil war onset (see table 6.1).

Additionally, the social structure of the population is important. Countries with
a dominant ethnic or religious group and a sufficiently large minority population are
at a higher risk for war. Accordingly, Mozambique, because of the dominance of
the Makua-Lomwé tribe and sizable minority groups, faced risks due to its social
makeup.[2]

Finally, structural factors, including a country's history and geography, are relevant. Civil wars are more likely to break out in mountainous countries with a recent
history of conflict. Although geography did not play a role, Mozambique's recent
emergence from an independence struggle left it vulnerable to a renewed insurgency.

The theoretical mechanisms driving these hypotheses must also be subjected to
scrutiny within the case study. Collier and Hoeffler link civil war outbreak to factors that make the organization of insurgency easier: "lootable" commodities;
mountainous terrain; and unemployed, potential recruits. In the face of these structural factors, they argue that the level of grievance is a less important influence.

Although the CH model makes an accurate prediction for the likelihood of
Mozambique's civil war, closer inspection reveals that it fails to highlight a set of
significant factors. The groundwork for civil war in 1976 was laid in the conflicts
emerging during the independence struggle and in the strategies chosen by the
victorious FRELIMO government immediately after independence in 1975. The
insurgency that aimed to topple the government came from outside the country,
mobilized discontented elites, and did not draw directly on an organized base of
peasant discontent.

Table 6.1 Mozambique in the World of Cases—Collier and Hoeffler's Best Model

Year	Secondary schooling	Annual GDP growth rate (previous 5 years)	Primary commodity exports	Ethnic frac.	Ethnic dom.	Length of peace	Population (mil.)	Population dispersion
1960	30		0.099	3,900	1	172	7.46	0.626
1965	3	1.854	0.099	3,900	1		8.34	0.626
1970	5	3.368	0.099	3,900	1		9.40	0.626
1975	4	-4.725	0.099	4,095	1	1	10.50	0.626
1980	8	-4.947	0.099	4,290	1		12.10	0.626
1985	10	-4.178	0.099	4,290	1		13.50	0.626
1990	10	0.292	0.099	4,290	1		14.20	0.626
1995	9	0.774	0.102	4,290	1	26	17.40	0.621
Sample mean (wars)	30.3	-0.226	0.149	52.63	0.452	221.0	32.7	0.603
Sample mean (no war)	44.39	1.74	0.169	38.64	0.465	334.2	46.0	0.569

Note: GDP = gross domestic product; Frac. = fractionalization; Dom. = dominance.

The Micro Story[3]

As the guerrilla struggle for independence from the Portuguese came to a victorious conclusion in 1974, the new Mozambican nation was seemingly united behind FRELIMO. Since its formation in 1962 in Dar es Salaam, FRELIMO had waged a successful revolutionary campaign against a strong colonial army. Moreover, FRELIMO sought, as part of its central mission, to build a deep sense of national unity among the ethnically and linguistically diverse population.

Yet, internal divisions wracked the national front from its inception. Eduardo Mondlane, FRELIMO's founder, had sought to unify a number of independent liberation movements. These groups included: UDENAMO (from Manica, Sofala, Gaza, and Lourenço Marques), UNAMI (from Tete, Zambézia, and Niassa), and MANU (from Cabo Delgado). Mondlane saw a unified front as the most effective way to fight the Portuguese because it would centralize the search for resources and external support and present a single mission of the liberation of the entire country. However, each of these movements came with its own leadership, different geographic bases of support, and distinct expectations about their role in the new, unified movement.

Following the mysterious assassination of Mondlane in 1969, the new FRELIMO leadership took a distinctly new tack; they began advocating the implementation of socialist strategies of development for Mozambique. This was met with stiff resistance by many of FRELIMO's founders, and the new leadership, in an effort to maintain its control of the movement, forced out dissenting members. A new movement, the Comité Revolucionário de Moçambique (COREMO), emerged to articulate an alternative revolutionary strategy.

Importantly, these divisions within the liberation movement had regional dimensions. Many interpreted the shift in strategy as an indication of "southern" dominance of the movement. When COREMO split from FRELIMO, southerners largely assumed the senior leadership, leaving those from the center and the north feeling disenfranchised. Many left FRELIMO to join COREMO or to become refugees in Zambia, Kenya, and Western countries to complete their studies (Hoile 1994; Vines 1991).

These splits within the liberation movement formed the foundation of a domestic base of discontent (directed against FRELIMO) that continued after independence. More importantly, the splits took on regional dimensions—"the rest versus the south"—that have been used by political elites to mobilize opposition ever since.

The immediate transitional and postindependence policies of the FRELIMO government only broadened this base of discontent. The new leadership made political opposition illegal, guaranteeing themselves full political power and the opportunity to set the future direction of the entire country. This tight political control was essential for FRELIMO to implement its socialist transformation, including nationalization of services, new systems of governance, and centralized production and control over resources.

Most damaging, the government set out to persecute those who had "benefited" most directly from the colonial leadership (Cabrita 2000).[4] FRELIMO took broad license to force citizens into reeducation camps and prison for supposed counterrevolutionary activities. Singled out for particular disdain were former Mozambican members of the police force, the army, and the intelligence units, including the *flechas,* a group of highly trained, special forces that operated as part of the colonial army against the guerrilla struggle (Flower 1987; interview, Maputo, March 2001).

Aside from these coercive measures, the postindependence government also faced the difficult task of governing and maintaining physical control over a vast country with limited resources (Lundin and Machava 1995). As a liberation movement, the FRELIMO guerrillas had barely penetrated most parts of the country before taking power. As a government, FRELIMO had to fill a vacuum left by the Portuguese without a sufficient capacity to manage the territory. Discontent simmered below the surface. In December 1975, an attempted coup by former FRELIMO guerrillas from northern provinces was crushed, but it exposed the internal weakness of the new regime (Cabrita 2000).

As Mozambique moved into its first full year of independence (1976), three structural factors put it at a significant risk for internal conflict. First, the legacy of infighting in the liberation movement had given voice to regional discontent (with deep roots in the colonial period) and rise to opposition groups with the capacity to challenge the new state. In addition, FRELIMO embarked on a politics of "transformation" that thoroughly isolated and oppressed large segments of the Mozambican population. Some of these discontents were already based outside of the country in Rhodesia, South Africa, and Portugal. Finally, the Mozambican state was weak, with few resources and a limited capacity to maintain territorial security, to control the emerging discontent, and to implement its policies of transformation throughout the country. Put simply, there was both grievance and opportunity for insurgency to develop.

Understanding the Outbreak of the War

The CH model and the preceding narrative highlight a number of factors that raised the risk of conflict in Mozambique. Collier and Hoeffler focus on the costs of organizing a rebellion. To them, Mozambique was likely to experience a war because, in a poor and shrinking economy, potential rebel groups had access to a large population of unemployed and uneducated men as potential recruits.

However, the CH model does not fit easily with the history of Mozambique's civil war. Although it correctly predicts that a war was likely to break out, in reality, war broke out for different reasons. In particular, the model misses the critical role of geopolitics: The Rhodesian government organized and financed the insurgency in Mozambique. Further, RENAMO emerged not from a pool of young, unemployed men, but instead from a collection of discontented soldiers and Mozambicans who were repressed in the new political system. The logic of the model is correct, though, in that this nascent rebel organization was able to grow and thrive because it faced a new regime, with a weak economic base and a lack of capacity to control all of the nation's territory. We draw on historical evidence and new data on the conflict to demonstrate that, at least at the outset, Mozambique's war was defined by external influences that played on internal grievances.

Birth of the Mozambican National Resistance

When FRELIMO came to power in 1975, it faced a complex regional and global situation. In particular, Mozambique was bordered by two white-colonial regimes, hanging on for survival and battling domestic struggles by African nationalist movements for liberation. Rhodesia, ruled by Ian Smith, faced its main armed threat from the Zimbabwe African National Union (ZANU), whose guerrilla army, the Zimbabwe African National Liberation Army (ZANLA), had been mainly operating from Mozambique since the early 1970s. Although the Rhodesians sought to counter this threat, with South African and Portuguese military assistance, these efforts were impeded when FRELIMO took power in Mozambique. In South Africa, as well, the African National Congress (ANC) had launched a campaign to unseat the apartheid regime that included domestic acts of terrorism, the training of recruits for the liberation army across the border in "friendly" countries, and an organized administrative apparatus for coordinating external support. Most importantly, Mozambique was South Africa's only unfriendly neighbor at the time. When the new government decided to offer safe haven to all the movements fighting for liberation across the continent, including the ANC and ZANU, FRELIMO immediately magnified the threats faced by Rhodesia and South Africa. In addition, FRELIMO joined the United Nations-sponsored sanctions against Rhodesia that prevented the Smith regime from accessing oil through the Beira pipeline and from using Mozambique's ports for its foreign trade. The Rhodesians interpreted these acts as, essentially, a declaration of war (Cawthra 1986; Moorcraft 1994).

Equally important, Mozambique achieved its independence at the height of the Cold War. At the time, the major world powers—the United States and the Soviet Union—were engaged in a competition for influence and control in Africa and other parts of the developing world. By throwing its support behind the liberation movements in South Africa, Mozambique established itself as an allied state to the Eastern bloc. Its transformation into an avowed Marxist state occurred, officially, in 1977, after the conflict began. By contrast, South Africa and Rhodesia were seen as the key bulwarks against communism in the region. They benefited from tacit, and often direct, support from the United States and other Western European powers. By aligning with the Eastern bloc, Mozambique took a principled stand in favor of African liberation, while ensuring South African and Rhodesian interest in the destabilization of their neighbor.

In 1976, Rhodesia launched an effort to establish a guerrilla force capable of fighting within Mozambique to defeat the ZANLA guerrillas. The security services invested significant resources in the development of this Mozambican insurgency, the MNR (Mozambican National Resistance), which later came to be called RENAMO (Flower 1987).[5] It recruited its first members from among discontented

Mozambicans based in Rhodesia, including a large number of former *flechas,* members of the colonial army and police service, and former FRELIMO guerrillas. Rhodesia trained, armed, and financed the insurgents, even paying salaries. To expand its base, the MNR, in partnership with the Rhodesians, targeted areas of discontent within Mozambique. They attacked reeducation camps and prisons in a search for new recruits. Many of those who were abducted by this new force were happy to fight FRELIMO.

The Mozambican insurgency, in its early stages, had a narrow domestic base of support. Recruits came largely from populations who were likely to oppose the new government, and little effort was invested in mobilizing civilian populations to support the new organization. Although discontent existed in the Mozambican countryside, the MNR made no attempt to build on these feelings against the government. Instead, the Rhodesians largely dictated strategy. Since the MNR lacked a strong domestic constituency, there was little effort to deviate from the Rhodesian orders. During this period of the insurgency, the MNR's strategy included brief incursions into Mozambican territory, relatively little effort in establishing local bases, and operations to destroy economic targets, often with backup from Rhodesian troops and airpower. The primary task, though, throughout this period, was to fight ZANLA guerrillas. Given that their bases were located along the border in southern and central Mozambique, the war barely spread outside of the borderlands in the Gaza and Manica provinces.

From External to Internal Conflict

Is this a sufficient explanation for the outbreak of civil war? We argue that it is, in part. The armed conflict in Mozambique falls neatly into two distinct periods: 1976–79 and 1981–92. The period 1979–80 was a watershed period for the MNR in two ways. First, the government of Rhodesia fell, and Zimbabwe achieved its independence through the Lancaster House Agreements. As a result, the MNR lost its financial and organizational base of support. Second, André Matsangaissa, the Mozambican commander of the MNR, was killed in battle with government forces in October 1979. Coinciding with the disappearance of its key sponsor, the MNR lost its most important leader.

If the argument about the primacy of the Rhodesian influence is true, we should expect to see a drop-off in civil war incidence after the Smith regime fell in 1979 and a fundamental change in the strategy and character of the war in the following period. Data on the incidence of civil war in Mozambique demonstrate the fundamental importance of external actors in defining the outbreak and conduct of the Mozambican conflict in the early stages.[6] Figure 6.1 shows that incidents of violence against civilians nearly dropped to zero in 1980, after reaching their peak in 1978 (in the early parts of the conflict). These incidents only picked up again after 1981. This gap in activity corresponds directly with the period in which RENAMO lost its external support and its leadership.

Figure 6.1 Regional Incidence of Violence Against Civilians

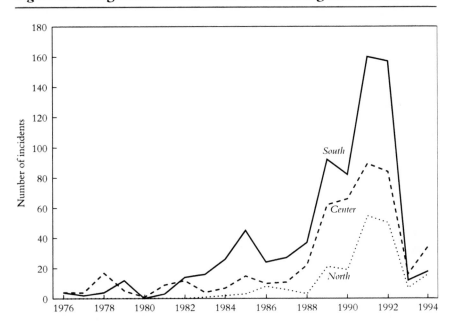

Figure 6.1 also provides evidence of a shift in strategy after 1980. In the early stages of the war, incidents focused largely on the center and the south. After 1981, the strategy shifted south, and violence against civilians was heavily concentrated in the southern provinces (though such incidents also occurred elsewhere in the country).

Further, in the first stage of the conflict, a high percentage of incidents took place in border provinces with Rhodesia and South Africa. This was particularly true in Manica and Tete, in central Mozambique, which shared the longest borders with Rhodesia. In the second stage of the civil war, the attacks shifted farther toward the sea and were now distributed throughout the country, as incidents also began to occur in the north. Importantly, incidents along the border do not appreciably decrease in the second stage owing to continued South African involvement and a more fundamental shift of activities to the southern provinces (two of which border South Africa) (see table 6.2).

Table 6.2 Incidents in Border Provinces (Percent of Total)

Period	South	Center	North
1976–79	77%	83%	0%
1981–92	76%	58%	28%

Finally, between 1976 and 1979, more than 73 percent of the incidents reported involved identified external forces. This includes incidents in which Rhodesia used conventional forces (including airpower) directly against Mozambique or in which expatriate soldiers were identified as part of a group attacking in Mozambique. After 1981, this percentage dropped to less than 1 percent of all attacks (figure 6.2). Clearly, external forces played a visible role both as perpetrators and strategists in the first part of the civil war.

The Emergence of RENAMO

The evidence suggests that the outbreak of civil war in Mozambique occurred in two stages. While 1980 was not a year of peace per se, with the fall of the Rhodesian government, it marked the collapse of the MNR.

Yet, the MNR was replaced by a "new" group, RENAMO, with many of the same commanders, but with a newfound autonomy to dictate strategy and to clarify its objectives, and the encouragement of its new backers to extend its reach throughout the country. How was RENAMO able to survive the collapse of the Rhodesian regime? Why did RENAMO emerge as an increasingly strong and autonomous rebel organization?

The role of geopolitics again emerges as a critical determinant. As the Lancaster House process drew to a close in 1979, the MNR's Rhodesian sponsors became acutely aware of the need to find a new home for the Mozambican rebels. With

Figure 6.2 **Responsibility for Violence Against Civilians**

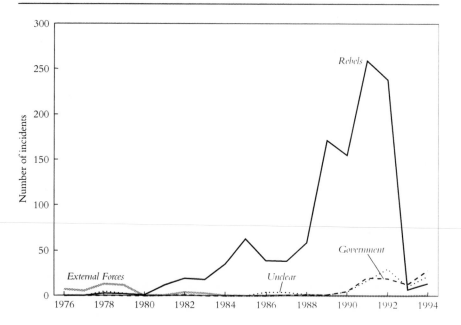

Rhodesian encouragement, the South Africa government moved to the fore; it transferred the remaining MNR rebels from Rhodesia to a new base in South Africa in late 1979. RENAMO was immediately incorporated into the structure of the South African Defence Forces (SADF), benefiting from its training, supply of weapons, and logistical infrastructure. However, in this new arrangement, the role of the external patron evolved. South Africa encouraged RENAMO to develop a clear political ideology and structure and gave the insurgency more autonomy in military strategy.[7]

However, external intervention is not sufficient to explain RENAMO's survival and, more fundamentally, its growth and shift in strategy. In this second phase of the conflict, the rebel organization encountered a growing dissatisfaction among the peasantry with the economic and political strategies of the FRELIMO government. A more hospitable environment for RENAMO penetration emerged, with clear sectors of the population opposed to the regime and, in some cases, actively resisting its policies. RENAMO was able to identify local "allies" and maintain these political connections as they marched through the countryside. Yet, it is important to note, that the fundamental strategy of recruiting by force did not change. We address this paradox of significant grievances coinciding with the use of significant coercion later in the chapter.

Internalizing the Conflict

The government of Mozambique mistakenly assumed that the MNR would disappear with the fall of Rhodesia. This was a fundamental miscalculation. South Africa not only filled the gap left by the Rhodesian security services, but the unanticipated side effects of FRELIMO's socialist transformation began to manifest themselves. RENAMO did not merely survive; it prospered. After FRELIMO adopted its Marxist platform at the Third Congress in 1977, the government embarked on an ambitious program of economic development. The new set of economic policies had its most devastating effects on the agricultural sector (Bowen 1989, 2000; Geffray 1991; Pitcher 1998). For example, FRELIMO introduced collective farming, a system in which peasants were required to devote part of their labor to work on *machambas do povo* (collective farms). Surpluses from these farms were taken away from the local areas, and peasants were left to survive on the meager produce from land that they could barely manage in their free time. At the same time that production was centralized, the government also eliminated the private sector and mandated that household goods could only be distributed through *lojas do povo* (government stores). This ushered in an era of scarcity in which peasants routinely visited stores with little on their shelves.

Opposition to FRELIMO grew, as well, in response to a set of policies aimed to transform social and political relations in the countryside (Alexander 1994; Coelho 1998; Lundin and Machava 1995). In particular, these policies were intended to eliminate old forms of local authority. During the colonial period, the authorities sought to gain the loyalty of traditional leaders by giving them an official title, *régulo,* as well as a set of responsibilities, a small salary, a bicycle, and a uniform.

For FRELIMO, the *régulos,* as symbols of colonial influence, had to be eliminated from rural life. The system of traditional leadership was banned; *régulos* were informed that their services were no longer required and the population was prohibited from traditional practices, including the consulting of *curandeiros* (traditional healers) and the rites of initiation. These changes created a vacuum in the rural political organization. Those individuals who had managed social life in the rural areas were now prohibited from taking part in political life. FRELIMO sought to fill this space with a system of local party secretaries, chosen from among the local population, without any clear criteria (interview, Sofala, May 2001). It was clear, only, that *régulos* and other traditional authorities were not welcome as new party secretaries. These changes created a set of discontented leaders, with deep local roots in their communities, who were forcibly isolated by the new regime.

The peasantry was affected more broadly by these changes in political and social organization. To ease the organization of production and the delivery of education and health services, Mozambicans were encouraged to move into *aldeais comunais* (communal villages) and to abandon their dispersed patterns of settlement. These communal villages were often far from the local *machambas,* on which rural people produced their own food, but served as a centralizing force for the government in providing services, controlling labor, and in spreading the political messages of the party.

Importantly, from as early as 1979, these policies of "transformation" in the countryside became a crucial part of FRELIMO's counterinsurgency campaign. People were forced to attend party meetings and to study party materials, and were prevented from expressing opinions that were in opposition to the FRELIMO doctrine. Moreover, freedom of movement was restrained by the party secretaries who kept constant watch over the civilians in their area of control. Civilians were required to obtain *guias de marcha* (traveling permits) for permission to travel outside of their home communities. These changes dramatically disrupted life in the countryside and were seen as unwelcome by many rural dwellers, particularly in the central and northern parts of the country.

Yet, the government was almost helpless to prevent RENAMO's onslaught. With a weak economy (further damaged by its rural economic strategy), the government found itself holed up in villages and towns as RENAMO marched through the countryside. Its macro-economy was in crisis, still struggling to recover from the huge economic losses sustained during the sanctions against Rhodesia. Further, its access to foreign currency was weakened as South Africa increasingly limited the migration of Mozambicans to work in the mines and held up the remittances of those who had completed their work. As a consequence, FRELIMO's soldiers were spread throughout Mozambique's vast territory, poorly reinforced and poorly supplied, and RENAMO was able to make significant advances. The rebels could move easily in the sparsely populated rural areas and could raid the concentrated settlements and escape relatively unharmed.

The Outbreak of Conflict: 1976 and 1981

Examining the outbreak of conflict in 1976 and its reemergence in 1981 underscores the centrality of foreign intervention as a proximate cause of conflict. In Mozambique, consistent external assistance provided "capacity" and "opportunity"— a revenue stream much like that provided by "lootable" commodities—to enable the rebel organization to take hold.

The rebels faced significant challenges as their key patron vanished. Their activity very nearly ceased. The insurgency rejuvenated itself, however, with the advent of a new external patron. With South African support, RENAMO encountered a Mozambican peasantry reeling from huge disruptions to their traditional ways of life. In this context, RENAMO reinvented itself—with newfound autonomy— and used the influx of arms and logistical support to spread across the country. In this effort, they found the symbols of FRELIMO control an easy and popular target. In addition, they found allies among the *régulos,* other traditional authorities, and individuals who had been ejected from political life. Surprisingly, however, RENAMO failed to mobilize actively much of this discontent. Coercive tactics, rather than mobilization, spurred the organization's growth. The reasons for this approach concern the internal structure of RENAMO.

Looking Inside RENAMO

A general question raised by recent studies of civil war is the relative importance of "preferences" and "constraints" in understanding the incidence of civil war. Do rebel organizations emerge as a result of the depth of grievances, or is their formation more directly determined by the opportunities to finance their insurgency? For the case of Mozambique, this issue can be rephrased in the following way: Was RENAMO a rebel organization driven by internal discontent or by the external forces that made its existence possible? More directly, did the opportunities provided by external finance and limited state control determine the growth and spread of RENAMO in the 1980s?

To answer these questions, we look inside RENAMO and focus on issues of microorganization. By examining the structure, growth, and strategy of RENAMO, we are able to explore the influence of preferences and constraints on a new layer of evidence. The evidence suggests that, while grievances shaped the choices of rebel leaders at the margin, the organization's structure and strategy were a direct consequence of the economic environment in which it emerged. External patrons attracted recruits by offering salaries or rewards and by providing a continuous supply of arms and ammunition that appreciably lessened the risks of participating in the conflict. When these backers disappeared, RENAMO developed alternative sources of income to maintain the organization; these resources were generated to pay off participants rather than to reinforce the movement. Political mobilization never emerged as a central organization strategy. The organizational culture was one of opportunism, rather than activism. Sustained coercion, in recruitment and the generation of resources, and violence against noncombatants were the unfortunate consequences of this structure.

Membership and Recruitment

Recruitment in RENAMO can be divided into two distinct periods. In the first period, under Rhodesian influence, the MNR targeted key groups of individuals who had been repressed by the new government. Attacks on reeducation camps, prisons, and recruitment among the diaspora in Rhodesia and South Africa ensured a group of soldiers with the capacity to fight. Some have argued that this pool of recruits was largely Ndau, an ethnic group based in central Mozambique. Evidence suggests that, at least among the commanders in these early years, there was a heavy Ndau influence. Was this heavy ethnic influence the result of a particularly profound grievance? More likely, the population pool available to the Rhodesian CIO and the MNR in Rhodesia and just across the border in Mozambique drove early recruitment strategies. Although a shared Ndau heritage may have eased communication, grievances were never articulated in ethnic terms. The key factor that brought people into the MNR, or kept them once they were abducted, was the salaries provided by the Rhodesians to the recruits. Paid, clothed, and fed, the recruits lived better than most in rural Mozambique.

After 1981, the pool of RENAMO recruits transformed dramatically.[8] The new soldiers were far less likely to have previous military experience, or even to have previously lived outside of their home areas. Recruits were largely peasants and came from a broad diversity of ethnic and linguistic groups all over the country. Part of the explanation for the growing diversity of RENAMO's army might be related to grievances. During this period of growth, the peasantry was beginning to feel the dramatic effects of FRELIMO's social and economic policies. As the war progressed, the probability that a peasant would end up fighting for one side or the other grew significantly. Facing severe shortages of food and consumer products and limited opportunities for work in rural areas, peasants had little to lose in accepting a military life. It is more likely, though, that RENAMO's newfound diversity was a function of the rebels' inward expansion into Mozambique. With bases spread throughout all the provinces, RENAMO's need to maintain a balance

Table 6.3 Growth of Forces (Trained Fighters)

Organization	1976–77	1978–79	1980–81	1984–85	1986–87
RENAMO	200–400[a]	2,000–2,500[b]	6,000–10,000[c]	20,000[d]	
FRELIMO				35,000[e]	65,000–70,000[f]

Sources: (a) Stiff (1999, 177); (b) Stiff (1999, 180); (c) Stiff (1999, 369); (d) Vines (1991, 120); (e) World Development Indicators; (f) Minter (1995, 193).

of forces with the government necessitated consistent recruitment regardless of region or ethnicity.

In terms of size, under Rhodesian leadership, RENAMO had remained small. In 1981, after South Africa's support was secured, the group grew rapidly in size. By the end of the year, the rebel organization had ballooned from around 2,500 active soldiers to approximately 8,000. Three years later, RENAMO consisted of close to 20,000 men (table 6.3). When the demobilization program was implemented in 1993, RENAMO brought forward 21,979 soldiers to the cantonment areas. This suggests that, between 1985 and 1992 (the most intense years of the war), RENAMO maintained the size of its force, recruiting consistently to replace killed and injured soldiers as well as deserters.

Underlying this demographic shift and process of growth, a consistent pattern of forced recruitment remained (Minter 1989). Although some in the diaspora joined voluntarily during the MNR's early days, the vast majority were abducted in raids in Mozambique. Likewise, after 1981, cases of individuals joining voluntarily were reported, but RENAMO soldiers took a large majority in attacks on villages and roads. Although we can point to a pattern of grievances that explains the shifts in RENAMO membership, there is little evidence that these grievances drove people to join. The decision was not left to the individual. Moreover, RENAMO did not "recruit" based on these grievances. Our field research suggests that little effort was made to identify willing volunteers, even in areas in which discontent with the government was high.[9]

Opportunity played a much larger role in shaping the patterns of RENAMO membership. Rhodesia's limited capacity to recruit outside of the diaspora and beyond the border areas of Mozambique fundamentally shaped the membership of the MNR. RENAMO's move into all of Mozambique's provinces enabled its base of new recruits to diversify in the 1980s. The critical question, though, is why the recruits stayed in RENAMO's army? Of course, one part of the answer is that they were brought in by force and interviews suggest that punishment for attempts to escape was severe. However, we also believe that decisions to stay were shaped by the opportunities that participation in RENAMO provided. In the early years, recruits received salaries directly from Rhodesia. Throughout the 1980s, RENAMO combatants benefited from the continual resupply of the South African government and were free to capture food, clothing, and property as part of their attacks. Given the poverty of life in the government forces, to which most peasants were headed anyway via conscription, life as a RENAMO soldier seemed a better option.

Sources of Funding

Throughout this chapter, we have emphasized the centrality of external financing in the formation and growth of the Mozambican insurgency. However, a solitary focus on Mozambique's neighbors, and on military supplies, neglects the diversity of revenue sources that kept this insurgency alive (figure 6.3).

While external assistance from Rhodesia and South Africa provided a continual resupply of arms, the rebel organization sought to boost its financial position for reasons other than the purchase of equipment. Rhodesia had provided salaries to many RENAMO soldiers, when the army was small, and South Africa continued making payments to the senior RENAMO leadership. But, as RENAMO grew to a force of almost 20,000 soldiers, it was imperative for the organization to diversify its sources of revenue. Commanders aimed to enrich themselves in the course of conflict, needed methods of remunerating the infantry soldiers, and sought to provide some goods to civilians in their zones of control.

RENAMO enhanced its revenue base through three main sources: looting, cross-border trade, and extortion. Looting of household goods, government stores and cooperatives, schools, and health posts was a consistent element of RENAMO attacks after 1982 (interview, Sofala, May 2001). Looted goods served a number of purposes. Primarily, looting was a way for RENAMO soldiers to improve their own personal economic situation (interview, Nampula, April 2001). The dramatic shortages of consumer goods at the time (particularly in RENAMO-held areas)

Figure 6.3 RENAMO's Sources of Revenue

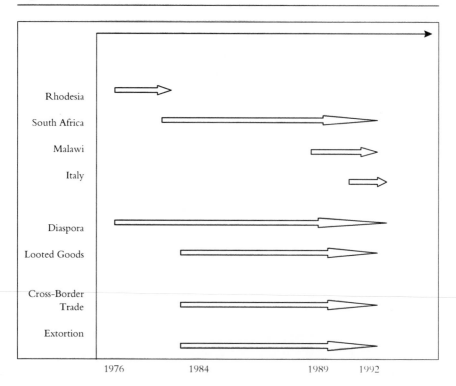

meant that attacks were the only avenue through which commanders and soldiers could gain access to clothing, pots and pans, mirrors, radios, batteries, and other household items. After an attack, RENAMO units would bring all the looted goods back to the base, with some later kept for personal use by the soldiers and others sold collectively across the border in Malawi and South Africa. This trade in looted goods was also a key part of an informal economy that developed around RENAMO bases. Infantry soldiers often left the bases and went into the civilian areas to exchange looted goods for farm produce (including goats, chickens, maize, cassava, etc.) (interview, Nampula, April 2001; interview, Sofala, May 2001). In this way, both soldiers and civilians were able to improve the quality of their lives. In addition, RENAMO would use looted goods to boost the collective morale and gain the loyalty of people in their areas. On occasion, RENAMO would return from an attack and distribute looted goods among the population, slaughter cattle and goats taken from government areas, and provide educational materials and medicines to schools and health posts operating among the civilians.[10]

Although the looting of primary commodities did not occupy a central place in the formation of RENAMO, revenue from cross-border trade provided a strong incentive for senior commanders to remain in the force. From 1982 until the end of the war, RENAMO was involved in the ivory trade, as well as the selling of game meat. Large amounts of foreign currency were generated from this trade. Some estimates suggest that in 1988 alone, the ivory captured in attacks on RENAMO bases by government forces was worth over $13 million (Vines 1991). It is important to emphasize that the revenue created by cross-border trade was not used to maintain the organization. Military supplies were guaranteed from elsewhere and there is no evidence that any income trickled down to the infantry. However, it played a critical role in maintaining the loyalty and commitment of RENAMO commanders.

RENAMO also obtained funds through extortion. In particular, the rebels negotiated with multinationals, including Lonrho, exchanging security guarantees for large sums of foreign currency (Vines 1998). Lonrho maintained profitable farms in all three regions of Mozambique almost until the end of the war. As part of these agreements, RENAMO was given permission to mount infrequent attacks on Lonrho facilities, with minimal damage, to keep up appearances. Malawi also was a victim of RENAMO's tactics of extortion. RENAMO negotiated payments in Malawian currency (to ease the purchase of salt, oil, and other consumer goods) in exchange for commitments not to attack trains carrying Malawian exports and imports along the Nacala rail corridor in northern Mozambique. Further, Malawi contributed to RENAMO's revenue growth by tacitly permitting cross-border trade along the frontiers of the Zambézia and Tete provinces. Of course, it is difficult to put a number on the scale of revenue created through extortion. However, in the course of the war, RENAMO surely generated tens of millions of dollars.

As the peace negotiations began and the war drew to a close in the 1990s, extortion took on a new form. Significant amounts of hard currency were used to strengthen RENAMO's incentives to lay down their guns. These payments for the "organizational growth" of RENAMO as a political party were also used to fatten the pockets of its leadership. We discuss the role of money in securing the peace deal in a later section.

Military Structure

From the very beginning, RENAMO was a highly centralized military organization. Rhodesian security officials worked with a small cadre of the senior MNR leadership to plot strategy. It is unclear to what extent the MNR influenced the choice of targets and strategies in these early years. However, without a doubt, decisions were made entirely at the top and orders were transmitted to lower levels of the organization.

This centralized structure continued after 1981, in spite of the change of leadership and of the external patron. The *Estado-Maior General* in Gorongosa, and later in Marínguè (both in Sofala province) coordinated the movement of troops, established new bases and fronts, and made decisions about when and where to launch attacks.[11] The information flow was consistently routed through the national command so that strategic planning was done with complete intelligence information from local areas. If a local commander wished to launch an attack, he would first need to receive clearance from the top (interview, Sofala, May 2001). Further, after an attack, decisions to vacate a village or town under occupation were always made by the national command. Any major strategic moves, such as the opening of a new front in Zambézia (1983) or in Nampula (1983/4), were also coordinated from Gorongosa.

Centralization went hand-in-hand with a strong and tight communications infrastructure. High-tech equipment provided first by the Rhodesians, and later by South Africa, along with the necessary training in communications, enabled the RENAMO command to monitor and control the activities of troops effectively throughout the country.[12] Units were required to provide regular updates (up to eight times a day) to their superiors. Even at the top, access to information about local conditions was excellent and immediate. The communications infrastructure also enabled RENAMO to harmonize its strategy and movements. Little was left to chance and local commanders were subject to direct orders and reporting requirements from above.

The system of resupply and logistics also reflected the highly centralized structure of RENAMO's military (Stiff 1999). Careful records were kept of South African airdrops and seadrops of equipment that were then transported by soldiers and civilians to central bases at the provincial and regional levels for redistribution to areas in short supply (interview, Nampula, April 2001). The logistics system focused not only on maintaining the supply of guns and ammunition. Attention was also given to ensuring that bases in isolated areas or those facing severe shortages were provided with food. There is evidence that RENAMO transported food from a "breadbasket" in Zambézia to bases south of the Zambezi River and to areas in which they faced difficult environmental and social conditions, including drought and a scarcity of civilians (Pereira 1999). Further, soldiers report leading hundreds of cattle from Nampula to RENAMO's central base in Maríngue in the late 1980s (interview, Nampula, April 2001).

Why did RENAMO develop such a centralized military structure? The fact that the bulk of military support came from external sources was a powerful influence on the military structure of RENAMO. A clear chain of command, with identifiable figures at the top, was essential to negotiate with the external patrons for continued support and supply during the conflict. To an external patron, the costs of dealing with a decentralized group would be far too high. Further, a centralized structure was crucial for the delivery of supplies provided through a single leadership structure. The *Estado-Maior General* was able to track the deliveries of guns and ammunition to different regions of the country and to redirect these supplies to the bases with the highest levels of need. The survival of each unit depended on its link to the central chain of command. The only alternative for getting guns involved direct fighting with government forces and that was a potentially costly venture.

Political and Civilian Organization

As a guerrilla force based inside Mozambique, RENAMO could not avoid repeated and sustained interactions with noncombatant populations. RENAMO relied on civilian support for the organization of resources, the provision of information and intelligence, and protection from government forces. But relations with civilians were more reflective of RENAMO's emphasis on coercion, rather than its political agenda.

On entering a new geographic area, RENAMO often intentionally made contact first with the *régulo*.[13] *Régulos* had a clear grievance with the FRELIMO government and instant credibility with the local population. RENAMO commanders would ask about the local customs, showing respect for the ancestors and traditional spirits, and seeking permission to operate in the area. Further, RENAMO would describe its purpose in waging a war against FRELIMO and indicate their commitment to reestablishing the traditional ways of living. Often, the *régulo* would perform a traditional ceremony to present the new arrivals to the ancestors and explain the purpose of the rebels' cause. These ceremonies would also serve as an introduction for RENAMO to the local population. It is important to emphasize, though, that while the *régulos* were targeted for a direct and political approach, civilians rarely received this treatment. Political education was limited, often occurring only during the first introduction. Although RENAMO had a system of political commissars in the army to coordinate the education of civilians, most interviewees remember receiving most of their political messages from the *régulo* and his associates. Direct political mobilization picked up as the war drew to a close because RENAMO was interested in establishing itself as a political party, but it played a minor role in relations with civilians during the 1980s.

The civilians who lived in RENAMO-controlled areas came via three paths. In some cases, after receiving permission from the *régulo* to set up a base, RENAMO entrenched itself in a local zone, working through the traditional authorities to maintain control (interview, Sofala, May 2001). Alternatively, RENAMO worked through *régulos* to move civilian populations from their current locations near areas of government control to more "secure" places by RENAMO bases (interview, Nampula, April 2001). Finally, and most often, civilians would be taken to RENAMO areas during attacks on roads and government zones (interview, Sofala, May 2001). It was easy for RENAMO to abduct large numbers of people since the government's policies that forced people to live in villages had concentrated settlement patterns and the military had a limited capacity to prevent incursions. On arrival in a RENAMO area of control, the new residents would be handed over to the *régulo* or another local authority who would provide them with a place to settle (interview, Nampula, April 2001).

Although RENAMO did not play directly on grievances in organizing civilians to move to their areas, the strategies used by the rebels to manage and maintain control had distinct political purposes and implications. Foremost among these was the reestablishment of traditional authorities. Civilian life in RENAMO zones was coordinated by the *régulo,* who worked with a team of traditional authorities below him to manage the civilian population (interview, Sofala, May 2001). RENAMO's decision to return power to the *régulo,* was often popular with the local population. *Régulos* often still commanded significant power among the peasants and RENAMO's capacity to mobilize and work through them eased its interaction with civilians in its zones. In particular, RENAMO coordinated a system of local police, the *mudjibas,* who assisted the *régulo* in monitoring the civilian population, resolving disputes, and, at some points, acting as middlemen between the civilians and the military (interview, Nampula, April 2001). Sometimes these *mudjibas* were trusted associates of the *régulo,* with positions in the traditional hierarchy predating RENAMO's arrival. However, a broad mix of civilians rose to fill these positions, not all of whom had instant credibility with the local populations.[14]

The *régulo* and his associates also played a central role in organizing the collection of food. Although RENAMO obtained food through attacks on villages or raids on fields, shops, and government stores in the early years, the control of civilian populations emerged as an essential tool of organizational maintenance as RENAMO grew. By the mid-1980s, RENAMO adopted a fairly uniform system of food collection that was apparent in most provinces in the country.[15] In this system, local villages were divided into zones (*Blocos*) that were responsible for a set contribution of food two or three times a week. In each zone, a specified individual (*Chefe de Bloco*) would come to collect each household's contribution and take the gathered food to the *Control* (interview, Sofala, May 2001). When a household was unable to make the required contribution, the *Chefe* would return to request a double contribution the following time (interview, Sofala, May 2001). It was not possible to free ride on the contributions of others. With the exception of the *régulo,* who was not required to contribute through this mechanism, every household (including the *Chefe's*) was responsible for the same amount of food. The *régulo* hosted RENAMO commanders and cadres regularly, providing food and shelter to the guests, and was therefore not required to make regular contributions. Civilians preferred this regularized system and appreciated that RENAMO soldiers no longer came arbitrarily to their homes asking for food, although many still felt burdened by the obligatory contributions.

Although many civilians welcomed the return of traditional authorities and their role in political organization, coercion characterized much of life in RENAMO areas. Most residents had been moved forcibly, having been abducted during RENAMO's attacks. And, on arrival, they faced a constant threat of RENAMO indiscipline, which included arbitrary killings, beatings, rape, and theft.

In regard to discipline, RENAMO had no consistent approach to handling behavioral problems.[16] In some cases, there were consequences for misbehavior; in others, there were not. When soldiers were punished for mistreating noncombatants, the consequences were largely at the discretion of each commander (interview, Nampula, March 2001). Soldiers who committed crimes against civilians might be punished publicly, in front of the aggrieved; privately within the base; or not at all, depending on the area.[17] Further, the choice about the kind of punishment each crime deserved was largely left to the local commanders.[18] Serious offenses, including rape and murder, sometimes warranted a direct report to a higher command and may have included a transfer of the accused soldier to another base (interview, Nampula, April 2001). Almost without exception, however, soldiers did not report the existence of a specified code of conduct or a process for determining the guilt or innocence of the accused. In practice, determination of right and wrong, and how punishment should be administered, fell to those in local control.[19] As a consequence, civilians from RENAMO zones recalled a constant fear of mistreatment at the hands of rebel combatants.

The realms of civilian administration and management more clearly demonstrate the influence of domestic grievances in shaping RENAMO's strategy. While RENAMO may not have emerged as a popular movement with the objective of resurrecting traditional leaders and providing better services, its strategies in building relations with local populations underscored political differences with the FRELIMO government. However, coercion still played a dominant role, even as these efforts to appeal to the peasants gradually contributed to the growth of a domestic base of support and gave civilians reasons not to flee RENAMO areas of control.

Competition from Other Groups

With our intensive focus on RENAMO and its structure, we have left an important question unanswered. Was RENAMO alone in mounting an insurgency against the FRELIMO government? The answer to this question may be important in determining the relative importance of "preferences" and "constraints" in the Mozambican conflict.

The "modernization" policies that FRELIMO implemented in the countryside were met with a number of forms of resistance. Much of this protest was on an individual level. People refused to work in the collective farms. They avoided moving into the communal villages, and when forced, illegally kept a second home near their *machamba*. Others lived in the bush, refusing to submit to the government's policies. Finally, Mozambicans continued reaching out to *régulos* and other traditional authorities for guidance in their communities.

There were also collective forms of resistance. Peasants collectively resisted FRELIMO's policies by sabotaging state farms. They would lay down their tools, refusing to work, and destroy equipment (Legrand 1993). In Maputo province, peasants resisted the government's changes through the FRELIMO party structures. New policies were denounced and coalitions formed that extended beyond the disenfranchised traditional leaders. Less than 1 percent of people moved into communal villages, even though the area was deemed a high priority for the government (McGregor 1998). These two examples suggest that, even as the MNR was taking shape under Rhodesia's leadership, Mozambicans were beginning to resist on their own.

RENAMO became the dominant rebel organization in Mozambique, but in the beginning, it was not alone. In 1976, a group called *África Livre* emerged in Zambézia. It was born with active Malawian support and headed by Gimo Phiri. The extent of external support that *África Livre* received is unclear. Between 1978 and 1981, *África Livre* expanded its operations from Zambézia into Niassa and Tete as well. They made these gains despite beginning as a "group of 10 ill-equipped men." Their growth was necessarily fed by some combination of external support from Malawi and internal success in capturing armaments from the government (Cabrita 2000). *África Livre* later merged with RENAMO in 1982, and Phiri rose to a senior leadership position under Dhlakama (Vines 1991). Phiri's forces were distributed among three RENAMO bases in Zambézia. However, although *África Livre* had emerged with Malawian assistance, it was resource-poor relative to RENAMO. RENAMO soldiers described the *África Livre* combatants as operating in a "rudimentary" manner, mainly relying on stones to fight FRELIMO. Moreover, the merger brought little in the way of armaments over to the RENAMO side.

Phiri broke with RENAMO in 1988, taking 500 men, and quickly turned his forces on RENAMO. This was the only major break within RENAMO during the course of the conflict. Phiri thought that he could compete with RENAMO, using the guns his followers took, by capturing new weapons from the government and by reaching out again to external backers. But his independent insurgency was short lived and Phiri turned himself into the government through the amnesty program in 1990.

While grievances created the conditions for armed resistance in Mozambique by the late 1970s, both cases demonstrate that external forces, and the financial backing that they provided, were critical factors that enabled the rebel organizations to emerge. The centralized military structure that RENAMO developed to coordinate its external supply system also weakened the capacity of internal agents to form splinter groups. Only Gimo Phiri could attempt to break off, with his previous experience of organizing *África Livre*. However, his new group, UNAMO, failed to survive. The external backers had already lined up behind RENAMO and, with only a small force, the costs of organization for Phiri's group were far too high.

This analysis of microstructures in RENAMO suggests that grievances shaped the strategies of rebellion at the margin throughout the conflict. External backers, however, and the sources of finance that they provided, played a more central role in shaping the membership, growth, and structure of the insurgent movement. Because of its access to external financing, RENAMO bypassed a process of political development; instead, material incentives became the main reason why people joined and stayed in the growing movement. As external backers disappeared, the organization faced the critical task of diversifying its revenue sources. Attacks on civilian targets became an important source of remuneration. Thus, in spite of domestic grievances, RENAMO survived and prospered through a combination of coercion and the provision of short-term rewards to its members and supporters.

Duration and Intensity of the War

Why did the war in Mozambique last for 16 years? In this section, we test two hypotheses, both emerging from theoretical arguments about war duration and from statistical results from a cross-section of cases. The first puts more emphasis on domestic social structures and the factors that enable groups to maintain cohesion. The second focuses on external factors and the issue of finance.

Collier, Hoeffler, and Soderbom (2001) argue that the fundamental problem faced by competing armies in a civil war is that of maintaining cohesion. For a war to last a long time, government armies and rebel organizations must maintain their capacity to fight the opposing forces and prevent their own group from splintering. Theoretically, they argue that ethnic identity or linguistic similarity is sufficient to maintain this cohesion; the costs of rebel coordination are lower in societies in which ethnic or linguistic groups are polarized such that the organization can rely on one part of the population for support as it sees itself in opposition to the rest.

Elbadawi and Sambanis (2000) accept Collier et al.'s argument with one critical extension. They argue that polarization is not a necessary cause of longer wars when external intervention is present. External forces reduce the costs of maintaining an insurgency, particularly for a small ethnic group, enabling the persistence of rebel organizations in highly fractionalized societies or in places where one group is dominant.

Mozambique is a crucial test case for these two theories. Collier and Hoeffler (2000) consider the country dominated by one ethnic/linguistic group. However, the minority populations are diverse, with many small ethnic groups and linguistic divisions.[20] In the view of Collier et al. (2001), this is a recipe for a short war. Cohesion in the rebel organization, in particular, ought to be difficult to maintain. Yet, the war lasted for 16 years, largely fueled by external intervention. The rebels were not organized along polarized ethnic or linguistic lines. Instead, the process of maintaining cohesion was influenced by external determinants.

To understand why the war lasted so long, it is a mistake to focus simply on factors shaping the cohesion of the rebel organization. RENAMO was unable to beat the government because FRELIMO augmented its capacity after 1984–85, increasing its military strength and drawing on external support to combat the strong insurgency. While the government resorted to force and coercion to conscript and control domestic populations, it survived only because it shifted the military burden away from its own regular ground troops, turning to air power, specially trained Mozambican forces, and the soldiers committed by Zimbabwe, Malawi, and Tanzania (interview, Maputo, May 2001).

External intervention lengthened Mozambique's civil war by strengthening *both* rebel and government capacity, enabling RENAMO to maintain internal cohesion, and assisting the government in lessening the burden on a demoralized army and population.

From Nkomati to Homoíne

The government attributed the expansion of RENAMO to one factor alone: South African external support. This belief shaped the Mozambican government's strategy to combat the insurgency through the mid-1980s (Hall and Young 1997; Vines 1991).

In an effort to put an end to South African support, FRELIMO initiated contacts with Pretoria in 1982. Over the course of two years, diplomatic negotiations took senior Mozambican and South African leaders back and forth across the border. The message delivered by the South Africans was clear: continued Mozambican support for the ANC would be met with harsh retaliation. A South African Defense Force (SADF) raid in Matola, a neighborhood in Mozambique's capital city, provided evidence of South Africa's determination. The use of "carrots and sticks" in Mozambique was part of South Africa's "total strategy" to dictate the rules of engagement in the region.

Both governments had something the other wanted, however. Mozambique was desperate to put an end to external military support for RENAMO and South Africa was anxious to weaken the ANC following its successful attacks on targets within South Africa. The two governments signed the Nkomati nonaggression pact in March 1984, cementing their commitments to end support for activities that destabilized their neighbors. The ANC was expelled from Maputo, its training camps were shut down, and its leadership was forced to move to Zambia. The South Africans committed themselves to ending military supplies and logistical assistance to the rebels in Mozambique.

The FRELIMO government had high hopes that the end of the conflict was near following the agreement. At the same time that the negotiations were underway, the government was preparing to launch a major military offensive against RENAMO, believing that the combination of diplomatic and military efforts would quash the insurgency once and for all. The culmination of this offensive in 1985 when FRELIMO captured RENAMO's central base at Gorongosa in Sofala province. However, as the military sifted through the remnants of the base, they uncovered evidence of continued South African assistance to RENAMO.[21] Diaries of Dhlakama's personal secretary indicated the schedule and contents of airdrops from South African planes to RENAMO positions after the signing of the Nkomati pact. Moreover, notes confirmed that high-level South African military officials had recently visited to reaffirm their continued commitment to RENAMO, irrespective of the agreement signed by their government.

FRELIMO had built its entire counterinsurgency strategy around the belief that RENAMO was entirely an external creation. The government's inability to put an end to South African assistance was, therefore, seen as a bruising defeat. However, the government continued in this mind set, refusing to acknowledge any responsibility for the conflict. FRELIMO assumed that everyone was on the side of the government—with the president handing out guns to the population to rid the countryside of the external agents. However, the situation on the ground was changing dramatically. Civilians were caught in the middle of two coercive forces and reluctantly accepted their fate to live on one side or the other. Soldiers fighting for the FRELIMO government had relatives or friends living with RENAMO. The war had taken on a local dynamic and both civilians and soldiers were keenly aware of the grievances articulated by the insurgents.

In 1986, the war escalated (interview, Maputo, May 2001). RENAMO had expanded throughout the north and was attempting to take all of Zambézia province, thereby cutting the country in two. With his continued focus on external forces, President Machel had pushed the Malawian government to cease its support for RENAMO. This meant, essentially, the closure and patrol of the Malawian borders with Tete and Zambézia. As a consequence, RENAMO was forced to move hundreds, or even thousands, of soldiers from bases and training camps in Malawi back into the country. RENAMO demonstrated tremendous strength during this offensive, taking control of 13 of Zambézia's 18 districts by the end of 1986. Military intelligence in Maputo feared that Dhlakama would march into Quelimane, the capital of Zambézia, and split the country into two parts.

However, RENAMO was never able to split the country. Since the fall of the Gorongosa base in 1985, the government had been steadily augmenting its capacity to fight the insurgents internally. Realizing the weakness of its conscripted forces, FRELIMO looked outside of the country for assistance. Furthermore, they attempted to transform the military, shifting the burden away from infantry soldiers toward more agile Special Forces backed up by air power. By late 1986, the FRELIMO government was fighting alongside troops from Zimbabwe, Malawi, and Tanzania. In addition, military advisors from the Eastern bloc and some Western countries (Portugal, France, and the United Kingdom) were assisting the four armies in combating RENAMO.

With external support, FRELIMO launched a major offensive to recapture Zambézia in 1987. It was the only time during the war that the military used all three branches of the armed forces—Army, Navy, and Air Force. The offensive was launched during the rainy season and caught RENAMO unprepared. The government had a tremendous advantage at this time of year because they were able to send in reinforcements by air. RENAMO, on the other hand, without mechanized transport, was unable to bolster its forces swiftly. In addition, Special Forces trained by the Russians were dropped throughout the province in small, efficient groups to uncover and attack the guerrilla bases. RENAMO was pushed back and lost control of most of the districts that it had gained.

At this point, the war was at a stalemate. RENAMO was a strong, centralized rebel organization with bases throughout the country. Continued financial assistance from outside and a sophisticated base of internal revenue sources had ensured the organization's sustainability and cohesion. RENAMO controlled most rural areas and had regained its former central base in Gorongosa as soon as Zimbabwean troops were redeployed to the Beira corridor. At the same time, the government, sensing its internal weakness, had turned to outsiders for help. Foreign soldiers secured most of the transport corridors that provided Mozambique with critical revenue. The army was reorganized to lessen pressure on traditional and unmotivated combat troops, instead prioritizing the training and deployment of specialized forces to counteract the guerrillas' advances.

In 1987, while the forces had achieved some sort of "parity," the intensity of the fighting picked up. Incidents of violence against civilians increased in number and in scale. In July, more than 400 civilians were killed in a RENAMO attack and government response in the Homoíne district (Inhambane province). Later that year, high-profile massacres also took place in Taninga and Mandlakazi—all in southern Mozambique.

The Magnitude of the Conflict

One important characteristic of Mozambique's conflict was the high level of violence committed against noncombatants during the conflict. This violence came to dominate international coverage of Mozambique's civil war and emerged largely in 1987, continuing through the end of the conflict. Two aspects of the violence merit closer attention: its perpetrator and its geographic concentration.

RENAMO was responsible for the vast majority of abuses committed against noncombatant populations during the course of the war (table 6.4). In a new data set that describes the incidence of civil war violence in Mozambique, rebel combatants are identifiably linked to over 80 percent of the recorded incidents (Weinstein 2003).

Table 6.4 **Responsibility for Incidents of Violence, 1976–94**

Type of violence	Government forces	Rebel forces	External forces	Unclear	Total incidents
Killing	29	692	41	67	829
Injury	27	499	37	52	615
Looting	36	396	9	27	468
Destruction	1	473	25	17	516

More importantly, the data provide evidence about the character of RENAMO attacks. Rebel combatants often engaged in looting and the destruction of civilian property as part of their combat missions. In addition, when RENAMO killed noncombatants, they tended to perpetrate massacres—killing six or more victims at a time in more than 40 percent of the recorded attacks (figure 6.4).

Although the magnitude of violence picked up in the later stages of the war, the data also suggest that its character did not become more indiscriminate and brutal over time. RENAMO attacks, even in the early stages of the conflict, were arbitrary, targeted large numbers of civilians, and involved the looting and destruction of civilian property.

A second facet of RENAMO's violence was its geographic concentration. Figure 6.1 demonstrates that across all three regions, the number of incidents increased rapidly after 1986. However, there is a clear bias toward the south. By the early 1990s, the southern provinces were experiencing nearly double the attacks as the center and the north (figure 6.5).

RENAMO soldiers again were responsible for the vast majority of these incidents in the south. Moreover, when civilians were targeted for violence in the south, they were killed in much larger groups. Over 70 percent of the incidents in which more than 15 people were killed took place in the southern provinces. By contrast, 67 percent of the attacks in northern Mozambique involved no killing or the killing of only one person. In the south, less than 50 percent of the incidents

Figure 6.4 Size of RENAMO's Victim Groups

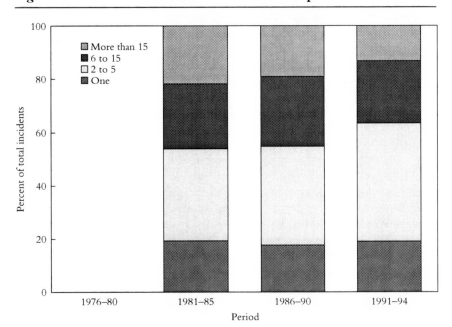

Figure 6.5 Geographic Concentration of RENAMO Violence

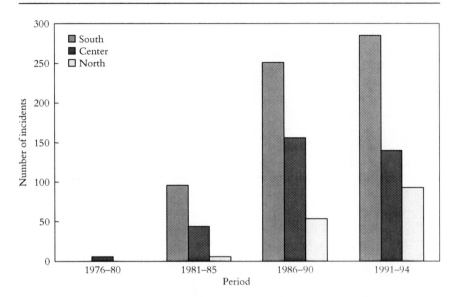

fell into this category. Finally, incidents of overkill (in which bodies were mutilated or burned as part of the killing) occurred overwhelmingly in the south. More than 80 percent of these incidents took place in the southern provinces.

Why did RENAMO perpetrate massive and indiscriminate violence against noncombatant populations? And why was this violence biased in favor of the south? These questions are not well addressed by the core models motivating the Yale–World Bank project, which focus almost exclusively on why wars begin and end. New microlevel research, however, offers two lines of explanation for the patterns that we observe with respect to the magnitude of the civil war.

RENAMO's behavior was in part a direct consequence of its internal structure. Weinstein (2005) argues that a rebel group's conduct is shaped by the pool of members that it attracts. RENAMO, by virtue of its sustained external support and the continuous flow of arms and ammunition, entailed a relatively low level of risk for potential combatants. Moreover, because the movement provided real, short-term payoffs to new recruits throughout the conflict, RENAMO attracted opportunistic joiners.[22] Thus, material incentives held the organization together and short-term considerations drove its strategy. Even when it sought to build a base of domestic support, RENAMO relied on coercive tactics to recruit soldiers, organize civilians, and extract resources necessary for conflict. Groups that develop in this type of context exhibit behavior similar to RENAMO's—characterized by high levels of violence, coercion, looting, and destruction.

But why the bias toward the southern provinces? Kalyvas (2000) argues that, because violence is a strategic enterprise used by both sides to elicit collaboration and prevent defection, how it is used is a function of the degree of rebel control.

Such control is necessary for combatants to solicit information about the behavior of civilians. His model predicts that where the level of rebel control is weak, as in Mozambique's southern provinces, one can expect high levels of indiscriminate violence. By contrast, where rebel groups exercise some control, selective violence is the norm. Kalyvas's theory provides one potential explanation for the geographic bias of violence in the Mozambican conflict.

Both of these theoretical arguments draw on insights from the core models motivating this project. They focus their attention, however, on how the organization of rebellion creates a set of strategic situations—both within the group and in its relations with noncombatants—that shape the magnitude and intensity of the conflict. Therefore, because coercion and violence play an important role in civil war, there is a need for a greater focus on the dynamics of conflict and not just its sources.

Conclusion

Our analysis of the Mozambican conflict suggests three conclusions relevant to the study of civil wars. First, we suggest that geopolitics is central to understanding the causes and consequences of civil conflict. Rhodesia and South Africa provided the financial and military means to mobilize domestic discontent. Continued assistance from external patrons, and broader support from right-wing activists around the world, contributed to RENAMO's growth and its transformation into a more internal political movement, and ensured that, in spite of its support from the Eastern bloc, FRELIMO would be unable to crush the insurgency. In this sense, external backers substituted for "lootable commodities" in providing the means to organize insurgency. The logic of the Collier-Hoeffler model thus finds support in the case of Mozambique.

In evaluating the relative importance of preferences ("grievances") and constraints ("opportunity") in Mozambique's conflict, we find first and foremost that this conflict was shaped by opportunity. Although no "lootable" commodities contributed to the war's initiation or continuation, the conflict was initiated and sustained with resources generated from external patrons. Shaped at first entirely by external agendas, the civil war gave voice to domestic grievances in its second stage. But it would be difficult to argue that these grievances were the proximate cause of the war. Indeed, no other rebel organization was able to form without external backing.

Second, FRELIMO's economic policies and social repression undoubtedly shaped the trajectory of the war, spurring RENAMO's growth and expansion throughout the countryside. Even though RENAMO recruited by force and utilized coercion to prevent civilian defection, FRELIMO's unsustainable social transformation made life with RENAMO an acceptable option for many civilians. Even when the capacity of the insurgent group to wage war is not dependent on social mobilization, as in the Mozambican case, grievances do shape the onset, duration, and termination of the conflict. Rhodesia acted on its desire to finance a cross-border insurgency in partnership with a set of discontented exiles based in Salisbury. RENAMO expanded inward in Mozambique and used the reappointment of traditional authorities as a political tool to maintain civilian cooperation. Finally, FRELIMO's decisions to mount political and economic reforms brought the two parties ideologically closer together, paving the way to peace in the late 1980s.

Third, the Mozambican civil war highlights the important role of coercion in civil conflict. Although ethnic and linguistic groups do provide linkages that ease mobilization and organization in Mozambique, these identities did not figure crucially in the conflict. Theoretical models that focus on these social factors in explaining group cohesion provide us with little leverage for understanding the organization and growth of RENAMO. On both sides in Mozambique, force was used to mount the struggle—in conscription, the collection of resources, the control of territory, and in selective and indiscriminate killing. But RENAMO emerged as a fundamentally corrupt force that abducted new recruits, paid them to stay in its military, and surrounded them with civilians taken from their homes to live in RENAMO areas. This behavior persisted in spite of the fact that many civilians were already prepared to resist FRELIMO. Levels of coercion did grow as the conflict hit a stalemate, but force was used from the beginning. Although RENAMO had a political purpose and was rooted in particular ethnic communities, they did not mobilize on either of those grounds. The Mozambican conflict thus highlights the important place of coercion in understanding the dynamics of civil war. In looking forward, an important next step involves understanding not only where conflict happens, but also why and where violence is likely to be most central.

Annex: Database on Civil War Violence

Over the last two decades, the quantitative study of civil war has gained prominence in the literature. Analyses of large-scale databases have provided for fruitful cross-country comparisons. In particular, statistical analysis has yielded new insights into the causes of civil war, forces impacting its duration, and the factors shaping its termination. However, the questions that scholars have been able to ask about civil war have been limited by the type of quantitative data that exists. Specifically, researchers have focused on the "civil war" as the unit of analysis. At this level, databases are composed of country-level indicators—including whether there was a civil war, how long it lasted, and when it came to an end—as well as a set of political and economic indicators of country-level characteristics.

Without more fine-grained information, it is impossible to examine systematically an additional set of issues, including the geographic spread of civil war, variation in the incidence of civil war over time, and the characteristics of civil war violence. These characteristics include details about the types of violence committed by soldiers during a conflict, the prevalence of these various types, the location, and details about the victims.

Scholars interested in quantitative research should not be limited to studies of the structural determinants of civil war initiation, duration, and termination. Although studies of the incidence and character of civil war violence have traditionally been largely in the domain of anthropologists and sociologists, it is feasible to develop a method for the systematic collection of cross-national quantitative data on the incidence and character of civil war. In this annex, we present the outline of one such method.

Structure

The violence database is collected with the following assumption in mind: Civilians are often the primary and deliberate target of combatants in civil wars. This is the result of a set of interrelated factors, including the weakness of military structures in irregular war, the absence of clear frontlines on which the parties fight, and the blurred distinction between combatants and civilians. Accordingly, an appropriate indicator of the "incidence" of civil war is the use of violence against noncombatant populations. A database constructed on this foundation yields significant information about the geographic location of civil war, how the level of violence varies over time, and the characteristics of those who are affected by the conflict.

In the database, the basic unit of analysis is the "event." An "event" refers to any interaction between soldiers (rebel or government) and civilians in which a "violation" is committed. "Violations" are instances of violence, including killings, mutilation, abduction, detention, injury, destruction, rape, looting, forced displacement, and overkill.[23] As a result, any one event may include a set of violations committed against the civilian population. Each event is characterized within the database in terms of the violations that it includes. Importantly, in the statistics presented in this chapter, the unit being counted is always the event.

In addition to coding the violations that occurred as part of an event, the database also includes important identifying characteristics for each event. These include: its geographic location, when it happened, who perpetrated the violence, the form of weapons they used, and whether rebel or government soldiers were also killed during the event. An effort is also made to capture detailed characteristics of the victims of civil war violence, including the number killed and injured, the number identified by name, their age, gender, and "affiliation." For purposes of understanding who suffered from civil war violence, victims are categorized into the following "affiliation" groups: religious leaders, professors and teachers, students, political leaders, traditional authorities, civilians (with a specified occupation), and those without any identifying characteristics.

Method

The violence database consists of events drawn from press sources. Local coders were trained to collect detailed event descriptions from daily newspapers in collections at the National Archives, local libraries, and from press reviews produced by local nongovernmental organizations. Coders gathered information from each published newspaper for each day during the entire period of armed conflict. More than 1,400 events were collected in a review of both government and opposition newspapers for the period 1976–94 in Mozambique.

Of course, the same events often appear in different sources. One newspaper might report that six individuals were killed, while another has information about only three. One story might indicate that a range of violations were committed, while another limits its description to the killing alone. Coders were required to complete a full event description each time the event was reported. In the process of building the quantitative database—transforming the event descriptions into numerical data—every effort was made to eliminate overlapping incidents. Moreover, a simple set of coding rules was established to resolve conflicting information about the same event.

Frequently, the data for an event is incomplete. A newspaper may report that individuals were killed, but lack information about the identities of the victims and the perpetrators. More often, specific identifying information including the affiliation, gender, and age of the victims is unavailable. The final structure of this database incorporates the incomplete information. Where no clear evidence is provided with which to code the individual variables, those entries are left blank. However, the events are still included in the dataset, even when some variables cannot be coded. Therefore, the summary statistics represent *certain* information recorded with respect to each variable.

Importantly, the violence database does not present a complete picture of civil war violence. Newspapers are unable to report every incident of violence that takes place in a conflict, because of material and security limitations. As a result, this database vastly understates the level of violence experienced in Mozambique. Nonetheless, the geographic, temporal, and characteristic patterns identified in the dataset match closely with the trajectory of civil war violence established in the historical record and narrative reports on the conflict. Moreover, the method enables the systematic collection of data on civil war violence across conflicts. Likely, the limitations in any one case are similar across countries. As a result, despite the weaknesses, the data gathered are comparable across conflicts, allowing for fine-grained comparisons of the incidence and characteristics of violence within civil war.

Notes

1. Our understanding of the internal structure of RENAMO is based on more than 60 interviews with former RENAMO combatants and civilians who lived in RENAMO-held areas. We guaranteed anonymity to our sources. As a result, references to the interviews refer only to the day on which the interview was conducted and its location. The research for this chapter was conducted in Nampula province (northern Mozambique) and Sofala province (central Mozambique) between February and June 2001.

2. It is important to emphasize, however, that in spite of the dominance of the Makua-Lomwé in terms of size, they have not come to dominate the political scene. Southern ethnic groups, with opposition from the center, have played a far more prominent role, and regional divisions have been the basis for conflict.

3. In this section, we draw largely on widely accepted facts about the emergence of the FRELIMO, from its anticolonial war to the beginning of its postindependence gov-

ernment. For example, see Hall and Young (1997) and Hoile (1994). For precolonial and colonial history, see Newitt (1995).

4. In Maputo alone, the government-established People's Vigilance Groups (GVPs) worked with over 17,000 informers to gather information about the activities of "potential counter-revolutionaries." President Machel disclosed that over 150,000 informers were working with the government nationwide. The government established reeducation camps in seven of Mozambique's 10 provinces, with nearly 75 percent of them established in the central and northern regions. Interestingly, FRELIMO's stronghold, Gaza province, had not a single reeducation camp.

5. The CIO's early efforts included the establishment of a radio station, *Voz da África Livre,* which broadcast from Rhodesia to Mozambican audiences. Civilians whom we interviewed in central Mozambique, in particular, recalled these broadcasts as their first contact with RENAMO (interviews, Sofala, May 2001).

6. In this chapter, we present a new methodology for measuring the incidence of civil war, enabling us to capture variation in the presence and character of conflict over time and across geographic space. In the annex, we describe the methods and sources of this new civil war database for Mozambique.

7. To this day, there remains significant debate about the extent to which RENAMO actually developed its own political strategy under South African leadership in the early 1980s. Critics of the South African government, often blinded to internal developments in Mozambique, claimed that the political propaganda emerging from RENAMO in the early 1980s was nothing more than a publicity stunt by the South Africans and far right-wing groups in Europe and the United States (Minter 1995; Vines 1991). Others argued that, under South African leadership, RENAMO achieved some autonomy for the first time, enabling it to develop its own political agenda (Cabrita 2000; Hoile 1994). Our interviews with civilians who lived in RENAMO zones lend some support to the claims of the latter. Civilians describe RENAMO efforts to establish liberated zones and educate those populations as beginning after 1982.

8. Our interviews of former combatants suggest how pronounced these changes actually were. The vast majority of RENAMO soldiers with whom we spoke, both in central and northern Mozambique, were recruited after 1981. These combatants were not mobilized politically before joining; with the exception of two interviewees, all were recruited by force, at young ages, and without previous military experience. They came from all social levels and ethnic groups within the peasantry in each of the regions that we visited.

9. Even in the locality of Metaveia in the northern province of Nampula, where RENAMO had a significant base of popular support during the war, both civilians and former combatants describe a similar process of forced recruitment. Surprisingly, even among RENAMO supporters, there is little effort to hide this characteristic of RENAMO's strategy (interview, Ribáuè district, Nampula province, April 1, 2001).

10. There are repeated examples of RENAMO sharing what it captured from attacks with the civilian population (interviews, Ribáuè District, Nampula province, April 1, 2, and 3, 2001; Marínguè district, Sofala province, May 19, 21, 24, 2001).

11. Former RENAMO combatants insisted that local commanders had no autonomy to mount their own attacks. One remarked that the soldiers would sit for weeks at a time, until word came from Gorongosa, after which an operation would be mounted within

days. Examples include interviews in Ribáuè district, Nampula province, March 31, April 2, and April 4, 2001; Marínguè district, Sofala province, May 19 and 21, 2001.

12. Units had members trained to handle the high-tech communications equipment. Regular updates were required with units required to provide significant details about their operations and attacks (interviews, Ribáuè district, Nampula province, March 27, 2001; Marínguè District, Sofala province, May 19 and 21, 2001).

13. When RENAMO arrived in Metaveia, the guerrillas asked the local population where to find the *régulo.* They explained their cause to him and asked for his support (and the support of the local spirits) to operate in the region. More practically, they asked the *régulo* to provide them with a geographical description of the surrounding areas (interview, Ribáuè district, Nampula province, April 1, 2001). In some cases, *régulos* didn't wait for RENAMO to arrive in their areas. A *régulo* in the Marínguè district described seeking out RENAMO to ask for their collaboration in fighting FRELIMO in his area (interview, Marínguè district, Sofala province, May 19, 2001).

14. We need to be clear that the partnership between *régulos* and RENAMO was a double-edged sword. In some places, the *régulo* brought RENAMO much-needed credibility and the population supported the partnership. In other places, the *régulo* lost his legitimacy with the local population by collaborating with the rebels. Finally, in an effort to manage the areas that they controlled, RENAMO sometimes elevated people to positions of traditional leadership, when it was not rightfully theirs, and this did little to build credibility with civilians. This elevation of non-*régulos* happened both in the Marínguè and Ribáuè districts.

15. Interviews, Ribáuè district, Nampula province, April 1 and 3, 2001; Marínguè district, Sofala province, May 21 and 24, 2001. One civilian insisted that the food system was proposed by the population to prevent the arbitrary practice of demanding food by soldiers individually. Others argued that it emerged from the RENAMO leadership (interview, Marínguè district, Sofala province, May 20, 2001).

16. In fact, many civilians did not report incidents of mistreatment to the commanders, fearing that the accused soldiers would emerge from the base and take retribution against them. This retribution actually happened, on occasion, demonstrating a further lack of control of soldiers' behavior within the RENAMO camp (interview, Marínguè district, Sofala province, May 22, 2001).

17. Stiff (1999) reports a story in which South African instructors staying at RENAMO's central base in Gorongosa awoke in the middle of the night to find a soldier stealing their supplies just outside their tent. Dhlakama was furious and told the instructors that the undisciplined soldier would be punished. The soldier was taken away but the South African instructors never learned what punishment was meted out.

18. Often, soldiers who committed "crimes" would be put in a prison-like facility within the RENAMO base (interview, Marínguè district, Sofala province, May 19, 2001).

19. A good example is the issue of rebels and women in the local villages. Authorities in RENAMO insist to this day that relations with women were prohibited for RENAMO soldiers. However, in practice, it was clear that RENAMO soldiers were permitted to have wives outside of the base. Punishment was applied only when soldiers brought women into the base (interview with a former captain in RENAMO's army, Marínguè district, Sofala province, May 18, 2001).

20. Although Mozambique is dominated by two major ethnic groups, the Makua-Lomwé (47 percent) and the Tsonga (23 percent), these major groups are highly fragmented. Experts suggest that the Mozambican population speaks at least 18 distinct languages, apart from Portuguese (the official language), making communication difficult even within ethnic groups. Further, Portuguese has never enabled groups to overcome these language boundaries; statistics show that only 6.5 percent of Mozambicans speak Portuguese with proficiency. Moreover, although political power has rested largely with the Tsonga of southern Mozambique, the founding members of RENAMO were from a small ethnic group, the Ndau, rather than the Makua-Lomwé (UNDP 2000).

21. RENAMO documents captured by the government in an attack on the main base at Gorongosa in 1985 provided detailed evidence of continued South African military assistance. The RENAMO leadership kept detailed notes of its meetings with the South African military leadership, recording the explicit promises of armaments and supplies and the timetable for airdrops. A combatant who fought in Nampula also described how supplies were delivered at least two times a year—by air—to RENAMO units in northern Mozambique (interview, Ribáuè district, Nampula province, March 30, 2001). His claims were supported in an interview in Marínguè as well (May 18, 2001).

22. This context stands in stark contrast with one in which rebel groups are unable to provide participants with any short-term payoffs to participation. Instead, promises are used to elicit cooperation. In such contexts, without resources of patrons to draw on, movements entail a far higher level of risk for potential recruits. Opportunistic joiners tend to be weeded out in the recruitment process (Weinstein 2003).

23. Each of these violations is defined in the codebook. The one violation which may not be immediately clear with readers is overkill. Overkill is coded for an incident in which bodies are excessively mutilated or destroyed in the course of killing or after the person is dead.

References

Alexander, Jocelyn. 1994. "Terra e autoridade política no pos-guerra em Moçambique: o caso da provincia de Manica." *Arquivo* 16.

Ball, Nicole, and Sam Barnes. 2000. "Mozambique." In *Good Intentions: Pledges of Aid for Post-Conflict Recovery,* ed. Shepard Forman and Stewart Patrick, 159–203. Boulder, CO: Lynne Rienner.

Bowen, Merle. 1989. "Peasant Agriculture in Mozambique: The Case of Chokwe, Gaza." *Canadian Journal of African Studies* 23 (3): 355–79.

——. 2000. *The State Against the Peasantry: Rural Struggles in Colonial and Post-colonial Mozambique.* Charlottesville: University of Virginia Press.

Cabrita, João. 2000. *Mozambique: The Torturous Road to Democracy.* Basingstoke: Palgrave.

Cawthra, Gavin. 1986. *Brutal Force: The Apartheid War Machine.* London: International Defence Aid Fund.

Coelho, João P. Borges. 1998. "State Resettlement Policies in Post-Colonial Rural Mozambique: The Impact of the Communal Village Program on Tete Province 1977–82." *Journal of Southern African Studies* 24 (1): 61–91.

Collier, Paul, and Anke Hoeffler. 2001. "Greed and Grievance in Civil War." Policy Research Working Paper 2355, World Bank, Washington, DC.

Collier, Paul, Anke Hoeffler, and Mans Soderbom. 2001. "On the Duration of Civil War." Policy Research Working Paper 2681, World Bank, Washington, DC.

Elbadawi, Ibrahim, and Nicholas Sambanis. 2000. "External Intervention and the Duration of Civil Wars." Policy Research Working Paper 2433, World Bank, Washington, DC.

Flower, Ken. 1987. *Serving Secretly: An Intelligence Chief on Record, Rhodesia Into Zimbabwe, 1964–1981.* London: John Murray.

Geffray, Christian. 1991. *A causa das armas: antropologia da guerra contemporânea em Moçambique.* Porto: Edições Afrontamento.

Geffray, Christian, and M. Pedersen. 1986. "Sobre a guerra na provincia de Nampula." *Revista Internacional de Estudos Africanos* 4–5.

Hall, Margaret, and Tom Young. 1997. *Confronting Leviathan: Mozambique since Independence.* Athens: Ohio University Press.

Hoile, David. 1994. *Mozambique, Resistance and Freedom: A Case for Reassessment.* London: Mozambique Institute.

Kalyvas, Stathis. 2000. "The Logic of Violence in Civil War." Unpublished manuscript.

Legrand, Jean-Claude. 1993. "Logique de guerre et dynamique de la violence en Zambézia, 1976–1991." *Politique Africaine* 50.

Lundin, Iraê B., and F. J. Machava (eds.). 1995. *Autoridade e poder tradicional, Vol. I.* Maputo: Ministério da Administração Estatal.

McGregor, Joanne. 1998. "Violence and Social Change in a Border Economy: War in the Maputo Hinterland, 1984–1992." *Journal of Southern African Studies* 24 (1): 37–60.

Minter, William. 1989. *The Mozambican National Resistance (RENAMO) as Described by Ex-Participants.* Report prepared for the Ford Foundation, Washington, DC.

——. 1995. *Apartheid's Contras: An Inquiry into the Roots of War in Angola and Mozambique.* London: Zed Books.

Moorcraft, Paul. 1994. *Africa Nemesis: War and Revolution in Southern Africa 1945–2010.* London: Brasseys.

Newitt, Malyn. 1995. *A History of Mozambique.* Bloomington: Indiana University Press.

Pereira, Fabião. 1999. "Historia social da guerra: camponeses, estado, guerra—estudo de caso de localidade administrativa de Mugeba." Unpublished thesis, Universidade Eduardo Mondlane.

Pitcher, M. Anne. 1998. "Disruption Without Transformation: Agrarian Relations and Livelihoods in Nampula Province, 1975–1995." *Journal of Southern African Studies* 24 (1): 115–140.

Stiff, Peter. 1999. *The Silent War: South African Recce Operations 1969–1994.* Alberton, South Africa: Gallagher Books.

UNDP (United Nations Development Program). 2000. Mozambique: Education and Human Development. Maputo: UNDP.

Vines, Alex. 1991. *RENAMO: Terrorism in Mozambique.* Bloomington: Indiana University Press.

——. 1998. "The Business of Peace: 'Tiny' Rowland, Financial Incentives, and the Mozambican Settlement." *The Mozambican Peace Process in Perspective.* Accord. Accessed at: http://www.c-r.org/accord/moz/accord3/index.shtml.

Weinstein, Jeremy. 2005. "Resources and the Information Problem in Rebel Recruitment." *Journal of Conflict Resolution,* Forthcoming.

Sudan's Civil War
Why Has It Prevailed for So Long?

7

ALI ABDEL GADIR ALI, IBRAHIM A. ELBADAWI,
AND ATTA EL–BATAHANI

"It is but the accident of Western rule that has brought peoples so completely different under one rule." *J. Spencer Trimingham, Secretary of the Church Missionary Society in Sudan*

"[T]he burden and incidence of neglect and oppression by successive Khartoum clique regimes has traditionally fallen more on the South than on other parts of the country. Under these circumstances, the marginal cost of rebellion in the South became very small, zero or negative; that is, in the South it pays to rebel." *John Garang de Mabior, Leader of SPLA/SPLM*[1]

Sudan has suffered two civil wars since independence. The first started in 1955 (but is usually coded in the literature as having started in the 1960s) and was settled in 1972. The peace that followed lasted a little more than a decade. The second war started in 1983 and is still ongoing (a peace agreement was reached in 2002). The two wars are not unrelated, and the peace interlude may have provided grounds for a better articulation of grievances from the first war.

Sudan's civil wars have been long and have caused untold suffering and destruction. Recent estimates suggest that more than

two million people have died as a result of the fighting over the past eighteen years; this includes victims of direct violence or conflict-related starvation and disease. Half a million refugees have spilled into neighboring countries, and roughly four million people have been displaced and driven from their homes within Sudan." (ICG 2002, 3–4).

Moreover, the economic cost of just four years (1986–90) of violence during a period of high-intensity conflict is estimated to have reduced national investment (relative to potential under normal conditions) by two thirds, and gross domestic product (GDP) by a cumulative rate of 8 percent (Elbadawi 1999).

Many historical narratives of the Sudanese wars have demonstrated that the preconditions for war were overly abundant, so there is little need to provide another such narrative here. This chapter, therefore, focuses on the most devastating characteristics of the Sudanese civil war: its intractability, long duration, and ethnoreligious character, "pitting Animist and Christian Southern Sudanese against the Moslem Arab and Arabized North Sudan."[2] As such, the analysis of this chapter is based on the strand of the literature that analyzes the duration and prevalence of conflicts (e.g., Elbadawi and Sambanis 2000, 2002) rather than focuses only on the onset of war (the Collier-Hoeffler [CH] model).

We begin with a historical overview of the country's recent colonial history. We then analyze the organization and growth of the rebel movement, focusing on the war of 1983, and explain the war's long duration. Models of the onset and continuation (prevalence) of civil war can explain the high risk of war in Sudan if they take into account the fundamental polarization between the North and the South. The North-South divide dominates Sudanese politics, despite substantial cultural and ethnic diversity, and explains the extensive external intervention in the Sudanese civil war. The combination of polarization and external intervention explains the higher risk of war in Sudan, compared with the median Sub-Saharan African country.

Background to the Conflict

The civil war in Sudan started prior to the country's independence during the last days of the Anglo-Egyptian colonial administration (1898–1956). Ali and Matthews (1999, 193) describe the atmosphere during these tragic days:

> Societal anxieties and tensions, coupled with administrative overreaction and ineptness, created a highly volatile situation in southern Sudan. Violence erupted in 1955, when the [southern part of the][3] Torit garrison mutinied and was joined by [southern] civilians, police and prison guards. For about two weeks, Equatoria Province [in southern Sudan] became the dying fields for northerners, most of whom were civilians, including women and children. Government punishment was brutal, though many mutineers had fled into the bush or to neighboring countries.

This tragic massacre, and what was perceived as a miscarriage of justice by the northern-dominated administration following the event, set the stage for a civil war that has devastated the country for all but 11 years (1972–83) of its independence since January 1956. Two key questions are: Why did such massive violence erupt around the period of de-colonization? And why was the war so protracted?

The literature on the Sudanese conflict suggests that history matters, especially recent colonial history prior to independence (e.g., Ali and Matthews 1999; Alier 1990; Beshir 1968, 1969). We review in detail the Southern Policy (SP) of the colonial administration, indicating how the SP shaped the initial conditions of the conflict. These initial conditions made Sudan ripe for a civil war, as would be predicted by the recent theoretical and empirical rational choice literature on civil war initiation. Our analytical review of the background of the civil war focuses on the implicit and explicit policies that insulated the South from the North. The SP had the fundamental objective of keeping the two entities apart while they were under one colonial administration and, thus, to facilitate the eventual partitioning of the country prior to independence. The South was to be integrated into East Africa when Sudan attained independence.

Just eight years before independence, the SP was reversed, but this reversal came after the SP had already divided the country for more than 40 years. When the SP was abandoned, the two entities were already drifting apart, having developed different "identities" and different rates of socioeconomic development, and the South was marginalized relative to the North. The new policy of unity was institutionalized in two major events associated with the Sudanese conflict. The first event was the first formal conference to be held under the auspices of the colonial government in 1947 in the southern capital of Juba, between representatives of the North and the South to discuss the future of the country. The second event was the "Independence Motion and Resolution" in Sudan's first parliament in 1955.

The Southern Policy

Most writers on the civil war in Sudan agree that the origin of the war is linked to the ill-fated Southern Policy of the colonial administration of Sudan over the period 1920–47. We now examine the implications of three aspects of the SP in more detail: the insulation of the South and the "closed districts" ordinance; educational policy; and development policy.

According to Beshir (1968), following the reconquest of Sudan in 1898 the British administration faced two urgent tasks in the South of the country: the establishment of an administrative system and the pacification of hostile tribes.[4] As in many other African colonies, the philosophy adopted for administering the country was that of "indirect rule," interpreted by Beshir (1968, 37) as "implying the protection of people against change," where the administration was left to the native authorities under the supervision of the government.[5] This applied equally to the North and the South. There is evidence that prior to 1920 there was no deliberate policy to separate the South from the North, although a number of steps were taken that had this effect: (a) reducing the demonstration effect of northern Muslim traders in various southern communities with the aim of curtailing the spread of Arabic as lingua franca; (b) the establishment of the Equatoria Corps as a southern military force composed of southern soldiers in 1917 as a counterweight to potential Arab rebellion in Sudan; (c) the recognition of Sunday as the official day of rest throughout the South in 1918; and (d) the adoption of English as the official language of the South in 1918.

A deliberate policy to separate the South from the North, on ethnic grounds, can be traced to a number of memoranda on the subject written in 1921 (Beshir 1968,

1969). Thus, for example, in one of these the Sudanese government noted that "the possibility of the southern (black) portion of the Sudan being eventually cut off from the northern (Arab) area and linked up with some central African system should be borne in mind." In another memorandum, the government suggested that the South "would have, eventually, to be assimilated to the government of other African possessions, such as Uganda and East Africa" contingent on the development of a Central African Federation.

Another important aspect of the SP was educational policy, which was designed to augment other measures of the colonial rule aimed at strengthening the divide between North and South. The dependence on missionary education in the South has not only meant a radically different educational system from that in the North, but also more limited access to education for those living in the South. According to a 1921 report by the Governor-General, education policy in the South was "not to substitute a government system of education for the missionary schools, but rather to attempt the regulation of the Missionary Societies along lines to be of more immediate benefit to government" (Beshir 1968). A system of grants-in-aid was devised and missionary elementary schools for boys increased from four, with 630 boys in 1926, to 33, with 3,103 boys in 1932.[6] In 1928 a new language policy was adopted according to which six language groups (Dinka, Bari, Nuer, Latuka, Shilluk, and Zande) were used in instruction in schools.

Apart from the restrictions on trade and labor mobility embodied in the various orders noted above, the Southern Policy did not have any declared economic development objectives. In the meantime, the two parts of the country were drifting further apart in terms of economic development in view of the huge investment in irrigated agriculture and the relatively large investment in transportation in the North. The motivation for investment in irrigated agriculture was not, however, a deliberate policy to develop the North in preference to the South, but rather to make the colony pay for itself. In the meantime, economic development projects in the South were limited to small rubber, cotton, and coffee-growing plantations; these plantations were established in the 1920s. The authorities in the South, similarly to their counterparts in other African colonies, had perverse ideas about economic and social development. The Governor of the Upper Nile province in his 1925 report noted that to

> provide means for the present generation to acquire sufficient wealth to enable them to obtain all the various luxuries civilization brings and to make it possible for such comparative wealth to be easily gained, would in my opinion, be disastrous. For this reason I am anxious that the price given for cotton should not be too high. (quoted in Beshir 1968, 44–45).

Reversal of the Southern Policy

During the early 1940s, the SP attracted a lot of criticism as the North was moving toward self-government and people were being trained for government positions.

In 1946, the old policy, aiming at separating the South from the North, was reversed.[7] The official statement of the new SP reads as follows:

[W]e should now work on the assumption that the Sudan, as at present constituted, with possibly minor boundary adjustment, will remain one: and we
should therefore restate our Southern Policy and do so publicly, as follows:"the
policy of the Sudan government regarding the Southern Sudan is to act upon
the fact that the peoples of the Southern Sudan are distinctively African and
Negroid, but that geography and economics combine (so far as can be fore-
seen at the present time) to render them inextricably bound for future development to the middle-eastern and arabized Northern Sudan: and therefore to
ensure that they shall, by educational and economic development, be equipped
to stand up for themselves in the future as socially and economically the equals
of their partners of the Northern Sudan in the Sudan of the future." (Beshir
1968, 119–21).

The reaction to the new SP by British administrators working in the South was
varied.[8] However, almost all of the reactions expressed the need for safeguards for the
South until it was able to stand on its feet to deal with the relatively more sophisticated North. Ideas of regional autonomy or federation were circulated.

The Juba Conference

Having made the decision to cast the future lot of the South with the North, the
central government went ahead with preparations for a Legislative Assembly for
the country. In 1947, a Sudan Administrative Conference was held to deal with the
issue of associating the South with the central and local government and its representation in the proposed Legislative Assembly. Despite the concerns just discussed,
the Juba Conference endorsed the new SP of forging a united Sudan. Naturally,
neither the new SP nor the outcome of the Juba Conference was acceptable to a
number of groups, including the missionaries.

According to the southern Sudanese account of the events, the agreement on a
united Sudan was conditional on explicit safeguards (Malwal 1987, 10), including:
(a) demand by southerners for the respect, preservation, and promotion of southern
cultures (languages, traditions, and heritage); (b) reconciliation over a blotted history
of relations between the two regions and commitment to equality for all citizens
in future Sudan; (c) racial equality; (d) promotion of accelerated educational and
economic development in the South; and (e) involvement of southerners in the
administration of the country at the national level coupled with self-rule in southern Sudan.

The critical issue here is not whether these concerns were formally enshrined in
the Juba agreement, but that they reflected the southern perspective of the events leading to independence. Again Malwal (1987, 10) argues that this was a "call by southerners for safeguards, in essence to preserve diversity and accelerated socioeconomic

development in the southern Sudan." He emphasizes that these safeguards were "endorsed by northern representatives at the conference," and characterizes them as having, "set the tone, the parameters, and the content of Sudanese national unity."

The Declaration of Independence and After

Between the Juba Conference and the declaration of independence by the Sudanese Parliament in January 1956, the Torit massacre and the subsequent reprisal had substantially damaged the relationship between North and South. In addition, the limited progress in the safeguards of 1947 did not inspire confidence. Against this background, southern representatives in the parliament demanded a pledge be made to establish a federal system of government in the future in return for their agreement to the declaration of independence. They received the consent of their northern colleagues to this proposal.

The account of the subsequent developments leading to the launch of the civil war from a southern Sudanese perspective is succinctly argued by Malwal (1987). He notes that the federal pledge was never considered by the northern-dominated governments during the period 1956–72, prior to the Addis Ababa agreement of 1972. Instead, he contends that the call for federation by southern Sudanese was construed by postindependence governments as a pretext for separation and that penal sanctions were imposed on those who stood for the federal principle. This led several political leaders and intellectuals to take refuge in neighboring countries and many of them joined the military personnel who fled the country after Torit to launch the insurgency. Moreover, according to Malwal, the attempt by the northern governments to promote the dominant religion and language in a "vain and costly effort to establish a nation state of cultural and religious homogeneity in the place of one of diversity" only exacerbated the grievances of the southern Sudanese. In the meantime, the already large gap of economic and social disparity between the two regions was allowed to increase even further.

The war can be explained both by an "opportunity cost" argument and "ethno-religious grievance" argument. The conflict has always focused on fundamental differences in culture, religion, and identity because the southern Sudanese resent the cultural, religious, and political hegemony of the North. But the substantial economic marginalization of the South in an already poor country also lends credence to the view that rebellion has had little or no opportunity cost for southerners.

External support has also been critical for both the onset and duration of the war. Support offered to the rebels by some of Sudan's neighbors has been partly motivated by sympathy with the rebels' cause, but it has also been influenced by the fact that these countries were largely undemocratic, with few constraints in meddling in each others' civil wars. The rebels have also received support from Christian missionaries and from nonneighboring countries motivated by strategic concerns or religious ties. On the other hand, a few Arab countries have supported various Sudanese governments.

As we will show next, most causes of civil war found in the literature seem relevant as explanations of the Sudanese civil war.

The Making of a Rebel Movement: SPLA/M

The emergence of the Sudan People's Liberation Army/Movement (SPLA/M) since 1983 stems from disillusionment with the regime. The experience of the earlier insurgency (Anyanya Movement: 1960–72) has also shaped the structure and dynamics of SPLA/M, as many in the SPLA fought in the Anyanya war.

The Anyanya movement emerged in the early 1960s as a loose alliance between army mutineers and politically active southern Sudanese, united against what they perceived as the hegemony of northern elites in newly independent Sudan. These groups nevertheless operated under dispersed and informal authority, at least throughout the 1960s. Factional fighting and lack of strong military command beset this movement. More importantly, because of its overt secessionist agenda, it failed to cultivate robust and steady external alliances, especially from neighboring African countries; some of these countries, like Ethiopia, were trying to cope with their own secessionist movements. Despite intense grievances, factional conflict and limited external support prevented the Anyanya movement from mobilizing a sufficiently large force to mount high-intensity warfare throughout the 1960s.

In the 1970s, however, the emergence of Israel as a military supplier and the ability of the military wing of the movement to consolidate power under one military leader, Joseph Lagu, allowed for the projection of a coordinated military campaign in the field for the first time since the launching of the insurgency (Johnson 1998). This enhanced military capability of the Anyanya movement partly contributed to the conditions leading to the peace agreement in 1972.

Origin of the SPLA/M

Following the end of the first civil war in 1972 and the signing of the peace treaty between the Nimeri regime and the Anyanya movement, Sudan entered into a peaceful period. However, political miscalculations by the Nimeri regime and the gross economic mismanagement of the peace dividend generated many grievances among southern Sudanese civil servants, students, and the military in the barracks, including former rebels subsequently absorbed into the army.

By the early 1980s, some rebels of the old Anyanya movement formed the "Anyanya 2" movement as an articulation of the widespread southern disenchantment with the peace process. However, armed insurrections remained isolated incidents that did not threaten the political grip of the Southern Regional Government in Juba (the capital of the South). It took a mutiny by two battalions in three Sudanese Army garrisons in southern Sudan (Bor, Ayod, and Pibor) in mid-1983 to provide the trigger event that heralded the outbreak of the present war, and the formation of SPLA/M.

Unlike Anyanya, the SPLA/M became a melting pot for all southern tribal differences and tensions. For the first time, many different groups were able to coalesce around a national objective. Whether this objective was expressed in the form of one united Sudan or "New Sudan" did not matter much to them. In terms of political and military organization and articulation of the political question, the SPLA/M was a better organized political and military instrument compared to Anyanya 2. It was the first armed group to be established by the people against the regime that also maintained deep tribal and sectional cleavages within its ranks.

In Equatoria, there was initially marked hostility toward the SPLA/M, especially at the level of the political leadership of the region. The SPLA/M was perceived as a Nilotic or Dinka movement whose objective was to reverse the division of the southern region, and to destroy the Equatoria region and impose Dinka hegemony. However, the organization received some support, especially among the people of the eastern banks of the White Nile. This occurred in spite of the fact that the Equatoria regional government's propaganda was directed against the SPLA/M. Nevertheless, Equatorians joined the SPLA/M in the tens of thousands.

Thus, by the time Nimeri decreed the division of the southern region, and imposed the *Sharia* laws,[9] he had offended nearly all the sections of South Sudanese society and prepared fertile ground for the war of national liberation. Many South Sudanese joined the SPLA/M to complete what the South Sudan Liberation Movement and the Anyanya had left unfinished in the 17-year war: the independence of South Sudan. By the beginning of 1983, the die was already cast in that southern Sudanese of different walks of life had already made their decision to join the liberation struggle.

In addition to attempting to minimize the tribal cleavages that beset the Anyanya movement, the SPLA/M leadership also internalized other lessons from the old insurgency. This leadership, which was mainly made up of army officers, moved quickly to establish a strong military structure and arranged robust external support, most notably from the Derg regime in Ethiopia. By eschewing the secessionist agenda of the Anyanya and instead espousing the ideal of a "new" united Sudan, the SPLA/M facilitated this support. This seemed to be a departure from the southern Sudanese elites' preferred solution to the problem of southern Sudan. From the start, the SPLA/M had declared that its overarching goal was the national "liberation" of Sudan and the establishment of a secular, socialist, and united Sudan. Despite the fact that some of its objectives kept changing, one objective remained constant: *changing the power structure at the center.* Moreover, to strengthen its appeal to the Mengistu Derg regime, the SPLA/M ascribed to socialist ideology. The movement quickly escalated violence to generate significant political and military impact and increase its external support.[10]

Leadership of the SPLA/M

Although it was senior and junior army officers who initiated the rebellion, the rebel leadership also later attracted many politicians, intellectuals, university lecturers, and students. Although the members of the Political-Military High Command, the highest institution of the SPLA/M, were mainly former military officers of the Sudanese army, it was presumed to represent a combination of political and military groups. However, subsequent developments in the movement and interventions by the main foreign sponsor, the Ethiopian regime, in the 1980s, tilted the balance of forces and eventually enabled the military officers to gain absolute dominance in the leadership.

This "militarization" of the movement resulted in an elitist vanguard whose members monopolized decision making and concentrated all powers in the hands of the person at the top. In the absence of collective leadership and accountability, the SPLA/M was slowly transformed into an autocracy. The ascension of Dr. John Garang de Mabior to the leadership of the SPLA/M was representative of this trend.[11]

Recruits were mainly drawn from the Dinka, the major ethnic-tribal group in the South. The leadership also accommodated representatives from other tribal and ethnic groups in the South and other marginalized areas in Sudan (the Nuba Mountains, the Ingessana, the Fung, the Beja, and Darfur). Its attempt to reach out to marginalized groups in the Muslim North and its professed commitment to the unity of Sudan set the SPLA/M apart from its predecessor, the Anyanya, which was openly secessionist. However, the SPLA/M also remained an overwhelmingly southern movement fighting an essentially "ethnic" civil war aimed at reshaping the Sudan in its own image.

SPLA as a Fighting Force

After the resolution of the leadership contest in the SPLA/M, the movement's first task was the reorganization and arming of the remnants of Battalions 104 and 105 (the two battalions that deserted from the Sudanese Army), and elements of Anyanya 2, which now formed the nucleus of the SPLA. The first wave of recruits, mostly secondary and university students and office workers, were given intensive training to form the Buffalo Battalion (1983). As time passed and the insurrection gained momentum, the Jarad Division graduated (1984), followed by the Mour Mour (1985), Kazuk (1986), Zaizal (1987), Intifadha (1988), and Intisar Divisions (1989). These were major divisions of the SPLA, composed of more than 15,000 officers and men.[12]

These divisions had graduated from the SPLA training camp in Ethiopia. There were auxiliary training camps in several locations, as well as mobile camps. The SPLA, by its definition, is a peasant army made up of volunteers. Apart from the initial tribal and other tensions, the members of the SPLA were propelled into action by nationalist and patriotic sentiments nurtured by deep-seated grievances. Its training was rigorous and the conditions in the training camps were severe and harsh. Nevertheless, the morale of the SPLA men and officers was very high, and this grew with every operational victory and its coverage by the international media. The frequency and pace of its military victories against the Nimeri regime, whose image and credibility were on the decline internationally as a result of the imposition of the *Sharia* and other oppressive laws, boosted the image and credibility of the SPLA.

Therefore, the SPLA grew rapidly in numerical and military strength. By 1991, and despite the breaking away of a splinter group from the main movement, the SPLA forces numbered between 100,000 and 120,000. The SPLA engaged the Sudanese army and its militia and scored remarkable victories. By 1990, the stretch of territory east of the Nile River, from the international borders with Kenya and Uganda up to the mouth of Sobat River, was under the control of the SPLA. The whole of western Equatoria, with the exception of Yei, Rokon, Terrikeka, and Juba towns, was administered by the SPLA. In rural Bahr el Ghazal, the SPLA controlled all the land routes.

However, the SPLA experienced a series of military defeats in the early 1990s, following the collapse of the Mengistu regime in Ethiopia, which had been the main foreign sponsor of the SPLA. There was also the split of a major faction from the movement, and the aggressive military campaign of the new "Islamist" military regime, which was determined to put an end to the conflict by imposing a crushing military defeat on the SPLA. However, the movement was able to restructure quickly the SPLA and reestablish external alliances with other neighboring countries, most notably Uganda, as well as northern Sudanese opposition parties. In a few years, the SPLA regained all of its lost territory. Moreover, through alliances with other marginalized minorities in the North, the SPLA managed, for the first time, to establish a presence in areas outside the historical region of southern Sudan. The leadership was thus able to restructure the SPLA into a "mobile" force of national character, and to mount a creative and flexible approach for cultivating local grievances (Johnson 1998).

Predation, Criminality, and Problems of Civil Administration

The positive image of the SPLA projected by its military victories and its politico-ideological agenda did not last long before it was tarnished by the behavior and conduct of some of its officers and men. At the early stages of the movement, reckless behavior had complicated the movement's goal of winning over the local population and establishing efficient civil administration in the areas under its control.

Again, according to an insider account (Nyaba 2000), "the SPLA/M, instead of being a genuine national liberation movement, degenerated into an agent of plunder, pillage and destructive conquest."[13] Also, according to Nyaba, these counter-productive acts could be explained by the goal of massive recruitment set by SPLA/M in its early stages:

> . . . accordingly, people of all walks of life flocked into the SPLA/M. Thieves, murderers, rapists and fugitives from the Sudanese justice system found a safe haven in the SPLA, and when an opportunity arose, they easily relapsed into their old practices. Many of the horrendous crimes committed against the civilian population were attributed to some of these social misfits masquerading as "revolutionaries." (Nyaba 2000)

Moreover, the absence of a program for reconstruction and rehabilitation and the failure to convert military victories into a political program for social and economic transformation were reflected by the continued dependence on external resources provided by relief agencies. This humanitarian aid relationship between the providers of relief aid and the receivers induced and reproduced the dependency syndrome in many communities in South Sudan.

The complete neglect of social and economic functions by the liberation movement meant that the SPLA could not rely on provisions from the people. Resources had to be imported. They could only be acquired from international humanitarian agencies, but since humanitarian assistance is only provided for the needy civilian population, the task of distribution of this assistance fell on specially selected SPLA officers and men who saw to it that the bulk of the supplies went to the army. Even in cases in which the expatriate relief monitors were strict and only distributed relief supplies to the civilians by day, the SPLA would retrieve that food by night. The result of this practice led to the absolute marginalization and brutalization of the civilian population.

Over time, the movement made considerable progress in addressing its failures in civil administration, leading to the emergence of a functioning civil authority in SPLA-held territory and a steady decline in the earlier egregious looting and human rights violations by the rebel army. The success of the SPLA in controlling large sections of the rural population is largely due to its success in civil administration (Johnson 1998).[14]

Duration of the Civil War

The civil war in Sudan is the longest running war in Africa, engulfing almost the entire history of postcolonial Sudan. Why has the war persisted for so long?

To address this question, we explore the determinants of war risk at every period. Consistent with the analytical literature on war initiation (e.g., Collier and Hoeffler 2004; Hegre et al. 2001) and war duration (Collier, Hoeffler, and Soderbom 2004), Elbadawi and Sambanis posit a model of war prevalence[15] that assumes that (a) economic development (high initial per capita income and low dependence on primary commodities) is negatively and significantly associated with civil war prevalence; (b) democracy reduces the prevalence of civil war; and (c) ethnic fractionalization is positively and nonmonotonically associated with civil war prevalence. This model suggests that ethnic polarization, rather than ethnic diversity, tends to be associated with high risk of conflict. The predictions of this model were strongly corroborated by the data on Sudan.

Another important factor, especially for Sudan, is external intervention. Intervention prolongs civil war duration (Elbadawi and Sambanis 2000; Regan 1996, 2000).[16] The weaker party is usually the main beneficiary of external interventions, which tip the military balance in its favor, diminishing the chance of a quick end to the war. Thus, we combine the prevalence model (Elbadawi and Sambanis 2002) with the external intervention model (Elbadawi and Sambanis 2000) to compute the risk of war onset and continuation in Sudan, once we take into account the effects of external intervention.

To summarize, there are several possible determinants of the risk of war onset and continuation in Sudan: social polarization and external interventions, as well as the economic and political preconditions discussed previously. Economically, the South was marginalized before the first war in 1956 and has been further marginalized since then. The CH model's focus on economic factors seems applicable to both insurgencies. But the CH model must be expanded to take into account other factors. Our analysis shows that the religious and cultural polarization between North and South better explains the protracted conflict in Sudan than the overall diversity in the country. This North-South polarization has also generated an ideological polarization and has invited external intervention.

Economic Preconditions

At independence in January 1956, Sudan's GDP was estimated as amounting to Sudanese pound (Ls) 284 million (US$795 million). Per capita GDP amounted to Ls 28 or about US$78, classifying Sudan among the poorest countries in the world. The South fared much worse than the northern regions with a per capita GDP of about Ls 14 (US$39), reflecting years of neglect and marginalization during the colonial period. Moreover, with agriculture accounting for 60 percent of the national economy and for 72 percent of the economy of South Sudan at independence, there was a clear dependence on natural resources. At independence, educational attainment in Sudan was very low, even by African standards, with average years of schooling at just 0.4 years. Still, educational attainment in the South was significantly lower than the national average.

In addition to these economic risk factors for civil war, other environmental variables in the CH model might have increased the hazard of civil war at independence. The vast and sparsely populated land area of the country could be an "environmental" factor contributing to higher probability of a civil war. As a measure of geographic dispersion, Sudan has a Gini coefficient of 38 percent compared with an African Gini coefficient of 55 percent. Moreover, other literature suggests that regional democracy and regional peace exert a moderating influence on the probability of civil wars in any given country in that region (Sambanis 2001). The evidence makes clear that the neighbors of Sudan have been neither democratic nor peaceful (Ali, Elbadawi, and El-Batahani, 2002).

In 1972, an end to the first civil war was achieved as a result of the Addis Ababa peace agreement between the main insurgency movement (Anyanya) and the military regime of General Nimeri. The achievement of peace served Sudan and the Nimeri regime well. For most of the 11 peaceful years (1972–83) Sudan's economy grew by more than 8 percent and substantial investment flowed into Sudan, including some to the South to finance postconflict reconstruction. The oil-exporting Arab countries provided substantial portions of these funds, following a "bread basket" strategy that they hoped would create a substantial agro-industrial base in Sudan. This was a pan-Arab strategy developed after the post-1973 oil boom and was designed to fill the food gap in the Arab world. This opportunity was squandered, however, and the growth spell gave way to a deep economic crisis that required economic adjustment under the auspices of the World Bank and the International Monetary Fund (IMF). If anything, these adjustments further deepened the crisis (e.g., Ali 1986). The economic crisis has contributed, at least indirectly, to the collapse of peace. Economic mismanagement and the ensuing economic crisis undermined the peace by encouraging autocratic governance.

At the level of the regional government in the South, plans for accelerated development of the economy did not proceed well. For example, during the five fiscal years 1972/73 to 1976/77 following the peace agreement, a "special development" budget of Ls 38.3 million was approved. However, implementation of the planned budget was very poor, averaging less than 20 percent (Yongo-Bure 1987). The same story could be told about implementation of investment projects in the South, as part of the national six-year economic and social development plan (1977/78–1982/83). If successfully implemented, this plan would have helped consolidate the cause of peace; the plan targeted the South and other marginalized regions of the country. It is not surprising that, prior to the start of the insurgency, the South remained very marginalized. For example, out of 5,912 public primary schools in the country in 1980/82, only 10 percent were in the South; and the shares of the South in public intermediate and secondary schools were even less at 7 and 8 percent, respectively.

Polarization and Political Institutions

We have so far described Sudan as a polarized society because of the ethnocultural and religious differences between North and South. This polarization implies that any war that pits the South against a northern–dominated government is bound to be an ethnic war or a "war of visions," as argued by a leading Sudanese scholar (Deng 1995).

At independence, the first population census of Sudan enumerated eight major ethnic groups comprising Arabs, Beja, Nubiyin, Southern Nilotic, Southern Nilo-Hamitic, Southern Sudanic, and Westerners. The distribution of population among these groups is given in table 7.1, where the number of specific ethnic groups is indicated.

Excluding foreigners, Sudanese with Arab origins constituted about 39.88 percent of the total population of Sudan in 1956. By comparison, Sudanese people of African origin had a 30.12 percent share of the total population. Excluding foreigners, an ethnic polarization index[17] of 0.625 is calculated for the country. If a polarization index in excess of 0.5 is considered high, then clearly Sudan is an ethnically polarized country.

Estimates of the religious composition of the population at independence distinguish three major religions: Christianity (mostly Catholic in the South), Islam, and indigenous beliefs (mostly in the South). Approximately 2.24 percent of the population followed the Christian faith, whereas 72.88 percent were Muslims. The balance of the population, 24.88 percent, followed indigenous beliefs. This yields a (high) religious polarization index of 0.7642 for Sudan at independence. More recent

Table 7.1 Population of Sudan by Major Ethnic Groups in 1956

Major ethnic group	Number of groups	Population	Share of population (%)	Comments
Arab	12	3,989,533	38.87	Major tribes include Baggara, Dar Hamid, Gawana'a-Budeiriya, Shukriya, Ga'aliyin, and Guhayna. Classification includes a specific group of "unknown."
Nuba	8	572,935	5.58	Specific groups relate to geographical locations in addition to Nuba-Mesiriya and a specific group of "unknown."
Beja	6	645,703	6.29	
Nubiyin	1	330,032	3.22	
Mainly Nilotic	9	1,982,503	19.32	Major tribes include Dinka-North Eastern, Dinka-Rweng, Dinka-Bor, Dinka-South Western, Fung tribes, Nuer. Classification includes "other Nilotic tribes" and "unknown."
Mainly Nilo-Hamitic	5	548,593	5.35	Major tribal groups include Ethiopian tribes, Bari speaking, Latuka speaking, Didinga speaking, and "others."
Mainly Sudanic	6	481,764	4.69	Major tribes include Moru–Madi, Bongo–Baka-Bgirma, Ndogo-Sere, Zande, "other," and "unknown."
Westerners	4	1,358,637	13.24	Includes tribes of western Darfur, French equatorial tribes, Nigerian tribes, and "unknown."
Foreigners with Status	NA	52,622	0.51	
Foreigners with no Status	NA	206,517	2.01	
Miscellaneous	2	93,695	0.91	People with no known tribe.
Total	53	10,262,536	100.00	

Source: Balamoan (1981, p. 152, table 35).
Note: NA = not applicable.

estimates, for 1995, place the population shares of the three major beliefs at 70 percent Muslims, 25 percent followers of indigenous beliefs, and 5 percent Christians. Thus, in 1995 the religious polarization index had increased to 0.785. The average for the period 1960–95 can be taken as 0.7746. The modified Esteban and Ray religious polarization index is 0.7496 for 1955 and 0.6994 for 1995 and thus the average for the period 1960–99 is 0.7245.

According to the most recent available information, the number of living languages in Sudan is 134. Linguistic studies show that the 1,500 African languages belong to five families: Afro-Asiatic, Nilo-Saharan, Niger-Congo, Khoisan, and Austronesian.[18] Sudan's languages belong to the first three families (population percentages are given in parentheses): 6 Afro-Asiatic (73.24 percent), 83 Nilo-Saharan (22.45 percent), and 45 Niger-Congo (4.31 percent). On the basis of this pattern of linguistic division, we can compute a linguistic polarization index of 0.738 for Sudan, indicating that the country is fairly polarized. If we measured linguistic diversity using the ethnolinguistic fractionalization (ELF) index,[19] the index value would be 0.41, which is consistent with high polarization.[20]

We have argued that some of this polarization was the result of the Southern Policy, which increased the cultural and religious differences between North and South. The civil war hardened these differences. Thus, polarization in Sudan is the joint outcome of cultural difference and politics and ideology and has evolved over time as the result of discriminatory governance that has victimized the South at the expense of the North.

Since independence, three major social groups have had the greatest influence in Sudan's politics and society: religious leaders, tribal leaders, and merchants. The emergence of the power of religious leaders was due to historical factors relating to the domination of religious life in northern society by Muslim Sufi religious orders, as well as to the indirect-rule policy of the colonial state. In the 16th to the 18th centuries, religious leaders consolidated their economic position by mobilizing small savings from their followers. The Mahdist revolution was the culmination of such Sufi influence on northern political, social, and economic life. Therefore, at independence, the most prominent political parties originated from religious orders. This historical precondition defines two important features of Sudanese politics, both linked to the civil war and the social divide between the two parts of the country.

First, the dominant political parties have essentially been confined to the North and have not yet been able to penetrate the South. Moreover, the fact that the two dominant parties consistently managed to muster more than 75 percent of the parliamentary seats meant that political bargaining processes were essentially determined by the northern parties.

Second, the capture of the postindependence Sudanese state by economic elites (with their religious followers) and the desire of these elites to maintain their monopoly on power partly explain the involvement of the military in the politics of the country. Over the period 1956 to the present, Sudan has had six alternating democratic and military regimes (see table 7.2). The military regimes have ruled during more than 70 percent of the postindependence era. Military rule has been devastat-

Table 7.2 Political Regimes in Sudan 1956–2001

Period	Regime type	Duration in months	Participation
January 1, 1956– November 16, 1958	Parliamentary- Democratic	35	Multiparty Bicameral Parliament
November 16, 1959– October 25, 1964	Military (Generals)	71	No Parties Single- Chamber Assembly
October 26, 1964– May 24, 1969	Parliamentary- Democratic	55	Multiparty Single- Chamber Parliament
May 25, 1969– April 5, 1984	Military (Young Officers)	178	One Party Single- Chamber Assembly
April 6, 1984– June 30, 1989	Parliamentary- Democratic	63	Multiparty Single- Chamber Parliament
June 30, 1989– Present	Military- Civilian	78	One Party Single- Chamber Assembly
Total	—	480	—

Source: Authors' compilation.

ing for the Sudan. It is associated with intensified violence in the civil war, and it has blocked various social groups from the institutionalized bargaining process available under democracy. It is not surprising, therefore, that under military regimes the political discourse descends to subnational (tribal and regional) levels. This appears to have reached a low point in the current military regime following the split in the ruling party.[21] Not surprisingly, the post–1983 grievance discourse by the rebel movement has been couched in terms of overcoming the problems created by the ruling elites.[22]

External Intervention

The Sudanese civil war is not seen just as a Sudanese conflict, but is rather described in more general terms as a conflict between Arabs fighting against Christians and Animists. This has led to several external interventions by third parties who feel that the war has important implications for their own societies (see figure 7.1). Some Christian organizations consider the war as an attempt to assert cultural and religious hegemony by the Arabized North. The war has also attracted the interest of Israel and several Arab and African countries as well as the United States since the 1990s.

According to a global index on the extent of external interventions in civil wars by third parties (developed by Patrick Regan), the civil wars in Sudan have experienced a relatively high degree of external intervention. The extent of external interventions in the second insurgency has been particularly high.[23] In both Sudanese wars, external intervention played an important role in the organization and financing of rebel movements. Neighboring countries acted on their own or as a proxy for distant powers in their interventions.[24] According to Human Rights Watch (1998), Ethiopia, Uganda, and Eritrea have all been involved in support of the SPLA/M. Until 1991, Ethiopia provided the main launching and training grounds and mili-

Figure 7.1 External Interventions in African Civil Wars by Regional and Global Third Parties

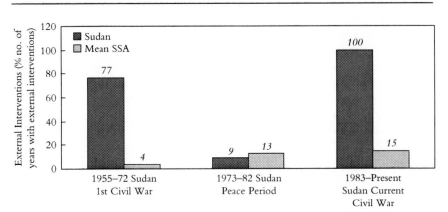

Note: Based on Regan (2000) data on external intervention, which covers economic, military, and mixed interventions. A country in a civil war is coded as experiencing intervention only if the extent of intervention surpasses a certain threshold. SSA = Sub-Saharan Africa.

tary supplies for the SPLA/M. Since the demise of the Mengistu regime and until 1995, the rebel movement lost the support of Ethiopia. Eritrea offered training bases in its western region starting in 1995 and publicly supported Sudan opposition forces; Eritrea also gave the National Democratic Alliance official headquarters. Similarly, Uganda supported the SPLA by providing access to arms and at "times sending its own troops across the Sudan border in military campaigns involving actual combat" (Human Rights Watch 1998, 47). The United States was also found to be involved in the conflict, albeit through proxies.[25]

The Empirics of Civil War

Before we analyze the relative contributions of the above factors in explaining the prevalence of civil wars in Sudan, we compare the estimated probability of prevalence under two approaches to social fractionalization in Sudan. One approach would be to adopt the relatively high index of ELF (equal to 73 percent), which is higher than the African median of 66 percent. This would suggest that Sudan has a diverse society. As we argued previously, this view, however, does not account for the fundamental cultural and ethnic divide that exists between the northern and southern parts of the country. According to this view, although both parts of the country are very diverse, the dominant factor affecting the prevalence of war is the social polarization between North and South. Therefore, the measure of ELF that is most relevant for the analysis should be based on the approximate population share of southern and northern Sudanese. According to 1983 population data, the shares should be 0.25[26] for the South and 0.75 for the North. These shares would produce an ELF equal to 38 percent.

Figure 7.2 provides the predicted probabilities under the "polarization" and the "diversity" cases for three periods covering part of the first civil war, the short-lived peace, and the ongoing second civil war. The polarization case resulted in predicted probabilities of 0.75 for the first civil war, 0.70 for the second, and 0.54 for the brief peaceful interwar period. On the other hand, the diversity case produces much smaller probabilities at 0.46, 0.41, and 0.33, respectively. It is very clear that the fundamental divide between North and South, which manifests itself in terms of social polarization or ethnic dominance, is more relevant for explaining the more than 37 years of civil wars in the history of postcolonial Sudan (1956–72 and 1983–present) and a short-lived uneasy peace (1972–83).Therefore, for further analysis regarding the question of why the civil war has persisted for so long in Sudan, we will use the model that assumes social polarization.This does not mean, however, that the overall social diversity is not relevant.As we argue elsewhere (Ali et al. 2002), the high degree of social diversity within the North and the South would have implica-

Figure 7.2 **Risk of Civil War**

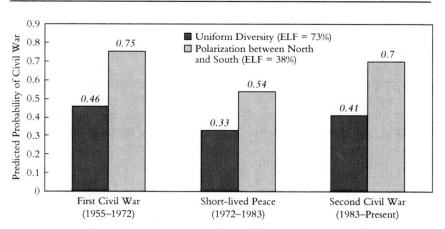

Note: Projected probabilities were based on an adapted model of prevalence (Elbadawi and Sambanis 2002), with "anticipated" external intervention added. The regression is:

$$Pw = 13.05 \ isxp - 26.40 \ isxp^2 - 0.03 \ poll \ 1 - 0.38 \ rgdplag + 0.03 \ ELF - 0.0003 \ ELF^2$$
$$+ 0.57 \log pop + 0.74 \exp int - 0.0086 \ ELF \cdot \exp int - 9.49$$

where *isxp* is primary exports to GDP, *poll 1* is the polity index lagged by one period, rgdplag is real GDP lagged by one period, ELF is ethnolinguistic fractionalization, log pop is the log of population size, exp int is expected intervention, and ELF.exp int is the interaction between intervention and ELF. Anticipated external interventions are derived from the predicted models below motivated by (Elbadawi and Sambanis 2000): P (external intervention) = −4.8 e-07 death & displacement −1.67 ethnic war −0.001 size of military (−1) −0.48 average regional democracy (−1) −0.16 regional dummy + 1.51 war (−1) + 4.3.

Predictions for the three episodes are based on the periods 1965–74, 1975–84, 1985–99, respectively.

The "uniform diversity" scenario takes the ethnoliguistic index (= 73) for the entire country, so it does not account for the polarization between North and South. The "polarization" scenario combines religious fractionalization to cultural and linguistic diversity. Under this scenario, despite the overall diversity of Sudan, we emphasize the fundamental divide between North and South. According to 1983 population data, southern Sudanese and other small minorities in the North account for about 25% of the total population of Sudan. The ELF index according to this polarization scenario is given by: $[1-(0.25)^2 (0.75)^2] \times 100\% = 38\%$.

tions for peace building and the type of economic and political governance in post-conflict Sudan.

To understand better the contribution of ethnic polarization, external intervention, and the other economic and political factors to the high risk of war in Sudan, we compare Sudan to the median for Sub-Saharan African countries (see figure 7.3). Compared to the risk of conflict faced by a median Sub-Saharan African country, the predicted probability in Sudan was higher by 0.47 and 0.51 during the first and second wars, respectively. Even during the short peaceful period, the risks of conflict remained high with a predicted probability of 0.54 compared with 0.32 for the median Sub-Saharan African country.

Moreover, external intervention and social polarization (as well as population size) are the main factors causing Sudan to be more prone to civil wars than the median Sub-Saharan African country (see table 7.3). The relative influences of the various determinants of war prevalence in Sudan relative to the median Sub-Saharan African country suggest a number of patterns.

First, while democracy is robustly and negatively associated with the risk of conflicts, it has virtually no role in explaining risk differential between Sudan and the median Sub-Saharan African country. This is to be expected, because in the Sub-Saharan African region the standard of democracy is rather low. Moreover, though Sudan has endured civil wars for most of its postcolonial history, it has, nevertheless, enjoyed some periods of genuine parliamentary democracy (1956–58, 1964–69, 1985–89).

Second, the net effect of economic factors (dependence on primary sectors and per capita income) suggests that, like political factors, these factors are not important in explaining the differential risks of conflicts between Sudan and the median Sub-Saharan African country. However, even though, like the rest of the Sub-Saharan African region, Sudan is desperately poor, the South is much poorer than the rest of

Figure 7.3 Risk of Prevalence of Civil War in Sudan Relative to Median Country of Sub-Saharan Africa (pw[Sudan] vs. pw[SSA])

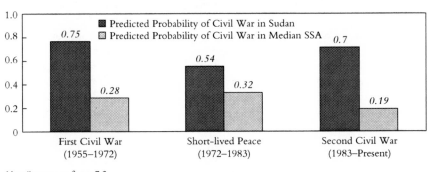

Note: See note to figure 7.2.

Table 7.3 **Explaining the Prevalence of Civil War in Sudan Relative to Sub-Saharan Africa**

	Sudan relative to Sub-Saharan Africa		
Factor	First war (1955–72)	Interwar (1972–83)	Second war (1983–present)
Dependence on primary sectors	0.13	−0.26	−0.09
Level of development (GDP per capita)	−0.02	0.02	0.03
Standard of democracy (Polity III)	0.04	0.04	−0.01
Social fractionalization (ELF)	0.09	0.14	0.11
"Anticipated" external intervention	0.48	0.49	0.57
Population size	0.28	0.60	0.38

Notes: The simulations are based on an estimated probability of "prevalence" of civil war based on a version of the Elbadawi and Sambanis (2002) model, which we explain in more detail in the notes to figure 7.2. The columns of table 7.3 include, for each factor and each period, the contribution to the predicted probability of civil war in Sudan minus the median probability estimate for Sub-Saharan Africa. The factors included in the model are described in the notes to figure 7.2.

the country. The region's economy is probably the most backward in the Sub-Saharan African region, and compared with northern Sudan, it has much lower levels of public services and literacy.[27] Because the Sudanese civil war has mostly been confined to the South, and the rebel organizations draw their fighting force almost exclusively from the South, economic factors are likely to be much more significant than what the model suggests, because the model draws on economic figures for the country as a whole. Indeed, as Dr. John Garang de Mabior (1997) argues, in the South "it pays to rebel."

Third, the population size in Sudan is larger than in the typical country in Sub-Saharan Africa, which contributes substantially to the higher risk of conflict in Sudan. Fourth, and as expected, social polarization accounts for a large share of the higher risk of conflict in Sudan, relative to the median Sub-Saharan African country. This polarization contrasts with cases of more homogenous or more diverse societies. Controlling for other factors influencing risk of conflicts, in more homogenous societies, political violence is likely to take different forms of expressions (e.g., coups, popular uprising); in very diverse societies, civil wars are not likely to be long even if they happen, because rebel movements have difficulty maintaining rebel cohesion (Collier et al. 2004).

Fifth, by far the most significant factor explaining the higher risk of civil war prevalence in Sudan is external intervention by third parties. This topic has been a subject of acrimonious exchanges in the Sudanese political debates on the genesis of the civil war and the obstacles to its termination. Southern politicians, for example, argue that deep-seated grievances are the only reason behind the civil war and accuse the northern political establishment of using the alleged "external intervention" as an excuse for maintaining the cultural and religious hegemony over the South and for justifying the military solution of the conflict (Ali and Matthews 1999).

The reality, however, is that external intervention in the Sudanese civil war has been substantial. The findings from this analysis as well as a great deal of other anecdotal evidence attest to this. However, to interpret better the role of external intervention, one would need to ask the question: Why does the Sudanese civil war attract so much external intervention, mostly in favor of the rebel groups? In our opinion this has a lot to do with the fact that a fundamental divide and not just a localized ethnic conflict drives the war. The fact that the Sudanese conflict is associated with other conflicts in the region would explain the involvement of neighboring countries. Part of the motivation for these countries' intervention may be an attempt to avenge the intervention of Sudan in their own conflicts. For example, Sudan supported the Eritrean rebels against Ethiopia, while the latter lent support to the southern Sudanese rebels during the fist civil war. And in the current civil war, Uganda provides considerable support to the SPLA/M, while Sudan provides support, albeit at a much lower scale, to Ugandan rebels active in northern Uganda.

Conclusion

The civil war in the Sudan was inevitable. It started even before independence. We have analyzed the reasons for the long prevalence of a very costly civil war. In addition to the standard economic determinants, which we do find to be relevant, we have argued that the long prevalence of the Sudanese civil war is due to social polarization between North and South Sudan and to extensive external intervention by third parties. These interventions have themselves been causally linked to Sudan's social polarization. Therefore, our key explanatory variable is social polarization. This understanding of the war also suggests strategies for conflict resolution. Interventions should attempt to transform the conflict away from a "war of visions" because no solution can be reached if the parties' interests are perceived as fundamentally irreconcilable. Any viable solution must recognize and work around Sudan's social diversity. Democratic transitions in both North and South could afford representation and redistribution that might be able to sustain a peace among Sudan's troubled ethnic groups.

Though a latecomer, oil has also been another very influential factor in the Sudanese conflict. Commercial production of oil and exports started in the late 1990s and has quickly started to make its impact on the Sudanese economy as well as on the strategic and military balance of power in the civil war.[28] Because most of the oil-producing cites are located in war-contested regions of Upper Nile of southern Sudan, securing the operation of the oil sector has been a major objective in the government's war effort. By contrast, stopping or disrupting oil production has been the primary military and diplomatic strategy of the rebels. In the process, the civilians living in the oil-producing regions have suffered the most (see Human Rights Watch 2003).

The strategic and military implications of the emergence of oil has been articulated in ICG (2002, 100): "Oil has raised the stakes of the war and given both sides an increased commitment to the battlefield. Any equitable peace deal will require some form of oil revenue sharing." As predicted by the ICG report, the emergence of oil as a potent influence in the Sudanese civil war has not only raised the stakes of the war, but has become a major factor in the ensuing peace process. Indeed, equal sharing of oil revenues between the federal government and the government of South Sudan (to be constituted following the final peace agreement) has now emerged as the key pillar of the already concluded agreement on "wealth sharing." Thus, oil, which led to intensified violence in the Sudanese civil war and invited the intervention of multinational oil companies, may now produce a positive externality for peace if it is equitably shared.

Notes

We are grateful to Håvard Hegre, Gary Milante, and John Randa for helpful suggestions and research support. The views expressed in this chapter do not necessarily represent those of the World Bank or the Arab Planning Institute.

1. John Garang de Mabior made this statement in his appeal to the Sudanese people on the "Founding of the Sudan's People Liberation Army (SPLA) and the Sudan's People Liberation Movement (SPLM)."

2. A recent book on the Sudanese civil wars begins by noting that sharply "divided by geography, culture, race, ethnicity and religion, Sudan is the world's foremost example of a seemingly intractable and endless civil war. Conflict has consumed the country for 34 of its 45 years of independence and remains the only constant factor in a land whose population has repeatedly been devastated" (ICG 2002, 3).

3. Bracketed words are authors' additions.

4. Alier (1990) notes the innate resistance of the tribes in southern Sudan to outside domination. Historical records show that "the Nuer were the most difficult tribe to pacify. In 1902 a force was sent against the Nuer witchdoctor Mut Dung. Other expeditions against this tribe were sent in 1910, 1911, 1914, 1917, 1920, 1923, 1924 and 1928. It was not until the early 1930s that the Nuer finally submitted" (Beshir 1968, 19). Similar military operations were undertaken against other tribes: Atwok Dinka (1907), Beir (1911 and 1912), Twig Dinka (1911), Anuak (1914), Latuka (1916), Aliab Dinka (1919–1923), and Toposa and Didinga (1922).

5. For a rich understanding of "indirect rule," see Mamdani (1996). Indirect rule was a response by the colonial state to resolve a central and overriding dilemma of how a tiny and foreign minority could rule over an indigenous majority.

6. Similarly, missionary elementary schools for girls increased from 9 in 1927 to 11, with 547 girls, in 1932. Missionary intermediate schools increased from one, with 35 pupils, in 1926 to three, with 280 pupils, in 1932.

7. The reasons that prompted the change in policy were enumerated in a 1946 memorandum on Southern Policy as follows: (a) "East Africa's plans regarding better communications with the Southern Sudan have been found nebulous, and contingent on the Lake

Albert Dam. Whatever the possibilities, we have no reason to hesitate between development of trade between the South and E. Africa and development of trade between the
Southern and Northern Sudan. Our chance of succeeding depends I think upon con-
fining ourselves to the one aim of developing trade in the South, and between the North
and the South"; (b) in education "while the South may hope to have a secondary school,
it cannot hope to support post-secondary education, and I believe that Southerners
should get that at the Gordon Memorial College"; and (c) "the distinctions in the rate of
pay and other conditions of government service, the artificial rules about employment of
southerners in the North, attempts at economic separation, and all similar distinctions are
becoming more and more anomalous" (see the text of the memorandum documented as
appendix 2 in Beshir 1968, 119–21).

8. See Beshir (1968, appendices 3–8, 122–35).
9. The *Sharia* laws are a penal code based on Islamic jurisprudence.
10. According to a former SPLA commander: "The SPLA/M leaders wanted to build a powerful military machine which could have immediate impact, not on the socio-economic
situation of the people, but on the political situation both inside the country and internationally. This military machine was therefore not a means for social transformation
but for impressing friends and foes alike and winning material support" (Nyaba 2000).
11. Dr. Garang de Mabior was a commander in the former Anyanya movement and a high-
ranking officer (a colonel) in the Sudanese army. Following the Addis Ababa peace accord
and the absorption of the Anyanya rebel forces into the Sudanese army, Dr. Garang de
Mabior went on to obtain a Ph.D. degree in economics from Iowa State University and
returned to teach at the Sudanese Military Academy, as well as the University of
Khartoum. Therefore, his academic and military credentials combined to make the best
qualified and suitable candidate for the leadership of this "revolutionary" armed struggle.
12. Unlike the normal army formation, the SPLA squad consisted of 17 men, a platoon
consisted of 51, a company was made up of 224, and a battalion consisted of 1,344 men.
This constituted an enormous volume of firepower. One SPLA battalion was similar to
a Sudanese government army brigade.
13. Nyaba continues: "The strong link between being a soldier in a national liberation movement and the solidarity with the people (which could have been provided by political
training and education of the SPLA combatants) was completely absent. The sad result
was that an SPLA soldier operating in an area different from his own home saw no difference between the civil population, for whom they had taken up arms, and the enemy.
The SPLA became like an army of occupation in areas it controlled and from which the
people were running away. This happened in Yambio and Tambura where, instead of
welcoming the SPLA, the Zande took to the bushes, leaving the towns to the 'liberators.' "
14. Johnson (1998, 65) makes this point: "The revival of the SPLA military strength was not
just the product of a reform in the military structure, or the advantageous network of
diplomatic alliances produced, in part, by Khartoum's alienation of Eritrea, Ethiopia and
Uganda after its support for Islamist and other dissident groups in those countries. All
these were significant factors, but they would not have come into play had the SPLA disappeared in 1992–4, as many external commentators expected. I suggest that it is within
the framework of a functioning civilian administration throughout the SPLA-controlled

territory that one can find the answer to the overall success of the SPLA in securing and holding on to large sections of the rural civilian population (that is, marinating [sic] a civilian base), despite the overwhelming military nature of the movement, and despite the political and military upheavals of the years after 1991."

15. Elbadawi and Sambanis (2000) estimate the probability that a civil war occurs at time t contingent on there being no war at time $t-1$ or that the war event in time t is a continuation of an earlier war event in time $t-1$. Thus, the probability of war prevalence in Elbadawi and Sambanis is the probability of war onset and continuation.

16. The analysis of Elbadawi and Sambanis accounts for the potential endogeniety of external intervention itself. They find that: (a) "external intervention is more likely in bloodier wars or when the government fighting the civil war is more democratic"; (b) "intervention is less likely to occur in ethnic wars"; and (c) "external intervention is less likely in civil wars where regions are characterized by high levels of democracy or when the state involved in the civil war has a strong military."

17. Note that this index is based on Reynal-Querol (2002), which is different from the ELF index. The polarization index proposed by Reynal-Querol is defined as: $IRC1 = 1 - 4[\Sigma(0.5 - \pi_i)^2\pi_i]$, where π_i is the share of the population group in total population and the summation is overpopulation groups. Maximum polarization attains at a value of $I = 1$, when a country is composed of two ethnic groups with equal weights. The other index of polarization used is $IRC2 = \Sigma\pi^{1+\alpha}$, where $\alpha > 1$.

18. For a fascinating summary of the development of African languages, see, for example, Diamond (1997, 381–86).

19. The measure, according to Mauro (1995, 692) is defined as $ELF = 1 - \Sigma(n_i/N)^2$, where n_i is the number of people in the ith group, N is total population, and the summation is over i ethnolinguistic groups.

20. Note that the ELF for the Sudan in the global databases frequently used by economists and political scientists is equal to 0.73 in 1960 (Mauro 1995, 710), which in this measure suggests diversity rather than polarization. This is because this measure assumes many smaller linguistic groups than the ones in table 7.1. We would argue that the classification in this table is more consistent with politically and culturally relevant determinants of the civil war.

21. A detailed account of the regional and tribal biases of the Salvation regime (1989– present) was documented in a recent report: "The Black Book on the Imbalance of Power and Wealth in the Sudan." The authors of this report chose to be anonymous, but they are widely believed to be defectors from the ruling party.

22. For example, in explaining the concept of "New Sudan" for which the SPLA/M is fighting, Dr. John Garang de Mabior (1997, 43–47) notes that the Sudan "we know from 1956 on, has been based on ethnic and religious chauvinism. So, it is that kind of Sudan, that is based on injustice, that is based on exclusivity, that has resulted in the present crisis." He characterized the objectives and commitment of the SPLA/M: "to create a Sudan that belongs to all of us, a socio-political commonality to which we pledge our individual allegiance irrespective of race, irrespective of religion, irrespective of tribe, and, women would add, irrespective of gender" (p. 51).

23. According to Johnson and Prunier (1993, 125), in "July 1983 the different groups of mutineers and Anya-Nya II guerrillas who had moved into Ethiopia met under the auspices

of the Ethiopian government and united in one Sudan People's Liberation Army, with a separate political arm named the Sudan Liberation Movement (SPLA/SPLM). On the insistence of the Ethiopians the army and the political wing were united under a single leader. It was Garang who ultimately received Ethiopian support, and there were some within the movement who felt that the Ethiopians imposed him on the rest."

24. An example of a neighboring country being the vehicle through which external intervention was mediated is the case of the unification of Anyanya in the 1970s under Joseph Lagu. According to Johnson and Prunier (1993, 118–19), for several years following the mutiny of 1955, "the exile political movement was fragmented, and guerrilla units were highly local and often in conflict with each other. The name Anya-Nya was not universally accepted or applied to all guerrilla groups until the late 1960s. The unification of the Anya-Nya army came about in 1970 largely because Joseph Lagu was supported by Israel through the brokerage of Gen. Idi Amin Dada, then chief of staff the Ugandan army."

25. "Uganda, Eritrea and Ethiopia have each received military and political support from the United States since 1995. At the end of 1996, the US also announced plans to provide the three frontline states with $20 million in what is termed 'non-lethal military aid' " (Human Rights Watch 1998, 48).

26. The 25 percent would constitute the share of the South (about 20 percent) plus other pockets of minorities in the North that are deemed to be culturally and religiously different from the rest of the Northern majority (5 percent).

27. An International Labor Organization report (ILO 1976, 199) suggests that, "The Southern Provinces are the poorest in Sudan; per capita income is about half that of the national average. . . . .They are relatively neglected in the provision of public services: with over 20 percent of the country's population hav[ing] little more than 10 percent of existing dispensaries and dressing stations, a similarly small percentage of post and telegraph offices, only 5 percent of bank branches, and the proportion of children in school is less than half that in the country as a whole. Communications are poor and much of the South is cut off from the stream of progress in the rest of the country." Five years later, the World Bank (1981, 47–48) comments on the devastation of the first civil war (1956–72) and observes that, "The illiteracy rate in Sudan (during the period) was 85 percent and was probably even higher in the South where a whole generation has grown up without education due to civil war."

28. The proven oil reserve volume is estimated at between 600 million and 1.2 billion barrels. New discoveries suggest that the reserve may be as large as 2 billion barrels. Most of these deposits are in war-contested regions of the South. However, the government has been able to secure these regions and to start production of oil in the late 1990s. Crude oil production has been rising steadily following the opening of the 1,600-km oil export pipeline in August 1999 as output increased from 40,780 barrels per day in 1999 to 262,128 barrels per day in 2003 and is expected to increase to more than 400,000 in 2005 as new capacity comes on stream.

References

Ali, A. G., ed. 1986. *The Sudan Economy in Disarray: Essays on the IMF Model.* London: Ithaca Press.

Ali, A. G., I. Elbadawi, and A. El-Batahani. 2002. "On the Causes, Consequences and Resolution of the Civil War in Sudan." Unpublished mimeo.

Ali, T. M., and O. Matthews. 1999. "Civil War and Failed Peace Efforts in Sudan." In *Civil Wars in Africa: Roots and Resolution,* ed. T. M. Ali and O. Matthews, 193–220. Montreal, Kingston, London, Ithaca: McGill-Queen's University Press.

Alier, A. 1990. *Southern Sudan: Too Many Agreements Dishonored.* London, Ithaca: Exeter.

Balamoan, G. A. 1981. *Peoples and Economics in the Sudan: 1884–1956.* Cambridge, MA: Harvard University Center for Population Studies.

Beshir, M. O. 1968. *The Southern Sudan: Background to Conflict.* Khartoum: Khartoum University Press.

———. 1969. *Educational Development in the Sudan.* Oxford: Clarendon Press.

Collier, P., and A. Hoeffler. 2004. "Greed and Grievance in Civil Wars." *Oxford Economic Papers* 56: 563–95.

Collier, P., A. Hoeffler, and M. Soderbom. 2004. "On the Duration of Civil War." *Journal of Peace Research* 41 (3): 253–73.

Deng, F. 1995. *War of Visions: Conflict of Identities in the Sudan.* Washington, DC: Brookings Institutions.

Diamond, J. 1997. *Guns, Germs and Steel: The Fate of Human Societies.* New York: Norton.

Elbadawi, I. 1999. "The Tragedy of the Civil War in the Sudan and its Economic Implications." In *African Perspectives Yearbook,* ed. K. Wohlmuth, A. Gutowski, E. Grawert, and M. Wauschkuhn. London: LitVerlag Munster.

Elbadawi, I., and N. Sambanis. 2000. "External Interventions and the Duration of Civil Wars." Policy Research Working Paper 2433, World Bank, Washington, DC.

———. 2002. "How Much War Will We See? Explaining the Prevalence of Civil War." *Journal of Conflict Resolution* 46 (3): 307–34.

Garang de Mabior, J. 1997. *The Vision of the New Sudan: Questions of Unity and Identity,* ed. E. Kameir. Cairo: Consortium for Policy Analysis and Development Strategies.

Hegre, H., T. Ellingsen, S. Gates, and N. P. Gleditsch. 2001. "Toward a Democratic Civil Peace? Democracy, Political Change and Civil War, 1816–1992." *American Political Science Review* 95 (1): 33–48.

Human Rights Watch. 1998. *Sudan: Global Trade, Local Impact: Arms Transfers to All Sides in the Civil War in Sudan,* 10 (4A). Available at: http://www.hrw.org/reports98/sudan.

———. 2003. *Sudan: Oil and Human Rights Abuses.* Accesed Nov. 25, 2003. Available at: http://www.hrw.org/reports/2003/sudan1103.

ICG (International Crisis Group). 2002. *God, Oil and Country: Changing the Logic of War in Sudan,* Brussels: ICG Press.

ILO (International Labor Organization). 1976. *Growth, Employment and Equity: A Comprehensive Strategy for the Sudan.* Geneva: ICG.

Johnson, D. H. 1998. "The Sudan People's Liberation Army & the Problem of Factionalism." In *African Guerrillas,* ed. Christopher Clapham, 53–72. Oxford: James Curie.

Johnson, D., and G. Prunier. 1993. "The Foundation and Expansion of the Sudan People's Liberation Army." In *Civil War in the Sudan,* ed. M. W. Daly and Ahmed Alawad Sikainga, 117–20. London: British Academic Press.

Malwal, B. 1987. "The Roots of Current Contention." In *The Search for Peace and Unity in the Sudan,* ed. Francis Deng and Prosser Gifford, 9–14. The Woodrow Wilson International Center for Scholars, distributed by UPA, Inc. and Lillian Barber Press.

Mamdani, M. 1996. *Citizen and Subject: Contemporary Africa and Late Colonialism.* Princeton, NJ: Princeton University Press.

Mauro, P. 1995. "Corruption and Growth." *Quarterly Journal of Economics* 110 (3): 681–712.

Nyaba, P. A. 2000. *The Politics of Liberation in Sudan: An Insider's View.* 2nd ed. Kampala, Uganda: Fountain Publishers.

Regan, P. 1996. "Conditions for Successful Third Party Interventions." *Journal of Conflict Resolution* 40 (1): 336–59.

———. (2000). *Civil Wars and Foreign Powers: Interventions and Intrastate Conflict.* Ann Arbor, MI: University of Michigan Press.

Reynal-Querol, M. 2002. "Ethnicity, Political Systems and Civil Wars." *Journal of Conflict Resolution* 46 (1): 29–54.

Sambanis, N. 2001. "Do Ethnic and Non-Ethnic Civil Wars Have the Same Causes? A Theoretical and Empirical Inquiry (Part 1)." *Journal of Conflict Resolution* 45 (3): 259–82.

Yongo-Bure, B. 1987. "Prospects for Socioeconomic Development of the South." In *The Search for Peace and Unity in the Sudan,* ed. Francis Deng and Prosser Gifford, 36–55. The Woodrow Wilson International Center for Scholars, distributed by UPA, Inc. and Lillian Barber Press.

World Bank. 1981. *Adjustment in Low Income Countries.* Report. Washington, DC: World Bank.

Algeria, 1992–2002
Anatomy of a Civil War

8

MIRIAM R. LOWI

Since January 1992, Algeria has been beset with civil war. The violence has pitted the military-backed regime and its allies against several armed groups that emerged out of the banned Islamist movement. At least 100,000—perhaps as many as 200,000—people have been killed.[1] Many, if not most, of the victims have been unarmed civilians.

The proximate cause for the outbreak of war was the military's annulment of the results of the December 1991 legislative elections, in which the constitutionally created *Front Islamique du Salut* (FIS) won 47 percent of the popular vote in the first round. In effect, the military canceled the transition to a multiparty system that had been decreed by the 1989 constitution after 27 years of an authoritarian, single-party state system. On January 11, 1992, the army staged a coup d'état, removed Chadli Benjedid from the presidency, and replaced him with a five-man *Haut Comité d'Etat* (High Council of State). A state of emergency was declared, the FIS was outlawed, and its leadership was imprisoned. Thousands of real or suspected members and supporters of the FIS were rounded up and detained, often without charges, and many were tortured. Outraged at the impunity with which the military had hijacked the transition and the ferocious repression that it was meting out to its challengers, new militants were radicalized overnight. Algeria exploded.

In this study, I seek to explain the inception, form, and persistence of violence in Algeria and explore some of the enigmatic features of this case that are at variance with the Collier-Hoeffler (CH) model. First, the violence took place in a relatively high-income country and has lasted a relatively long time. Second, the violence is located in the most densely populated and urbanized regions of the country. Third, despite the ethnic dominance of Arabs in relation to Berbers,[2] there is no significant ethnic dimension to this conflict, and despite the discourse of Islam, religious claims are not a major stake, either. Fourth, the country's oil wealth, while neither "lootable" nor "easily appropriable," has played an important, albeit indirect, role in the onset, organization, and persistence of violence.

I make the following linked arguments. First, the violence emerged as an expression of political contestation within the context of an obdurate political system and a brutal socioeconomic crisis. For decades, political freedoms had been woefully absent and the oil-rich economy was poorly diversified, but the population had been appeased and remained relatively comfortable through redistribution (Lowi 2004). However, with the fall in oil prices after 1982, the combination of a sharp decline in living standards, rising inequalities in a context of severe institutional rigidities, growing unemployment, and, by 1986, the end to redistribution brought acute social conflicts to the fore. Second, the violence took on a religious guise because religion (Islam) provided a critique of Algerian politics and society, and offered a formula for a better life. In Muslim societies with authoritarian political systems, Islam has been one of very few tolerated forms of (political) expression, and its message resonates strongly with its adherents. However, the discourse of contestation expounded from the pulpits attracted to its ranks not simply those who viewed an "Islamic alternative" as the preferred one. The insurgency, couched in religious garb, has been a magnet for those who felt excluded and came to view the *maquis* (the resistance) as the antidote to exclusion. Third, over time, the interests of the insurgents and incumbents evolved; violence became self-sustaining and progressively depoliticized, as both insurgents and incumbents developed economic stakes that depended on the continuation of war. Insurgents became more interested in looting, while incumbents fought to protect their control over the country's oil wealth. The latter received external support from parties coveting Algeria's oil wealth and wary of "Islamic radicalism."

Violence continued because both insurgents and incumbents benefited from the status quo. The Algerian war became more a war over the appropriation and utilization of a hydrocarbon rent than a conflict between two irreconcilable conceptions of how to organize society. Grievance was indeed the "start-up tool" for the violence in Algeria, and grievance was linked to the interaction of political and economic variables: a sharp decline in living standards, combined with rising inequalities and the absence of political freedoms (Elbadawi and Sambanis 2002). However, opportunity, in the form of both material and political resources, sustained the conflict, and this is consistent with the CH model.

I turn next to an overview of the Algerian economy and society in the years leading up to civil war and I consider how well the CH model fits this case. I then turn to the microlevel, and examine the formation, growth, and character of the insurgency movement(s), and offer an explanation for the latter's wide appeal. Following that, I discuss the government's responses to the insurgency and their effects. Next, I analyze the geographic concentration of the violence. I conclude by summarizing the argument and evaluating the links between the Algerian case and the CH model.

Background to the Outbreak of Violence

At independence in 1962, Algeria had a population of 10 million. It has tripled since then, approaching 33 million in the year 2002. Because of the country's extensive surface area of 2.38 million square kilometers, overall population density today is only 13 per square kilometer (World Bank 2001). However, as more than four-fifths of the country is desert, 90 percent of the population remains concentrated in less than 12 percent of the total land surface in the northern portion of the country along the Mediterranean coastline. Here, population density is roughly 105 per square kilometer. The desert begins south of the Saharan Atlas, the southernmost of three mountain chains that extend from east to west in the north of the country, and stretches to the borders with Mauritania, Mali, and Niger. It is in the south that the country's oil and natural gas endowment are concentrated. Oil and gas exports constitute 95 percent of total exports and 60 percent of government revenues.

Algeria is not religiously divided. The population is composed of three Muslim communities: Arabs constitute the majority, Ibadis of Mzab a tiny minority, and Berbers represent roughly 20–25 percent. There are four different Berber groups, of whom the Kabyles are the most culturally assertive. Although the regime resists acknowledging the cultural distinctiveness of Berbers, the Berbers have not developed secessionist tendencies of note. To the contrary, their contributions to Algerian nationalism have been enormous. The Algerian nationalist movement, which emerged in France in the 1920s, was spearheaded by the Kabyle émigré community (Harbi 1980). Some of the most prominent nationalist figures are Berbers, including Abane Ramdane and Hocine Ait Ahmed. The Berbers have also consistently occupied important positions in the bureaucracy of the independent state. Ethnic fractionalization has not played a significant political role.

At independence, an authoritarian single-party state, dominated by the military, was established. Similar to Nasser's Egypt, it propounded an Arab socialist ideology and a welfare statist discourse of egalitarianism and inclusion. However, reality kept flying in the face of rhetoric and inequalities grew. For example, despite the lip-service paid to "arabism," francophone Algerians have consistently received preferential treatment in the marketplace, while unemployment rates among their arabophone compatriots have remained higher (Carlier 2002, 89). Linguistic fragmentation has had some divisive social consequences. In addition, a private and lucrative trading sector flourished behind-the-scenes in "socialist" Algeria, privileging the political-military oligarchy and its clients. Institutions remained hollow shells; corruption was pervasive. At the same time, the only public place where political expression was tolerated was the mosque.

Economy and Society

Since the death of President Houari Boumedienne in 1978, Algerians experienced a progressive degradation of their quality of life, combined with growing inequalities, corruption, and an absence of opportunities for political participation (Hassan 1996; Hidouci 1995).

A Soviet-style development strategy, which combined *dirigiste* central planning and controls, guided the economy for much of the Boumedienne era (1965–78). During this time, a heavy industrialization program, financed by oil revenues and severe constraints on personal consumption, was the engine of growth. Until the early 1980s, economic growth indicators were impressive. Hovering around 8.5 percent in the 1970s and averaging 7.5 percent between 1965 and 1980, they were the highest among oil-exporting developing countries (Gelb 1988). Nonetheless, severe distortions characterized the economy, and their effects became increasingly evident. As much as four-fifths of the oil windfalls in the 1970s were invested. Not only was precious little saved, but the government augmented the windfalls with massive foreign borrowing that would begin to fall due in the mid-1980s (Auty 2002, 4). Over 90 percent of that investment was in the public sector and primarily on capital-intensive industrial projects. But Algerian industry was not competitive internationally, and it created few jobs. Unemployment, which had fallen from 28.5 percent in 1970 to 16.2 percent in 1980, climbed to 20 percent in 1990 and close to 24 percent in 1992 (Aissaoui 2001, 238). Agriculture, which had produced a surplus before independence, shrunk considerably. By the 1990s, Algeria was importing as much as 75 percent of its food (Auty 2002, 4). The neglect of agriculture and the rural sector encouraged migration from the countryside, exacerbating the precariousness of socioeconomic conditions in urban areas.

Indeed, Algeria exemplifies many of the characteristic features of oil-exporting states with authoritarian political systems, as elucidated in the rentier state literature.[3] The almost total dependence of economic activity and government revenues on the export of a single high-valued commodity (oil and gas exports were 95 percent of total exports in 1985–1995) that is subject to exogenous shocks has profound repercussions on the domestic political economy. Oil and gas exports as a percentage of gross domestic product (GDP) were 38 percent in 1975, 25.8 percent in 1985, and 30 percent in 1995. In Algeria, oil and gas exports provided approximately 60 percent of government revenues in the 1980s and 1990s. The lure of easy wealth encourages short-sighted economic policies and fosters a resistance to reform. As hydrocarbon rents accrue directly to governments, which may disburse them as they choose, corruption and clientelism are reinforced and democratization is eschewed.

With the international recession and the gradual depletion of oil revenues as of 1982, followed by the 40 percent collapse in oil prices in 1985–86, Algeria's external revenues declined by more than 50 percent: Export earnings from hydrocarbons fell from a peak of $14.2 billion in 1981 to $7.3 billion in 1986 (Aissaoui 2001, 15; ICG 2001a, 7). Around the same time, international borrowing possibilities dried up. Making matters worse, Algerian debt was already onerous. The debt service ratio had increased from 33 percent in 1982 to 68 percent in 1986; it would reach 86 percent in 1988, just as government revenues—reflecting 27.56 percent of GDP, as opposed to 38.18 percent in 1984 (and 29.53 percent in 1992)—were at an all-time low.[4] Rather than implement decisive reforms—as Indonesia, for example, did at that time, by devaluing its currency substantially and broadening the tax base to boost the nonoil tax share—the government simply curtailed imports and held back on redistribution (Auty 2002, 8–11). There were massive shortages of essential goods. Per capita gross national product (GNP) declined by roughly 2.5 percent annually, from a high of $1,789 in 1985 to a low of $1,370 in 1994: a drop of 24 percent in nine years (ICG 2001a, 7). As in several other countries, in Algeria, this period of growth collapse was one of high risk for domestic political stability.

The country's financial woes were made worse by demographic pressures. By 1980, the population of Algeria had reached 20 million, having doubled in less than two decades. Although population growth had fallen from 3.2 percent in the 1970s to roughly 2.6 percent during 1985–88, the labor force, because of a disproportionately large young population, was growing at more than 3.8 percent (World Bank 2001). Since 1980, more than 70 percent of the Algerian population has been under 30 years of age. Masses of young people were entering the work force precisely when the economy was shrinking. Unemployment would reach 28 percent in 1995 and 30 percent in 2000 (Aissaoui 2001, 238).[5]

In addition, a private trading sector had emerged at the interstices of the state-capitalist system, benefiting mostly former military officers, high-ranking administrators, and the few local entrepreneurs. State use of hydrocarbon rents to finance expensive importation programs also generated revenues, in the form of commissions, for the masters of the *dirigiste* economy and their clients (CHEAr 1997; Hadjadj 1999, 90–113, 197–211). State-directed economic patronage nurtured state power, the personal enrichment of a few, and large-scale corruption.

Emergence of Opposition

By the mid-1980s, as oil revenues declined, the rationing system began to create very large rents, just as the economy as a whole was getting poorer. This created enormous opportunities for contraband activities of all sorts; goods were acquired increasingly through smuggling networks and exchanged on the black market. Moreover, as inequalities and unemployment worsened in Algeria by the end of the 1980s, contraband activity, or *trabendo* as it is called, seduced the unemployed, disillusioned, and marginalized of Algerian society into its smuggling and distribution networks. In this way, they became linked to the private trading sector (Martinez 1998). Together, they have nourished the parallel economy, the extent of which has been thought to account for anywhere from 30 to 70 percent of GDP, depending on the source (ICG 2001a; Henni 1991; Talahite 2000). The parallel economy would eventually attract insurgency groups, who would exploit it for financing and recruitment by linking up with *trabendo* networks and engaging in smuggling and racketeering. With time, it would contribute to the violence. The infrastructure of parallel economies provides those involved with an organizational advantage for perpetrating violence, insofar as they operate "in the shadows" and evade the state with relative ease.[6] Indeed, the three sets of actors—the state-sponsored private sector, *trabendo* networks, and insurgents—were living vicariously off each other in their dealings with the parallel economy, and off the climate of fear and uncertainty that reigned in the country (Martinez 1998; Talahite 2000). There was a conjoining of interests between those who practiced violence initially for political motives (insurgents) and those who were well placed for engaging in violence (public-private sector *mafia*).

Recall that in this highly authoritarian system, there existed no institutional space for debate about political, economic, or social matters among competing interests.[7] From 1962 to 1989, the mosque was the only place where political expression was tolerated. It is not surprising, therefore, that it was from the mosque that an organized opposition to the state would emerge. By the end of 1982, when Abassi Madani, who would later cofound the FIS, led antistate demonstrations for the first time, Islamist opposition had become a distinctive feature of the landscape. The first demands of the FIS—for economic liberalization and investment of oil revenues in local economic projects—threatened the interests of the politico-military oligarchy (CHEAr 1997). Around the same time, the Bouyali group[8]—the first guerrilla formation in the history of independent Algeria and the precursor to the armed Islamist groups of the 1990s—emerged and started an armed conflict against the regime. By 1987, Bouyali was dead, but during the previous five years, his movement, called the MAIA, with only several hundred members, managed to launch spectacular operations against the state (Moussaoui 1994, 1324–25). Bouyali became something of a mythic hero, inspiring *maquisards* in the 1990s. A "return to Islam" as the antidote to the Algerian predicament was gaining adherents. It was the only articulated alternative.

Opposition culminated in a popular uprising in October 1988 and was followed by a constitutionally approved transition to a multiparty system (during 1989–91). The coincidence of a shaky political transition with economic growth collapse increased the risk of civil war, consistent with general findings in the civil war literature (Hegre 2002). The reformist government of Mouloud Hamrouche (1989–91), which had been mandated with resuscitating the domestic political economy, was sacked, and the transition was brutally called off.

Civil War Models and the Algerian Case

The insurgency that began in the spring of 1992 occurred in the wake of economic collapse, during an attempted political transition, in the mountainous terrain of a country characterized by ethnic dominance. These features fit the CH model. Other factors do not fit the CH model well: Algeria has a highly concentrated population (the violence-ridden north has the greatest population density and highest degree of urbanization) and, according to the CH model, this should give it a very low risk of conflict. Moreover, the violence in Algeria is concentrated in the north, not in the south, where the country's oil and gas reserves are located. In the desert conditions of the south, the opportunity to rebel is constrained, given the flat, treeless topography and the sparse population base from which to draw recruits and sustenance. Furthermore, anticipating that hostile forces might try to take control of the oil wells, the Algerian regime, assisted by its Western allies, has stationed 45,000 men in the region to safeguard its control, and entry into the zone is granted only with special authorization (Ait-Larbi et al. 1999).

In keeping with the CH finding that the risk of conflict peaks when primary commodity exports constitute around 32 percent of GDP, hydrocarbon exports represent 30 percent of GDP in Algeria. But the CH model does not tell us how oil increases the risk and persistence of civil war. One mechanism is through the corrosive effect that oil wealth has on governance in authoritarian environments: Oil-rich regimes are resistant to reform and Algeria is no exception (Lowi 2004). Another mechanism is the increased vulnerability of oil-dependent economies to external shocks that affect the price of oil. In Algeria, the plummeting of oil revenues in the 1980s exacerbated the economic crisis that contributed to the mobilization of opposition against the state.[9] In nondemocratic, weakly institutionalized regimes such as Algeria, some redistribution is needed to keep the peace. When redistribution came to an end, largely as a result of dwindling oil revenues, so did the peace. A third mechanism is that control of oil rents provides a motive for capturing the state. It is, indeed, the ultimate prize. While oil created incentives for violence, it was not used to finance rebellion in Algeria. This seems contrary to the CH model. Furthermore, the Algerian diaspora has not been a major financier of the war. Despite some support for the insurgency in the early years, external support has weighed in heavily on the side of the regime.

Historical precedents have also mattered for the onset of violence. The seven-year-long war of liberation against French settler colonialism (1954–61) demonstrated the capacity of Algerians to combat oppression successfully, and that experience remains prominent in the Algerians' collective memory. The Bouyali group offered an important demonstration effect as a local example of Islamist guerrilla activity that could destabilize the state. The Bouyali group also used tactics that had been used during the Algerian war of independence.[10] The insurgency also was inspired by the precedent of a successful Islamist revolution in Iran against the Pahlavi monarchy (Moussaoui 1994). Indeed, fundamentalist trends expressed themselves in the mosques built by the hundreds as of the 1970s, and radical Islam witnessed diffusion and success from Afghanistan to Lebanon.

Tables 8.1 and 8.2 compare Algeria to other countries (with and without civil war). With respect to primary commodity exports, income, mountainous terrain, income inequality, democracy level, and previous war history, Algeria is close to the mean for the cases of civil war. In other respects, Algeria is much closer to cases of no war; therefore, it does not fit the CH model in those domains (e.g., diaspora, forest coverage, geographic fractionalization, population density, religious fractionalization, and length of time at peace since the previous civil war).

The Universe of Protagonists

Formation and Growth of the Rebel Organization(s)

During 10 years of civil war, there were at least as many insurgency groups in Algeria; at any one point, between two and five operated. Main groups were: *Armée Islamique du Salut* (AIS), *Front Islamique du Djihad en Algérie* (FIDA), *Groupe Salafiste Combattant* (GSC), *Groupe(s) Islamique Armée(s)* (GIA), *Groupe Salafiste pour la Prédication et le Combat* (GSPC), *Groupe Salafiste pour le Djihad* (GSPD), *Houmat Eddaoua Salafia* (HES), *Ligue Islamique de la Da'wa et du Djihad* (LIDD), *Mouvement pour l'Etat Islamique* (MEI), and *Mouvement Islamique Armée* (MIA). Of these, the AIS and the GIA were the two most important groups from 1994 to 1997, when the violence was at its peak (Ait-Larbi et al. 1999). Since 1998, only the GIA and the GSPC (and the related GSC, GSPD, and HES), representing an estimated 600–700 men, remain active. The MIA was dismantled in 1994, and the AIS and LIDD called a truce and

Table 8.1 Algeria Versus Civil War Group (n = 78)

CH variable	Mean	SD	N	Minimum	Maximum	Algeria 1990
Primary commodity exports	0.149	0.114	72	0.122	0.176	0.179
Real per capita GDP	1,645.000	1,353.000	62	1,298.532	1,991.468	2,777.000
Diaspora	0.004	0.005	39	0.002	0.006	0.0001851
Male secondary education	30.300	26.100	66	23.825	36.775	67.000
Growth of real income	−0.226	4.312	54	−1.411	0.959	−1.465
Forest coverage	27.810	21.180	71	22.747	32.873	1.710
Mountainous terrain	24.930	24.030	78	19.453	30.407	15.700
Geographic fractionalization	0.603	0.015	72	0.600	0.606	0.916
Population density	62.000	69.000	74	45.848	78.152	NA
Urban population	32.700	19.970	76	28.088	37.312	NA
Ethnolinguistic fractionalization	52.630	29.060	73	45.780	59.480	44.000
Religious fractionalization	37.700	24.900	74	31.871	43.529	2.000
Polarization index	0.076	0.038	73	0.067	0.085	0.123
Ethnic dominance	0.452	0.501	73	0.334	0.570	1.000
Income inequality	41.000	10.450	46	37.884	44.116	38.730
Land inequality	0.631	0.131	78	0.601	0.661	NA
Democracy	1.821	2.740	72	1.171	2.471	0.400
Previous war	0.538	0.501	78	0.424	0.652	1.000
Peacetime since last war	221.000	177.400	78	180.567	261.433	324.000

Table 8.2 Algeria Versus No Civil War Group (*n* = 1,089)

CH variable	Mean	SD	N	Minimum	Maximum	Algeria 1990
Primary commodity exports	0.169	0.193	1,011	0.157	0.181	0.179
Real per capita GDP	4,219.000	4,403.000	978	3,942.906	4,495.094	2,777.000
Diaspora	0.018	0.030	610	0.016	0.020	0.0001851
Male secondary education	44.390	30.980	893	42.357	46.423	67.000
Growth of real income	1.740	3.760	807	1.480	2.000	-1.465
Forest coverage	31.330	23.780	1,029	29.876	32.784	1.710
Mountainous terrain	15.170	20.350	1,089	13.961	16.379	15.700
Geographic fractionalization	0.569	0.234	949	0.554	0.584	0.916
Population density	156.000	539.000	1,029	123.051	188.949	NA
Urban population	46.000	25.560	1,060	44.461	47.539	NA
Ethnolinguistic fractionalization	38.640	28.220	1,027	36.913	40.367	44.000
Religious fractionalization	35.980	23.950	1,066	34.542	37.418	2.000
Polarization index	0.077	0.040	1,027	0.075	0.079	0.123
Ethnic dominance	0.465	0.499	1,027	0.434	0.496	1.000
Income inequality	40.580	10.270	672	39.803	41.357	38.730
Land inequality	0.641	0.170	701	0.628	0.654	NA
Democracy	4.070	4.270	908	3.792	4.348	0.400
Previous war	0.185	0.388	1,089	0.162	0.208	1.000
Peacetime since last war	334.200	159.800	1,089	324.704	343.696	324.000

disarmed in 1997 (Maiza 2002; Zerouk 2002). All groups donned a religious mantle and none demonstrated a coherent political discourse (Izel 1999; Kepel 2002, 256–72; Interviews: 2/26/02, 3/4/02).

The fractionalization and radicalization of the Islamist opposition resulted from the decimation of the FIS by the state security forces in the aftermath of the 1992 coup d'état. The apparatus of the FIS was weakened tremendously by repression. First, the charismatic leaders, and then hundreds, perhaps thousands, of members and supporters of the Front were targeted by the security services. The FIS was a confederation of local groups organized around individuals who were responsible for strategic matters and, at times, had rival ambitions that were teased by hopes of acceding to power. The arrest of the FIS leadership left militants without elaborated directives and with hardly any clear strategies outside of a few simple slogans. In this context, the temptation toward extremism was strong (CHEAr 1992–97).

The leaders of the FIS, imprisoned or under house arrest in Algeria, or living in exile abroad, lost control of the situation on the ground as well as access to information. This deficit of political and moral authority over a clientele that had no affinities to other local political forces led to the proliferation of very small, dispersed, and heterogeneous opposition groups that were poorly coordinated and uncontrollable. The motivations of these small groups have varied from religious exaltation to outright banditry. In the absence of a sophisticated political discourse and the means to express one, the only way in which these groups could gain recognition, or gauge their importance and their impact on the environment, was by demonstrating and exercising a capacity for maximum disruptiveness, especially relative to their rivals. Maximalist strategies of outdoing one another through violence became the order of the day (CHEAr 1992–97).

The generic term GIA is often used to refer to the ensemble of these small groups. However, there is no recognized hierarchy or concerted strategy within this collective. Profiting from the void left by the massive arrests of the leaders of the FIS in 1992 and 1993, the new chiefs of these small bands engaged in desperate, gratuitous violence. They won over, through threats and seduction, many of the former clients of the FIS who had originally been attracted to Islamism by the populist rhetoric of the traditional Islamist opposition. The differences among these groups are more apparent than real. While there is no evidence of real ideological or tactical distinctions, apart from the suggestion that the AIS and the GSPC did/do not target civilians, there are strong indications that splits derive largely from personality conflicts and struggles for power and access to resources (Interviews: 3/4/02, 3/6/02). The GSPC, for example, originated in a rift within the GIA leadership and was composed, at least initially, of former GIA fighters. The movement was founded in 1998 by Hassan Hattab, who had begun his career in the FIS before adhering to the short-lived MEI, and then, in 1994, to the GIA (Salgon 2001; Zerouk 2002).[11]

The combination of these three factors—group fractionalization with internecine battles, weak leadership, and the cult of personality—accounts for the failure of the Islamist opposition to organize and institutionalize itself. Furthermore, fractionalization has obstructed the potential for a negotiated settlement. In spite of the unilateral truce declared by the AIS in October 1997, and adhered to by the LIDD as well, violence has continued. The GIA and the GSPC especially have remained active, and the death toll, albeit significantly lower than the average 1,200 deaths per month between 1994 and 1998 (ICG 2000), registered an average of 200 per month between 1998 and early 2001 (ICG 2001b, 4), with up to 400 during several months in 2001 (Fakhri 2002, 21).

Recruitment and the Origins of Rebel Groups

The insurgency groups emerged from four principal sources. First, former "Bouyalists" were among the first members of both the MIA and the GIA (Maiza 2002, 3; Willis 1996, 269, 279–81). The MIA seems to have been (re)created in 1991 from the remnants of Bouyali's MAIA (Labat 1995, 89–90; Moussaoui 1994, 1324–26).

Second, so-called "Afghans"—Algerians who had fought alongside the Afghans in their war with the Soviets during the 1980s—have figured prominently in the Algerian insurgency. Some have played important roles in the FIS, while others have been among the leaders of the first armed groups, and they have also comprised some portion of the rank and file of these groups, at least in the early years of the insurgency.[12] From 1986 to 1989, between 2,000 and 3,000 Algerians joined the Afghan struggle and were trained in Afghanistan (Bouzghaia 2002, 17; Mokeddem 2002). They were recruited in poor neighborhoods in Algeria and through local mosques, or while on pilgrimage in Saudi Arabia (Interviews: 2/26/02, 3/4/02). Consistent with the CH model, those who were attracted to the Afghan resistance were primarily those with very low economic opportunity costs (e.g., the unemployed).[13] Recall, as well, that the "freedom fighter" is a glorified figure in Algerian history and society, and fighting an occupying power—France in Algeria, or the Soviet Union in Afghanistan—is a path to social mobility, bringing social status and material benefits. To wit, veterans of the Algerian war of liberation, and their children, have consistently enjoyed preferential treatment (Interview: 6/28/00). For both "Bouyalists" and "Afghans," there was also an international dimension to the organization of rebel groups. Financial support came from fundamentalist Islamic forces in Saudi Arabia, Pakistan, and Afghanistan, and moral/ideological support came from Iran and Egypt (Kepel 2002, 172–76, 256–71).

Third, members and supporters of the banned FIS constituted an important base for these movements. Government repression radicalized persecuted members of the FIS. This is consistent with other cases (see Wickham-Crowley 1990, on insurgency movements in Latin America). Upon their release from detention, hundreds, if not thousands, would join what would evolve into a highly fractionalized resistance. Both the AIS and the GIA recruited heavily from among former internees (Martinez 2000, 213).

Fourth, migrants from the Algerian countryside formed the core of the rank-and-file of the insurgency. In Algeria—as in Turkey and Sierra Leone on the eve of their civil wars in the 1970s and 1990s, respectively—the rural exodus overwhelmed the urban fabric. The cities could not successfully absorb the increased numbers (Bozarslan 2001, 9–10; Davies and Fofana 2005). With the intensification of socio-economic dislocation and marginalization, the pool of potential insurgents grew significantly. In Algeria, the depressed peripheries of urban areas, and especially the overpopulated and less-urbanized suburbs of Algiers—Baraki, Les Eucalyptus, El Harrach—as well as the smaller towns of the neighboring Mitidja plain—Boufarik, Larbaa, Meftah—provided the bulk of recruits (Labat 1995, 92; Martinez 2000). Rural exodus, therefore, not only has been an important sociological effect of demographic growth and economic development, but it also became a principal venue for politicization.[14]

Finally, in Algeria as elsewhere, membership in these armed groups has been filled primarily by young, unemployed men. One analysis of *repentis*—those who surrendered to government authorities after the presidential elections of November 16, 1995—indicated that 70 percent were between the ages of 20 and 35, and 80 percent were unemployed (Willis 1996, 374).

Objectives and Financing of the Insurgency

The insurgents' objectives have evolved over time due, first, to their failure to capture the state and, second, to the financial benefits of the insurgency. In effect, a politically motivated insurgency quickly turned into an instrument of predation. Initially, the declared goal of insurgents was to reinstate the 1991 election results. The MIA, AIS, and GSPC insisted on this in public statements, and explained their use of violence as a response to state repression (ICG 2001a). Nonetheless, as the insurgents failed to gain popular support, their interest in capturing the state faded (Charef 1998, 26; Interviews: 2/26/02, 3/3/02, 10/27/02).

At the outset, and in keeping with the preference to capture the state, the insurgents' tactics demonstrated a will to weaken incumbents. During the first phase of the violence, from 1992 through 1994, insurgents targeted symbols of state power and confined their activities to the district of Algiers, the seat of power and authority (Ait Larbi et al. 1999). It was during this period that the insurgency grew significantly. From an estimated 2,000 men in 1992, guerrilla forces reached an estimated 27,000 men with the creation of the GIA in 1993 and the AIS in 1994, according to the military (Maiza 2002; Zerouk 2002).[15] The financial needs of the insurgency soared. Meeting those needs in an environment of persistent economic crisis and woefully inadequate regulatory institutions, but a flourishing informal sector, would have a strong impact on preferences. Similarly, the coincidence of mounting financial needs with the increasing fractionalization of the insurgency, its difficulty imposing itself, and the intensification of incumbents' response, would also affect preferences. An attitude of "catch as catch can" reigned supreme.

The initial means of financing the insurgency through raids and armed robberies, especially of military outposts and financial or commercial institutions, quickly gave way to extortion and looting of various forms: pillaging commercial traffic, "taxing" local populations, and seizing property (land, livestock, etc.) (Hadjadj 1999, 240–54).

The next step was involvement in the parallel economy and contraband trade. The GSPC, for example, is said to have controlled an important portion of the contraband traffic operating between Tunisia and Algeria, and in doing so, forged a commercial alliance with the traditional mafia. As a result, it has reaped fantastic profits from the illicit trade in hashish, vehicles, and food products (Salgon 2001, 68). Over time, these activities have become increasingly common, increasingly competitive, and increasingly difficult for the state to confront. Controlling roads, for example, became a major objective of guerrilla strategy and a major source of rivalry among insurgency groups, particularly in the mid-1990s between the AIS and the GIA. Moreover, the mounting financial needs of the insurgency coincided with the regime's half-hearted acceptance in 1994 of an International Monetary Fund (IMF)-backed structural adjustment program. The measures that were part of the reform package—especially, the abolition of price controls and liberalization of access to foreign exchange—enhanced guerrillas' access to financial resources and allowed them to get involved in business and trade (Hadjadj 1999, 92–94; Martinez 2000, 202–3, 213–18;). By 2001, the number of import-export agencies, ". . . dealing mainly with imports on which commissions are skimmed . . . ," and better known as import-import firms, were reported to exceed an alarming 27,000. At the same time, registered bona fide import companies numbered little more than 3,000 (ICG 2001a, 6). According to one keen observer of Algerian affairs, "Now that administrative barriers have been removed without having been replaced by the rules and institutions of the market, corruption, offences and economic crimes have no limits" (Talahite 1998).[16]

The possibility of rapid enrichment through such activities would seduce large numbers of young men, feeding the ranks of the insurgency and creating new networks of "political" banditry. It would also incite a profound change in preferences. As the violence became increasingly articulated within the microeconomy, the interest in capturing the state gave way to looting it and, eventually, to holding the state at bay so as to focus squarely on gaining and maintaining access to resources. Violence and the Islamist insurgency provided a cover for corruption and contraband; in essence, the violence represents a struggle for control over the rent, in which several different parties are involved—sometimes as rivals, sometimes as collaborators. The cement monopoly is a case in point: Armed groups managed to destroy the state-owned cement enterprise, which has favored import networks in the hands of the mafia (Hadjadj 1999, 250). Also, the transport of building materials in the east of the country, between Constantine and Tebessa, requires a stamped permission slip, after payment of a fee, from Hassan Hattab, who, although the leader of the GSPC, functions like a member of the regime.[17] Similarly, Mokhtar ben Mokhtar, a rebel leader linked to the GSPC, is known to cooperate with the military. It has been suggested that he was responsible for the kidnapping of the 32 European tourists in the south of Algeria in February/March 2003. The conclusion of this episode was curious. Although there have been suggestions that a ransom was paid, the regime announced that the military had stormed the rebels' hideout. Half the hostages were rescued unharmed, and their captors fled (Interview: 5/20/03). Finally, there is credible evidence that Djamal Zitouni, leader of the GIA from October 1994 to July 1996, was an agent of the Algerian security services and, in that capacity, carried out the GIA-attributed attacks in Paris in 1995.[18] In sum, having lost the political battle, in an environment in which the economic stakes loomed large but regulatory institutions were weak, the insurgency transformed itself progressively into a loot-driven operation that would persist over time. A veritable "market of violence" was created: The interests of those who practiced violence initially for political objectives would coalesce with those who, by virtue of their involvement in economic activities that required evading the state, were well placed for carrying out violence.

The Attraction of the Insurgency

Although it is true in the case of Algeria, as in the CH model, that the vast majority of fighters were young, poor, and unemployed, it would not be correct to suggest that poverty is what drives people to rebel. Only a small minority of the poor and unemployed will join insurgency movements.

There is an array of reasons why people would join a rebel group. No doubt, Islamist propaganda and social action resonate with many. Nonetheless, some people do not join voluntarily. In Algeria, many were recruited through threats and manipulation (AI 1997; Interviews: 3/3/01; 3/8/02). Among those who joined voluntarily, the reasons were sometimes political; many individuals considered the political alternatives proposed by the insurgents as preferable to those offered by the state and other political forces. Others had economic reasons; the insurgency provided an occupation and source of livelihood. Psychological reasons existed as well. For example, revenge was a powerful individual motive: revenge for mistreatment at the hands of the state or even rival insurgency groups.[19] Moreover, by joining the *maquis,* the individual could enhance his self-esteem, as he gained social status. Those who advanced through the ranks of the movement could eventually become "*emirs*" and turn their status into profit by becoming successful businessmen (Martinez 2000). Furthermore, rallying to Islamist ideology wins delinquents some grace: for some, "*jihad*" became a means of salvation (Moussaoui 1994). Finally, joining the insurgency was an antidote for deep feelings of exclusion. As the biographies of some of the alleged members of the *al-Qa'ida* movement suggest, for those suffering from anomie, joining such a group gives meaning to one's life: It provides an identity and membership in a community.[20]

Government Responses

The state had at its disposal about 160,000–200,000 soldiers, over 100,000 gendarmes, and 125,000 police (Garçon 1998; Interview: 3/6/02). In addition, an elite army corps specializing in antiguerrilla operations was created, numbering 15,000 men in 1993 and up to 60,000 by 1995 (Martinez 2000, 147–49). Thus, the state's armed forces numbered around 450,000 men.[21]

Two principal state factions emerged with different views of how to settle the conflict: "Conciliators," represented by former president Liamine Zeroual and his military advisor, Mohamad Betchine, advocated a politically negotiated settlement of the war and a more inclusive form of government that would integrate the FIS. "Eradicators" advocated a military solution and the political and physical eradication of all Islamist groups including the FIS. They were represented by the head of the General Staff, Mohamad Lamari, and the head of the *Direction du Renseignement Sécuritaire* (DRS), Mediène (Bedjaoui 1999, 321–22). Despite this lack of cohesion, the state pursued a fairly clear set of responses to the insurgency. A strong military response was favored, combined with some attempts at accommodation to win over the population.

Government forces engaged in fierce repression of the "Islamist threat" during the initial phase of violence (1992–1994). Torture, disappearances, and executions were used against the insurgents (AI 2000). But these tactics backfired: Armed Islamist groups grew from approximately 2,000–4,000 fighters in 1993 to perhaps as many as 27,000 in 1995. Moreover, the next phase of the violence, from 1994 to 1998, witnessed, alongside the rapid growth and fragmentation of the insurgency, the greatest mass terror and highest degree of victimization of the civil war years (Ait Larbi et al. 1999, 24–25).

The Algerian state armed civilians, encouraging them to create anti-Islamist militias to protect their communities. A special fund from the president's office financed these local militias (CHEAr 1997). There is no reliable information regarding the size of the militias, although estimates vary from between 100,000 and 300,000 (AI 2000). Hence, a total of up to 750,000 men were armed by the state and engaged in the war either through the regular army or irregular forces.

The two principal types of militia groups—the *Groupes de légitime défense* (GLD) and the *Patriotes*—were established to take responsibility for self-defense and resistance, respectively. The GLD tend to be composed of villagers who carry out territorial surveillance and are often associated with particular political parties or regional associations (Ait-Larbi et al. 1999, 74). In contrast, the "Patriots" are veterans of the Algerian war of liberation, organized into what are essentially combat units that work in conjunction with state security forces. They, too, are often affiliated with local officials (Ait-Larbi et al. 1999, 119–20; Bedjaoui 1999, 318).

As with repression, the effects of countermobilization via the creation of civilian militias led to conflict escalation. First, the escalation of violence since 1994 is related in part to the presence of these irregular forces. Although the GLD and the Patriots are, in principle, supervised by the regular forces, in practice, they function autonomously outside any legal framework, and are authorized to retaliate against "acts of terrorism or subversion" (Zerouk 2002, 21). Not surprisingly, there have been numerous cases of militia abuses, including the killing of many civilians (AI 1997; Garçon 1997). At times, these killings have taken place under the leadership of local authorities (Garçon 1998; El Watan 2002). Second, government-created militias have also been loot seeking, just like the insurgents. Functioning in a weakly regulated environment, with a dilapidated economy but a flourishing parallel sector, many of them sustain themselves through racketeering, organized crime, and revenge killings (ICG 2000, 4; Garçon 1998; El Watan 2002). Because these financial benefits are so attractive relative to their alternatives, militia members, like insurgents, are reluctant to see the violence end.

In its efforts to win over the population, the state may have used violence against civilians, attributing that violence to insurgents. For example, the massacres in the Mitidja plain in 1997/98 have been the subject of much controversy, with allegations that government forces perpetrated or facilitated the killing of civilians (Aboud 2002; Charef 1998; Souaidia 2001; Yous 2000). Either the state acted directly, disguised as Islamist guerrillas, or it arranged for an infiltrated group, presumably the GIA, to do the job. Whatever the logistics, military-backed assailants terrorized a target population so that it would condemn the insurgents and transfer their loyalties to incumbents (Bedjaoui 1999, 312–18).

The state has also tried some efforts at accommodation, including negotiating with the rebels and calling for elections. In October 1997, negotiations between the Zeroual government and some of the rebel groups culminated in a truce with the AIS and the LIDD. The latter recognized, and accepted, that they had lost the political battle. Then, in April 1999, President Bouteflika offered a conditional amnesty, through his *Concorde Civile,* to members of armed Islamist groups (ICG 2001b). The effects of these efforts have been mixed. Following the truce and the dissolution of the AIS, violence subsided significantly. The death toll in 1998/99 reflected a drop of 600 percent over the 1994–98 period, and the cities returned to some semblance of normalcy (ICG 2001b, 4; ICG 2000). By early 2000, however, and despite the surrender of some 6,000 men, violence was again on the rise (AI 2000). The most intransigent groups, the GIA and the GSPC especially, rejected the amnesty and continue the struggle. As for elections, they have tended to incite more violence. Election periods are often moments of violent upsurges. This was certainly true during the months leading up to and immediately following the 1995 presidential elections, but somewhat less so with the spring 2002 legislative elections (Ait-Larbi et al. 1999, 23–43; Maiza 2002, 7).

Three conclusions can be drawn regarding the effectiveness of government responses. First, repression is counterproductive as it leads to violence escalation and mobilizes the population against the state. Second, countermobilization through the creation of civilian militias makes the negotiation of an end to the violence more unwieldy and difficult. Third, violence can be a source of political capital. Government-perpetrated terror that is blamed on insurgents delegitimizes insurgents and wins support for incumbents (ICG 2001b, 5). Furthermore, by privatizing war through the creation of civilian militias, over-stretched military forces are relieved, their losses are minimized, and cheap repression is facilitated (Garçon 1998). In sum, incumbents use terror in order to preserve their comparative advantage in the control of political and economic resources. Holding onto power means retaining a monopoly over the oil rent and, in authoritarian environments, remaining above the law.[22]

Financing the Counterinsurgency

By cleverly equating Islamism and terrorism, the military-backed regime has received much support from Western governments and international institutions.[23] First, many

Western powers supported the coup that brought the democratic transition to an end (Bedjaoui et al. 1999, 695). Second, Western powers have consistently rejected demands from Algerian nationals and human rights organizations to create international tribunals to adjudicate government abuses of human rights (Interview: 3/6/02). Third, in 1994, the international community provided the Algerian government with about $6 billion through several different arrangements to support economic liberalization, in conjunction with an IMF agreement in April of that year (Martinez 2000, 228–31). In fact, the two agreements for debt-rescheduling in 1994 and 1995 gave the state about $20 billion that included deferred payments and IMF credits, as well as credits made available by the European Union and the European Investment Bank (Talahite 2000). The perception of an "Islamist threat" promises uninterrupted external support for incumbents. Moreover, by transforming the oil fields in the south into heavily guarded zones of exclusion, the regime has convinced foreign oil companies that it is safe to continue to invest in the Algerian hydrocarbon sector: the only sector of the economy that attracts foreign capital and the most important source of large-scale corruption (CHEAr 1995).

Both incumbents and insurgents have benefited, in a variety of ways, from ongoing and relatively low-intensity conflict. The dynamics of violence, previously described, and the financial interests in the war economy favored the status quo. For these reasons, the violence persisted as long as it did, despite a combination of factors that would predict otherwise: that external interventions have been subtle; that there are no major stakes in the conflict linked to national sovereignty, as in Palestine or Chechnya, for example; and that Algeria is a relatively high-income country.

The Geography of Violence

Initially, violence in Algeria took the form of an urban civil war. As long as capturing the state was the principal goal of insurgents, destabilizing the capital and surrounding areas was the main strategy. Once insurgents lost the political battle and were considerably weakened, that goal gave way to survival concerns. Hence, looting gained in importance and was effective where the opportunity structure favored it.

Between 1992 and 1998, the most affected districts were in the north-central portion of the country, in the districts of Algiers, Blida, and Medea, and the Mitidja plain.[24] This area is surrounded by high mountain ranges—the Ouarsénis and the Blida Atlas—that are part of the extensive Tellien Atlas configuration, stretching across the north of the country from Tlemcen in the west to Tebessa in the east. This small portion of the country is the most fertile, the most urbanized, the most densely populated, and of greatest economic potential.

Until 1994 and the end of the first phase of civil war, the principal scene of violence was the district of Algiers. From there, it spread westward, toward the districts of Relizane, Mascara, Oran, Sidi Bel-Abbès, and Tlemcen. In the northeast, violence concentrated in and around Jijel and Batna, at the foot of the Jijiloua and Aurès mountain ranges, respectively. And Kabylia, the Berber heartland to the east of Algiers, has witnessed increasing, albeit sporadic, violence since 1994, and an important upsurge since 2001.[25] Table 8.3 summarizes the key phases of the war.

In contrast, the arid and sparsely populated south, where Algeria's hydrocarbon reserves are located, has been spared. How is it that this resource-rich region has remained safe from violence? Have insurgents been unable, or are they unwilling, to target this resource? Recall that the oil fields and surrounding areas have been heavily guarded, and therefore, relatively inaccessible. Furthermore, oil and gas are the lifeline of any regime in power in Algeria. Hence, as long as their intentions were to capture the state, insurgents would have been unwise to damage the resource endowment, which was the ultimate prize. As the civil war dragged on, however, oil and gas pipelines further north were obstructed intentionally on at least one occasion. There was, for example, a spectacular attack in February 1998 on the Trans-Maghreb pipeline, one of two pipelines which provide Europe with 20 percent of all the gas that it consumes (Joffé 2002). Until then, there had been no attacks on the hydrocarbon sector, despite the fact that pipelines, even those underground, are well marked. Given the infrequency of such obstructions, and despite the remarkable capacity of insurgents to disrupt, there may be collusion between insurgents and incumbents in the form of an understanding that the resource endowment is "off limits." The effective safeguarding of the hydrocarbon sector suggests that this conflict is about control over oil revenues.

By far, the region with the worst violence has been the vast Mitidja plain, southwest of Algiers and within the districts of Blida and Algiers. It is part of the Mitidja— an area of about 150 km², between the towns of Baraki, Larbaa, and Blida—that has been dubbed the "triangle of death." It is here that two of the most notorious massacres in the history of the civil war, that of Rais and Bentalha, with the highest number of victims (1,690 deaths), occurred in the summer and fall of 1997 (Yous 2000).

As land in the Mitidja is both highly arable and intensively cultivated, the plain is Algeria's breadbasket. Moreover, because this land is in close proximity to the coastline, it is prime real estate. Because of its high value, land in the Mitidja has been appropriated outright by members of government and their clients. This type of looting is not new: On the eve of independence, officers of the disbanded *Armée de la Frontière* simply established themselves on this land (Interview: 2/26/02). This practice has continued over the years by ex-*mujahideen* (former guerrilla fighters) converted into businessmen, state bureaucrats, and army officers engaged in part-time business. It was especially pronounced in the 1980s, the years just preceding the violence (Hadjadj 1999, 100–103).[26] Most recently, counterinsurgents-turned-businessmen have themselves become involved in such appropriations (Interview: 6/3/02).

The localization of violence in the Mitidja derives from several factors. First, the Mitidja is strategically located: It borders Algiers, is surrounded by forested mountain ranges, and is part of the first military zone of the country. As such, it has always been a heavily armed region (Interview: 3/1/02). Second, it is the region with the greatest economic potential. Thus, violence in the Mitidja corroborates the strong correlation found elsewhere between the economic potential of a region and the

Table 8.3 **Phases of Violence**

Phase	Years	Protagonists	Goals	Type	Location	Tactics	Death rate	Outcomes
1	1992–1994	FIS/MIA vs. government	Reinstatement of 1992 election results & capture state for Islamists vs. retention of status quo ante & hegemony of military-backed regime	Urban civil war	District of Algiers	Targeted killings vs. fierce repression of Islamists	<1,200/mo.	Growth of insurgency; radicalization
2	1994–1998	AIS/GIA/MEI/LIDD vs. gov't & allies (civilian militias)	Financing networks; capture/replace state vs. "total war" against insurgents	Privatization of violence; collapse of state monopoly over violence	Southwest of capital; Mitidja plain; mountainous zones	Mass terror; massacres; thuggery & criminality; counter-mobilization of population	1,200/mo.	AIS/LIDD sign truce; GIA/GSPC continue struggle
3	1998–2002	GIA/GSPC vs. gov't & allies	Economic & political survival; maintain status quo	Low-intensity conflict	West & east of capital; mountainous zones	Random violence; criminality	200/mo. (1998–99); 400/mo. (2000–)	

presence of armed groups. Here, insurgency movements and anti-insurgency militias could accumulate resources. Third, the majority of the population of the Mitidja has its roots in the peasantry, many of whom had either worked as laborers on colonial estates or had migrated in the early years of independence to what were then the outskirts of the capital. In the Mitidja, they would come into contact first with European settlers and then with the privileged of Algerian society. The population of the Mitidja perceived both the settlers and privileged Algerians as their oppressors. This, in combination with their humble origins and proximity to the capital, the seat of power and wealth, would heighten their feelings of resentment, marginality, and exclusion. As a community, they were drawn to traditions, and increasingly, to opposition to the regime in power. Hence, they were easily enticed by Islamist groups that excelled as "service providers," replacing the state and demonstrating the irrelevance of the state (Carlier 2002, 91; Humphreys 2002, 12). Not surprisingly, the Mitidja was a bastion of support for the FIS. In the 1991 elections, the population voted heavily in its favor, as did virtually the entire "green belt" surrounding Algiers. It remained loyal to the Islamist opposition in general, and in large measure because of its own antistate proclivity. Because of this very important sociological dimension, in addition to the topographic, strategic, and economic features that favored insurgency, the Mitidja also was a coveted region for every insurgency group, beginning with the "Bouyalists" in the 1980s. The region provided a built-in support system, including a base for recruitment, and it had the resources for not only financing the insurgency, but enriching insurgents as well.

Conclusions

As suggested by the CH model, grievances are at the source of the violence in Algeria. Grievances were related to political exclusion and economic hardship which, in turn, derived from the distortions of single-resource-dependent economies, falling living standards, and the absence of political freedoms. However, the Algerian case illustrates three features of violence that the CH model fails to capture. First, the violence occurred in a relatively high-income country and continued for a long time. Second, the violence was located in the most densely populated and highly urbanized regions. Third, natural resource wealth played an important, but indirect, role in the onset, form, and persistence of violence, in ways that are peculiar to oil.

The persistence of violence in a relatively high-income country derives from two important aspects of the conflict. First, the economic downturn since 1986 had such profound social consequences that it negated the effects of relatively high per capita income. Thus, change in per capita income and the economic dislocation of large segments of the population were more significant for outcomes than the level of income. Had per capita income growth been more constant or had the state provided a safety net for the unemployed urban migrants, Algeria may well have been more stable politically. Similarly, important political reforms could have averted the descent into violence. Second, both the self-sustaining dynamics of violence (where repression led to cycles of escalation and revenge) and a profitable war economy encouraged ongoing, low-intensity conflict. In the absence of a stable, growing economy, the war offered more economic opportunities to the young unemployed men in large urban centers. In this regard, the CH model also seems applicable.

The fact that most of the violence is located in regions with high population density can also be seen as broadly consistent with the CH model, but it would require a different interpretation of the population density variable than the one offered by CH. Those regions offered a positive opportunity structure for rebellion, including large pools of unemployed migrants, newly arrived from rural areas, as well as important pockets of population and other resources, which could be appropriated relatively easily, to help sustain the insurgency.

The role of oil in the onset of violence is also different from that suggested by CH. Because oil is subject to exogenous price shocks, oil-dependent economies are subject to distortions. Moreover, oil has a corrosive effect on governance insofar as it enhances the patrimonial tendencies of rulers. In Algeria, the socioeconomic and political consequences of an oil-dependent political economy, combined with an illusory nationalist ideology, incited popular grievances. Oil would also affect the form of violence. When capturing the state was the principal objective of insurgents, the oil wealth was critical in that it raised the premium for organizing violence with the ultimate aim of removing incumbents. This also explains the determination of incumbents to retain power at all costs. Oil raises the stakes of fighting by making it a zero-sum-like struggle over control of the state. However, the importance of oil persisted as the preferences of insurgents were replaced by material objectives to sustain themselves. Oil wealth distorts in ways that present certain groups with "organizational advantages for behaving extra-institutionally."[27] In addition, the oil wealth helped the state and its counter-insurgency campaign. Government revenues from the sale of oil were used to arm the security forces of the state, as well as the civilian militias, and finance their operations. Furthermore, external support for incumbents derives largely from the lure of the country's oil wealth. Oil has played a crucial, albeit at times indirect, role in the persistence of violence.

Notes

In preparing this study, I have incurred enormous debts to the many Algerians, inside and outside Algeria, who have shared their knowledge and thoughts with me about the ongoing crisis in their country. Although they must remain anonymous, I thank them for their generosity. In addition, I thank the World Bank/Yale University project organizers who have funded this research; the participants at the Yale workshop (April 2002), Paul Collier, Ibrahim Elbadawi, Nicholas Sambanis, Indra de Soysa, Lucette Valensi, and Isabelle Werenfels, for commenting on an earlier draft; the organizers of the International Symposium on Terrorism and the Algerian Precedent, Algiers, October 26–28, 2002; and Joao Neves and Vanessa Tuason for research assistance.

1. There has been much debate among Algerians about whether this is a civil war. The conflict meets the definition of civil war (see Elbadawi and Sambanis 2002).
2. "Ethnic dominance" occurs when the largest ethnic group constitutes 45–90 percent of the population (Collier and Hoeffler 2001, 14).

3. See, inter alia, Mahdavy (1970) and Beblawi and Luciani (1987).

4. The debt service ratio would remain at those levels until the government embarked on an IMF-style economic restructuring program in 1994. After that, it fluctuated between 30 percent and 50 percent, until it dropped to 20.9 percent in 2000 (Dillman 2000, 34; ICG 2001a, 7). I am grateful to Marta Reynal-Querol for providing me with data for Algeria, 1960–2000, from the World Bank Data Base.

5. The fraction of the Algerian population living in poverty doubled through the 1990s: from 12.2 percent in 1988 to 22.6 percent in 1995 (World Bank 2001).

6. I am grateful to Indra de Soysa for clarifying this relationship.

7. Indeed the only forum for "debate" has remained the FLN party and its various appendages, such as the RND (*Rassemblement Nationale Democratique*) and the Organization of Mudjahidins, and in which the different currents within the army participate actively. However, the only issues at stake is access to oil rents. Note, in this regard, that to legitimize the interruption of the electoral process in 1991–92, the Algerian regime asked the French government: "Would you accept that the oil rent fell into the hands of the Islamists?" (Communication with a former member of the Mitterand government, 5/26/03).

8. Mustafa Bouyali was a veteran of the Algerian War of Independence. His group proclaimed the intention to establish an Islamic government.

9. On the relationship between economic crisis and popular mobilization, see Goldstone (1991).

10. Just like the wartime FLN, the MAIA, in the 1980s, was organized into cells, each with its own leader. Moreover, it divided the territory strategically among the different cells and cadres, reminiscent of the FLN's Wilaya system (Moussaoui 1994).

11. An earlier rift within the GIA was responsible for the creation of the LIDD in 1995 or 1996. Composed primarily of those who had seceded from the GIA, it then allied with the AIS against the GIA (AI 2000; ICG 2000).

12. Although there are rumors that the first cells of the Algerian Islamist resistance were created in Peshawar (Pakistan) in the late 1980s, it has been confirmed that Said Mekhloufi, a dissident member of the FIS and founder of the MEI, Aissa Messaoudi of the shadowy *al-Takfir w'al Hijra* group, and Kameredine Kherbane and Abdallah Anas, two of the leaders of the four-man "Executive Authority of the FIS Abroad" were all veterans of the Afghan war (Martinez 2000, 199, 206–19; Mokeddem 2002; Willis 1996, 228–9, 268–70).

13. One of my Algerian interlocutors spoke of a high school student from a middle-class background and son of a veteran of the war of liberation. Uninterested in his studies, he dropped out of school and, as there were few work opportunities in Algeria in the mid-1980s, went to Afghanistan (Interview: 2/26/02). Interestingly, enlistment in the Afghan resistance was condoned by the Chadli regime; it was viewed as a temporary relief for the employment crisis.

14. Bozarslan (2001, 17) notes that roughly two-thirds of militia members in the Turkish insurgency issued from the rural exodus.

15. A prominent human rights lawyer (Interview: 10/29/02) suggests that the number of insurgents has never exceeded 7,000, while Martinez (2000, 212–15) presents a figure of 40,000 for the AIS alone.

16. The Algerian diaspora appears relatively insignificant for financing the insurgency, even though the FIS and the GIA tried in the early years of the violence to establish themselves in European countries where there already was an Algerian immigrant population. It has also been suggested that since late 1998, the GSPC—rumored to be linked to *al-Qa'ida*—has set up networks in Europe with the aim to collect funds for insurgents. Although we have few details on these efforts (Angoustures and Pascale 1996, 531–33; Salgon 2001, 57), it seems that the armed groups lack a mass base among the émigré community (Interview: 2/26/02).

17. Alain Chouet, "Terrorism and Political Violence in the Middle East and North Africa," talk delivered at the Transregional Institute, Princeton University, April 14, 2003.

18. See the powerful documentary, "Attentat de Paris: Enquete sur les Commanditaires," by Jean-Baptiste Rivoire and Romain Icard, produced by Canal Plus, France, November 4, 2002.

19. It is said that the father and at least one brother of Antar Zouabri, leader of the GIA from July 1996 to February 2002, as well as the brother of Mokhtar ben Mokhtar, had been killed by government forces or a rival group (Interviews: 2/26/02, 3/3/02, 5/20/03).

20. See the biographies of Mohamad Atta and Zacarias Moussaoui, as well as the American John Walker Lindt, the British Richard Reid, and the French citizens who were found among the Taliban in Afghanistan in fall 2001, as described in *Le Monde*, the *New York Times*, and the *Washington Post* newspapers (fall/winter 2001/02).

21. However, this was a conscription army with only a few professional soldiers. In the 1990s, the army had recruitment problems that affected its morale and effectiveness.

22. The "Pinochet factor" also weighs heavily on the Algerian leadership: incumbents are fearful of what could befall them if they lost power. See the triple lawsuit in France against former Algerian defense minister, Khaled Nezzar (2001), submitted by the family of an Algerian victim of torture, plus two survivors (Algeria Watch).

23. It has also received, especially since 9/11/01, much sought-after equipment for fighting the insurgency, such as infrared night lights (*New York Times* spring 2003; Interviews: 10/28/02, 10/29/02).

24. See Ait-Larbi (1999, 52–56) for a tabulation of massacre episodes, their date, location, and number of victims.

25. A fourth phase, of a quite different form, would intervene during the spring of 2001. In response to the death of a Kabyle youth in police custody, civilians, rather than "Islamist" insurgents, challenged the regime through massive demonstrations that turned violent. Although the violence began in Kabylia, it elicited widespread support. The regime responded with severe repression. Moreover, to prevent the popular revolt from developing into a nationwide uprising, it maneuvered quickly to quarantine the region, and subjected it to considerable manipulation—of identity, "communal differences," and interests (Interview: 2/26/02). The regime has insisted that the revolt was a form of cultural contestation—a "Berber problem." This, however, was not the case. The violence immediately assumed an important socioeconomic dimension, with demands for not only official recognition of the Berber language, but also social justice: improved living conditions and life chances, and an end to the glaring inequalities (Yacine 2001). The government

response to the rebellion has bought off some and radicalized others, creating a very dangerous situation (Algeria Watch; ICG 2003).

26. Mouloud Hamrouche, who led the reformist government of 1989–91, initiated an investigation into such activities; his efforts were impeded by powerful interests in the military.

27. I am grateful to Indra de Soysa for this observation.

References

Aboud, Hichem. 2002. *La mafia des généraux*. Paris: J. C. Lattès.

AI (Amnesty International). 1997. "Algeria: Civilian Population Caught in a Spiral of Violence." MDE/28/23/97.

———. 2000. "Algeria: Truth and Justice Obscured by the Shadow of Impunity." MDE 28/011/2000.

Aissaoui, Ali. 2001. *The Political Economy of Oil and Gas*. Oxford: Oxford University Press.

Ait-Larbi, M., M. S. Ait-Belkacem, M. Belaid, M. A. Nait-Redjam, and Y. Soltani. 1999. "An Anatomy of the Massacres." In *An Inquiry Into the Algerian Massacres*, ed. Youcef Bedjaoui et al., 13–195. Geneva: Hoggar Books.

Algeria, Democratic and Popular Republic of. 1966/67, 1976, 1980–1981, 1985/86, 1994–2001. *Annuaire statistique de l'algérie*. Algiers: Ministère de la Planification et de l'Aménagement du Territoire, Direction des Statistiques et de la Comptabilité Nationale.

Angoustures, Aline, and Valerie Pascale. 1996. "Diasporas et financement des conflits." In *Economie des guerres civiles*, ed. François Jean and Jean-Christophe Rufin, 494–542. Paris: Hachette.

Auty, Richard M. nd. "How Natural Resources Can Generate Civil Strife." Working Paper. Lancaster University.

———. 2002. "Integrating Industrialising Oil-Exporting Countries into the Global Economy: Egypt and Algeria." Working Paper 0102, prepared for MNSIF, World Bank, May 13.

Beaugé, Florence. 2002. "Antar Zouabri, chef du GIA algérien, a été tué par les forces de sécurité, vendredi, à Boufarik." *Le Monde* 2 (2): 5.

Beblawi, Hazem, and Giacomo Luciani, eds. 1987. *The Rentier State*. London: Croom Helm.

Bedjaoui, Youcef. 1999. "On the Politics of the Massacres." In *An Inquiry Into the Algerian Massacres*, ed. Youcef Bedjaoui et al., 305–72. Geneva: Hoggar Books.

Bedjaoui, Youcef, et al. 1999. *An Inquiry Into the Algerian Massacres*. Geneva: Hoggar Books.

Bouzghaia, Djamel E. (Colonel). 2002. "Le terrorisme Islamiste" une "menace transnationale." Paper prepared for the International Symposium on Terrorism, Algiers, October 26–28.

Bozarslan, Hamit. 2001. "Le phénomène milicien: Une composante de la violence politique en turquie des années 70." *Turcica* 31.

Carlier, Omar. 2002. "Civil War, Private Violence, and Cultural Socialization: Political Violence in Algeria (1954–1988)." In *Algeria in Others' Languages*, ed. Anne-Emmanuelle Berger, 81–106. Ithaca, NY: Cornell University Press.

Charef, Abed. 1998. *Algérie: Autopsie d'un massacre*. Algiers: éditions de l'Aube.

CHEAr (Centre des Hautes Etudes de l'Armement). 1992–97. "Reflections on the Crisis in Algeria." Laboratoire Minos No. 16, Paris.

Collier, Paul, and Anke Hoeffler. 2001. "Greed and Grievance in Civil War." Policy Research Working Paper 2355, World Bank, Washington, DC.

Davies, Victor, and A. Fofana. 2005. "Diamonds, Crime, and Civil War in Sierra Leone." Paper presented at the Yale conference on the Economics of Political and Criminal Violence, New Haven, CT, April 2002.

Dillman, Bradford L. 2000. *State and Private Sector in Algeria: the Politics of Rent-Seeking and Failed Development.* Boulder, CO: Westview Press.

Elbadawi, Ibrahim, and Nicholas Sambanis. 2002. "How Much War Will We See? Explaining the Prevalence of Civil War." *Journal of Conflict Resolution* 46 (3): 307–34.

El Watan. 2002. "L'Affaire Hadj Fergane fait encore des vagues." Algiers, February 28.

Fakhri, Nahid. 2002. "L'Echec de la concorde civile: le retour de la violence?" *Les Notes de l'IFRI.* [Institut Français des Relations Internationales], special issue. "L'Algérie: une improbable sortie de la crise?" 37: 19–30. Farouk, M., et al. 1999. "Voices of the Voiceless." In *An Inquiry Into the Algerian Massacres,* ed. Youcef Bedjaoui et al., 196–265. Geneva: Hoggar Books.

Fearon, James. 2001. "Why Do Some Civil Wars Last So Much Longer than Others?" Paper presented at World Bank [DECRG] conference, "Civil Wars and Post-Conflict Transition," University of California, Irvine, May 18–20.

Garçon, José. 1997. "Quatre questions sur la tragédie." *Libération* August 30.

———. 1998. "La dérive sanglante des milices en Algérie." *Libération* April 15.

Gelb, Alan. 1988. *Oil Windfalls: Blessing or Curse?* New York: Oxford University Press.

Goldstone, Jack. 1991. *Revolution and Rebellion in the Early Modern World.* Berkeley: University of California Press.

Hadjadj, Djillali. 1999. *Corruption et démocratie en Algérie.* Paris: La Dispute/Snédit.

Harbi, Mohamad. 1980. *Le FLN, mirage et réalité.* Paris: éditions J. A.

Hassan. 1996. *Algérie, Histoire d'un Naufrage.* Paris: Le Seuil.

Hegre, Havard. 2002. "Some Social Requisites of a Democratic Civil Peace: Democracy, Development, and Armed Conflict." Paper presented to the American Political Science Association Annual Meeting, Boston, MA., August 29–September 1.

Henni, Ahmed. 1991. *Essai sur l'economie parallèle.* Algiers: ENAG.

———. nd. "Algérie: Violences, pétrole et société." Unpublished manuscript.

Hidouci, Ghazi. 1995. *Algérie: La libération inachevée.* Paris: éditions La Découverte.

Humphreys, Macartan. 2002. "Economics and Violent Conflict." Working Paper. Harvard University, August.

ICG (International Crisis Group). 2000. "The Algerian Crisis: Not Over Yet." *Africa Report* 24, October 20.

———. 2001a. "Algeria's Economy: The Vicious Circle of Oil and Violence." *Africa Report* 36, October 26.

———. 2001b. "La concorde civile: Une initiative de paix manquée." *Africa Report* 31, July 9.

———. 2003. "Algeria: Unrest and Impasse in Kabylia." *Middle East/North Africa Report* 15, June 10.

Izel, B., et al. 1999. "What Is the GIA?" In *An Inquiry Into the Algerian Massacres,* ed. Youcef Bedjaoui et al., 373–457. Geneva: Hoggar Books.

Joffé, George. 2002. "The Role of Violence within the Algerian Economy." *Journal of North African Studies* 7 (1): 29–52.

Kalyvas, Stathis N. 1999. "Wanton and Senseless? The Logic of Massacres in Algeria." *Rationality and Society* 11 (3): 243–85.

Kepel, Gilles. 2002. *Jihad: The Trail of Political Islam*. Cambridge, MA: Harvard University Press.

Labat, Séverine. 1995. "Le FIS à l'épreuve de la lutte armée." In *L'Algérie dans la guerre,* ed. Rémy Leveau, 87–110. Paris: Éditions Complexe.

Lowi, Miriam R. 2004. "Oil Rents and Political Breakdown: the Case of Algeria." *Journal of North African Studies* 9 (3): 83–102.

Mahdavy, Hossein. 1970. "The Patterns and Problems of Economic Development in Rentier States: The Case of Iran." In *Studies in the Economic History of the Middle East,* ed. M. A. Cook. London: Oxford University Press.

Maiza, A. (General). 2002. "L'Engagement de l'armée nationale populaire face au terrorisme." Paper presented at the International Symposium on Terrorism, Algiers, October 26–28.

Martinez, Luis. 1998. *La guerre civile en Algérie.* Paris: Karthala. [English version, 2000. *The Algerian Civil War 1990–1998.* New York: Columbia University Press]

Mokeddem, Mohamed. 2002. *Les Afghans Algériens: De la djemaa à la Qa'ida.* Algiers: éditions ANEP.

Moussaoui, Abderrahmane. 1994. "De la violence an Djihad." *Annales HSS.* 6, November/December: 1315–33.

Ross, Michael. 2001. "Natural Resources and Civil Conflict: Evidence From Case Studies." Prepared for the World Bank/UC Irvine workshop on "Civil Wars and Post-Conflict Transitions," May 18–20.

Salgon, Jean-Michel. 2001. "Le groupe salafite pour la prédication et le combat (GSPC)." *Les Cahiers de l'Orient* 62 (April/June): 53–74.

Souaidia, Habib. 2001. *La sale guerre.* Paris: La Découverte.

Talahite, Fatiha. 1998. "La corruption: Le prix de la contre-reforme." *Libre Algérie* 5: November 9–22.

———. 2000. "Economie administrée, corruption et engrenage de la violence en Algérie." *Revue du Tiers-Monde* 41: 161.

United Nations Development Program. 1995. *Human Development Report.* New York: Oxford University Press.

Wickham-Crowley, Timothy P. 1990. "Terror and Guerrilla Warfare in Latin America, 1956–1970." *Comparative Studies in Society and History* 32: 201–37.

Willis, Michael. 1996. *The Islamist Challenge in Algeria: A Political History.* New York: New York University Press.

World Bank. 1960–2000. *Data Base: Algeria.* Washington, DC: World Bank.

World Bank. 2001. *World Development Indicators.* Washington, DC: World Bank.

Yacine, Tassadit. 2001. "La juste révolte des Algériens." *Libération* June 27.

Yous, Nesroulah. 2000. *Qui a tué à Bentalha?* Paris: La Découverte.

Zerouk, M. (Lt. Colonel). 2002. "Le terrorisme: Le précédent Algérien." Paper presented at the International Symposium on Terrorism, Algiers, October 26–28.

Senegal and Mali | 9

MACARTAN HUMPHREYS
AND HABAYE AG MOHAMED

In mid-December 1983, hundreds of demonstrators—armed with spears, machetes, and hunting rifles, covered in protective charms, and chanting incantations to render them invulnerable to bullets—invaded the streets of Ziguinchor to call for the independence of a region in the southwest corner of Senegal—the Casamance.[1] The government responded with a heavy hand, leaving an official toll of 80 injured and 29 dead.[2] A handful of those retreating, led by veterans from the Senegalese army, under the banner of the *Mouvement des Forces Démocratiques de Casamance* (MFDC), headed to the mangroves and dense forest of lower Casamance to set up rebel bases. They started military training and planning attacks on government positions. In doing so, they began a guerrilla war that has left thousands killed and the south of Senegal strewn with land mines. After 20 years of failed negotiations and aborted attempts at achieving military victory, no end to the war is in sight.

The civil war in Mali started very differently. On the morning of June 28, 1990, a small group of Libyan-trained fighters belonging to the *Mouvement Populaire de Libération de l'Azawad* (MPLA), also hoping to gain independence for their region, Azawad, attacked a small government position in Tideremen in the far northeast of Mali. They killed four and gained control of a dozen automatic rifles. Moving southwest, the group attacked more government positions that same evening. In an attack at the town of Méneka, they seized 124 automatic rifles. These attacks were the beginning of a war that would engulf the region in intercommunal conflict, pitting northern "whites" against northern "blacks." After extensive and broad-based negotiations, the war ended with a weapons-burning ceremony in 1996.

These two conflicts between north-south groupings in neighboring countries provide a rich environment in which to study both the causes of conflict and the determinants of war duration. In the study of conflict onset, these two relatively low-intensity conflicts allow us to analyze the extent to which insights developed in the study of larger wars extend also to smaller conflicts. Although the two wars are large enough to enter a number of civil war data sets, neither is coded as a civil war by

Collier and Hoeffler (2001). The five years of conflict in Mali likely produced at least 6,000–8,000 deaths[3]; the Casamance conflict has probably produced about 3,000–5,000 over 20 years.[4] Rebel groups fighting smaller wars have similar economic concerns as those engaged in wars that end up as large conflicts, notably the need to recruit and to finance an organization. Yet macroeconomic information of relevance to small wars—such as the local distribution of natural resources, or the relative sizes of different groups in their local context—is no longer discernible once data are aggregated to the national level. Studying these conflicts using disaggregated data provides a way of checking whether the logic of theories that have been developed for large wars continues to function at a more microlevel.

To do so, we consider the predictions for war onset probabilities in Senegal and Mali that result from the Collier-Hoeffler core model, alongside predictions from a model developed by Fearon and Laitin (2003), and consider the evidence for the argument that these conflicts were driven by greed or local access to natural resource-based financing. As both wars are secessionist wars, we consider claims that these two zones are especially different from the rest of the country from which the rebels aim to secede, as well as arguments that focus on grievances and arguments that focus on opportunity-costs. We find no support for the greed hypothesis in either case, and we find mixed support for a grievance-based explanation for Casamance and strong support in Mali. We find support for opportunity cost arguments that focus on variation in state strength and local unemployment rates. Although we find spillover effects from neighboring countries, such as ideological support and interethnic solidarity, we do not find evidence that the movement of fighters across borders or regional arms markets were an important contributory factor to war onset in these cases. Whereas in the study of war onset we compare aspects of these two conflicts with ideas developed in the study of larger wars, we can use variation *between* these two conflicts to study war duration.

The two countries have similar geographies—more forested areas in the south and Sahelian or Saharan belts in the north—as well as similarly structured economies and ethnic demographics. In both cases, the rebel groups launched the conflicts ostensibly with a view to obtaining independence for their regions rather than to control the state. In both cases, the rebel groups have taken, to varying degrees, ethnic modes of organization. The roots of both conflicts predate independence. And in both cases, rebels have been able to draw on support from bordering countries. Yet although in Mali the war was of relatively short duration and was successfully ended through negotiation, in Senegal, the war has been protracted: Attempts at resolution have repeatedly failed. Explaining this variation is a central aim of this study. We do so by considering features of variation across the two countries that are missed by aggregate data.

One such point of variation is the location of the conflicts within the countries. Casamance—divided since 1984 into two administrative regions, Kolda and Ziguinchor—constitutes just 14 percent of Senegal's landmass. It lies in the south of Senegal, in an agriculturally rich part of the country, cut off from Senegal's capital,

Dakar, by the Gambia. The conflict in Mali, however, took place in the vast desert and mountainous regions of the far north of the country, a region—referred to as the "Azawad" by the rebel movements—that constitutes two thirds of the national territory but that is relatively poor in natural resources. Nomadic pastoralist populations, Tuareg and Arab,[5] are concentrated in this area, living alongside long-established sedentary communities, notably the Songhoi. These differences in the location of the conflict have had implications for the sustainability of the struggles. In both cases, the types of resources available locally led to poorly centralized rebel organizational structures, which in turn have made a negotiated resolution difficult, but only in Casamance have sufficient resources been available to sustain a protracted military conflict.

Ethnic demographies also differ across the two countries. Whereas data that concentrate simply on the number and size of groups fail to distinguish between Senegal and Mali, the structure of ethnic divisions within Mali is perceived very differently from that within Senegal. In Mali, as for example in Sudan or Mauritania, ethnic groups are perceived to be aggregated broadly into two racial blocks, the whites (the Tuareg and the Arabs) in the north and the blacks in the south. In Senegal, racial divisions do not reinforce ethnic cleavages. These differences in the structure of ethnic divisions correlate with variation in the extent to which the conflicts have become ethnically polarized.

The political backgrounds of the countries provide another point of variation. The Casamance conflict originated within a country with a relatively robust democracy and a relatively strong state. Independence leader and later president, Léopold Sédar Senghor voluntarily stepped down from office in 1981. His successor, Abdou Diouf, also handed power over peacefully, this time after electoral defeat in March 2000 to Abdoulaye Wade. Throughout, the state has received strong support from France. In contrast, immediately after independence, the First Republic of Mali, led by Modibo Keïta, set up a single-party socialist state. From 1968 a military regime led by Moussa Traoré governed a Second Republic until, faltering at the early stages of the rebellion, it was eventually overthrown in 1991. Although democratic institutions and a strong state are often described as facilitating conflict resolution, the experiences in Senegal and Mali suggest that these features may have insulated the state from international pressure to respond to the rebellion at home.

More broadly, the local geostrategic importance of the conflicts differs. We argue that although the Casamance conflict has typically had little negative impact beyond Senegal's borders—and, if anything, has benefited neighboring countries—countries surrounding the north of Mali, Algeria in particular, have been fearful of similar rebellions at home and have been keen to intervene to bring the conflict to an end.

Many of these factors that we identify—the location of the conflicts relative to the national distribution of resources, the form of ethnic cleavages, and the geostrategic stakes—are points of variation that have, to date, been absent from cross-national quantitative studies of war duration. This chapter is structured as follows. For Casamance in Senegal and Azawad in Mali, we provide a narrative charting the origins and course of the rebellion. We then consider, in turn, factors that led to the onset of the conflicts and those that determine conflict duration. A final section concludes.

Chronologies of Conflict

Senegal

PRELUDE TO REBELLION. Contemporary Casamance regional politics began with the 1947 founding of a political party, the MFDC, by a multiethnic group of leaders. The party, although not calling for outright independence, aimed to represent regional interests. President Senghor responded to the centrifugal threat of a regionalist party by co-opting much of the leadership into national political parties.[6] The present MFDC, reborn at the beginning of the 1980s, now claims that in exchange for this co-optation, Senghor promised Casamance independence within 20 years of Senegal's own independence in 1960. More generally, there is a belief in the region that Senghor would invest heavily in the development of Casamance. The failure of the state to invest is often seen as a cause of rising frustrations in the early 1980s.[7]

Frustrations, which activists link to a lack of investment and to discrimination against Casamance populations with regard to education and land policies (and even to the treatment of the Casamance football team on the pitch), led to a series of peaceful demonstrations in the early 1980s. Capitalizing on these frustrations, the future leader of the MFDC, Fr. Augustin Diamacoune Senghor, in a speech delivered in August 1980, drew on colonial history to lay the ideological foundations for rebellion:

> By what right did France, at the moment of Senegalese independence, attach Casamance to that country? Casamance has no link with Senegal, neither a historical link, nor an economic link nor an ethnic link. It was simply for bureaucratic convenience [for the French] that it was administered together with Senegal.[8]

SPEARS AND MACHETES. On December 26, 1982, the MFDC organized a peaceful march through the streets of Ziguinchor, culminating in the lowering of the Senegalese flag at key government buildings and the raising of a white flag in its stead. This time, Senegalese forces responded by violently dispersing the march, killing a number of activists and arresting many more.[9]

In anticipation of further problems, the government increased its security operations in the zone. These included a raid on a gathering in a sacred Diola forest on the outskirts of Ziguinchor in early December 1983. In reaction to the perceived violation of the forests, three of the gendarmes were immolated. These sacrifices were followed by more in an attempt to undo the damage to the forests.[10] Through this act of cult, Casamance stumbled into a new stage of violent resistance. The political stakes were raised when a few days later, 19 Casamançais were charged with attempting to subvert the state. Nine of them, including Diamacoune, were sentenced to 10 years for violating territorial integrity. With tensions mounting, a larger and more aggressive demonstration in Ziguinchor was again dispersed violently, leaving an official toll of 29 dead.

A group of those not killed or arrested left Ziguinchor to found a new armed branch of the MFDC, *Atika* ("warrior" in Diola), in the dense forests outside Ziguinchor, dedicated to achieving independence for the region.[11] At their head were veteran Senegalese army soldiers Sidy Badji and Léopold Sagna.[12] In moving to the *maquis*—or rebel base—the veterans and their followers were ill prepared for a violent struggle. Armed with traditional weapons and a small number of hunting rifles, most of the group had had no prior military training. And *Atika* had no military or political plan.

In fact, the group took almost no military actions until late 1986. Nevertheless, the government responded. By using an administrative reorganization, it removed the term "Casamance" from official usage. As steps toward appeasement, two Casamançais ministers were added to the cabinet. The mayor of Ziguinchor was replaced by a Casamançais.[13] And public investments were reoriented toward the region.[14] Dakar also placed the region under special governance with an army general assigned as governor for the region of Ziguinchor. Throughout the mid- and late 1980s, intelligence and torture were used to undermine the organization. Reflecting on the conflict in 1990, Mamadou Dia wrote:

> Casamance [. . .] is under a state of emergency with a governor drawn from the army who has been granted full powers. Unable to put their hands on the guerrillas, the administration arrests civilians without evidence. [. . .] We are seeing a wall of silence even though the press is billed as free and independent. Ignoble things are happening. Young people, women, old men are being stretched naked on trees under the sun, tortured. All this to get dubious statements and admissions.[15]

Atika nonetheless continued its low-intensity actions through to the end of the 1980s, gaining in intensity only in 1989. At a moment when relations with neighboring Mauritania and Gambia were becoming strained, the MFDC stepped up its military campaign, using automatic rifles and hand grenades for the first time, attacking government positions on the Gambian border in the north and by the border with Guinea-Bissau in the south. The MFDC also brought insecurity into Ziguinchor, taking direct action against civilians,[16] forcing the populations to take a position in favor of or against independence, and attacking people suspected of collusion with the Senegalese state. Meanwhile they established networks to manage recruitment and to collect "subscriptions" for the movement.

By this time the numbers in the *maquis* had, according to members of the MFDC, swollen into the thousands. The Senegalese army responded with crop destruction, internment, summary executions, and, in some cases, the clearance of entire villages.

In May 1990, the intensity of the fighting was such that the Senegalese army, pursuing rebels into Bissau, nearly sparked an interstate war, with direct engagement of Senegalese and Bissau troops on May 19–20. Casamançais refugees settled in the thousands in Guinea-Bissau and Gambia, sheltered by cross-border coethnics and kin. Hundreds more internally displaced swelled the suburbs of Ziguinchor.

The step-up in government action against the rebellion coincided with a report by *Amnesty International* criticizing Dakar for the practice of torture between 1983 and 1989.

TREATIES AND DIVISION. The publication of the *Amnesty International* report was bad timing for a government that, faced with a collapsing tourist industry and a decline in government revenues, was financially reliant on the donor community. In late 1990, the government opted for dialogue.

First meetings were held between a commission of Casamançais members of parliament and a team of MFDC military leaders. These were followed up by meetings between the government and military leaders of the MFDC in Guinea-Bissau. The amorphic political leadership, largely in prison in Dakar, had limited participation. The accord that resulted from these meetings—the Bissau Accord of May 31, 1991[17]—was later bolstered by an amnesty law preventing any penal proceedings against any party in relation to the conflict. In principle, the war was over.

The Bissau Accord is an extraordinary document. Just one page in length, it contains three short lines of operative clauses stating that the parties agree to: "(1) The cessation of all armed activity; (2) The return of all armed forces and forces of intervention to their barracks; and (3) The free circulation of individuals and goods." The missing element from this—and from all accords signed between 1991 and 2004—is a treatment of the stated fundamental concern of the MFDC: the constitutional status of Casamance.[18] Despite accepting the accords, internal meetings—according to the files of the MFDC—were still resulting in motions for the immediate independence of Casamance.

In an attempt to manage these divisions, exchanges with the government led, for the first time, to the formal development of an organizational structure for the political wing of the MFDC. At a meeting in Cap Skirring, the *maquis* nominated Diamacoune as Secretary General.[19] A follow-up meeting in April 1992 in Guinea-Bissau produced an agreement that gave rise to further dissension within the MFDC. In an organizational restructuring, the head of the *maquis* and the politically more moderate, Sidy Badji, took on the position of deputy secretary general, while more radical elements were expelled. Diamacoune soon thereafter denounced the accords and sided with the increasingly hard-line Léopold Sagna—who, taking over from Badji as head of the *maquis,* created a new focal point for militant rebels, the *Front Sud.*

Supporters of Badji, now grouped into the *Front Nord* and ostensibly abiding by the Bissau Accord, retired from military action. Keeping their weapons and maintaining effective control of a zone within the department of Bignona, the *Front Nord* has since been active in the timber and, reportedly, the cannabis industry (Evans

2002) and has, with government or donor support, been benefiting from a series of postconflict development projects.

RISE OF THE FRONT SUD. With the movement split, the Senegalese government took steps to consolidate its control over the situation on the ground,[20] increasing its military presence. By early 1993, close to a third of the Senegalese army, or about 5,000 troops, were stationed in Casamance.

After a yearlong lull in activities, the army began a new offensive with a bombarding of villages in lower Casamance along the Guinea-Bissau border, and a rise in arrests and summary executions. The *Front Sud* extended its zone of operations into Kolda, an area previously relatively untouched by the war (Marut 1992, 225). It had numerous successes in attacking government positions, and in particular in ambushing army convoys. In one coup in February 1993, the MFDC launched rocket attacks on Ziguinchor airport.

The period was marked by an increase in attacks on civilians, a rise in banditry, and the increased reliance on financing from the natural resources of the region. Looting activities were centered on holdups of public transport vehicles and the pillaging of stores in Casamance villages. The MFDC killed civilians on the basis of their place of origin, on suspicion of collaboration with the government, or, occasionally, on the basis of their ethnic identity.[21] They extended the zone of conflict to areas of high economic value, with fighting taking place in zones of importance to the cannabis and cashew nut industries,[22] peaking in this period with the taking of areas adjoining those controlled by the pacified and economically successful *Front Nord*.[23] In parallel, Senegalese army units reportedly benefited economically from the conflict through their control of timber industries (Evans 2002). The Casamance economy was crippled, with a reduction of regional income at the beginning of this period of as much as 80 percent by some estimates.[24] By the late 1990s, violence against civilian populations became more widespread and more arbitrary with the introduction of land mines to the conflict from 1997.[25] The conflict, punctuated by attempts at negotiation in 1993[26] and 1997,[27] short lulls in fighting, and returns to violence—exacerbated at one point by the disappearance of four French tourists— produced occasionally relatively heavy losses for the army.[28] War-weary populations, traumatized by the high level of arbitrary attacks and killings and dubious of the prospects of victory, began to take explicitly propeace stances through marches and projects organized by nongovernmental organizations.

The relative success of the *Front Sud* in this period and the increased reliance on financing from looting was accompanied by a new set of internal divisions. One major division took place around the persons of Léopold Sagna and Salif Sadio. Sadio, a younger *maquisard* appointed to the position of Number 2, was widely held to be responsible for the growth in success of operations and rose as a rival to Sagna. After Sagna met with President Diouf, apparently undertaking fresh negotiations without consultations with the wider organization,[29] a radical wing of the MFDC moved to replace him with Sadio. Upon his return to the *maquis,* Sagna was "arrested" and has since probably been killed. Diamacoune continued to recognize Sagna as a military leader and a group of Sagna loyalists still occupy *maquis* along the Bissau border. The Sagna faction has since divided into at least two parts, with one group working along the Bissau border and a second operating further to the north.

The strengths of these different factions during this period varied as a function of events in neighboring countries. Events in Guinea-Bissau in 1998–2000 provide a case in point. Ansoumane Mané, after being accused by President João Bernardo Vieira for trafficking arms to the MFDC, staged a revolt in June 1998. As a result, the theater of the Casamance conflict temporarily shifted to Guinea-Bissau: Senegal sent troops to oppose Mané while the MFDC sent hundreds of *maquisards* to support him.[30] The MFDC helped frustrate Senegal's efforts to capture Mané. Salif Sadio was a clear winner of the interlude. With the support of the now President of Guinea-Bissau, Ansoumane Mané[31]—playing the role of godfather to the Sadio grouping—Sadio grew in political and military strength[32] and reportedly began to model himself on Charles Taylor. Partial reversal occurred, however, when, with the election of Kumba Yalla at the end of 1999 and the death of Mané in November 2000, Bissau moved to normalize relations with Dakar and launched attacks on Sadio's positions along the border.

A TOLERABLE STALEMATE. In March 2000, elections in Senegal brought a change in the executive. Expectations of a resolution to the conflict were high, as the new president, Wade, had claimed even in opposition that he would have the problem solved within three months of taking office.[33] Wade put a stop to any work being done by civil society groups, intermediaries, diplomatic or nongovernmental, attempting to deal with the conflict.[34] While claiming to put its faith in negotiations, the Wade government put a price on the head of Salif Sadio and continued to attempt to negotiate with the increasingly irrelevant Diamacoune.[35] The MFDC in contrast began pushing for greater internationalization of the process.[36] The result of Wade's maneuvers to date has been a peace accord signed in March 2001 and another in December 2004. These accords have had few substantive innovations on previous accords and, because of the divisions within the MFDC and the narrowness of the negotiations, have had difficulty in securing the broad support of the movement.

The MFDC is now going through an unprecedented level of organizational confusion with the armed wing divided into at least four factions and no consensus within the political wing either regarding how the MFDC should be structured or who the present leadership is. However, since the signing of the December 2004 agreement guns have been silent. Mines and small-scale pillaging still cripple the local economy and rebel fighters remain in their bases.

Mali

PRELUDE TO REBELLION. The rebellion in the north of Mali in June 1990 had historical antecedents. Previous attempts at rebellion, such as those in 1894 and 1916, had been met with harsh repression. But most immediate to Tuareg activists was the 1962 rebellion against the newly independent Malian State.[37] The repression of the rising by the Keïta regime included the sacking of the region of Kidal, the poisoning of wells, and the killing of an estimated 1,000 members of the Tuareg community, resulting in an exodus by nomad groups toward southern Algeria. As in Casamance, the government instituted military rule in the rebellious province. And until 1987, communication with the Adrar region in the north was cut and access to the zone was prohibited to outsiders.[38] The history of this rebellion in Mali provided fresh grievances: Many of those who took part in the 1990 rebellion were among those who had quit the country following the reprisals against the North; among them, many had had parents killed in 1962–63.

The numbers of Tuareg-in-exile swelled when a series of droughts—beginning in 1968 and reaching extreme levels in 1973–74 and in the late 1970s to mid-1980s (Bernus 1990; Clarke 1978; Keck and Dinar 1994)—destroyed their livestock. Tuareg and Arab groups moved to Algeria, Mauritania, and, especially, Libya. They were joined there by a new class of Tuareg intellectuals, who, benefiting from the tardy introduction of education to the transhumance zones found few employment opportunities within the Malian state.[39] The immigrating population in Libya increased greatly after Mouamar Ghadaffy invited Tuareg populations to Libya in 1980, pledging to help them to "liberate" their countries. In return for training, Ghadaffy gained fighters for his Islamic legion, active in Lebanon, Palestine, Syria, and Chad.

Alongside training, emigrants in Libya engaged in political organization, founding the *Mouvement Tuareg de Libération de l'Adrar et de l'Azawad,* an organization dedicated to the liberation of the northern areas of Mali and Niger and the introduction of a popular republic *Jamahiriya.* In a move ostensibly promoted by Libya, the Malian section of the movement, splitting from the Nigerien section, transformed into the *Mouvement Populaire de Libération de l'Azawad* (MPLA) in 1988 and came under the leadership of Iyad ag Ghali.[40]

However, over the course of the late 1980s, Libya became an increasingly unwelcome place for Tuareg immigrants. The end of the oil boom led to a contraction in the demand for immigrant labor, and the defeat of Ghadaffy in Chad in 1986 led to the redundancy of Tuareg fighters. The government of Mali meanwhile, aware of Tuareg dissidents training in Libya, increased intelligence-gathering operations, arresting suspected returnees in early 1990.[41] A clampdown by the Nigerien and Malian governments followed an outbreak of fighting with Tuareg in Tchin-Tabaradene, Niger, in May. Fearing a destruction of the movement before the rebellion even started, the MPLA decided to strike.

REBELLION. In contrast to the improvised beginnings in Casamance, the war in Mali began as a planned action by a group coming from the outside with a political agenda and a military strategy. The war began in June 1990 with a string of attacks on government posts by members of the MPLA returning from Libya. The government responded with an attempted repetition of the repression of Kidal 30 years previously.[42] Militarily, however, the MPLA turned out to be strong. In one battle at Tuxemene in September 1990, the movement defeated the army with up to

200 troops lost on the government side. The defeat increased the flows of young Tuareg and Arabs to join the *maquis*. By the end of the year, the *maquis* comprised an estimated 3,000 fighters.[43] Some bases, particularly in the west, were comprised almost entirely of volunteers who had never emigrated or trained in Libya. With an inferior command of the desert, and frustrated by a failure to engage directly with the rebels, the army struck at noncombatant Tuareg communities, staging a series of beatings and public executions. Criticism of the military response came both from the international community and from the south of Mali, where communities, already dissatisfied with the Traoré regime, were conscious of the marginalization of the northern zones.[44]

In response, the government adopted a new approach. Drawing on its capital with traditional Tuareg leadership, it encouraged the traditional elites to try to resolve the problem in house. The chief of the *Iforas* group, Intalah ag Ataher, attempted an initial round of talks. At the same time, the government paper *L'Essor* ran articles quoting traditional Tuareg and Arab leaders proclaiming their support for the administration and the territorial integrity of the country, and their condemnation of the actions of what they claimed to be an unrepresentative minority.[45] These approaches produced considerable division within the MPLA, with some subsets forming alliances with traditional leaders and others insisting that their grievance was with the state and that they ought to negotiate directly with the state.

The government responded to the call for direct talks, accepting Algeria's demands to act as mediator. A hasty set of negotiations in Tamanrasset, Algeria, on January 5 and 6, 1991 ensued. Following a brief intervention by Algeria, the MPLA underwent a reorganization, now assuming the name *Mouvement Populaire de l'Azawad* (MPA); it dropped the contentious "*Libération,*" signaling even before the talks began a willingness to compromise. The Arab components meanwhile distinguished themselves formally from the larger movement taking the title *Front Islamique et Arabe de l'Azawad* (FIAA). In doing so, they became the first group to take an explicitly ethnic and religious title.

The accords that ensued seemed generous. They provided for a gradual demilitarization of the northern regions and the elimination of military posts and military activity, especially near Tuareg camp or pasture sites. And they provided for advanced administrative decentralization, according a "*statut particulier*" to the three regions of the North with a high degree of autonomy.[46] In terms of more material returns, the accords promised the creation of jobs through the replacement of the Malian army by civilians in the regional administration and the integration of insurgent combatants into the national army. The accords also promised an allocation of 47.3 percent of funds from the fourth national investment program to the North, dwarfing all previous investment allocations.

UNEASY PEACE. The Tamanrasset Accords led to a decline in organized violence. However, the regularity of seemingly isolated attacks suggests that neither the government nor the rebel groups had full command over their fighters.[47] The Traoré regime, having refused to publicize the terms of the Accords—fearing apparently that the accords would be interpreted as a surrender by the South—took contradictory public stances, at one point denying on national radio that there would be any *"statut particulier"* for the North (Gaudio 1992, 191).

For reasons largely unconnected with the conflict, Moussa Traoré was overthrown on March 26, 1991. The transitional government, the CTSP, led by Amadou Toumani Touré, moved quickly to register its acceptance of the Tamanrasset Accords and assigned two seats in the CTSP to the MPA/FIAA. The transition in Bamako, however, was accompanied by a worsening of conditions in the North. Financing was not available to implement the terms of the accords. Frustration with the loss of status of the army and public concerns with the recently published Tamanrasset Accords, which were widely interpreted as giving autonomy to the North, led to more attacks conducted by dissatisfied sections of the armed forces, notably in Gao. Tuareg and Arab fighters, now with increased freedom of movement and still armed and frustrated at not seeing the material benefits of an ostensibly successful campaign, used their position to exact revenge and, through banditry, to make material gains. The army responded in kind. In one of the most publicized incidents, on May 20, 1991, the army, after rebel groups had left town, rounded up and executed an estimated 48 Tuareg and Arab traders and notables in the village of Léré.[48] By mid-1991 public displays of violence, such as the public burning of a nomad[49] or the destruction of premises owned by Arab traders, led to enormous refugee flows from the white settled as well as nomadic populations. By the end of the summer, Timbuktu was all but deserted by white groups. In areas where nomadic populations were killed or fled, sedentary populations benefited economically from the goods left behind, which, in the opinion of many in the rebel movements, implicated the black populations in these attacks.

With ex-combatants turning their attention from military targets to sources of revenue, sedentary populations increasingly became the victims of their actions.[50] And with a rise in polarization, the criterion used to select targets by the rebels was the same as that used by the army to vent their frustrations: race. The result in early 1991 was a gradual rise in interethnic violence and the first reporting of black defense militias.[51]

Throughout the rise in violence, the MPA retained its position of support for the application of the Tamanrasset Accords and formally maintained its cease-fire, responding to the rise in violence with increased levels of coordination with the government and with traditional Tuareg authorities. This conciliatory position placed great stress on the movement and led rapidly to greater fragmentation of the organization. The FIAA grouping returned to the *maquis* and by May a further group split to form the *Front Populaire pour la Libération de l'Azawad* (FPLA),[52] frustrated both by the inaction of the MPA and by the ideological jettisoning of the principles of the rebellion. A second split, this time largely from the FPLA, produced a fourth movement, the *Armée Révolutionnaire pour le Libération de l'Azawad* (ARLA). Both groups, returning to the ideology of independence and employing a discourse of social revolution, rejected the Tamanrasset Accords.

The Tamanrasset Accords—imprecise, unimplemented, unpopular among the army and among sedentary populations, and rejected by fragments of the rebel groups—were quickly becoming irrelevant. The task of finding an alternative political solution to the Tuareg problem was deferred in order not to complicate the August 1991 National Conference set to determine the constitution of the Third Republic. To address the problem, the government of Mali set up an international mediation team that began its work by facilitating the organization of the disparate groups into a coordinating body, the *Mouvements et Fronts Unifiés de l'Azawad* (MFUA), and by running a series of consultative meetings in Algeria. Fighting raged in parallel with the meetings, with, in December, FIAA attacks on Timbuktu and the execution of Tuareg taken from the Méneka market. Nonetheless, the meetings led to a new agreement, termed the *National Pact,* signed on April 11, 1992 in Bamako (Government of Mali 1992) and initialed by the leaders of three of the four factions forming the MFUA.

The pact, like the Tamanrasset Accords, contained a mixture of material benefits and political reforms. The material benefits for the fighters and their communities included jobs in the army and in the administration, investment promises, and support for small to medium sized enterprises, as well as two funds—one for civil and military victims and one for social assistance for victims of insecurity. The pact, explicitly recognizing the economic marginalization of the North, provided for a 10-year plan to "redress the economic, social and cultural inequalities between the North and the rest of Mali."

The constitutional reforms, while not threatening the territorial integrity of Mali, did allow for considerable autonomy for the North. The decentralization provided for in the pact was at least as broad as that in the Tamanrasset Accords. It included not simply extensive control over issues of regional interest, but also envisaged a role for regions to be involved in international coordination and for cross-regional coordination, with provisions for redefining regional boundaries within the state.

Unlike the Tamanrasset Accords, the pact was a carefully developed document with well-specified institutional details and a timetable for implementation. Institutions to be set up to facilitate implementation included a high-profile *Commissariat du Nord,* a cease-fire commission, and, on the ground, mixed military patrols.

In practice, the National Pact suffered from problems similar to those of the Tamanrasset Accords. The Pact was developed with minimal consultation with the sedentary populations and, while members of the MFUA were to be allocated central roles in the transitional bodies, the pact contained no mechanisms to allow sedentary populations to be involved in its implementation.[53] Again, promises of material benefits were made without the resources in place to fulfill them.[54] The result was that implementation of the National Pact, like the implementation of the Tamanrasset Accords, was painfully slow.

The period following the signing of the pact was one of relatively low conflict intensity. As after Tamanrasset, the signing of the agreement was followed by a shift in regimes in Bamako, in this case with Konaré formally taking over as President of the Third Republic two months after the signing of the pact. A slow implementation of the pact, coupled with the failure of the leadership of the MFUA to discipline its forces, led to a return of banditry, which, in a familiar pattern, resulted in reprisals against noncombatant Tuareg.[55] This time banditry was accompanied by fighting within the MFUA. As a result of poorly coordinated acts of banditry, fighting broke out between the FIAA and FPLA in late 1992.[56] Disagreements over how to allocate the benefits of the pact, notably positions within the army, seem to have had been "resolved" by a call by the MFUA to the government to increase the size of the pie. After negotiations in April and May 1994, the MFUA increased its demands for army positions for ex-combatants.[57]

By early 1994 the continued insecurity and increasingly routinized banditry, coupled with seemingly extravagant demands for benefits exclusively for members of the MFUA, were wearing on the patience of sedentary communities. Problems became more complicated when, in April, increased tensions within mixed patrol units led to the shooting by integrated nomads of sedentary soldiers in their units.[58] Retaliatory action led to a collapse in the system of mixed patrols and the return of nomad soldiers to the desert.

INTERCOMMUNAL CONFLICT. On May 19, 1994, Captain Abdoulaye Hamadahmane Maïga, a member of the sedentary Songhoi community, deserted from the Malian army. Claiming frustration with the failure of the army to act effectively to restore security to the North, Maïga founded a civil militia: the *Ganda Koy* (literally: "masters of the land" in Songhoi). The formation of the *Ganda Koy* marked a transition of the war from a struggle directed against the central government to an intercommunal conflict. In this transition, ethnic and racial affiliation took center stage.

In one of their first actions on May 30, the *Ganda Koy* pursued and killed nine supposed cattle rustlers. In response, the MFUA head of the cease-fire commission, moved in on the *Ganda Koy* base at Fafa.[59] Encountering a regular army unit on their return, the MFUA forces were routed. There followed a rapid rise in race-based attacks and a steep escalation of violence. In August a leader of the FIAA declared "total war" and claimed responsibility for multiple attacks, many against civilians.[60] Attacks on the Tuareg and Arab communities continued apace. The escalation was accompanied by a new radicalization of political positions with new calls for an independent Azawad.[61] Interracial tensions reached such a point that many of the few Tuareg who had been integrated into the government in Bamako from the time of Traoré now went into exile. By the end of 1994, peace could not have seemed more distant.

TERMINATION. Despite the seemingly impossible situation in late 1994, the conflict in Mali fell silent within one year. In March 1996 the *Ganda Koy* and the four member organizations of the MFUA disbanded at a ceremony that included the burning of 2,700 weapons.

There was some variation in the processes that led to the cessation of activities by the different groups. The MPA had, since 1991, retained close relations with the government and had been active only in policing activities within its zone of influence. The FIAA, the group involved in some of the most bitter tit-for-tat relations with the *Ganda Koy* and seemingly the most opposed to a rapprochement, was eventually defeated, largely by military action. On January 17, 1995, their base in Tin Adema fell subsequent to action by the army, with the help of other MFUA organizations. Of the two more radical Tuareg groups, the ARLA imploded largely as a result of its defeat by the MPA. Its members split to join the MPA and the FPLA. In November 1994, the FPLA, financially exhausted, starting negotiating with the *Ganda Koy*. The negotiations, largely organized by community groups, soon included other groups from the MFUA and the communities from both sides, resulting in the signing of several accords throughout 1995. The accords provided for coordination between the sedentary and the nomadic communities to prevent banditry and to demilitarize the zone. For the brunt of the *Ganda Koy*, whose chief concern was the security of their economic activities, the accords were satisfactory.[62]

While conflict is sometimes associated with a collapse in state strength, the increase in the capacity of the Malian state—particularly its capacity to control its own army—contributed to the termination of the conflict in Mali. The localized nature of the conflict, and the fact that at no point did the rebellion aim to overthrow the state, meant that the strength of the Malian state was not endogenous to conflict. In fact, during the mid-1990s there was a strengthening of the state, which finally began to receive support from the international community and to gain tighter control over its army. Whereas in the immediate aftermath of the Tamanrasset Accords, many elements of the army were acting independently of civilian control, in the mid-1990s there was a series of security sector reforms, including a U.S.-sponsored International Military Education and Training program to reformulate the role of the military in Mali's new democracy.[63] The result was an opportunity to improve relations with northern populations: The government replaced senior army commanders, and by the end of 1994 Konaré was able to withdraw troops from the region that had been involved in massacres.[64]

While formally the terms of the *National Pact* remained in place, intercommunal meetings were used to respond to inadequacies of the agreement, leading ultimately to a division of the spoils (counted in jobs) that also benefited the sedentary populations.[65]

Causes of Conflict

Lessons from Statistical Work

We begin our analysis of the causes of these conflicts by considering the predicted probability of war onset from two econometric models: the Collier-Hoeffler core model (figures 9.1 and 9.2) and the Fearon and Laitin model (figures 9.3 and 9.4).

The Collier-Hoeffler model predicts war onset risk using four time-varying variables—the share of primary commodity exports in gross domestic product (GDP), and past levels of education, population, and per capita income growth—along with a number of time-invariant variables—notably the level of ethnic fragmentation and country size. The average predicted probability of war onset in a five-year period sub-

Figure 9.1 Probabilities of Civil War from the Collier-Hoeffler Model

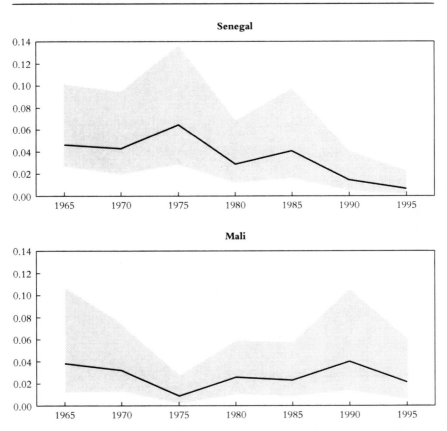

Note: The solid line gives the predicted probability of civil war onset in Senegal and Mali based on estimates and data from Collier and Hoeffler (canonical equation). The shaded area records a 95 percent confidence interval around these predictions.

sequent to 1965 is around 3 percent in Mali and 4 percent in Senegal; the population frequency is 7 percent.

The level predictions of the model appear unsuccessful: The model predicts that these two countries have well-below-average probabilities of having conflicts (as defined by Collier and Hoeffler), despite the fact that both countries did indeed have sizable civil wars. The model does not appear to be successful in terms of comparative statics predictions either: The period in which the Casamance conflict actually started was a period in which the model predicted a below-average likelihood of civil war *even in terms of Senegal's already low probabilities*. Similarly, the period in which the war escalated—around 1990—corresponds to a dip in predicted probabilities. The model seems to perform better for Mali, with predictions peaking in the period in

Figure 9.2 **Factors Contributing to Variation in the Probability of Civil War Outbreak in the Collier-Hoeffler Model**

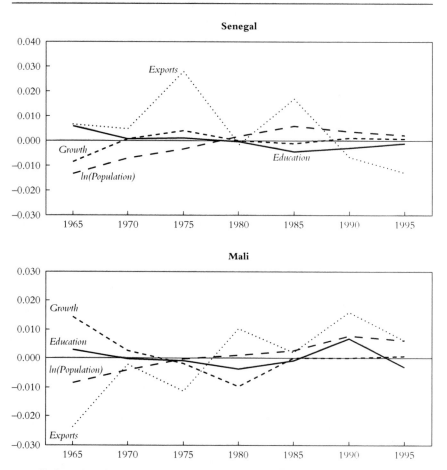

Note: This figure shows how the predicted probability of civil war differs from what it would have been had different variables from Collier and Hoeffler (2001) remained at their period average.

which the conflict did in fact break out; however, these predictions are, in absolute terms, very low throughout and never predict a conflict for any given year. Even so, it is reasonable to ask whether the changes in predicted probabilities that are observed are related to factors of importance to the conflicts.

We answer this question by considering a "decomposition" of the predicted probabilities in which we consider how changes in the time-varying explanatory variables account for changing predictions of war onset.[66] The decomposition for Mali shows that the peak in 1990 can be attributed in part to a continuing rise in popu-

Figure 9.3 **Probabilities of Civil War from the Fearon–Laitin Model**

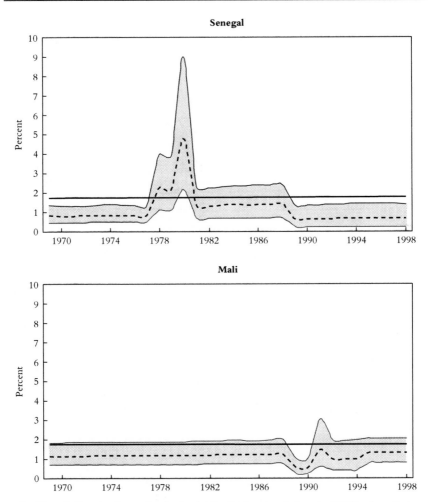

Note: The marked line gives the annual predicted probability of civil war onset in Senegal and Mali based on estimates and data from the Fearon and Laitin model. The shaded area records a 95 percent confidence interval around these predictions. See Fearon and Laitin (2003) for details regarding the estimation of the model and data used.

lation and fall in education rates, but, most importantly, to a peak in the relative value of exported primary commodities to GDP. Similarly, the Senegal decomposition (figure 9.2) suggests that intertemporal variation in predicted probabilities is driven overwhelmingly by changes in the value of primary commodity exports. Primary commodity dependence may put a country at risk though a number of mechanisms, such as by increasing inequality, producing an economic structure with a low inten-

Figure 9.4 **Factors Contributing to Variation in the Probability of Civil War Outbreak in the Fearon-Laitin Model**

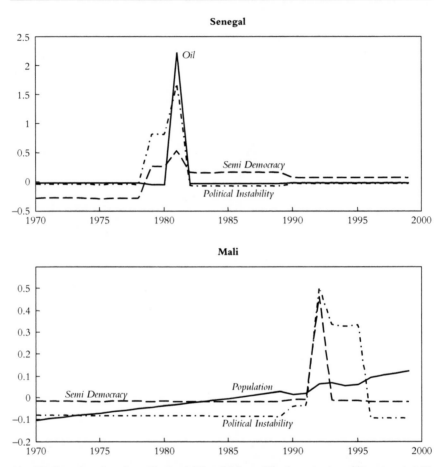

Note: This figure shows how the predicted probability of civil war differs from what it would have been had different variables from Fearon and Laitin (2003) remained at their period average.

sity of internal trade, or producing an economy especially vulnerable to terms of trade shocks (see Humphreys 2002; Ross 2002). In the next section we consider the greed mechanism suggested by Collier and Hoeffler—that control of (or the desire to control) primary commodities provides either the start-up capital or the motives for would-be rebels.

The predictions of the Fearon and Laitin model are presented in figure 9.3. This model predicts the probability of the outbreak of a conflict in any given year (rather than for a five-year period) based on the wealth and population of the country as well as a number of binary variables, notably whether or not the country is a semi-democracy[67] or has had a large change in its political institutions.[68] As with the Collier and Hoeffler model, this model predicts both countries as having below-average chances of having a civil war. Although the comparative statics do not suggest conflict is particularly likely in Mali in 1990,[69] the model does predict that Senegal's chances of having a conflict rise dramatically in 1981—right before the conflict actually starts (although again the predicted probability of conflict is still extremely low).[70]

To evaluate these predictions we again perform a decomposition (see figure 9.4).[71] We find that the spike for Senegal in 1981 derives from just two features—institutional change in 1978 and an increase in oil exports in 1981—neither of which is obviously related to the Casamance conflict. In Fearon and Laitin's model, the political reform in 1978 classified Senegal as a semi-democracy, which increased the chance for conflict onset over the period 1979 to the present.[72] This change in political institutions, though undertaken at a moment of institutional strength, is classified by Fearon and Laitin as a moment of political instability. The imputed instability leads to higher probabilities of war onset particularly in years 1979–81. The peak in 1981 arises from these effects coupled with the classification of Senegal as an oil-exporting country for that year.[73] Fearon and Laitin argue that oil producers have weaker state apparatuses and that the availability of oil revenue raises the value of taking the state. The revenues of the Senegalese state do not, however, derive primarily from oil; more importantly, oil revenues in Senegal in the period did not derive from domestic production but rather from re-exports (Enda-TM 1994). These less lucrative oil re-exports are a poor proxy for state strength. Moreover, the MFDC at no point aimed to gain control of this industry.[74]

Greed

The aggregate data used in econometric work to measure the resources available to insurgents in Casamance—capturing fluctuations in the yields and price of fish, groundnuts, cotton, and oil re-exports—do not reflect the resources that are most relevant to the conflict. Although the expansion of some of these industries by *nordistes* working in Casamance has fueled the complaints of the Casamançais, none of these has been used to finance the war in Casamance and there has been no attempt by the *maquisards* to gain control of them. There are high-value, lootable natural resources in Casamance—notably cannabis, timber, and cashew nuts—but the chronology of the rebellion does not support the greed hypothesis with regard to these commodities either, because these resources increased in importance many years after the conflict began. Furthermore, although we argue that access to natural resources in the region has contributed to the duration and plausibly the intensity of the Casamance conflict, these resources were not accessed by the MFDC in the early stages of the rebellion, when the rebellion relied much more on subscriptions from local populations.

It is also difficult to make a case that the conflict in Mali was driven by the desire to control stocks of natural resources. Gold is Mali's third largest export after cotton and livestock, with a 1994 value of $67 million, accounting for 20 percent of exports.

The country also has diamond deposits (van Oss 1994). Furthermore, the CH model suggests that variation in the value of primary commodities is largely responsible for the intertemporal variation in the predicted probability of war occurrence in Mali. There is, however, nothing linking these gold and diamond deposits directly to the conflict. Although there are gold and diamond deposits in the Adrar des Iforas, these remain untapped because of high extraction costs. Instead, gold is mined and exported in the south of the country, far from the conflict. At no stage was a bid made by any of the rebel groups to gain access to the mines or the revenues from them. The one lootable resource that did help fuel the war was cattle. Cattle are, however, typically "diffuse" both in their supply and their marketing and, although access to cattle may have motivated individual fighters, the difficulty in deriving a centralized revenue stream makes it implausible that cattle were an important motivation for the leaders of the rebellion.

Regional Specificity

The two conflicts, it seems, were not initiated with a desire to control lucrative natural resources. Nor did either rebellion at any stage attempt to gain, or claim to be fighting for, control of the state. The MFDC are fighting, they claim, for the independence of Casamance, or more precisely, for the recognition, not the granting, of the independence of the Casamance. The MPLA initially had a more complex project involving the piecing together of nomadic areas across a range of countries in the region. In both cases, the arguments that are used to justify the independence struggles rely on a notion that these regions are "particularly different." An important comparative question then for the study of secessionist struggles is to what extent some regions, and not others, differ in ways that make bids for secession germane.[75] We turn now to consider the arguments that the exceptionalisms of the Casamance and the Azawad are politically relevant.

POLITICAL GEOGRAPHY.   We noted that Senegal and Mali share similar physical geographies with great internal ecological variation. With the political center of Senegal based in the north of the country and the political center of Mali based in the south, a shared feature of their political geographies is the fact that the would-be seceding regions are "distant," constituting in each case the *most* remote region relative to the political center (at least in travel time). For all intents and purposes, Casamance is disjointed from the rest of the country, separated by the Gambia. An overland route through Senegal exists, but requires a 20-hour drive to bridge the 300 miles between Dakar and Ziguinchor. Otherwise transit from the north to Casamance passes either by sea or by air or through the Gambia. Casamançais nationalists liken the situation to that of East and West Pakistan and see in the map of Senegal a confirmation of the legitimacy of their struggle.[76] Their thesis finds some support in econometric work that finds that noncontiguity is positively associated with conflict (Fearon and Laitin 2003). A similar situation prevails in Mali. While again the north is formally contiguous with the south, the desert zones are relatively inaccessible from the capital, although this is due to sheer distance and a lack of infrastructure rather than shape. Travel from Bamako to Gao by road takes approximately 35 hours, including an overnight wait for a ferry. If the Niger water levels are not right or the ferry is out of order, a trip to Timbuktu can take 48 hours, while travel to Kidal is likely to take four or five days.

COLONIAL HISTORY. While geography suggests a particularity to these regions, rebelling groups can also point to the fact that colonial administrators treated these regions as exceptional. Casamance had an ambiguous and now hotly contested administrative status under colonialism, especially from 1854 to 1939,[77] partly because, unlike other areas of the country, the French did not succeed in gaining full control over the area until early in the 20th century.[78] The north of Mali, a region of extended armed resistance, was also relatively late in coming under French control. Timbuktu was taken in 1894, followed by Gao in 1899 and the *Adrar des Iforas* only in 1909. The status of the North remained exceptional, being the only region of the country that remained under military rule up until 1958. Indeed shortly prior to Malian independence, the French entertained the idea of separating the North from the rest of the country with the formation of the OCRS.

We have then that in each case the conflicts that ensued were linked to a longer tradition of local resistance and special forms of governance. However, although econometric studies take account of histories of conflict postindependence, they fail to include measures of the degree and location of conflict during the colonial period. The exceptional histories of these regions are linked to the present conflict in at least four ways. First, variation in the histories of resistance in different areas signal prior motivations for armed struggle in these areas—fixed effects. Second, the fact that colonialism took so long to take hold in the region reduced the degree of homogeneity that was introduced in other regions of the countries under colonial rule.[79] Third, the history of conflict in the areas led to local militarization as well as—and this is particularly clear in the case of Azawad—to grievances resulting from past conflicts. Finally, the history of resistance can be used to motivate and legitimate new actions. Fr. Diamacoune, for example, makes use of the administrative history of Casamance, as well as of the history of resistance to colonial rule, to argue that Casamance was colonized by France independently of Senegal.[80]

ETHNIC AND RELIGIOUS COMPOSITION. Both Casamance and Azawad, while each ethnically diverse, have very different ethnic and religious demographics relative to those in Senegal and Mali more generally. Can the simple distribution of groups help explain the tendency for secessionism? Lower Casamance is the most ethnically heterogeneous region of Senegal, and, like Senegal as a whole, has a dominant—albeit internally fragmented—ethnic group, the Diola.[81] Mali, like Senegal, is ethnically heterogeneous with a dominant group—the Bambara—active in the political center of the country. The Tuareg and Arabs, however, are almost entirely based in the northern regions, comprising a majority in the far north. The demographics are consistent with the notion that regional concentration within states that have another dominant group are especially prone to secessionist bids.

However, the argument for ethnic exceptionalism is weak. In neither country are these the only regions with local dominant groups; furthermore, in neither case is there an attempt to create a state with a permanent ethnic majority. The dominance of the Diola does not extend to the entire region, as Peuls and Mandinka dominate in upper and middle Casamance respectively, nor would Tuareg and Maure groups form a majority in an Azawad region that contains, particularly along the banks of the Niger, a large sedentary community composed mostly of Songhoi and Peul.

Nor do differences in religion help to explain the specificity of Azawad: nomadic and sedentary groups in the north are overwhelmingly Muslim within an entirely Muslim country. Casamance has more religious diversity than other parts of Senegal, with a large Christian population within a country that is 94 percent Muslim. Nonetheless, Casamance is not the only region with a Christian concentration[82] and, more importantly, religion has not been an important organizing force in the conflict: The leadership of the MFDC has been both Muslim and Christian, seemingly without great attention being paid to the balance.

Of perhaps more importance is the *qualitative* nature of the differences between the ethnic groups. Although each country is ethnically heterogeneous, the Tuareg and Arab groups are often considered in Mali to be racially rather than simply ethnically distinct from other groups in the country and are referred to as whites or reds.[83] These perceived racial differences, absent in Senegal, have affected the course of the conflict. Interviews also suggest that racial differences motivated at least in part the desire for independence.[84]

NATION. In both Casamance and Azawad, intellectuals working with the rebel groups argue that the struggles are for the independence not simply of a region but of a nation. The geographic and historical exceptionalism discussed above does not, however, imply the existence of the sense of "nationhood" that appears necessary to these movements as they motivate their struggles. In both cases, providing arguments for the existence of nations that correspond to the contested territories has been difficult. Intellectuals in the movements draw heavily on ethnic rather than regionally relevant motifs and have made little effort to develop more inclusive notions of an Azawad or Casamance nation corresponding to the regions being fought for.[85] The discourses attempt to found a notion of national identity upon characteristics of ethnic identities while refusing to identify nation with ethnicity. This strategy has been unsuccessful in both cases. In Casamance the movement has failed to generate support sufficiently broad so as to allow for the organization of mass actions such as electoral boycotts.[86] Nationalist aspirations in north Mali were short lived, even among the rebel leaders who rapidly adopted more "patriotic" positions.[87]

Grievances

Arguments presented by rebelling groups to justify the onset of the conflicts in Senegal and Mali draw heavily on perceived grievances. In both cases, the list of grievances is long. And indeed in both cases—at least in the early stage of the conflicts—there was widespread local recognition of the grievances that were articulated by the rebels. As, arguably, any groups can identify *some* grievances, our concern is to see whether there exists observable indicators of grievances that demonstrate that the grievances suffered in Casamance and Azawad are more pronounced than those in other parts of Senegal and Mali.

ECONOMIC GRIEVANCES. Casamance rebels complain of the economic treatment of the province since independence. The area does indeed suffer from severe poverty and underinvestment in infrastructure. Basic services are lacking: Casamance has only one hospital and no university. In many parts of the region, child malnutrition rates are high, and there is poor access to health services and drinking water.[88] Furthermore, the rebels argue, what wealth has been generated has been distributed unevenly, with *nordistes* benefiting disproportionately from Casamance's resources. They argue that Casamance has great potential for wealth but that the region remains poor due to extraction and a lack of investment in public goods by northerners.

The analytic question remains, however: To what extent are these grievances specific to Casamance? It turns out that many of the grievances are shared with other regions within Senegal, resulting from decades of development policy that has privileged the capital at the expense of the regions. From table 9.1 we see that, at least based on data produced by the Senegalese government prior to the outbreak of the conflict, Casamance was not the most badly treated region in the country. Although road infrastructure was essentially ignored, medical services were no worse than elsewhere, and government investment in telecommunications infrastructure, though worse than the regional average outside Dakar, made disproportionate gains in the 1960s and 1970s. Strikingly, with data available that distinguish between the two regions of Casamance, Kolda and Ziguinchor, we see that for a wide range of measures, Kolda ranks as one of the worst-off areas of the country, while Ziguinchor— the zone where fighting and recruitment is most concentrated—is one of the best off (see table 9.2), with particularly high levels of primary education.[89]

Of more relevance perhaps, but more difficult to evaluate, are notions of a shortfall between economic expectations and economic outcomes. The sense of economic marginalization may arise from the sense that, on the basis of the fertility of the land,[90] the region ought to be *particularly* wealthy. Casamançais argue, for example, that investments in sugar cane and rice ought to have been undertaken in Casamance, where, they argue, these investments would have been more productive, rather than in other regions, notably in the Senegal river valley.[91]

A final salient aspect of economic grievances relates to the redistributive politics of economic development, and especially to the political economy of land rights. The *Loi sur le Domaine National,*[92] introduced in 1964 but implemented in Casamance only in 1979, made the Senegalese state the formal owner of all nonprivatized land (Hesseling 1994, 243, 250). The law had repercussions throughout Senegal and was felt strongly among the Diola.[93] By treating land development as the primary criterion for private ownership, state-appointed rural councils used the law to reallocate

Table 9.1 Evidence on Economic Grievances Prior to 1982

Region	Population, 1978	People per doctor, 1978	Surfaced roads (km)		Telephone lines		People per telephone line, 1978	Total and percentage increase in lines, 1962–78
			1972	1979	1962	1978		
Casamance	776	32,342	0	0	419	979	793	560 or 134%
Other regions								
Cap Vert (Dakar)	1,038	3,832	101	105	19,673	32,126	32	1,2453 or 63%
Diourbel	449	34,590	54	5	545	1,064	423	519 or 95%
Senegal River Basin	556	21,413	3	41	1,193	1,208	461	15 or 1%
Louga	438	10,9741		111	—	479	916	—
Eastern Senegal	299	42,826		0	121	335	895	214 or 177%
Sine Saloum	1,059	52,997	57	57	797	1,603	661	806 or 101%
Thies	733	28,207	159	167	1,041	2,648	277	1,067 or 54%
Senegal	5,353	13,691	374	486	23,789	40,442	132	16,653 or 70%
Source	GoS, 1979, Table 11	GoS, 1979, Table 11	GoS, 1979, p. 294	GoS, 1979, p. 294	GoS, 1979, p. 319	GoS, 1979, p. 319	Authors' calculation	Authors' calculation

Note: GoS = Government of Senegal.

Table 9.2 Evidence on Economic Grievances 1980s and 1990s

Region	Population (thousands), 2000	Average household Income ('000 CFA), 1995	Human poverty index, 1999	Human development index, 2000	Primary school participation rates (%), 1991/92	% of population with access to drinking water, 2000	Gini coefficient measure of income inequality, 1995	Ethnic fractionalization, 1995	Between-group inequality, 1995	Male unemployment rate 1988, age 15–29
Casamance										
Kolda	797	805	62	41	40	27	.56	.58	22%	4
Ziguinchor	544	2,053	39	53	94	38	.71	.73	6%	16
Other Regions										
Dakar	2,327	3,773	30	62	93	93	.67	.74	0%	33
Diourbel	902	1,361	52	37	25	78	.63	.60	3%	6
Fatick	629	1,479	56	41	42	50	.62	.68	13%	3
Kaolack	1,101	1,936	52	41	37	49	.63	.55	4%	5
Louga	555	2,311	57	42	35	57	.62	.48	2%	5
St Louis	842	4,020	49	46	42	64	.81	.51	4%	16
Tambacounda	518	1,376	59	42	36	40	.64	.62	9%	5
Thiès	1,311	1,657	48	48	59	65	.64	.68	8%	10
All Casamance	1,341	1,456	53	43		32		.77	1%	8
All Senegal	9,527	2,597	44	43	56	64a	.70	.75	5%	13
Source	BADIS p.16–25	ESM	BADIS p.51	BADIS p.52	RDP A2.4	BADIS p.181	ESM	ESM	ESM	BADIS p.129

a. Recorded as 64 but figure based on data above is 73.

Notes: ESM = Enquête Sénégalaise Auprès des Ménages, Government of Senegal Statistics Office, 1995; BADIS = Banque de Données des Indicateurs Sociaux, Government of Senegal Statistics Office.

land to nonresidents to be used for tourism, fishing, and orchards.[94] The reallocations, stressing economic productivity, took on a political, and in particular ethnic character, with a reported 6,000 cases of expropriation, primarily of Diolas and Mancagnes from lower Casamance.[95] Land politics are seen as one indication of a more general domination of the modern sector by northern groups, the impact of which was amplified by changing economic conditions. When falls in production in the 1970s led to the need to engage with the market, Diola producers in Casamance found that markets—in transport, fishing, and commercial agriculture—were already dominated by northerners.[96]

It is difficult, however, to find data to compare the levels of unequal treatment in other regions of the country. To check the hypothesis that there exists politically relevant inequality within the region, we use household data from 1995 to estimate the total inequality in each region that can be explained by between-(ethnic)group inequality.[97] We find that, consistent with the complaints of the MFDC, the two regions of Casamance are among those with the greatest horizontal inequality— that is, in which income cleavages are most reinforced by ethnic cleavages. The between-group inequalities are driven by gaps between Wolof and Diola in the region of Ziguinchor and between Wolof and Peul in Kolda (see table 9.2).[98] As with other objective measures of economic grievances, however, this measure identifies the region of Kolda rather than the region of Ziguinchor—where in fact the conflict has concentrated—as the most conflict-prone region.

Economic grievances, dating back to the colonial period, are less ambiguous in northern Mali. Chief among these is the colonizer's drawing of boundaries through the desert. The drawing of national boundaries was of singular economic importance in the North—interrupting caravan routes and, at least formally, preventing access to traditional pasture zones, limiting the capacity of nomadic pastoralists to spread their risks. The effects of this compartmentalization became most strongly felt with independence and the breakup of French West Africa. In this regard decolonization had a deeper economic effect on the economic lifestyle of the Tuareg than did colonialism (Hawad 1990). The problem is attributed in part to differing conceptions of property between nomadic and sedentary communities—claims of traditional complementarities between nomadic and sedentary modes of production notwithstanding.[99] The legal apparatus assigning and protecting property rights developed by the Malian state, allowing the state to claim rights to unregistered land[100] and to land left fallow, was seen as privileging sedentary communities.[101]

The economic marginalization of the North subsequent to independence was felt as keenly by sedentary populations as by nomadic groups and was quickly acknowledged in the national press and by the transitional CTSP government.[102] Even the Traoré government, attempting to demonstrate its dedication to the North by noting major investments in the area in the first *Livre Blanc* (1990), was only able to list a phosphate factory in Bourem and a salt project in Taoudenit, the latter in fact being a prison. Besides the lack of investments in the region, complaints center on inequalities in the provision of health and education in the regions. The data in table 9.3 support the view that in the early and mid-1990s, the North was not

Table 9.3 Socioeconomic Conditions by Region

Region	Population (%)	School attendance rates, 1995/96 (%)	Malnutrition 0–3 years; rates (%)	Vulnerability to extreme food insecurity 1996 (%)
Original data source	DNSI (Direction nationale de la statistique et de l'informatique) Commissariat au Plan	"Report on the analysis of the situation in Mali." UNICEF, 1996	Population and health survey, 1995–96	FEWS data for 1996 and 1997
Kayes	14	35	38	0
Bamako	9	131	29	0
Koulikoro	16	44	41	0
Sikasso	17	38	44	0
Segou	18	37	41	0
The North				
Mopti	16	23	41	10
Timbuktu	6	23	41	28
Gao	4	31	41	61
Kidal	1	19	41	83
Total	100	42	40	7

Note: Based on data presented in WFP Country Program Mali (1999–2001), *Agenda Item 7;* FEWS = Famine Early Warning Systems Network.

just badly off in these regards, but was in an exceptionally poor condition relative to other regions of the country.

POLITICAL GRIEVANCES. Rebels argue that economic marginalization has been accompanied by political marginalization. The advent of independence is represented in Casamance as the simple replacement of one foreign-language speaking administration with another.[103] To demonstrate political exclusion, Casamançais point to a low proportion of Casamançais in public offices, especially heading up local and regional administrations (positions of governor or prefect); even the representatives of Casamance in the national parliament were disproportionately from the region of Saint Louis and the position of mayor of Ziguinchor was, before the rebellion, filled by a Toucouleur who was seen as a *nordiste*. Attempts to place Casamançais as governors in other regions were rejected. However, the case for political exclusion, at least at the center, is not entirely compelling. There is no evidence that Casamance has been treated worse than other regions in its political appointments, and indeed many prominent cabinet positions—such as minister of defense or minister of the armed forces—have been allocated to Casamance politicians throughout the postindependence period.

Again, the political marginalization of the nomadic groups in Azawad is more convincing. In Azawad, as in Casamance, independence was seen as a shift in the identity of the colonial power. But, largely in response to the Tuareg uprising of 1962, political marginalization in the North was exceptionally harsh. The North for much of the period was under military rule and governors appointed, if from the region (broadly defined), were drawn from the Songhoi group.[104] There was a total of just two Tuareg and two Arabs appointed as ministers in all postindependence cabinets up to 1990, with three of these appointed toward the end of the 1980s. In the same period, there were only two Tuareg officers in the Malian army; there were no Tuareg national heads of administrative departments within the civil service and there had been only one Tuareg inspector of education throughout the educational sector.

A final form of political marginalization, as articulated by the insurgents in Mali, relates to in-group politics. The insurgents, initially drawn from groups that had quit Mali after the droughts of the mid-1970s, felt socially marginalized by the Tuareg elites who remained behind. Tuareg elites had been given limited privileges by the Traoré regime and were held responsible for the diversion of food aid sent in response to the droughts.[105] The marginalization of the combatants from the traditional elites meant that the former had no access to the albeit limited channels of political communication that had been established by the state.[106]

CULTURAL GRIEVANCES. Members of the MFDC stress cultural grievances more than economic grievances, noting prejudices encountered when dealing with *nordistes* in administrative positions in Casamance. They see the imposition of the Wolof—the *lingua franca* of the North—in the media, in the administration and in their schools, as a denigration of their own languages.[107] Similarly, besides economic marginalization, Tuareg groups complain of a denigration of their culture, epitomized by the attempt by the Malian administration to replace the *Tamacheq* script, *Tifinagh,* with a Latin script.[108]

Cultural disdain of this sort remains, however, difficult to measure, even within a single country and fails to feature in most cross-national econometric work. Fearon and Laitin (2003) failed to find evidence that state discrimination against minority languages or religions is associated with conflict. Yet no cross-national measures exist of attitudes that groups have toward each other. Stereotyping, existing prior to the outbreaks of the conflicts, nonetheless appear germane in both the Senegal and Mali cases, with, in both cases, the rebelling factions coming from groups that are negatively stereotyped. The stereotype of the Casamançais reported by compatriots is one of "forest people, pagans, palm-wine drinkers (or drunkards) and pork eaters."[109] The image in the North of the working Diola is of the housemaid, at the lowest rank of the Dakar pecking order. Attitudes of "West Africans" to the Tuareg meanwhile were described thus by a Malian officer: "West Africans tend to view the Tuaregs as lazy, prone to violence and criminality, opportunistic, ethnically chauvinistic, and unpatriotic" (Keïta 1998, 9).

Opportunity

Plausibly, the onset of conflict may not be due to extraordinary grievances or atypical levels of greed, but rather to the fact that the costs associated with engaging in violent action happen to be unusually low. If this argument is correct, differences in the local availability of arms, variation in the relations that exist with neighboring countries, and variation in the degree of state strength and in local economic conditions may determine conflict onset.

ARMS. Explanations for conflict onset based on variation in opportunity costs suggest that, given that grievances are ubiquitous, the existence of a vibrant regional arms market or a drop in the cost of arms may determine rises in the chances of conflict. We find, however, that the onset of the conflicts in Mali and Senegal cannot be attributed to such features.

In both cases, the conflicts began before fighters had access to significant supplies of arms—the MFDC did not have any access to modern arms and automatic weapons until the very end of the 1980s, while the Tuareg fighters, despite having taken arms from Libya, in fact had had these arms stolen before the conflict began.[110] Furthermore, when arms were accessed, they were largely accessed from nonmarket sources. In Casamance, arms transfers from regional governments have been more important than the regional arms market. In contrast, although for Mali there was a general availability of arms in the region[111] and arms could be bought from dealers in Mauritania and Algeria or from the *Polisario,* the majority of arms accessed, particularly in early stages, were taken from government stocks rather than from markets.[112]

TROUBLE WITH THE NEIGHBORS. Research has suggested that there is a contagion effect to civil wars—the likelihood of a civil war is increased by the existence of civil wars in neighboring countries (Sambanis 2001). A number of mechanisms may lie behind this relationship—including ideological contagion, ideological support, and the availability of supplies, arms, and combatants. Many of these mechanisms serve to reduce the costs of conflict to belligerent groups.

In the region, the only conflicts that preceded Senegal's were the independence struggles, notably of Guinea-Bissau and Guinea Conakry. Guinea-Bissau's struggle played a particularly important role. Early relations between Casamance and Guinea-Bissau developed in part *because* the two zones were under different colonial administrations. Casamançais resistors to French colonial rule took refuge in Guinea-Bissau or used the Portuguese-held area as a base and, in return in the 1960s and early 1970s, the independence movement PAIGC, used Casamance as a base during their own independence struggle. The first mechanism through which the Bissau struggle mattered for Casamance is through ideological contagion. The MFDC viewed the PAIGC as having been fighting for the same aims—the removal of a colonial power—and, importantly, as having been successful in their actions. The second mechanism is through intraethnic solidarity developed in part from a shared history of resistance. The debt to the Casamançais is used to explain the fact that, since the beginning of the revolt, the MFDC has expected to be able to use Guinea-Bissau as a location for bases, as a source of arms, and as a market for goods. A third mechanism, often cited but for which we have not found evidence, is that the MFDC has been able to access arms used by the PAIGC during their own struggle.

An important role model in the Malian case was provided by the conflict in Algeria in 1954–62. During the Algerian War of Independence, FLN representatives mounted information campaigns in the area, engaging in significant fund raising and awareness raising throughout the North, particularly in the Adrar and the region of Timbuktu. On an individual basis, Tuareg also participated in the Algerian conflict.

Conflicts in the region also lent ideological support to the fighters. The ideological support was derived from the commonality of the cause with those of other liberation fighters in Niger and Western Sahara in particular. These groups trained together in Libya and supported each other, with Niger—by providing refuge for Malian rebels—playing a role similar to that of Guinea-Bissau in the Casamance conflict.

There is evidence too that both arms and fighters spilled across borders. Arms originated from the conflicts in Chad, Western Sahara, and Niger, and also from the conflict between Senegal and Mauritania,[113] while a small number of fighters also migrated to northern Mali after other conflicts in the region (Maïga 1997, 268).

But perhaps the most important neighborhood effect for Mali was the Libyan effect. Libya's impact on the conflict was not due to civil wars in Libya but rather to the international engagements of the country and the use it made of Tuareg fighters. By taking part in Libya's offensives, particularly in Chad, young Tuareg men were able to receive military training and developed both competence in and a commitment to the use of force. In turning their attention to problems at home, a violent campaign was the obvious option for them.

ECONOMIC AND POLITICAL CONDITIONS. Consistent with the logic in Fearon and Laitin (2003), variation in state strength can help explain the timing of conflict. Plausibly, Casamance rebels hoped to benefit from the moment of transition of power in Dakar to capitalize on transitory fragility of the Senegalese state.[114] The change in leadership at the center also reflects a change in the manner in which the Casamance dossier was managed. Whereas Senghor, a Catholic Sérère, succeeded in negotiating effectively with discontented Casamançais, Diouf's response to the protests of December 1982 and 1983 was less sophisticated. Responding with a clampdown, he confirmed feelings of marginalization and helped to radicalize the movement. Sending one group fleeing to the forests, he stimulated the creation of the *maquis,* and sending another to prison in Dakar, he facilitated the organization of the political wing.[115]

Like Senegal, this was a period of political transition in Mali. In 1990, the government of the second republic was already going through a state of crisis, and indeed was to fall within seven months of the start of the rebellion.

Interviews in Mali suggest, however, that despite state weakness and the fact that government installations were poorly defended in northern Mali, the factor in the forefront of the minds of the leaders of 1990 was their rapidly declining status in exile. An important factor of timing in Mali seems to be the correlation between increased levels of education with economic downturn. Economic downturn reduced possibilities in Mali; more important, however, was the recession in Libya, where, with the fall in oil prices in the mid-1980s, a concomitant decline in demand for immigrant workers, and the dissolution of the Islamic league, there was reduced demand for Tuareg immigrants, both military and intellectual. The downturn, combined with the increased levels of education among the immigrants, left, alongside the Tuareg soldiers, a class of nomad unemployed intellectuals no longer welcome in Libya.

As in Mali, a number of more local economic conditions of the mid-1970s seem important in Senegal. In response to the economic downturn faced by Senegal following the droughts of the mid-1970s, northerners turned more intensively to the resources of Casamance. This, too, was a difficult period for the Casamançais, with a decline in revenues and a local economy that was dominated by northern groups. As in Mali, as a result of higher levels of education in the region at least since the 1960s, by the early 1980s, the economic crunch left Casamance with intellectuals with poor employment prospects who rapidly articulated strong critiques of the center.[116]

Duration and Termination

Financing Rebellion

We find that the forms of financing available to the rebel organizations help to explain the duration of these two conflicts. A key aspect is the extent and exhaustibility of financing—whether or not the resources are sufficient to sustain an extended conflict. A second aspect is the control of sources of funding, whether control is held by sources with an interest in conflict perpetuation or in conflict resolution. A third key aspect is the impact of different forms of financing on rebel organizational structures.

Over the course of the conflict, the Casamance rebels have increasingly become financed by renewable sources that diminish the incentives for conflict resolution and, plausibly, contribute to the fragmentation of the rebel organization. Although financed in the 1980s largely by subscriptions,[117] by the 1990s, voluntary contributions were replaced by nonvoluntary war taxes, in cash or in kind, including looting and livestock rustling. At least since the early 1990s, however, natural resources—notably cannabis, cashew nuts, and timber—have been playing a central role in sustaining the *maquisards*. The cashew nut industry for the region has an estimated value of $2.5 million,[118] whereas the Gendarmerie reported the seizure of 106 tons of cannabis in 1999 valued at $10 million.[119] Control of the latter industry would likely shift in the absence of the conflict.[120] These resources are *diffuse* in the sense that they require no centralization either for their production or for their exportation (see Le Billon 2001); they allow for subgroups to split and finance themselves independent of other factions. Nonetheless, income from these revenue sources does not appear to be evenly distributed within the MFDC.[121] If common valuations of these trades are correct, the implication is that the conflict is a highly profitable endeavor for some elements of the MFDC leadership.

Unlike Casamance, north Mali, already the poorest area in the country, did not have the resources to sustain a protracted conflict. The financing of the Tuareg groups depended largely on lifting stocks of resources such as cattle and vehicles.[122] Like the natural resources in Casamance, accessing these goods did not require centralized structures. But unlike the resources in Casamance, these goods were not to be replenished annually. Dwindling stocks left groups, including the leadership of the organizations, living increasingly from hand to mouth. In this context, a negotiated solution with the offer of a salary as part of the package was increasingly attractive.

In the Mali case, important funding came from voluntary sources. But these sources had an interest in war termination. Funding for the FIAA was drawn in part from financial capital from Arab traders in exile hoping to be able to return to the zones. The returns to these investments for the Arabs depended not on the duration of the conflict but on its termination. The *Ganda Koy*, operating from the towns rather than from bases, and functioning within the sedentary community, drew its financial support largely from the communities.[123] To the extent that the *Ganda Koy* was a service provider, a private supplier of violence, it was also called upon by communities and business interests to provide services of economic value not relating to the conflict, including occasionally taking action against other Songhoi communities.[124] Their freedom of action was limited by the demands of those communities. In particular, hard-core elements, unlike those in the Casamance, had no direct control over their sources of funding. Once communities and business interests reached agreements with rebel groups, radical elements that had a more racially motivated agenda lost their means of functioning.

Rebel Organization

Researchers have suggested that we should expect a positive relationship between the cohesiveness of a rebel organization and the duration of a conflict.[125] The experiences of Senegal and Mali, however, both suggest that if anything the *lack* of cohesiveness leads to longer conflicts. We contend that while cohesiveness may improve the fighting capacity of a group and thereby delay any military victory over the group by the government, in a context in which military victory is unlikely, cohesiveness may instead lead to an improved ability to reach a negotiated settlement.

The MFDC is a severely fragmented organization. The military wing of the MFDC is now divided into at least four armed factions, and the political wing, itself internally divided, is also divided from the military wing.

We noted that the resources of the region are such that subsections of the MFDC can benefit without need for a disciplined organization. In consequence, pressures to achieve cohesion within the movement are weak. Divergent preferences further motivated the splits. The two most important policy dimensions that we could expect to be the subject of MFDC-government negotiations are the constitutional status of the region and the allocation of resources to the region by Dakar. Although there may be some incompatibility between these two goals, all members of the MFDC claim that they want more rather than less of both. They differ, however, in their willingness to trade off political autonomy for economic resources. Hence, for example, the acceptance of the Bissau Accords by the *Front Nord* is interpreted by the government and local nongovernmental organizations as an opting by the *Front Nord* for the economic benefits that would accrue from peace and investment from the North over a continued struggle for independence.[126] In the language of the *Front Sud,* the *Front Nord* sold out. While the *Front Sud* claims a hard-line position vis-à-vis independence, similar divisions exist within it. The Sadio faction seems to have benefited more from the ongoing conflict and is less keen on the prospects of any form of negotiation with Dakar.[127]

The disarray within the political wing is palpable—members of various political factions are quick to share their complaints about other parts of the organization with outsiders and coalitions are formed and overturned rapidly and publicly. Complaining of the lack of a constitution for the group, the political leaders are unsure of what procedures ought to be followed in order to accord weights to the different historical leaders, or when a self-proclaimed secretary general ought to be accepted or rejected. For a long time, Fr. Diamacoune was the only element in the political structure that all could agree upon, mainly for the symbolic role that he plays. The rebel priest was removed from the position of secretary general in August 2001. However, even though Fr. Diamacoune commands little authority *de facto* and *de jure,* negotiations have continued to pass largely through him.

Finally, there is a disarticulation between the political wing(s) and the military wing(s). Although the political wing supposedly sets the overall strategy for the movement, in practice the operations of the military wing are largely independent of it. And even though the political wing makes commitments on behalf of the military during negotiations, this is done frequently without consultation with the military wing and always without a structure to ensure compliance. Many of the political leaders of the MFDC are isolated from the *maquis* and have not been required to live with or to operate alongside the *maquisards.* Similarly, with the insulation of the military wing from the political wing, attempts by the government to co-opt political leaders have had little impact on the functioning of the *maquis.*

The mechanisms through which the fragmentation of the MFDC prevents effective negotiation include a failure on the part of the MFDC to formulate a coherent ideology and an inability to convince the Senegalese state that it can deliver what it offers. The movement suffers from the absence of a clear political project. The ideology of the MFDC is centered around the single word "independence." In the absence of a debate within the MFDC regarding the *content* of independence, or what steps should be taken to achieve it, the result is that negotiators fall back to all-or-nothing demands.[128]

The fragmentation of authority prevents the movement from being able to convince the government that it can deliver what it offers. A culture of unilateral bargaining has produced a series of failed accords. Although the literature on bargaining (e.g., Schelling 1960) suggests that fragmentation, by producing limited mandates, may strengthen a negotiator, this logic only holds when these limits still leave ratifiable options available to the negotiators. The constraints imposed by Sadio, however, seem to hinder the negotiation of any credible deal.[129]

The lack of cohesiveness was at least as pronounced among the rebel groups of Azawad. Splits occurred within the movement during and immediately after the signing of the first accords. These splits occurred in part because of different evaluations of the importance of the goal of independence relative to economic benefits, but the splits also took place in part along geographic and subethnic lines. The goal of an independent Azawad was abandoned by the leadership of the MPLA, and gradually too by the brunt of the organization. A consequence was that the focus of negotiations shifted from policy-oriented politics to the attainment and division of private goods. Concurrently, groups affiliated with regions or traditional factions began forming, with a view to altering the share of the pie allocated to their zones. Unlike the Casamance case, however, there was no division between the political and military wings. The military leaders were active throughout the negotiations and the intellectuals who were central to the negotiations were expected to train militarily and take part in missions.

As in the Casamance case, the fractionalization did not lead to a military victory by the state over the groups. The lack of cohesiveness slowed the resolution of the conflict and played a role in transforming it from a rebellion into an intercommunal conflict. Nonetheless, in Azawad, unlike in Casamance, the different factions did succeed in 1992 and again in 1995–96 to overcome their fragmentation enough to be able to negotiate as a single entity with the government and to agree on a division of the spoils between them. The critical difference with the Casamance case was that by the mid-1990s the most important private benefits—access to jobs in the army and civil service and the securing of local investment—required a return to peace. The benefits of these goods could only accrue if the parties could jointly agree to an allocation and abide by its implementation. To this end, the rebels were required to produce a public good—coordinated security. As a result, the splits served to signal the determination and strengths of parties and affected the bargained allocation within the movement but did not preclude joint negotiation.

Ethnicity

The experience in Mali is consistent with the hypothesis suggested by Collier and Hoeffler (2001) that the relationship between ethnicity and violence is often one where, rather than ethnic hatred causing violent conflict, conflict becomes organized along ethnic lines because of reduced costs of organization within ethnic groups.

The salient features of ethnicity in Mali that help to explain the course of the conflict include the broad "racial" division between black and white groups and variation within the ethnic blocks and within the Tuareg group in particular. Ethnicity in Mali was used to organize fighting groups. Ethnic variation within the Tuareg groups helps to explain the fragmentation of the rebel movements, whereas variations in the relations between ethnic subgroups help to explain variation in the success of negotiations. Such variation is missed by methods used to capture ethnicity in econometric work on conflict.

Although the Tuareg and Arab fighters were ostensibly motivated primarily by the economic marginalization of the North—a subject of concern to sedentary and nomadic communities alike—and the rebels received some aid from black sedentary groups in the early stages, they made no effort to recruit outside the white populations.[130] Indeed, the organization of politics around race has a long pedigree in the North[131] and was evoked explicitly by the *Ganda Koy*.[132] Throughout the intercommunal conflict, each side accused the other of being motivated primarily by racism.[133]

Why did race come to structure the conflict? In contrast with Casamance, an "ancient hatreds" explanation was very fast in appearing publicly in Mali.[134] The explanation has some merit. Some historical grievances in the region *are* structured along racial lines and what grievances exist appear to be more easily evoked across racial groupings rather than within them. One of the most common popular criticisms of the Tuareg is of their history as slave owners. Strikingly, however, almost all groups in Mali historically had slaves, and the Songhoi group in particular was as stratified as the Tuareg groups, with a caste of tradable slaves (*Ciré-bania*) and non-tradable slaves (*Horso*) (Maïga 1997, 102).[135] The relevant fact, however, is that slavery by the whites, unlike that by other populations, had a racial component. With slave relations *within* black populations more quickly forgotten, it has been the racial organization of slavery, rather than the fact of slavery per se that continues to inform attitudes representing the Tuareg as a barbaric group.

Phenotypical differences—a very imperfect proxy for ethnic self-identification in any case—are not, however, sufficient to account for ethnic polarization.[136] The Mali case suggests that polarization resulted in part from the effect that phenotypical differences can have strategic choices in environments with imperfect information. In Mali, racial coding was used to distinguish enemy from ally.[137] Race was used to structure recruitment. But race was also the organizing principle used to effect retaliation.[138] The result was the rapid creation of a new set of grievances and fears. Even if reprisals by the army may have been in part a response to the actions of the rebels, the effect for noncombatant white groups was an increased fear of the army, not of the insurgents, and the new grievances that resulted were held against the army. Most importantly, the actions of the army helped convince whites who were slow to join the rebellion that they were now considered enemies of the state. In many cases, this meant that actual affiliation with the rebel groups was an optimal response. Similarly, the *Ganda Koy*, rather than mounting attacks on rebel bases, attacked light-skinned targets often indiscriminately.[139] The resulting dynamic was a cycle of tit-for-tat racial killings.

Qualitative divisions between subgroups and the variation in the relations between different subgroups across ethnic lines also help to explain both the fragmentation of the rebel movements and the variation in the course of negotiations. Tuareg populations can be divided vertically into a series of castes and spatially into a series of confederations and clans. The groups vary in their practices and in the extent to which their economic activity is dependent on exchanges with sedentary communities. These differences in part structured the divisions within the rebel groups. Furthermore, while much is made of the "economic interdependence" between the nomadic and sedentary communities,[140] in fact this interdependence varies across subgroups and the variation can help to explain the process of war termination.

The MPA drew its support largely from the *Kel Adrar* who operate far to the north and, except for market exchanges, have limited contacts with the sedentarists. In contrast, the FPLA drew support largely from the *Chamanammas* Tuareg clan, which has been based closer to the Niger river and has highly complementary exchanges with sedentary communities. The FIAA drew support from Arab traders who, if anything, are in direct competition with the traders supporting the *Ganda Koy*. This variation in economic relations across subgroups correlates with the different levels of violent engagement between groups during the conflict and the success of negotiations. The FIAA, beginning with plans to assassinate a list of leading Songhoi citizens in Timbuktu,[141] was involved in the greatest levels of conflict with the sedentary community. The FPLA was successful in negotiating with the *Ganda Koy* and drew upon traditional community structures to facilitate its exchanges. The MPA meanwhile remained largely removed from the intercommunal aspect of the conflict.

It is less easy to find a relationship between ethnicity and duration in Casamance. Although the organization of the rebellion in Casamance has made use of ethnic institutions, the conflict has not yet become an ethnic conflict; so far there has not been an intercommunal dimension to the conflict and no significant self-defense militia have been formed. Even in attacks dubbed as ethnic by Senegalese and foreign media, the targets, when not arbitrary, have been determined on the basis of their regional origin rather than on the basis of their ethnicity alone.

Despite the claims by the MFDC that the movement is fighting for a nationalist and not an ethnic cause, the movement has been largely a Diola project, at least in its early phases.[142] It is difficult to argue, however, that the predominance of a single group facilitated organization. The Diola form a highly internally fragmented grouping that has not in the past been successful at organizing for collective action. Furthermore, the MFDC has recruited also outside the Diola grouping, with non-

Diola leaders such as Salif Sadio controlling sections of the movement without relying on Diola institutions.

Terrain and Population Density

The two cases are consistent with the positive correlation between forest cover and conflict duration found in Collier et al. (2001). Mali has about 9 percent forest cover to Senegal's 38 percent. One plausible mechanism behind the correlation is that forest cover, by preventing access for the government to rebel bases, makes a decisive victory by the army more difficult. The forest cover in Senegal has been an aid to the members of the MFDC who have made strategic use of the thick forests running along the southern border to frustrate the Senegalese army. However, the desert areas in Mali posed the same problems of pursuit for the Malian army. Indeed, it appears that the Senegalese army, largely composed of Casamançais soldiers, was if anything more likely to venture into forested areas than was the Malian army to venture into desert and mountainous areas.[143] Hence, variation in forestry per se does not provide sufficient variation in the strategic advantage of the rebels to help explain variation in war duration between these countries. Rather we suggest that forest cover, along with other topographical features, by facilitating a guerrilla insurgency, can reduce the likelihood of a *military* victory. But whether or not this translates into longer wars will in turn depend on factors that affect the ability of groups to achieve a negotiated settlement.[144]

We also fail to observe relevant variation when we consider the role played by population density. Political scientists, drawing on the logic of collective action, have argued that population density should have an impact on the likelihood and success of conflict—although whether the impact of density is to increase tensions, increase the group's ability to organize, or increase the government's ability to monitor it is a subject of some dispute.[145] The war in Mali took place in the least densely populated parts of Africa, with just 1.2 people per square kilometer and considerably less in the northern stretches.[146] The conflict in Senegal, however, took place in a relatively densely populated area of the country with 28 people per square kilometer.[147] Nevertheless, we found no relation between variation in population density and conflict duration. The original collective action problem was solved by Tuareg groups in concentrations outside of the country, whereas collective action problems have remained insoluble for Diola groups living in close proximity.

Negotiations: Government Strategies and International Actors

Government Strategies

The government of Senegal has used three approaches to respond to the Casamance conflict. A first response was to ignore the political nature of the conflict and to respond with force. That, and subsequent attempts to achieve a military victory have, to date, failed. But with few exceptions the failures have been inexpensive for the government.[148]

The second approach has been to address the "root causes" of the conflict. By unilaterally addressing some of the grievances that led to initial popular support for the campaign—including improvement in land allocation processes and the appointment of more Casamançais to positions of authority within the region—the government has narrowed the support base of the MFDC: Casamançais who were more concerned by the treatment of the area than by its constitutional status have stopped supporting the MFDC. Hard-core elements, including those who have passed through rituals swearing dedication to the cause, have not been convinced, nor have those who benefit materially from the conflict.

Finally, starting one decade after the conflict began, a series of negotiated settlements have been attempted, mostly with Fr. Diamacoune. To date, these have failed to address the constitutional concerns of the MFDC. And their negotiation, unlike the Malian case, has not involved broad consultations or public debate. By disallowing any deliberations over issues pertaining to the territorial integrity of the country, the government has probably succeeded in deflecting attention from the superficiality of the MFDC's independence project, and, by preventing discussion of the relative merits of different degrees of regional autonomy, has added to the discrete nature of the bargaining space. The superficial nature of those negotiations that have taken place is reflected in the texts of the agreements, which rarely surpass a page of bullet points. The negotiations have, however, succeeded in containing the scale of the conflict by leading to splits in which one group stops fighting in return for economic benefits. In limiting discussions in these ways, the government has accepted the risk of prolonging the conflict in Casamance.

Plausibly, Dakar has been slow to respond to the conflict in Casamance because, for the most part, it has not been hurt by it. The conflict has mostly been relatively low intensity and with the actions of the MFDC being local in nature, the suffering has been felt most strongly locally.[149] According to government officials, the financial burden of the war on the Senegalese budget has been low.[150] And with some exceptions, such as in the early 1990s, the Senegalese state has not been put under pressure from the international community to resolve the conflict. Indeed, a hypothesis suggested by the Casamance case is that the war has lasted long *because* it is low intensity.

Because of domestic and international pressure, as well as the intensity of the fighting and the extent of the national territory involved, Malian governments have been much more proactive in seeking an end to the Azawad conflict. The government of Mali's initial reaction in 1990, like that in Senegal, was to ignore the political aspects of the conflict—referring to the attacks as being the actions first of a group of "armed bandits" and then of "our lost brothers" (*"frères égarés"*). From June 1990, the Traoré government attempted to crush the rebellion militarily. However, following military defeats much more severe than any suffered by the government of Senegal, and facing an increasingly hostile population in Bamako, the government chose to resolve the problem through negotiations, and, with rapidly shortening time horizons, was content to offer promises of political and economic advantages to the Tuareg.

The Touré regime took office with much greater popular support than that available to Moussa Troaré. Under less pressure from the democratic movements in Bamako, Touré was able to take a more open position with respect to negotiations. In a strategy combining tough military action—the army had more free rein to strike rebel groups as well as civilian populations—with a series of much more inclusive meetings and dialogues, organized in concert with international mediators, the Touré government succeeded in obtaining broad agreement for the National Pact.

The strategy employed by Konaré, taking office in 1992, was consistent with that of Touré: maintaining military pressure; persistently engaging international actors—notably Mauritania, Burkina Faso, Algeria, and Libya—to maintain their support and to engage them to place pressure on the movements; and involving a very broad set of actors in a discussion of the contents of the accords. The strategy led eventually to agreements between the rebel movements and civil militias.

International Actors

The government and rebel groups in Mali, unlike those in Senegal, came under considerable international pressure to find a resolution to the Tuareg problem. France placed pressure on Mali from the beginning of the conflict. With France adopting a new hardened opposition to military regimes in Africa toward the end of the 1980s, relations between France and the Traoré government worsened. France ran a media campaign highlighting abuses by the Malian government and, reportedly, in supporting opposition groups in Bamako, it contributed to the fall of the Traoré regime. France's position with respect to the Casamance conflict has been less activist. Unlike its opposition to Traoré's military regime, France maintained strong relationships with Senegal and, with occasional exceptions, has not taken a prominent diplomatic position to help resolve the Casamance conflict.

Ultimate adherence to the agreements in Mali resulted in part from sustained international pressure on the rebel groups. Exposed to risks of similar conflicts within their own borders, none of the neighboring countries had interests in an extended conflict. Mauritania, Libya, and Burkina Faso each contributed to bringing the conflict to an end. Mauritania placed pressure on the movements to accede to agreements through its control over the 80,000 refugees inside its borders. With many of the Tuareg still in Libya, Libya had some control over incentives for Tuareg to move to join the movements in Mali. To prevent a swelling in the number of combatants, Ghaddafy acted to improve conditions for Tuaregs in Libya. Finally, Burkina Faso, with 35,000 Malian refugees and controlling the conditions for some of the FPLA leadership in exile, succeeded in bringing the FPLA in line with the other movements to accept the National Pact.

The greatest influence, however, was probably that exerted by Algeria. The Azawad conflict took place in a region bordering southern Algeria—a region home to Berber populations living in similar conditions to those of Tuareg groups in Mali.

With fears of a spread of the conflict to Algeria and fearful of the possibility of a Berber state on its borders, Algeria was strongly opposed to the independence of Azawad and keen for the conflict in Mali not to drag on. Algeria was able to place pressure on the movements because of its control over supply routes and over Tuareg exiles and refugees in Algeria. And, as a major supplier of oil as well as military and economic aid, Algeria was influential in Bamako. Its determined opposition took the issues of Azawad independence and territorial integrity off the agenda and thereby helped overcome a stumbling block that has plagued negotiations in Casamance.

Countries neighboring Senegal did not have the same fears of a spread of the conflict. With small Diola populations, there seemed to be little risk of copycat conflicts. Neither Guinea-Bissau nor Gambia had strong motivations to bring the conflict to an end. Indeed by many accounts, both countries have benefited from the war economy associated with the conflict—Guinea-Bissau, through the routing of cashew exports through the zone and by acting as a market to areas more isolated from Senegalese markets, and Gambia, through its involvement with the routing of cannabis and wood exports through the country (Evans 2002). The ambiguity of these countries toward the conflict has led to ill-fated diplomacy, and material support to MFDC fighters, many of whom have lived and operated, in different moments of the conflict, across the border in these neighboring states.

Conclusion

In this chapter we have described cultural and historical particularities that have shaped the conflicts in Senegal and Mali, contributing to an explanation both of their origins and of the variation in duration. Table 9.4 provides a summary of mechanisms linking explanatory variables to outcomes and reports arguments for which we have found evidence. In some instances we find that the logic developed in econometric work is supported by these cases; in many we find that the logic of the conflicts differs from what econometric work leads us to expect. Some mechanisms, we find, have been ignored in econometric work; whereas for others we find that the aggregate data that have been used fail to capture key points of variation taking place at the microlevel.

We have presented evidence relating to the claims of the rebel groups that their motivations derive from grievances. We find that the relevant grievances derive not from aggregate levels of inequality—as typically tested in econometric models—but from horizontal inequality: a correlation between the economic, political, and cultural factors on the one hand and membership of politically relevant groupings, either regionally or ethically defined, on the other. In contrast, we have found no evidence for a greed-based explanation for the origins of the conflicts, although control over natural resources does help to explain the different lengths of the two conflicts. Nonetheless, economic arguments do apply. Economic opportunity costs faced by rebels seem to have been important in both cases: Both conflicts were sparked by groups with high unemployment rates and relatively poor economic prospects. And, the rebellions occurred at moments of national political instability—although in the

Table 9.4 Variables and Mechanisms of Civil War in Mali and Senegal

Variable/Mechanism	Mali	Senegal
Onset		
Natural resources and the start of the conflicts		
• Provide start-up capital	✗	✗
• Rebels motivated by greed	✗	✗
Regional exceptionalism		
• Region is more "remote" from the political center than other regions	√	√
• Region has had a unique history of conflict and an exceptional colonial history.	√	√
• Region, unlike other regions, has concentrated ethnic or religious majorities.	✗	✗
• Region has a historically developed notion of a nation distinct from that of the rest of the country.	✗	✗
Grievances relative to other regions of the country		
• Economic grievance	√	Mixed evidence
• Political grievances	√	Mixed evidence
• Cultural grievance	√	√
Mechanisms through which conflicts in neighboring countries facilitated conflict		
• Ideological contagion	√	√
• Ideological support	√	√
• Intraethnic solidarity	√	√
• Access to arms	Limited	Limited
• Access to combatants	Limited	✗
Factors affecting opportunity costs of conflict		
• Availability of arms	✗	✗
• Poor employment prospect	√	√
• Weakened State	√	√
Duration		
Mechanisms relating rebel financing to duration		
• Resources makes financing of conflict possible even without popular support.	✗	√
• Resource financing makes conflict more lucrative than peace for some groups.	✗	Mixed evidence

(continued)

Table 9.4 **Variables and Mechanisms (*Continued*)**

Variable/Mechanism	Mali	Senegal
• Resource financing reduces rebel cohesion; makes negotiations more difficult.	Mixed evidence	✓
• Resource financing signals viability of independent state and makes compromise on independence less attractive.	✗	✓
• Financial backers sought a return to a "peace economy."	✓	✗
Topographical features		
• Make military victory less likely (desert, mountains, forests)	✓	✓
Ethnicity		
• Descent into interethnic conflict	✓	✗
• Ethnicity has helped maintain group cohesion.	Mixed evidence	Mixed evidence
Interests of international actors		
• Benefited from war economy	✗	✓
• Threatened by prospects of secession	✓	✗

Senegal case this related to a change in leadership rather than to institutional change. In neither case, however, can we find evidence that the wars were caused in part by the availability of arms in the region.

In both cases, we found that international factors mattered for conflict onset. Guinea-Bissau, and its history of fighting for independence, played an important part as a role model for many MFDC fighters, and interethnic solidarity across the border opened access to MFDC fighters to ready military bases and armaments. In the case of Mali, we argued that the most important neighborhood effects resulted not from any civil conflict among its neighbors, but from features not presently considered in econometric work: the ideological and security priorities and the international military engagements of neighboring states.

In explaining the duration of the conflicts, we find that a fundamental difference between the two countries is that in Mali the insurgents belonged to the natural resource-poor part of the country, whereas in Senegal the rebels belonged to a natural resource-rich part of the country. This single point of variation, though unobservable from aggregate data, has had multiple implications. The variation in resources available to fighting groups has affected the extent to which the welfare of fighters depends on the termination of the conflict. In the language of political scientists (Zartman 1995), the variation in resources across the countries produced a "hurting stalemate" in only one of the countries. In Casamance, the stalemate seems tolerable to sections of the warring parties, if not to the populations that they are affecting. The local distribution of resources has also affected the course of negotiations. In Senegal, the high value placed by both groups on the question of independence versus integration has led to a "discrete" bargaining space. In Mali, by contrast, the expected economic difficulties of an independent Azawad have produced a more "continuous" bargaining space, with multiple forms of autonomy and regionalization considered and attention shifting to jobs and the allocation of government expenditure.

Resources also relate to organizational structures and the prospects for collective action. Whereas in economic models of civil wars the ability of groups to solve collective action problems leads to shorter conflicts, the evidence from Senegal and Mali suggests the opposite relation, at least when military victory does not seem to be a viable option. Hence, we expect to see a negative term in the interaction between factors that facilitate collective action and factors that militate against negotiated resolutions. As suggested elsewhere (Le Billon 2001; Ross 2002), we find a relationship between the diffusion of resources and rebel group cohesion. In both cases, diffuse resources meant that there were weak financial consequences for the groups from their lack of cohesion. In contrast, we found that as stocks of lootable goods became exhausted, as in Mali, the economic benefits that fighters hope to achieve (especially government jobs) depend on the joint production of peace.

Ethnicity also has had implications for the duration of the wars that are not presently captured in econometric work. Our study suggests that although ethnic groups and ethnic divisions are constructed, not all differences are equivalent and, in particular, measures of ethnicity need to be enriched with some measures of distance between groups. Such measures need to account for the ability of individuals to *place* other individuals, either on the basis of phenotypical or behavioral characteristics of groups. We have noted that the intensity of intercommunal violence observed in Mali has not occurred in Senegal despite similar levels of criminality and violence, a similar imposition of costs on local populations, an identification of the rebellion with a particular ethnic group, and the existence of a rival large ethnic group in the area. We attribute this to variation in the form of ethnic differences in Azawad, relative to those in Casamance. The ease of placing individuals into friend or enemy categories has led, in northern Mali, to strategies that polarized groups around ethnic lines. Such strategies are more difficult in the more phenotypically homogenous Casamance.

A last point of variation between Mali and Senegal that explains variation in duration has been the geostrategic and commercial interests of external actors in the conflict. The interests of neighbors explain much of the pressure on both sides to negotiate in good faith in Mali and the lack of pressure on parties to the Casamance conflict. Information on the interests of neighboring states is difficult to measure and is presently absent from econometric work. The evidence from the Senegal and Mali cases suggests nonetheless that such variation features prominently in the calculations of governments and rebels.

Notes

1. See *Jeune Afrique Plus,* No. 10, January/February 1991.

2. The actual number of deaths among the insurgents is uncertain, with most of the bodies of the insurgents reportedly removed by the retreating group. The MFDC Web site reports more than 100 killed and 700 arrested.

3. The 6,000–8,000 figure is from Lode (1997); MFUA (see below) sources place the number of deaths on the nomad side alone at at least 8,000.

4. There is great uncertainty over the numbers of deaths in Casamance. As indicators of the human consequences, the United Nations High Commissioner for Refugees (UNHCR) estimates about 13,000 refugees in Gambia and Guinea-Bissau in 2000, whereas the numbers of internally displaced are generally put at around 40,000. *Source:* Interviews in Dakar, June 2001.

5. A common term used in the region for Tuareg groups is the "*Kel Tamacheq*" or speakers of *Tamacheq*. The term "Maure" or "Moor" is commonly used in Mali to describe Arab groups. Since the group self-identifies as Arab, we use this term throughout the text. Collectively, Tuaregs and Arabs are termed "whites."

6. Senghor subsumed the MFDC into his *Bloc Démocratique Sénégalais* (BDS). The merger resulted in the formation of a more radical breakaway group, the *Mouvement Autonome de Casamance* (Autonomous Casamance Movement) led by Assane Seck. By 1956 Seck had joined Senghor's *Bloc Populaire Sénégalais.*

7. In the words of Mamadou Dia, head of the Senegalese executive prior to independence: "The promises made in the early years of independence that Casamance would become the breadbasket of Senegal were not kept [. . .]. Twenty years after independence the regional economy is still blocked, is still an enclave, with hardly any links to the larger Senegalese markets." "Senegal, by breaking its promises, left Casamance feeling betrayed and prepared to take fresh steps to move, pacifically, towards independence in 1982." (Dia 1981)

8. Diamacoune, "*Message de la Reine Aline Sitoé,*" MFDC Archives.

9. The MFDC Web site reports 200 deaths and 400 arrests; a more likely figure reported in interviews by the leader of the armed wing of the MFDC, Sidy Badji, is three deaths among the protesters; other sources report only a single death among the gendarmes. *Jeune Afrique Plus* reported two gendarmes killed (January/Feburary 1991, 23).

10. Other measures reportedly had to be taken to purify the sacred forests, sullied by intrusion by foreigners, notably the sacrifice of Ameth Kounda, an older resident of Ziguinchor who was taken and immolated in the forests on December 18 (*Jeune Afrique Plus,* No. 10, January/February 1991).

11. In some documents the MFDC date the founding of *Atika* to early 1984.

12. The MFDC's files record 1,000 men joining the *maquis* on December 6, 1983, a date that would indicate the formation of the *maquis* after the immolation of the gendarmes rather than after the Ziguinchor march.

13. The previous mayor had in fact been born in Casamance, but with one Casamance Diola and one northern Toucouleur parent, he was broadly perceived as a representative emanating from the North (Foucher 2001).

14. According to Minister of Agriculture and Mayor of Ziguinchor Robert Sagna: "in the last decade [since 1983], no region has received as much investment." See: *Jeune Afrique Economie*, No. 170, August 1993.

15. *Sopi*, September 14, 1990.

16. These included the launching of grenades on Muslims in prayer at the Place de Gao, Ziguinchor, immolation of villagers in the sacred forests, holdups on thoroughfares, robbing boutiques, and burning homes.

17. Signed by Sidy Badji for MFDC and Médoune Fall, on behalf of the Republic of Senegal, and witnessed by two representatives of Guinea-Bissau, acting as guarantors.

18. April 17, 1992 (Cacheu); July 8, 1993 (Ziguinchor); December 25, 1999 (Banjul); December 2000; March 16 and 23, 2001 (Ziguinchor), December 30, 2004 (Ziguinchor).

19. MFDC Archives, *Chronologie des Rencontres Importantes;* accessed June 2001.

20. As part of the strategy, the government successfully organized a series of high-profile events in the region—such as the African Nations' Cup and a papal visit.

21. According to *Amnesty International* (1998), civilians were killed in this period for opposing the MFDC publicly, for participating in the 1993 elections, and for welcoming Diouf to their homes.

22. *Source:* Interviews with army personnel, Ziguinchor, July 2001. In one such operation the army set about trying to root the MFDC from Guidel valley, some 15 km from Ziguinchor. According to a senior Senegalese army officer, "the valley is strategically important to the *maquisards* because of the supply of cashew nuts and because the soil is good for growing profitable crops like cannabis" (*Le Soleil*, November 3, 1997, 9, 10).

23. Local nongovernmental organizations argue that the redeployment of *Front Sud* forces in the North is driven by a desire to control zones of cannabis production (Sindian, Diakaye, Baila, Marsassoum). *Source:* Interviews, Ziguinchor, July 2001.

24. *Jeune Afrique Economie*, May 1993, 167.

25. A small number of land mine victims were reported during the period 1988–96, but widespread use of mines began only in 1997. The highest level of reported victims from land mines occurred in 1998. See Handicap International (2000), see also *Jeune Afrique Economie*, May 1998, 127.

26. Hence, for example, seemingly from nowhere a new peace agreement, the Ziguinchor Accord, was signed on July 8, 1993. In a move that signaled a willingness to begin to consider the question of the constitutional status of Casamance, the parties asked France to make a statement on the legal history of Casamance. France appointed Jacques Charpy, who presented his report in December 1993, concluding that Casamance was, in fact, historically a part of Senegal. It was immediately rejected by the MFDC.

27. In 1997, France offered to intervene to help facilitate. Discussions started up in June but were abandoned after a rise in violence culminated in August in the massacre at Madina Mancagne of an elite army unit.

28. One confrontation during this period resulted in the death of 23 soldiers. The attack took place at Babonda; see, for example, "23 Militaires Tués en Casamance" (*Le Soleil*, August 3, 1995).

29. Adherents of Sagna explain this action by claiming that Sagna was in fact kidnapped by government forces.

30. According to leaders of the MFDC interviewed (July/August 2001), "the MFDC will never tolerate enemy troops taking positions in Guinea-Bissau or Gambia—this is an issue of the utmost importance for the security of the MFDC and the independence struggle."

31. *Le Matin,* February 17, 1998.

32. Reportedly, the general thanked the MFDC through military aid. For the first time the *maquisards* gained access to heavy arms, 82-mm and 105-mm shells, heavy machine guns, and RPG 7s and 9s.

33. More specifically, Wade had claimed that it would take him three months to provide a definitive solution to this problem that has been causing Diouf headaches for a decade (*Jeune Afrique Economie,* May 1993, 167).

34. *AFP/Le Soleil,* August 8, 2001, 4. In limiting in particular the roles of Gambia and Guinea-Bissau, Wade appears intent on limiting the extent to which the conflict is internationalized. *Walfadjri,* December 16–17, 2000, 2; *Sud Quotidien,* December 1, 2000, 4.

35. Meetings with Diamacoune since 2001 have been met with much criticism from inside the MFDC.

36. See, for example, the editorial in the MFDC's *Journal du Pays,* January 2001: 48 and *Le Soleil,* December 2000: 20.

37. With independence ambitions, the 1962 rebellion attempted to revive an older project for managing an independent Saharan zone, the *Organisation Commune des Régions Sahariennes* (OCRS). The OCRS, as much a project of business interests in France hoping to gain rights to oil reserves as that of nomads attempting to avoid a dismemberment of their zones, had been opposed on both sides of the Sahara: by Algeria and Mali.

38. Bourgeot 1990.

39. Ibid.

40. Notably the title of the new movement dropped the reference to "Tuareg," allowing for the easier integration of Malian Arabs.

41. This increase in government activities took a particularly callous form in April 1990. In an operation organized by the International Fund for Agricultural Development, returnees expelled from Algeria were enclosed in camps by the Malian army and prohibited from circulating, producing a humanitarian crisis. The army meanwhile, through arrest and torture, used the occasion for intelligence gathering (see, for example, the account in Gaudio 1992, 184).

42. Examples include the public beating of the chief of the Idnane group and public executions in Gao (Gaudio 1992, 186).

43. *Source:* Interviews, Bamako, July 2001.

44. Sedentary populations too, sympathetic to the rebellion, lent logistical support to the rebels in these early stages. See, for example, Lode (1997).

45. "Les cadres et chefs de fraction Tuaregs condamnent avec vigeur les actes criminals des bandits armés," *L'Essor,* September 19, 1990.

46. The text provides for "local assemblies with legislative and executive branches that will regulate all economic, social and cultural issues that concerns them."

47. In the first follow-up meetings to Tamanrasset in Gao on March 26, 1991, the government accused the rebel groups of failing to respect the cease-fire, pointing to two killings by the rebel groups (*Livre Blanc,* published in *Amawal,* No. 6, January 31, 1995).

In contrast, nongovernmental sources point to a sustained series of killings by government troops (see, for example, Gaudio 1992).

48. See *Association de Refugiés et Victimes de la Répression de l'Azawad* (1992). Contemporary newspaper reports recording the same story report a lower number of deaths—between 20 and 30.

49. "Guerrilla, Satanisme et Paix," *Aurore,* July 4–11, 1991.

50. Interviewers note that in these early stages the targeted populations were southern blacks, while northern sedentary groups were largely spared.

51. "Guerrilla, Satanisme et Paix," *Aurore,* July 4–11, 1991.

52. Plans to launch the FPLA began at the time of the signing of the Tamanrasset Accords. The choice of title indicated an intention to rejuvenate an older FPLA founded prior to the political independence of Mali.

53. In one representative expression of the frustration, Mohomodou Atayabou, in an open letter complained that "the National Pact, designed and signed without consulting the true population of Gao and Timbuktu [. . .] is nothing more than the handing over of the zone to the *arabo-tamacheqs*." (*Le Républicain,* No. 112, p. 3, November 1994). In fact the design of the new political institutions made no explicit mention of membership of the MFUA; Ethnic divisions *within* the North were entirely ignored by the document.

54. At a moment when financial support from the international community would have been most beneficial, none was forthcoming. See Poulton and ag Youssouf (1998).

55. See, for example, "Le Destin du Mali de doit pas être entre les mains d'un bandit ou d'un badaoud," interview with Iyad ag Gahlli, *Aurore,* July 30, 1992.

56. The disputes, threatening to pit Tuareg against Arabs, were resolved through negotiation by March 1993. Similar tensions arose between the ARLA and the MPA, this time driven both by class and ethnic divisions and by rivalry over control of turf. See: "Iyad nettoie le nord," *Aurore,* April 28, 1994.

57. Poulton and ag Youssouf (1998, 70).

58. *Aurore,* "Le nord s'embrase," April 28, 1994 and "Nord: le volcan qui dort," May 5, 1994.

59. In one account the leader, Zahaby—also a FIAA leader—attacked the base; in another, Zahaby's attempts to arrest members of the *Ganda Koy* under his authority as a member of the cease-fire commission led to fighting.

60. Including attacks on a market in Bamba. See articles in *Le Républicain,* July 27, 1994 and *L'Essor,* July 28, 1994.

61. See "L'Independence totale de l'Azawad d'ici le 1er Janvier 1995," *Le Tambour,* No. 61, November 8, 1994.

62. The accords were less appealing to those with more racially motivated concerns. Cracks within the *Ganda Koy* were signaled by the departure at this time of the hardline chief of staff and a group of loyalists.

63. Keita (1998, 40).

64. New, retrained army units, including mixed patrols, were put in place. These had less aggressive relationships with the local communities and were given a more humanitarian role (Keita 1998, 21).

65. Lode (1997), Poultan and ag Youssouf (1998), and articles in *Tambour,* September 26, 1995 and October 3, 1995.

66. Because the model employed by Collier and Hoeffler is nonlinear, changes cannot be decomposed into the impact of changes in each of the variables. To approximate such a decomposition we measure for each variable the extent to which the predicted probability of civil war is higher or lower at the beginning of a given period than it would have been had that variable remained at its average level for that country. Hence, if $\hat{y}_{i,t} = f(x_{i,t}, x_{-i,t})$, we calculate for each t and each i, $f(x_{i,t}, x_{-i,t}) - f[E(X_i), x_{-i,t}]$.

67. The term used in Fearon and Laitnin (2003) is "anocracy" and corresponds in practice to a score of between −5 and 5 on the combined Polity autocracy democracy scores (that range from −10 to 10).

68. Other binary variables include whether or not the country has just been founded, is noncontiguous, or has had a war in the previous year.

69. In the case of Mali, an increase in predictions occurs a year after the onset of the war as a result of the collapse of the Troaré regime, which counts as a moment of political instability and marks a period in which the Malian state is coded as a semi-democracy; the effect is dampened however, in the graph because of the effect of the ongoing war from 1990 onward.

70. Based on their battle deaths criteria, Fearon and Laitin code the Casamance conflict as a war in 1989.

71. In the Fearon and Laitin model, a conflict in the preceding period prevents the probability of the outbreak of a conflict in the next period; Fearon and Laitin code the conflict in Senegal and Mali as beginning in 1989, which explains the dip in predicted probabilities in each case from 1990 onwards.

72. In 1978, Senegal became a multiparty democracy with four parties competing in the legislative elections.

73. The dollar value of oil exports approximately doubled in 1981 (see, for example, EIU country data).

74. In principle, however, oil reserves off the coast of Casamance may have played a role in the thinking of the MFDC, but these reserves are unrelated to the rise in exports in 1981.

75. A more complete study would need to compare these countries with countries that have not had secessionist conflicts. This is beyond the scope of our case study; however, the study should help inform attempts to develop cross-nationally comparable measures of vulnerability to secession.

76. N'krumah Sané, making use of the political geography, wrote in the MFDC journal "Senegal and Casamance are in fact strangers to each other, just like the two rivers that they are named after. The two stretch to the Atlantic, but never cross each other's paths" (*Voix de la Casamance,* December 1994, 47: 24).

77. After 1939 the French incorporated the "Territoire de la Casamance" into the rest of Senegal. See also the Charpy report and responses by Fr. Diamacoune (1995). The lateness of integrating the region resulted, according to Dominique Darbon, from the fact that "the French colonial administration never intended to join the Casamance to the rest of Senegal . . . indeed originally the Casamance was a trading area and there were no plans for it to be a colony at all" (Darbon 1988).

78. In 1917 the Governor General of French West Africa noted: "We have never managed to become masters of lower Casamance; In that area we are simply tolerated." Van Vollenhoven, *Archives du Sénégal,* 13 G 384.

79. Indeed Foucher (2002) argues that the fact that the region preserved its traditions intact to a much greater extent than elsewhere in Senegal led the Senegalese state to attempt to capitalize on the Casamance by advertising it to tourists interested in a more exotic African experience than they were likely to find in Dakar or along *la Petite Côte*. Foucher argues that this "exoticization" helped to promote a Casamançais identity.

80. *Source:* MFDC correspondence with the French government, MFDC files.

81. Government of Senegal 1979, 24.

82. In this and in other aspects, the *Petit Côte* area of Senegal has much in common with Casamance.

83. Even though communities that are popularly classified as black in Mali, the *Haratines* and *Bellahs*—historically slaves or servants—also form part of the Arab and Tuareg communities.

84. White Malians register frustration at not being identified by non-Malians as Malian (*Source:* Interviews in Mali, July 2001). Black militia groups meanwhile argue that the rebellion was motivated by the refusal of whites to live in a majority black country.

85. Diamacoune's nationalist discourse draws heavily on Diola motifs, frequently conflating Diola with Casamançais. See also discussions in Foucher (2002). Similarly, Tuareg intellectuals such as Aboubcarine Assadeck ag Indi justify the Azawad project with reference to the historic notion of a "Tuareg nation"—*Temoust*, in Tamasheq. For debates on the issue, see Claudot-Hawad (1987, 1990) and Bourgeot (1995).

86. In this context, President Wade argues that the massive acceptance of the new Constitution in January 2001 by referendum was an endorsement by the people of Casamance of their position inside the Senegalese state. "Wade Says Casamance Has Said 'No' to Independence," PANA, January 21, 2001.

87. In one such instance, a leader of the FIAA described relations between the rebelling groups and the government thus: "This is about the children of a single country who at some stage have had their differences and who are now working at multiple levels to try to reestablish peace and confidence among the population." See: "Iyad est à féliciter," *Aurore,* May 5, 1994.

88. At 41 percent, the child malnutrition rate in Kolda is the highest in Senegal. In the Department of Sédhiou it takes an expected 85 minutes to reach a health clinic, as opposed to a national average of 40.

89. See also Foucher (2002).

90. It is estimated that Casamance alone could provide for the food needs of all of Senegal (EIU 2001, 22).

91. Andriamirado argues that these decisions were made for security reasons in response to the separatist threat; they were, however, interpreted locally as a slighting of Casamance; see "Violence en Casamance," *Jeune Afrique Plus,* January/February 1991.

92. *Loi sur le Domaine National,* No. 64–46, June 17, 1964; *Journal Officiel,* 3690, July 11, 1964, 905.

93. Senegalese government minister Moctar Kébé, analyzing the causes for the revolt, argued that Casamançais failed to benefit from the provisions of the law in part because of contradictory conceptions of appropriate land use—with Casamançais valuing the sacred properties of land and the *nordistes* focusing on its economic value. Interview in *Le Soleil,* July 19, 1990, 11.

94. In fact the *Loi* and traditional land rights systems formally forbade the allocation of land to nonresidents.

95. This figure is given by Pierre-Xavier Trincaz, quoted in Omar Diatta, "Les Terrains de la Colère," *Sud Quotidien,* July/August 1991. The clearing out of the Kadior neighborhood in Ziguinchor to make way for the Socitour construction company in the 1970s was one example that was made public with a court case. After the failure of the action, plaintiffs played a prominent role organizing the December 26, 1982 demonstration. See Ansoumana Abba Bodian's open letter to the Public Prosecutor in Casamance, reproduced in the MFDC's *La Voix de la Casamance,* December 1994, 47: 13–15.

96. In particular, the trading sector was controlled by northerners; the profitable fishing industry was controlled by Sérères and Toucouleurs, while the Wolof had moved rapidly into commercial agriculture—particularly in the upper Casamance. Groundnuts were introduced to upper Casamance around 1935 (Marut 1992). According to Sall, crisis in the groundnut basin led to migrations from the north to Kolda, threatening local forests. In 1996–97 alone, 30 new migrant villages had been founded in rural Kolda (Sall 1997). Northern Islamic leaders meanwhile attempted to gain large areas of land for their *talibés* (Hesseling 1994, 252).

97. Using the decomposable GE(2) index.

98. This claim is based on data from the *Enqûete Senegalaise Auprès des Ménages,* 1995.

99. A debate on rival property rights regimes took place in parallel to the conflict, with *"Ganda Koy"* representing private ownership and nomadic groups promoting instead *"akall ohar"* or "shared land." See "Irreductable rebelle hier, se redouvre des qualités d'homme de paix. Qui trompez-vous?" article signed by "M.A.B-M.S.C., member of *Ganda Koy," Le Tambour,* No. 46, July 26, 1994.

100. Government of Mali, *Code Domanial et Foncier,* 1986.

101. Law dating from February 4, 1983 (see Poulton and ag Youssouf 1998, 32). Policies disfavoring nomadic lifestyles were in fact inherited from the older French system of "nomadic licences" (see Boilley 1999).

102. See, for example, *L'Aurore,* August 8–22, 1990.

103. Senegalese Minister Robert Sagna speaking on national radio Sud FM, November 1999.

104. Although three Tuareg governors were appointed to regions in the South.

105. Interviews by authors in Bamako 2001. See also "Tales of Timbuktu," *Newsweek,* February 17, 1992 and "Les Tuaregs paysans du Mali," *Le Monde,* January 25, 1990.

106. We find, however, no evidence to support the view that the Tuareg rebellion was primarily an uprising against traditional Tuareg societies. The rebels, we have seen, focused on military targets in the early stages and, except for limited fighting between factions, selected primarily out-group targets in later stages. Although purportedly assassination lists of traditional elites were composed in Libya, no concerted actions were in fact taken to forcibly remove the traditional elites.

107. Casamançais explain these prejudices by referring to ethnographic descriptions of the differences between Casamance and *nordiste* (Diop 1994; Diouf, 1994). These describe Casamance cultures, and the Diola in particular, as being founded on religious beliefs that are closely linked to the earth, rice, and the forests. They write that Diola culture is horizontally structured, individualistic, and radically egalitarian. Unlike the Wolof, the Diola have not fought politically for the goods of modernity and have not engaged

aggressively with the modern economy. See Diouf (1994); see also Sidi Diop, *Le Populaire,* December 12, 2000, 5.

108. ag Mohamed (1994).

109. *Source:* Multiple interviews, 2001.

110. Left with a single automatic rifle, the first actions of the group were to get arms from the Malian army. *Source:* Interviews in Mali 2001.

111. Due less to the domestic history of conflict than to the history of conflicts in neighboring countries since the mid-1970s, notably in Chad and Western Sahara.

112. The most important raids included the initial attack on Ménéka and Touxmen, which gave the groups access to RPG 9s, grenades, heavy machine guns, and automatic weapons. Arms transfers were also made from the government of Mali to self-defense militias. Interviews with army officers, 2001; see also Keita 1998, 20.

113. This route is somewhat indirect. In fact the Malian army armed self-defense groups around the Mali-Mauritania border who were being raided by Mauritanians in reprisals for cattle thefts by Senegalese herders. Interviews with officers in the Mali army, Mali, 2001.

114. The moment of Senghor's withdrawal from politics may also be relevant in light of reported deal making between the Casamance leadership and Senghor in the 1950s, in which Casamançais leaders claim that Senghor promised independence for Casamance around 1980. The disappearance of Senghor from the scene dashed any hopes that any such promise of independence would be honored.

115. Indeed according to Diamacoune's account, the two most prominent early political leaders, Diamacoune and N'krumah Sané, were introduced to each other in prison after their arrest by the Senegalese authorities.

116. See Foucher (2002) for more on the role of scholarization and the Casamance conflict.

117. In the enthusiasm of the early 1980s, these contributions of approximately $2 were made in exchange for membership cards and collections were organized in part by local communities. Even if in the heyday one subscription was paid by every single household, total revenues could not have surpassed $100,000.

118. Based on 10,000 tons of annual production and a per kilo price of $0.25 (Interviews Casamance, July 2001 and EIU 2001), although the MFDC share by some accounts is as little as 3 percent (Evans 2002).

119. Total annual volumes may be considerably higher. It is unclear how much of this trade is controlled by the MFDC. See Cissé (2001) and *Observatoire Géopolitique des Drogues* (1997) for similar size estimates for other years.

120. In particular, the illegal nature of the industry makes it difficult for belligerents to be guaranteed control over the industry in the absence of conflict.

121. The organization seems unable to provide basic services to its members, such as access to medication and basic foodstuffs. There are multiple reports of a state of destitution in some of the *maquis;* and *maquisards* engage in small-time extraction—driven, seemingly by hunger, to hold up small shops and travelers and to steal bicycles and side-mirrors from cars. Indeed, in an unusual twist, the Diouf regime and army troops supported operations by Caritas to deliver food aid to the *maquis.* The inability of the organization to access heavy artillery until a very late stage in the struggle or to pro-

vide public goods for the *maquisards* indicates either a poor centralization of financing or a stockpiling of financial revenues by a concentrated elite.

122. With tiny communities outside of West Africa, Diaspora financing was unavailable to the Tuareg groups. And there is no evidence of substantial flows from other Berber groups or from French sympathizers. Small transfers in cash and in kind were made from UNHCR sources via the refugee camps in Mauritania. The size of these supplies, never large, would fluctuate as a function of Mauritanian policy toward the camps.

123. Two other sources of financing for the *Ganda Koy* were transfers from the Songhoi Diaspora, notably in Ghana (See "Le *Ganda Koy* devoile son visage," *Le Tambour*, No. 60, November 1, 1994) and, reportedly, from the government of Mali. The government of Mali denies claims that it helped to establish or fund the *Ganda Koy*. However, a representative of the *Ganda Koy* in Paris, Mahmoud Alpha Maiga, claimed in 1995 that "relations are very good between us and the army [. . .]. In fact, the deserting officers that joined the *Ganda Koy* continue to receive a salary from the Malian army." See "Nouvel enlisement des espoirs de paix dans le conflit Tuareg au Mali," *Le Monde Diplomatique,* April 1995. Furthermore, at least some of the sedentary group militias were armed by the army (see, for example, Keita 1998, 20).

124. See, for example, the protests by representatives of the sedentary population of one neighborhood in Tondibi regarding the use of *Ganda Koy* forces to support another neighborhood of Tondibi in a land dispute (*L'Indépendent,* No. 22, July 13, 1995, 3).

125. Collier, Hoeffler, and Söderbom (2001), for example, argue that "[many] rebel organizations face severe problems of maintaining cohesion: hence the much shorter duration of such wars." As suggested by Nicholas Sambanis in comments on this paper, a useful distinction may be drawn between the ability of leaders of a given group to enforce orders, and the existence of multiple factions, each with their own leadership structures. Lack of the former type of cohesion may make military victory for the government more likely, whereas lack of the latter may prevent negotiated resolution. Our concern in this text is with the latter form of cohesion.

126. The moderation of the wing and their position in favor of peace gave them access to government favors and the praise of the progovernment Senegalese press (Marut 1992, 222).

127. *Source:* Interviews with fighters, Casamance 2001.

128. In August 2001 Alexandre Djiba, hinting at some room for negotiation around the term claimed "we have been fighting for our independence for 18 years and in that period nobody [in the Senegalese administration] has asked us what we mean by the term." (Interview, Banjul, August 2001.) See as an exception to the trend: Jean-Marie François Biagui's contribution to the 1999 MFDC meetings "Territoire de Casamance." www.ifrance.com/Casamance/Communication%20Lyon.htm.

129. In a letter dated August 26, 2000 addressed to Diamacoune, Sadio, writing in the name of the *maquis,* recognized the authority of Fr. Diamacoune as head of the organization but set down what he took to be the limits of the mandate of the secretary general. Reaffirming a hard-line position, he wrote that the MFDC was struggling "for the national independence of Casamance, not for autonomy still less, regionalization . . ." (*Le Matin* December 2–3, 2000, 3).

130. Indeed, Tuareg leaders now lament the fact that when black sedentary populations asked to join the rebel movements in early stages they were turned away. *Source:* Interviews, Bamako, July 2001.

131. Claudot-Hawad (1997) cites the *Rapport Politique du Cercle d'Agadez* that claims in September 1916 that the "Tuareg have no more reason to continue to exist than did the Redskins [in America]. Unfortunately the desert climate and the extraordinary camel present us with obstacles that the Americans did not have to face."

132. The name, *Ganda Koy,* literally means "masters of the land." As noted by one columnist, "the central objective of the *Ganda Koy*—as its name suggests in Songhoi, was to remind everyone that the sedentary populations were first occupants and the true owners of the region." (*L'Indépendant,* July 13, 1995, 22.) The *Ganda Koy* in the *Voix du Nord* (1992), accusing the *"rebelles-bandits-armés"* of themselves being racist, argued: "[T]hey have always been bandits, living from theft, harassment and brigandry. The people of the north are a foreign body in the social fabric [. . .] Let us close the border [with Mauritania], let us create a no-man's land 100 km wide, and let the army and the sedentary populations clean out the area." By 1994, the *Ganda Koy* had toned down its rhetoric and claimed to have a minority of Tuareg and Arab members. (See statements by Abdoulaye Hamadahamane Maïga, "Le *Ganda Koy,* la conscience noire s'impose," *L'Aurore,* September 1, 1994, 2.)

133. Tuareg intellectuals likened the militias to the Rwandese *genocidaires,* while the *Ganda Koy* likened the aims and methods of the rebelling groups to European fascism (see *Ganda Koy,* "Appel aux patriots maliens").

134. In one of the very first analyses published in the Malian press, an Algerian author provided a primordial explanation of the conflict, claiming that in the North there is "a hatred that can be easily re-awakened, once we know the history that separates the blacks, the 'ancient slaves' from the Tuareg, the 'ancient masters.' " (*L'Aurore,* August 8–22, 1990, 3, citing *Algerie Actualite,* July 19–25, 1990.)

135. Furthermore, the Tuareg group that was largely responsible for initiating the rebellion, the *Kel Adrar,* historically used salves the least. In principle, the southern blacks in the Malian army, coming from areas with little contact with the North, should not have in been any more affected by the history of Tuareg and Arab slavery as by the history of slavery by the Songhoi or by black populations elsewhere in the continent. See Ibrahim ag Litny and Pierre Boiley, "Une Histoire Méconnue," *Tidmi,* No. 14, 6, February 21–27, 1995.

136. In particular, as is clear from the cases of Burundi and Rwanda, conflict may become highly ethnically polarized without sharp phenotypical differences. As a striking point of comparison, the cotemporaneous conflict in Niger did not involve a grouping together of Tuaregs and Arabs but, rather, conflict between them.

137. In fact the ability to identify and classify people using phenotypical evidence is imperfect in Mali. Poulton and ag Youssouf (1998) describe groups whose "ethnic identity" has mutated from Tuareg to Moor to Songhoi; they note that inhabitants of the North speak multiple languages and that among the Tuareg there is considerable diversity in complexion.

138. Reporters in Mali noted "the soldiers [. . .] no longer distinguish between 'having white skin' and being a rebel." *L'Aurore,* "Etablir La Verité," Editorial, June 13, 1991. In explanation, one Malian officer argued that rebels put civilian populations at risk precisely in order to capitalize on the backlash against the inevitable army reprisals. This strategy is denied by rebel leaders. *Source:* Interviews, Bamako, Summer 2001.

139. Describing a strategy of retaliation, Omar Hamida Maïga of the *Ganda Koy* reported simply "if they killed 15 blacks [*nègres*], we then killed 20 *Tamacheqs*." (Reported by Thomas Sotinel, *Le Monde,* January 31, 1996. http://gouna.avenir.free.fr/tombouctou/fichiers/articles/horizons.htm.) Justifying the strategy, the Paris representative of the *Ganda Koy* explained: "the Tuareg and Arab populations are more or less complicit in the rebellion. We are willing to assume the right to judge them and to punish them." ("Nouvel enlisement des espoirs de paix dans le conflit Tuareg au Mali," *Le Monde Diplomatique,* April 1995.)

140. There is considerable evidence that the nomadic and sedentary communities were engaged in complementary production that gave rise to relationships based on gains from trade, complementary resource usage (with pastoralists accessing postharvest stubble on fields used by agriculturists), and also on the ability of the communities to engage in classic insurance activities. See examples given in Poulton and ag Youssouf (1998) and Maïga (1997).

141. December 15, 1991, see Poulton and ag Youssouf (1998, 63).

142. Explanations of the grievances motivating the struggle relate largely to specifically Diola concerns. Furthermore, the institutions used to recruit and organize—the sacred forests—are ethnic institutions. With access to the areas forbidden to noncoethnics, initiation rituals cannot cross ethnic lines. Interviews suggest that in practice these ceremonies have from the start been conducted almost exclusively in Diola forests.

143. Indeed when there were victories against the movements, such as the taking of the FIAA base, these occurred only with the aid of other rebel groups that had already ended their fight against the government.

144. An alternative mechanism suggested by the cases of Mali in Senegal is that forest areas are more "liveable" than desert areas and can support groups divorced from a productive economy longer.

145. Similar arguments based on *local* population density can be used to motivate a relationship between organization and the dispersion of population. Collier (2000) argues: "Geography matters because if the population is highly geographically dispersed, then the country is harder for the government to control than if everyone lives in the same small area." In direct contradiction, King and Zeng (2001) argue that density makes conflicts more likely as "internal conflict requires people to be near others who might disagree."

146. Government of Mali, 1994.

147. Government of Senegal, 2000.

148. The military costs incurred by the army due to the Casamance struggle are, according to the government at least, negligible.

149. According to the World Food Program, there are now 60,000 internally displaced people in Casamance. There were 32,684 displaced people in the Department of Ziguinchor alone between 1990 and 1996 and a further 2,299 in Oussouye. Recorded violence between August 1997 and January 1998 has included 132 land mine victims, 152 bullet wounds, and 16 grenade injuries. Economic costs include a 30 percent drop in rice production in the 1990s.

150. *Source:* Interviews, Dakar, June 2001.

References

ag Mohamed, Habaye. 1994. "Violations quotidiennes des droits d'un peuple." *Tifinagh* 1: 3–4.

Amnesty International. 1994. Mali: Conflit ethnique et massacres de civils. Report.

———. 1992. *Mali, Afrique*. 206–208. Report.

———. 1998. *Senegal: Climate of Terror in Casamance*. Report.

Association de Refugiés et Victimes de la Répression de l'Azawad. 1992. *Rapport sur la Tuerie avant le Pacte National*. Report, ARVRA Archives.

Barbier-Wiesser, François George (ed.). 1994. *Comprendre la Casamance: Chronique d'une integration contrastée*. Paris: Karthala.

Bernus, Edmond. 1990. *Dates, Dromedaries and Drough*. New York: Guilford Press.

Boilley, Pierre. 1999. *Mali: Stabilité du Nord-Mali*. Writenet Paper 11.

Bourgeot, André. 1990. "Quadrillage et pâturages: des touarègues sacrifies." *Bulletin de l'Association Française des Anthropologies* 40–41: 136–146.

———. 1995. *Les sociétés touarègues: Nomadisme, identité et résistances*. Paris: Karthala.

Cissé, Lamine. 2001. *Carnets secrets d'une alternance*. Dakar: Édition Gideppe.

Charpy, Jacques. 1993. "Casamance et Sénégal au temps de la colonisation française." Testimony.

Clarke, Thurston. 1978. *The Last Caravan*. New York: G. P. Putnam.

Claudot-Hawad, Hélène. 1987. "Lin de pen dance." *Ethnies* 6 (7): 15–19.

———. 1990. "Honneur et politique, les choix stratégiques des Tuaregs pendant la colonisation française." *Revue du Monde Musulman et de la Méditerranée* 57: 11–17.

———. 1997. "Question Touarègue, un silence éloquent." *La République des Lettres*. www.republique-des-lettres.com/h2/hawad.shtml.

Collier, Paul. 2000. "Economic Causes of Civil Conflict and Their Implications for Policy." Working Paper, World Bank, Washington, DC.

Collier, Paul, and Anke Hoeffler. 2001. "Greed and Grievance in Civil War." Policy Research Working Paper 2355, World Bank, Washington, DC.

Collier, Paul, Anke Hoeffler, and Måns Söderbom. 2001. "On the Duration of Civil War." Working Paper, World Bank, Washington, DC.

Darbon, Dominique. 1988. *L'Administration et le Paysan en Casamance essai d'anthropologie administrative*. Paris: Pédone.

Dia, Mamadou. 1981. "La Casamance, 20 ans après: Une région trahie." *Àndé Sopi* 47.

Diop, Momar-Coumba, (ed.) 1992. *Sénégal: Trajectoires d'un état*. Dakar: Codesria.

———. (ed.) 1994. *Le Sénégal et ses voisins*. Dakar: Sociétés-Espaces-Temps.

Diouf, Makhtar. 1994. *Sénégal: Les ethnies et la nation*. Paris: L'Harmattan.

EIU (Economist Intelligence Unit). 2001. Senegal: Country Profile. London: EIU.

Enda-TM. 1994. *L'énergie en Afrique: Situation énergétique de 34 pays*. Dakar: Enda-TM.

Evans, Martin. 2002. "The Political Economy of War in the Casamance." Working Paper, SOAS, London.

Fearon, James, and David Laitin. 2003. "Ethnicity, Insurgency and Civil Wars." *American Political Science Review* 97: 75–90.

Foucher, Vincent. 2002. "Les 'évolués', la migration, l'école." In *Sénégal: Trajectoires d'un état*, ed. Momar-Coumba Diop, 375–424. Dakar: Codesria.

Gaudio, Attilio. 1992. *Le Mali*. Paris: Karthala.

Government of Mali. 1990. *Livre blanc sur les évènements survenus en VI et VIIe régions du Mali,* Bamako, December.

———. 1992. "Pacte national conclu entre le Gouvernement de la République du Mali et les Mouvements et Fronts Unifiés de l'Azawad." *Journal Officiel de la République du Mali* 34: 3.

———. 1994. *Livre blanc sur le "Problème du Nord" du Mali,* Bamako, December.

Government of Senegal. 1979. *Situation economique, 1959–1969.* Dakar: Ministry of Finance.

———. 2000. *Banque de donnees des indicateurs sociaux.* Dakar: Ministry of Finance.

Handicap International. 2000. *Les victimes de mines en Casamance (Sénégal) 1988–1999.* Report.

Hawad. 1990. "La teshumara antidote de l'état." In *Tuaregs, exil et résistance.* Edisud.

Hesseling, G. S. C. M. 1994. " 'La terre, à qui est-elle?" Les pratiques foncières en Basse Casamance." In: *Comprendre la Casamance,* ed. F. G. Barbier-Wiesser, 243–262. Paris: Karthala.

Humphreys, Macartan. 2002. "Economics and Violent Conflict." Framework Paper, Harvard CPI Portal on Economics and Conflict. http://www.preventconflict.org.

Keck, Andrew, and Ariel Dinar. 1994. "Water Supply Variability and Drought in Sub-Saharan Africa." Report, World Bank, Washington, DC.

Keita, Kalifa. 1998. *Conflict and Conflict Resolution in the Sahel: The Tuareg Insurgency in Mali.* Strategic Studies Institute Report, US Army.

King, Gary, and Langche Zeng. 2001. "Improving Forecasts of State Failure." *World Politics* 53: 623–58.

Le Billon, Philippe. 2001. "The political ecology of war: Natural resources and armed conflict." *Political Geography* 20: 561–84.

Lode, Kåre, 1997. "Civil Society Takes Responsibility—Popular Involvement in the Peace Process in Mali." Report. Norwegian Church Aid and PRIO.

Maïga, Mohammed Tiessa-Farma. 1997. *Le Mali: De la sécheresse à la rebellion nomade.* Paris: L'Harmattan.

Marut, Jean-Claude. 1992. "La Casamance: du particularisme au séparatisme." *Hérodote* 65–66: 207–32.

Observatoire Géopolitique des Drogues. 1997. *World Geopolitics of Drugs 1995/96.* Annual Report.

Poulton, Robin-Edward, and Ibrahim ag Youssouf. 1998. *A Peace of Timbuktu: Democratic Governance, Development and African Peacemaking.* New York: UNIDIR.

Ross, Michael. 2002. "Oil, Drugs, and Diamonds: How Do Natural resources Vary in Their Impact on Civil War?" Working Paper, UCLA.

Sagna, Robert. 1999. Sud FM Interview, November.

Sall, Abdou Salam. 1997. *Pauvreté rurale au Sénégal.* Report, Government of Senegal.

Sambanis, Nicholas. 2001. "Do Ethnic and Non-Ethnic Civil Wars Have the Same Causes? A Theoretical and Empirical Inquiry (Part 1). *Journal of Conflict Resolution.* 45 (3): 259–82.

Schelling, Thomas. 1960. *The Strategy of Conflict.* Cambridge: Harvard University Press.

Senghor, Augustin Diamacoune. 1995. "Casamance, pays du refus. Une réponse à Monsieur Jacques Charpy." MFDC Publication.

van Oss, Hendrik G. 1994. "The Mineral Industry of Mali." Report, USGS.

Zartman, William. 1995. *Elusive Peace.* Washington, DC: Brookings Institution Press.

Conclusion

Using Case Studies to Refine and Expand the Theory of Civil War

10

NICHOLAS SAMBANIS

The previous chapters have offered rich historical narratives of civil war onset and avoidance, explaining the organization of rebellion and analyzing the dynamics of violence in several countries. They have evaluated the fit between the cases and the core economic model of civil war that we used to structure each case. In this chapter, I try to synthesize the many lessons and insights that we can draw from the cases. I use those insights to suggest possible revisions and refinements to the Collier-Hoeffler (CH) model and to identify a number of ways in which we can expand the theory of civil war.

Measurement and Theory Refinement

One of the main functions of the case study project was to analyze the usefulness of empirical proxies used in the quantitative analysis of civil war. Many of our cases suggest better ways to code explanatory variables so that there is a closer connection between the theoretically significant variables in the CH model and the proxies used in empirical testing. Improving the selection and coding of such proxies can reduce the uncertainty associated with our causal inferences from the CH model.[1]

Have We Coded All the Wars and Can We Predict Their Occurrence?

One source of measurement error is lack of clarity in the definition of civil war and difficulties in coding war onset and termination (see Sambanis 2004b).[2] Some of the case studies in our project suggest revisions to the CH list of civil wars. Accurate coding of the dependent variable should improve the accuracy of the model's predictions.

Many of the predictions of the CH model seem accurate: some of the country-years (five-year periods) with the highest estimated risk of civil war were actually periods when war occurred (e.g., the Democratic Republic of Congo [DRC]/Zaire in 1995–99). The tables with statistical results included in the introduction can be used to make predictions for the cases included in our project. Case study authors have looked at those predictions to figure out if the model "fits" their case. By looking at "wrong" predictions, we can explore if and how problems with the measurement of the dependent variable reduce the predictive accuracy of the CH model.

There are several problems with the model and the data. First, the CH data set sometimes codes no war in country-periods in which the cases indicate that a war did occur. Thus, if the model predicted a high risk of civil war in that country-period, then we would think that the prediction was wrong, when it was in fact accurate. This seems to be the case in Burundi in 1965–69.

Second, it is frequently the case that country-periods that are coded as being "at peace" are in fact experiencing significant political violence that does not meet the definition of civil war. In those cases, if the predicted probability of civil war in the CH model is high, the model would appear to be making an inaccurate prediction, when in fact it is correctly predicting the occurrence of political violence. The model cannot distinguish between predictions of civil war and predictions of other violence, because the theory underlying the CH model could potentially apply to lower-level insurgencies, terrorism, coups, and other violence, including organized crime. I return to this point later and argue that we need to develop a model that attempts to explain the organization of violence into different forms and the transition from one form to the other.

Third, the flipside of the problem that I just raised is that several cases of civil war in the CH data set are not necessarily civil wars. For example, both the death toll in Romania in 1989 and the level of organization of the opposition do not meet the CH definition of civil war. Several other cases of war in the CH data set are coded in countries that were not yet sovereign states, like Angola before 1975 or Guinea-Bissau in the 1970s. These are better characterized as extra-state wars or civil wars in the territory of the colonial metropole.[3]

Classifying an armed conflict as a civil war is not straightforward. Ross (volume 2, chapter 2), for example, argues that Indonesia has had only one civil war with two phases (Aceh in 1990–91 and 1999). This war is not coded in the CH data set. Other armed conflicts in Indonesia that are often considered civil wars in commonly used data sets are not classified as civil wars according to Ross (e.g., East Timor, 1975–99). Similarly, Collier and Hoeffler do not code a civil war in several of the countries in which chapter authors argue that a civil war has occurred (e.g., in Senegal and the United Kingdom). Case studies can help us establish with greater certainty if an armed conflict meets the definition of civil war.

The lack of many time-sensitive variables in the CH model, combined with errors in coding the dependent variable, may result in poor predictions of civil war risk because of the overwhelming importance of the "peace-time" variable in the model. (Remember that, the longer a country has been at peace, the lower is its estimated risk of a new war.) In Burundi, the fact that Collier and Hoeffler do not code a civil war in 1965 leads them to underestimate the risk of a civil war just before war broke out in 1972. In Algeria, the predicted probability of civil war is heavily influenced by the peace-time variable and declines steadily from 45 percent in 1965 (high because of the proximity of the postindependence strife in 1962) to 30 percent in 1975, and 17 percent in 1990. Although at 17 percent this point estimate is almost three times the population average (0.067, with a standard deviation of .08), the model still produces a declining trend in the risk of civil war in Algeria and war actually occurred in a period of relatively low risk (as compared to previous periods).

The CH model cannot make accurate predictions of the timing of civil war onset and this is partly due to coding errors in the data. A case that illustrates this point is the DRC. The fact that several wars in the DRC are not coded in the CH data set (e.g., the Kisangani mutiny of 1967 and the Shabba wars of 1977–78) decreases the accuracy of probability estimates derived from the model (the standard errors of point estimates will be very large). Collier and Hoeffler predicted probabilities of civil war for the Congo ranging from 8 percent for 1975–79 to 77 percent for 1995–99. At 8 percent the estimated risk of civil war is only marginally higher than the mean risk for the population (but it is within the bounds of the confidence interval for the average probability). These estimates for the DRC should have been much higher: The DRC has lower income, lower growth, higher dependence on natural resources, and a larger and more highly dispersed population—all of which increase war risk. What pulls probability estimates downward is the peace-time variable, which is coded with error in this case.

In Nigeria, the model runs into similar problems. We have both false-positive and false-negative predictions in this case. The model predicts a high risk of civil war in the 1990s, when a war did not occur. The economy was deteriorating and oil production was declining, while expansion of the oil pipeline allowed even more regions to claim a piece of the oil resources. But, although the model is technically incorrect here, it does capture something important, given that several episodes of intercommunal fighting have caused thousands of deaths in that period (Zinn, volume 1, chapter 4). What distinguishes these events from civil war is that the state was generally not involved directly in the fighting and the death toll was sometimes low in individual events. Thus, the model actually predicts violence accurately; and part of the problem with predicting war is related to the rather arbitrary ways we distinguish civil war from other political violence. Zinn (volume 1, chapter 4) identifies up to 60 violent conflicts in Nigeria from 1985 to 1989, during a time when the country is coded as being "at peace" in the CH data set. The operationalization of the peace-time variable in the CH model (years at peace since the previous war) does not allow us to capture the consequences of such ethnic violence and turmoil in Nigeria. If a different version of "peace time" is coded that can capture the history of all organized domestic political violence, the model's predictions of war onset in Nigeria and other countries should improve.

Economic Variables: Gross Domestic Product, Growth, and Education

The key proxies used to test the CH opportunity cost hypothesis are gross domestic product (GDP) per capita, secondary education, and economic growth. Collier and Hoeffler find that high values of these variables reduce the risk of civil war.

Consistent with this result, many countries included in our project had low and declining income and low education levels in the years leading up to the war. Although the CH hypothesis is consistent with these cases, there can be different ways to interpret the association between civil war and these economic variables. The case studies help us sort out the mechanisms underlying this correlation.

GDP per capita is also a proxy for Fearon and Laitin's (2003) state weakness hypothesis, and they argue that state weakness leads to civil war. If this measure (GDP) can be used as a proxy for two competing hypotheses, then we cannot easily distinguish among these hypotheses with statistical analysis. Given the lack of clarity about what exactly GDP measures, one wonders why we do not use more direct measures of the potential rebel supply (which should be affected by the opportunity cost of violence in a metaphorical "labor market" for insurgents). Unemployment, especially among young men, should be a better measure of potential rebel supply. In Mali and Senegal, local unemployment was greater in Azawad and Casamance—the two regions where the insurgency took place (Humphreys and ag Mohamed, volume 1, chapter 9). In prewar Yugoslavia, while income per capita was two or three times the average for civil war countries (thereby lowering estimates of relative risk in Yugoslavia), unemployment had surged and in some regions reached 40 percent of the adult population (Kalyvas and Sambanis, volume 2, chapter 7).

Turning to education, our case studies suggest that the relationship between schooling and war are complex and might vary across regions. While African cases seem broadly consistent with the CH hypothesis that low secondary school enrollment is found in countries with civil war, Eastern European and Middle Eastern cases pose a problem for the hypothesis. There, high levels of education are found in civil war countries (e.g., Yugoslavia, Georgia, Russia, Lebanon). Lebanon's civil war was among the longest in the region, but its education levels are also among the highest in the Arab world with a 60 percent adult literacy rate (Makdisi and Sadaka, volume 2, chapter 3). In Saudi Arabia, by contrast, the secondary schooling rate was low (4 percent), but there was no civil war.

What is missing here is an explanation of *how* schooling influences civil war risk. The CH interpretation is that schooling increases the opportunity costs of violence because educated people face higher economic opportunity costs if they join a rebellion. Although this seems like a reasonable argument, it does not consider interactive effects: How do educated people behave if the political economy of their countries does not provide them with opportunities for productive activity? The case studies of civil wars in Lebanon or in countries in the Caucasus pose particular problems for this argument. In those countries, the curriculum has been the primary mechanism of inculcating children with nationalist ideology, and education may, therefore, encourage violence. It is not surprising that this mechanism is absent from Collier and Hoeffler's thinking about schooling, because nationalism plays no role in the CH model and is dismissed as rhetoric. But others (Darden 2002) show that there is a close correlation between nationalist education and the persistence of nationalist ideology. Darden's argument about the galvanizing effect of mass schooling in forging and hardening a national identity that can be used to mobilize support for conflict—

including violent conflict—can go a long way toward explaining cases such as Lebanon, where education was as sectarian as the country's politics. (The flipside of this argument is that a strong and widespread national identity can dampen support for secession and violence against the state.)

Several of the case studies are consistent with the CH argument that economic growth, the third proxy for the opportunity cost model, reduces the risk of civil war. Growth was negative before a war started in Senegal, Mali, Bosnia, Azerbaijan, and other countries among our cases. However, this relationship, too, may be complicated with potentially two-way causal effects. First, something that all quantitative studies miss is that low-level violence typically precedes civil war and this should reduce both income and growth by reducing investment and encouraging capital flight. Second, once violence reaches the level of civil war, it further undermines economic activity, reducing growth. Civil wars in the Caucasus caused massive drops in income (Zürcher, Baev, and Koehler, volume 2, chapter 9), as they did in the DRC, Burundi, and in all countries with recurrent or long wars. If some of the decline in growth is influenced by previous values of the dependent variable (war), then we have a feedback effect that has not yet been properly modeled in empirical tests of the CH model or other studies.

Third, in some cases, rapid growth may actually increase the risk of civil war. In Lebanon, growth averaged 7.5 percent for the 1950s, 6–6.6 percent for the 1960s; and 7 percent for 1970–74 (Makdisi and Sadaka, volume 2, chapter 3). In Indonesia, rapid growth indirectly reinvigorated the Acehenese rebel movement (GAM) because it led to the expansion of the extractive resource industry and an increase in the number of migrants, leading to land seizures in Aceh (Ross, volume 2, chapter 2). Thus, while it was not growth per se that increased the risk of war, there seems to have been a positive correlation between growth and war in Aceh, as a result of government policies during high-growth periods. The government aimed at increasing migration into Aceh and its policies favored migrants at the expense of the autochthonous population. This is a mechanism that increases the potential for violence. But migration was part of a deliberate government policy of repression. So, without placing migration in the context of a deliberate policy of repression, it is hard to argue that migration *caused* the violence any more than high economic growth did.

The difficulties associated with distinguishing between rival mechanisms on the basis of limited quantitative results are becoming clearer. Consider what the CH model would predict as a result of declining income per capita. If the opportunity cost argument is correct, then the risk of civil war should increase. But, if we had interpreted GDP per capita as a measure of state strength, as Fearon and Laitin (2003) do, then the same empirical result would have led us to different inferences that support a different theory. Indeed, several of our case studies seem to support the hypothesis that state strength reduces the risk of war. Woodwell's (volume 2, chapter 6) study of the war in Northern Ireland is explicit in arguing that the violence there stayed protracted, but of low intensity, largely because it was taking place in a highly developed country.[4] The "Troubles" and their aftermath were the worst political violence in Western Europe, causing 3,281 deaths and dozens of thousands of injured (Smith 1999).[5] According to Woodwell, part of the reason that the conflict did not escalate into a larger war had to do with the strength of the British state, which forced the insurgents from the "Troubles" of 1969 until 1994 into a strategy of low-level urban violence and terrorism.[6]

Woodwell is explicit in his discussion of the strength of the British army, which deterred conflict escalation. (The strength of the army as a measure of state strength is not something that either Collier and Hoeffler or Fearon and Laitin explore in their studies.) What this explanation probably leaves out is the role of civil society and public opinion in the United Kingdom and neighboring Ireland. A more intense war campaign by the IRA and a more decisive response from the British army could have backfired, causing protest from civil society institutions. In an established democracy like Britain, war-fighting tactics like the ones that Russia has used in the second Chechen war (e.g., bombing Chechnya's capital, Grozny) are not viable— indeed they are unthinkable. In other words, the state strength argument may be conflated with the liberal-democratic characteristics of the British state.[7]

An example that helps disentangle the complicated relationship between GDP and state strength is Kenya, because there we have a weak economy and a strong authoritarian state (strong in terms of the state's penetration of society and its ability to defend itself against challenges). The absence of war in Kenya may be a consequence of the state's strength (Kimenyi and Ndung'u, volume 1, chapter 5). Despite intense ethnic antagonisms, electoral violence, and a coup attempt in August 1982, no civil war has occurred in Kenya.[8] However, in this case GDP per capita is low. The state has exercised control over Kenyan territory through corruption. Local police violently repress those opposition groups that could not be bought off with gifts of public land. The problem here is that a low GDP is not a good measure of the Kenyan state's capacity to prevent a civil war. Although the case study helps identify this problem, it introduces another: We now cannot distinguish between the effects of state strength and the consequences of weak civil society institutions. Clearly, to sort out the relative significance of these explanations, we must return to large-N data analysis. But case studies help us identify plausible candidates for large-N analysis.

On the whole, the cases support the CH hypothesis about the negative association between economic development and civil war onset. But they also indicate that the CH model does less well in proposing theoretically consistent mechanisms that explain these correlations.

Natural Resources

The resource predation hypothesis is central to the CH model, which argues that looting of natural resources is a way in which rebels can finance their insurgency. This is certainly a plausible argument, and it seems to apply well to several cases. But some cases do highlight problems both with the argument and the empirical measures used to test it. First, the CH model is unclear if resource predation is a motive for violence, and it cannot distinguish between looting as a motive and looting as a means to sustain rebellion. Second, empirical tests of the hypothesis are weakened by the fact that Collier and Hoeffler measure resource dependence as the ratio of primary commodity exports over GDP. Using this very broad measure, they find that the risk of civil war onset is maximized when the share of primary commodity exports to GDP is around 25–32 percent.

Although this is a useful result, it is obvious that the proxy includes agricultural commodities that are not easily looted unless the rebels gain control of the state. Some case studies suggest that the correlation between dependence on primary commodities and civil war may be spurious. In several resource-dependent countries with civil wars (e.g., Nigeria, Mali, Senegal, Azerbaijan), the occurrence of civil war seems to justify the CH model's predictions, but the narratives in this volume show that those natural resources were neither a motive for the war nor a means to sustain rebellion. (In the case of the Biafran rebellion, the prospect of control of oil reserves might have been a factor, according to Zinn, but it was not in the Maitatsine rebellion.) A more targeted test of the resource predation hypothesis would, first, disaggregate the components of the primary commodity exports, focusing on easily lootable resources,[9] and, second, establish whether the civil war actually took place in resource-rich regions. Most of our case studies suggest that primary commodity exports do not influence decision making about civil war onset, though many cases did identify a link between war and oil, diamonds, or other high-value lootable commodities.

The DRC is a good example, suggesting a refinement of the resource predation hypothesis. According to Ndikumana and Emizet (volume 1, chapter 3) most of the Congolese rebellions originated in the resource-rich regions of Katanga, Kivu, and Kasai. The DRC has massive mineral deposits, including diamonds and gold, and most of them are concentrated in the east. The authors argue that it is not resource dependence per se that increased the risk of war, but rather the territorial concentration of these resources. Dominant ethnic groups in resource-rich regions demanded secession and the government, which could not afford to lose control over this natural wealth, responded violently. By contrast, if resources had been evenly distributed across the country's territory, the government's response might have been different.

The mechanisms that link natural resources to civil war also become clearer in the case studies. Some chapters have argued that natural resources were unimportant as both motives for rebellion and sources of rebel financing once the war had begun. But in several of those cases, we see a lot of looting of other assets to finance the insurgency (e.g., Bosnia, Lebanon, Burundi, Georgia, and Mozambique). Looting in resource-poor countries takes the form of small theft, looting houses and businesses, car-jackings, extortion, and kidnappings. Looting, therefore, seems to be a mechanism to sustain rebellion in the absence of external support for insurgency. If they are available, natural resources will also be looted. Thus, the cases suggest that looting is a mechanism to sustain rebellion even where resource predation is not a motive for war. This is not to say that resources never create incentives for violence. In Indonesia and Nigeria—two countries with sizable oil and natural gas reserves—natural resources provided motives for rebellion. But what ultimately determines whether claims on natural resources will lead to war is the state's response to those claims. An accommodative state may prevent conflict escalation into war (more on escalation later). But the state's reaction is a function of its dependence on the resources and this, in turn, is a function of the territorial concentration of resources (see Sambanis and Milanovic 2004). Thus, government response may be a mechanism that can connect resource dependence and war outbreak.

Four other data and measurement issues confound the interpretation of the CH empirical results on resource predation. First, sometimes natural resources can create motives for war even when the country's dependence on primary commodity exports is low. This is the case of Nigeria in 1967 (with primary commodity exports at 9 percent of GDP), where exploitation of recently discovered oil deposits was a key motive for the Biafran rebellion (Zinn, volume 1, chapter 4).[10] Second, in some cases, no war is coded by the CH model in a country with high levels of primary commodity exports (as in Nigeria in the 1980s). This results in underestimating the effect of resource dependence on civil war risk. Third, large fluctuations to a country's ratio of primary commodity exports over GDP can be due to international economic conditions and price shocks. These shocks would affect the coefficient for the resource/GDP ratio in the civil war regression, but they do not make the country any less dependent on resources, nor do they make resource predation any less useful in supporting insurgency. (A drop in the price of coffee in a country like Burundi may actually increase the available pool of rebel labor by increasing the pool of unemployed young men.) Controls for trade flows might capture these international or regional price shocks.[11] Finally, dependence on certain commodities, such as oil, may influence civil war risk through its effects on regime type. Many oil exporters have autocratic systems (Ross 2000; Wantchekon and Neeman 2000) and can use oil revenues to repress political opposition violently.

Thus, we need to pay more attention to the mechanisms through which resource dependence influences war risk. The difficulty in sorting out several plausible mechanisms in quantitative studies demonstrates the usefulness of the case studies, which have suggested that the CH model would benefit from considering interactions between resource dependence and other covariates (e.g., regime type, level of development, trade).

Population, Dispersion, and Terrain

Population size is one of the most significant variables in the CH model with a large positive coefficient. The CH hypothesis is that the larger the population, the easier it should be to find a group that wants to challenge the state, *ceteris paribus*. Although the quantitative evidence shows a correlation, several cases pose a challenge to the logic underlying the CH hypothesis. Many civil war countries are small: Burundi, Rwanda, Georgia, Azerbaijan, Cyprus, Lebanon, Mali, and Senegal all have small populations. Moreover, the argument clashes with some of the policy recommendations that flow from the CH model. The authors are reluctant to propose partition as a solution to secessionist war, although in principle a state divided into smaller parts would contain smaller ethnic majorities, thereby reducing the risk of civil war by the logic of their argument.

It would be useful to consider ways to refine the theoretical links between population size and war. A potentially significant variable that the CH model does not consider is population growth. Changes to the demographic balance of antagonistic populations may increase a country's propensity to war and such changes might be more common in very populous countries. But, in this case, the mechanism through which population size is linked to violence is ethnic mobilization of groups whose relative size decreases vis-à-vis other groups that are perceived as hostile. The absolute size of each group need not matter much in this case.

Related to population (but also to income level), urbanization may be an important variable in tempering the prevalence of civil war. Several insurgency scholars have pointed out the difficulty in sustaining urban warfare.[12] Urbanization is, of course, a function of GDP per capita, but it also provides an additional explanation for the fact that most long civil wars tend to occur in peripheral areas of relatively sparsely populated countries (as predicted by the CH model). Thus, population density—not just population size—is important in identifying where a civil war might break out.

Density (or rather, dispersion) is crudely measured by Collier and Hoeffler, but it is nonetheless part of the model. But many of our case studies are ambivalent about this variable. In some cases, high dispersion works to facilitate insurgency because a country with large unpopulated regions may offer hideouts to the rebels. But, in other cases, the same condition can have the opposite effect: High dispersion reduces the effectiveness of rebellion because the rebels cannot establish control over a population large enough to hide them or support them through material or other contributions.

Rough terrain (mountainous and/or forested terrain) is related to population dispersion. Mountains and forests offer hideouts to the rebels. Yet, again, our cases point to the need to refine the argument, because rough terrain is more likely to be associated with war duration than with onset. In expectation, perhaps rough terrain does influence war onset, if rebels plan on hiding in mountains once the insurgency is under way. But a study using several different definitions of civil war has found that the CH results on rough terrain are not robust and that this variable is not statistically significant (Sambanis 2004b). Indeed, even in areas without rough terrain, rebels can find sanctuary across the border if foreign governments are sympathetic to their cause. So, rough terrain (as measured in the CH model) is not necessarily a critically important determinant of the technology of insurgency.

Diasporas

One of the key variables in the CH model, measuring international assistance to the organization of rebellion, is the size of the ethnic diaspora, measured as the ratio of nationals of the war-affected country living in the United States as a proportion of the national population at home. The larger the diaspora, the greater should be the ability to organize and finance a rebellion. (Collier and Hoeffler use a statistical correction to account for the endogeneity of the diaspora variable.) There are several cases that motivate this hypothesis, including Irish American support of the IRA, Canadian Tamil support of the LTTE, German Albanian support to the KLA, and financing of the Chechen rebellion from Chechens living in Russia, but outside Chechnya.

Many case studies suggest that we must broaden the definition of diaspora and refine its measurement. In most cases, it is the presence of migrants in neighboring countries (not in the United States or in countries of the Organization for Economic Co-operation and Development, OECD) that increases the risk of civil war onset. Diaspora communities can also include refugees living in camps across the border. Having ethnic kin across the border is likely to nurture irredentist and unification nationalisms, fueling secessionist movements (Hechter 2001; see also Woodwell 2004).

Diasporas can not only finance rebels at home, but they can also influence the foreign policies of their host countries. In the case of the Yugoslav conflict, the Croatians were the big winners of the diaspora influence, as their large lobby in Germany decidedly influenced the German government's decision to recognize Croatia's bid for independence in 1991–92 (see Woodward 1995). Ethnic lobbies play a significant role in influencing the foreign policies of developed, multicultural countries such as the United States and the United Kingdom. Moreover, a complication that is hard to accommodate in the CH model is that diasporas do not constitute a unified entity that supports a single party to a war. Multiethnic states could have multiethnic diasporas, each supporting a different party, including the government. In Yugoslavia's wars, all three groups (Croats, Serbs, and Bosniacs) received diaspora support (Kalyvas and Sambanis, volume 2, chapter 7).

Finally, perhaps we should consider a broader concept of diaspora, one that incorporates all shared transnational networks and cultural communities that can influence the pattern of civil war. In some of our cases, Islamist militants joined Muslim groups fighting wars in the Balkans and Central Asia (see Zürcher et al., volume 2, chapter 9). Such transnational networks are becoming increasingly important in world politics.

Ethnicity, Social Fragmentation, and Polarization

One of the key findings of the CH model is that ethnic diversity does not increase the risk of civil war. This result counters widely held assumptions about the causes of civil war in the popular press and scholarly literature. Several of our case studies illustrate why Collier and Hoeffler might be right. The primary mechanism through which social (ethnic and religious) fractionalization contributes to peace is by increasing the costs of coordinating a rebellion against the government (see the Nigeria chapter, as an example).

While higher fractionalization need not make civil war more likely, Collier and Hoeffler argue that ethnic dominance raises the risk of civil war. Several case studies agree with this hypothesis. There are several plausible mechanisms. Perhaps the most important is that dominance raises the minority's fears of victimization or exclusion, particularly when ethnic divisions overlap with class cleavages. The case of Northern Ireland suggests that the mechanisms through which ethnic dominance influences the risk of civil war are economic and political.

In two of our cases of war avoidance, Macedonia and Côte d'Ivoire, we also had ethnic dominance.[13] But in both cases, war was avoided by virtue of strong political institutions that, in the case of Macedonia, allowed a policy of cultural accommodation vis-à-vis the Albanian minority. In the Côte d'Ivoire, a system of fiscal transfers (often informal) to northern regions that were not well-represented in the government reduced the minority's fears of exploitation by the ethnic majority. Here, again, institutions are an important intervening variable in the process of ethnic competition.

In other cases, we find indirect evidence of the CH hypothesis about ethnic dominance. Collier and Hoeffler measure dominance by the index of ethnolinguistic fractionalization (ELF) and characterize ethnic dominance as occurring when the majority group is between 45 and 90 percent of the population. But in some cases, even when the ELF index suggests a high degree of fractionalization (i.e., when it does not fit the "dominance" scenario), the country may well be deeply polarized. In Mali, despite high fractionalization (the ELF is equal to 78/100), there is deep polarization between the Tuareg and Arabs in the north, each fearing domination at the hands of the other (Humphreys and ag Mohamed, volume 1, chapter 9). Similarly, in the Sudan, the Arab North has dominated political life and sought to limit the cultural autonomy of Christian and Animist South, and this cleavage has dominated the country's political life and has been centrally associated with the civil war (Ali, Elbadawi, and el-Battahani, volume 1, chapter 7). These cases point to deficiencies in the way in which ethnic dominance is measured in the CH model.

Several case studies discuss at length problems associated with ethnic dominance and ethnic fractionalization and explain that domestic political institutions are an important variable to consider in interaction with ethnic dominance. But the cases also suggest that, to understand the role of political institutions, we must look beyond the blanket measures of democracy currently used in quantitative studies and we must consider, for example, how different electoral systems and constitutional arrangements might influence the risk of civil war in multiethnic states.

Political Institutions—Which Ones Matter, When and How?

The message from the CH model is that grievances do not matter once we control for the opportunity to rebel. Collier and Hoeffler show that democracy does not reduce the risk of civil war significantly (see the results of their "combined" model in chapter 1). This negates theories about the positive effects of democratic institutions and contradicts the empirical evidence that has been presented to support those theories (Esty et al. 1995; Gurr 1993, 2000; Hegre et al. 2001). The impact of democratic institutions on the probability of civil war is still heavily debated in the literature. The case studies suggest several ways in which we could qualify the statement that "democracy does not matter" and modify the specification of the CH model to better capture the effects of political institutions.

ESTABLISHED VERSUS NEW DEMOCRACIES. Gurr's (2000) distinction between established democracies and new democracies is an important one. Newly established democratic institutions may not be credible or effective in resolving social conflicts. Ross's chapter (volume 2) offers an example from Indonesia: Trying to respond to demands for greater autonomy in Aceh, the newly elected democratic government in Indonesia implemented three legislative changes in late 1999, passing decentralization laws that would increase Aceh's administrative and cultural autonomy. Decentralization should have reduced the risk of violent conflict according to theories of nationalist conflict (e.g., Gurr 2000; Hechter 2001). However, these changes were noncredible, given the previous governments' track record in Aceh and the government's apparent inability to prevent attacks on civilians by the military. Government *credibility* and *legitimacy* are crucial components of democratic regimes that cannot easily be coded in quantitative studies. But they are important dimensions that differentiate new (and unstable) democracies from old (and stable) ones.

Beyond the question of institutional stability, we must also contend with the degree of institutional openness and social inclusion. A country may be coded as democratic on the basis of the criteria in the "Polity" database used by Collier and Hoeffler, while not being truly inclusive. In some countries, a relatively high democracy "score" implies that the government will accommodate its ethnic minorities, averting the escalation of ethnic conflict, as was the case in Macedonia (Lund, volume 2, chapter 8). But in other countries, democracy is shallow. In Lebanon, electoral democracy was based on sectarianism, restricting the operation of the parliamentary system (Makdisi and Sadaka, volume 2, chapter 3).

The concentration of power is another important dimension. Federal institutions have been offered as a solution to ethnic competition. But they do not always work. In Nigeria, federalism failed to control ethnic competition over resources. Colonial legacies intensified ethnoregional conflict, as British rule had pitted the northern and southern protectorates against each other. Just as in the case of Cyprus (Sambanis 1999), which inherited a consociational system from the British colonial rulers in 1960, so in Nigeria the system endogenized ethnic conflict; it did not resolve it. Thus, although on paper a federal system might appear as a balanced solution to ethnic competition over the distribution of resources, the central government might not be able to offer credible guarantees about minority rights and regional institutions can be manipulated by local elites to demand more autonomy and secession.

In addition to the fact that the CH concept of democracy does not distinguish between new and old, liberal and illiberal, and federal and centralized democracies, the CH model may also suffer from important selection effects, which may explain the nonsignificance of democracy. Democratic institutions may be endogenous to previous war outcomes (Elbadawi and Sambanis 2002) and/or to levels of economic development (Przeworski et al. 2000). To date, these complex relationships have not been studied adequately, with the possible exception of Hegre (2003), who argues that we should study the risk of civil war in poor and rich democracies separately. Since poor democracies tend to be unstable, they cannot provide effective conflict resolution mechanisms to prevent the onset of war. But more stable democracies in richer countries will be more effective in managing conflict. Tilly (2003) also pursues a similar argument as he considers how high-capacity democratic regimes differ from low-capacity regimes with respect to the type and intensity of political violence that we are likely to see in each of these regime types. Other selection effects or nonlinearities in the data may also be present. For example, some of the variables (democracy, in particular) may have different effects on civil war risk before and after the end of the Cold War, perhaps because several new, unstable democracies were established with the end of the Cold War (see Sambanis 2003 for some preliminary results).

POLITICAL INSTABILITY AND POLITICAL SYSTEMS. Moving from levels of democracy to the process of democratic change, the case studies make clear that there are dangers associated with failed democratization. In Burundi, challenges to Tutsi elites from the Bururi region during democratization was causally linked to the onset of the civil war of 1993 (Ngaruko and Nkurunziza, volume 1, chapter 2). Other cases offer similar evidence. A massive political transition to independence and Marxist revolution in Mozambique added to the burdens of a young and weak state and gave way to infighting in various regions of the country in 1976 (Weinstein and Francisco, volume 1, chapter 6). In Bosnia, state failure as a result of the crumbling Communist Party apparatus gave way to nationalist violence in Croatia, Bosnia, and later Kosovo (Kalyvas and Sambanis, volume 2, chapter 7). None of the conflicts in the Caucasus can be understood outside of the context of the collapse of the Soviet state (Zürcher et al., volume 2, chapter 9). In Kenya, ethnic violence started as a result of a political transition to a multiparty system in 1991 (Kimenyi and Ndung'u, volume 1, chapter 5). And the failed democratic transition of Zaire in 1960 is an example of how ethnic competition, compounded by external intervention, can undermine the peace (Ndikumana and Emizet, volume 1, chapter 3).

Quantitative studies of civil war have also identified a risk of war associated with regime transition. What these studies do not capture, however, is the increased risk of political violence that can result from a *power transition* even without a *regime transition*.[14] Consider the case of a change in leadership in a dictatorial regime. The Polity database would still code the country as autocratic, if the institutions of dictatorial exclusion are preserved through the leadership change. But disaffected elites with access to war-making capital may strike at the new leadership and a civil war can occur from a military coup, particularly if the military splits, each supporting a faction of elites. All this could happen without a substantive change in the underlying "polity" score. Indeed, violence in authoritarian regimes can occur precisely in an effort to prevent such leadership change, as in the case of Kenya during the Rift Valley riots.

The risks associated with political instability seem to be magnified with economic transition. Declining growth in the early 1990s and negative growth since the mid-to-late 1990s exacerbated the political conflict in Kenya's Rift Valley. In Azerbaijan, Chechnya, and Georgia, it was not only the disintegration of the USSR, but also the transition to a free market that magnified the political conflict between titular nations and ethnic minorities. The selection effects mentioned previously are relevant again here, as economic decline weakens political institutions and makes them even less able to respond to crisis.

Several cases, particularly the wars in the Caucasus, suggest that broad-ranging political instability is a necessary but not sufficient condition for violence. Of all the former Soviet Republics, only a small number actually descended into violence. We learn three important lessons from careful case studies of that region. First, not all regions had the same level of latent nationalist sentiment, and the potential for nationalist mobilization and conflict differed according to the level of nationalist education that they had received in the pre-Soviet period (Darden 2002). Second, in several former Soviet and former Yugoslav Republics, the collapse of the USSR spelled conflict between ethnic minorities and politically dominant titular nations that were previously forced to coexist by an authoritarian and repressive central administration (Glenny 1999; Zürcher et al., volume 2, chapter 9). Third, these latent ethnic conflicts were likely to escalate to civil war because of external interference or political failure of the dominant elites to assuage the fears of ethnic minorities. In Georgia, Russian interference took the form of bussing Chechen fighters to support Abkhazian demands for self-determination. In Chechnya, collapse of the USSR meant a chance to pursue a long-held desire for national independence. In all these places, we had civil wars.

But in other areas of the former USSR, political instability and economic strain did not translate into civil war partly because of the strength of local institutions. The comparison between Chechnya and Dagestan (Zürcher et al., volume 2, chapter 9) is instructive. The 1994 constitution and the informal *dzhamaat* system fostered stability in Dagestan, despite the tensions that might have otherwise emerged due to Dagestan's high ethnic fractionalization. By contrast, no political institution was left standing after 1991 in Chechnya and there was no continuity in political elites— both of these developments made the state-building challenge harder in Chechnya.[15]

Less democratic solutions to political conflict may eventually yield democratic outcomes, though the transition may be difficult and long. State oppression can certainly result in (a perhaps unjust) peace and in the long run it may lead the way to a more open political system. This was the case of the Greek civil war, where oppression of leftists in the 1950s and 1960s gave way to a successful democratic transition in the mid-1970s and 1980s (Iatrides 1993). But, although authoritarianism can work in some cases to prevent war onset or war recurrence, it is not always straightforward that supporting local warlords will eventually lead to representative government. A recent finding that autocracies are less stable than democracies (Hegre et al. 2001), in conjunction with other findings that regime change increases the risk of civil war and that this risk is even greater in states that transition out of nondemocratic regimes (Elbadawi and Sambanis 2002), suggests that the strategy of supporting authoritarian governance after civil war need not yield stable polities or peaceful societies.

Civil wars frequently result in patterns of minority exclusion if postwar institutions reify old (prewar) identities (Rothchild 2002, 118). If the war ends in a negotiated settlement and not a decisive victory, then there can be a number of group-based mechanisms to design an equitable polity, three of which are "proportional distribution," "proportional representation in electoral systems," and "cultural and social protections." To negotiate postwar institutions, the first hurdle is that all parties must be included for a stable power-sharing system to be established. In Cambodia, even the homicidal Khmer Rouge leadership was included in the Paris Agreements (Doyle 1997).

Proportional distribution of political power is one way to manage multicultural societies after civil war. Consociationalism (proportional representation and a minority veto) can in theory at least be good solutions to manage ethnic conflict,[16] but in reality these institutions are difficult to create and credibly maintain as mechanisms of adjudicating ethnic antagonisms (Horowitz 1991). That is why the empirical record of proportional distribution of power in postwar systems is mixed (Rothchild 2002).

Another way to manage multiculturalism is through parliamentarianism. Parliamentary systems may be better than presidential systems in managing conflict because of dispersion of political authority, which makes minority exclusion harder (Linz 1996; Sisk 1996). This is not yet a fully tested hypothesis, but some preliminary statistical evidence demonstrates the peace "dividend" of parliamentary systems (Reynal-Querol 2002). Another solution at the level of electoral rules in a centralized political system is to foster multiethnic proportionality in the central government and reward leaders for "interethnic moderation" (Horowitz 1991). The advantage of such a system is that it could be self-enforcing, if voter preferences and electoral districts are not organized in such a way as to create powerful ethnic majorities. But caution is needed in advocating the adoption of multiparty democracy. First, statistical studies have not necessarily demonstrated an effect of proportional representation systems as compared to presidential systems, while taking into account the factors that explain the prevalence of those systems in the first place. Second, multiparty elections alone are an insufficient inducement for cooperation because democratic institutions in postwar situations can be hijacked by warlords (Walter, 2002, 29). Power-sharing agreements can help in implementing the terms of civil war settlements. The difficulty in estimating the effects of such agreements is in controlling for the fact that the power-sharing systems themselves are likely to be the consequence of the previous war, thus making it hard to identify their impact using quantitative analysis.

It is difficult to apply insights from the literature on political institutions (consociationalism, parliamentarianism, etc.) to the question of how to prevent civil war and to do so in the context of the CH model, because the model does not consider political grievance as a significant cause of civil war. Thus, effective political institutions in multiethnic states need not influence the risk of civil war, if that risk depends more on organizational capacity and on the "technology" of insurgency. But the case studies and the brief analysis presented here suggest that the CH model might have produced different empirical results if it had taken into account those dimensions of political institutions that I have mentioned here: how new/old the regime is; how liberal and open it is; and what electoral mechanisms it has instituted to manage multiculturalism. Interaction effects between political institutions and the different "structural" characteristics of countries (such as their ethnic diversity or their growth patterns) must also be considered carefully.

To address these complicated questions on the link between political institutions and civil war, the CH model must be revised and expanded, and different econometric techniques must be used to estimate a model that accounts for interaction and selection effects. This brief review of how the CH model fits the case studies offers insights into how the model might be revised and expanded. I make some suggestions below.

Drawing on the Case Studies to Expand the Theory of Civil War

A number of theoretical extensions to the CH model are suggested by the case studies. This section outlines some of them.

First, we must take better account of escalation dynamics and government repression to explain the outbreak of war. Second, we must reconceptualize the relationship between ethnicity and violence. Third, we must model the regional and international dimensions of civil war. Fourth, we must consider violence as a recurring phenomenon and rethink the meaning and definition of civil war and the similarities between civil war and other forms of political violence. Fifth, we must account for case heterogeneity; the model's fit to the data might be influenced by variables such as the rebels' ideology and war aims or the type of warfare. Sixth, we need to understand better the role of elite preferences and the organization and growth of rebel movements. And, finally, we need more nuanced analyses of the impact of different kinds of inequality; regional inequalities, for example, may matter more for secessionist war than for popular revolutions. I take up each of these topics briefly.[17]

Escalation Dynamics

Case studies can describe social protest and low-level violence leading up to civil war and can give us a view of the sequence of protest events. Several of the case studies in our project focused on the government's reactions to nonviolent protest as a key variable influencing conflict escalation and civil war outbreak. This dynamic perspective is missing from the CH model and other quantitative studies of civil war onset.

In Nigeria, what triggered the war in the 1960s was the demand for independence by the leadership of the Biafra region. Faced with such a demand, the government could have responded with repression, accommodation at the center, increased independence (regional autonomy, or de facto independence as in the cases of the regions of Somaliland, Abkhazia, and Trans-Dniestria). State capacity is what largely decided the approach to be used. Strong states have the capacity to either accommodate or suppress demands for self-determination at low cost (Gurr 2000, 82). It is easier to gain concessions from the government by pursuing non-violent movements that do not threaten state security.

One of the main insights from the case study project is that government repression increases opposition and, if repression is incomplete, it can lead to violence.[18] It may be the case that there is a causal link between regime type and ability to repress effectively and this link may explain the higher risk of war in so-called anocracies: Democratizing states lose the ability to use their repressive apparatus with impunity and open the door to protest and rebellion. Several of our case studies (e.g., Burundi, Nigeria, Indonesia) suggest that the lack of government legitimacy and loss of control over the military and police (especially in periods of transition) undermine the government's ability to provide credible guarantees that satisfy the demands of minority groups.

This raises an interesting question: Under what conditions will governments be accommodative? And when will policies of accommodation be credible and effective in reducing the threat of war? These questions have not yet been answered in the literature and suggest fruitful ways to expand the CH model so as to link the economic theory of war onset that it provides to political theories about the uses of institutions to reduce social conflict and violence.

Ethnic Fractionalization, Dominance, and Polarization

Whereas the CH model seems to be correct in identifying the increased civil war risk associated with ethnic dominance, the case studies suggest several ways in which we must reconceptualize the relationship between ethnicity and violence. The ELF index used by Collier and Hoeffler and others is a very crude measure if what we care about is politically relevant fractionalization.[19] For example, Côte d' Ivoire has more than 70 ethnic groups and, according to its ELF score, is highly fractionalized. However, natural aggregations of these groups result in three or four major ethnic groups, the largest of which, the Akan, makes up 42 percent of the population and has been politically dominant by controlling the state since independence (Azam and Koidou 2003). Similarly, most of the 40 large tribes of Kenya were excluded from government after Kenyatta's postindependence government instilled ethnic favoritism and this is not captured by the ELF index. In Nigeria, we have a nominally highly fractionalized country that includes more than 250 ethnic groups. Yet, the country is effectively polarized along the Muslim North versus the Christian and Animist South (Zinn, volume 1, chapter 4). In these and other cases, the ELF index often does not allow us to identify the political dominance of an ethnic group.

The ELF index also does not allow us to account for the role of race or religion in shaping ethnopolitical action.[20] Several case studies in our project indicate that this is a mistake. In the case of Lebanon, religious fractionalization was more salient that other forms of ethnic division. Christians and Muslims constituted around 45–55 percent of the population; but each group within each cleavage was not larger than

20–25 percent of the population, which would suggest no ethnic dominance even though, on the basis of religious affiliation, we had an intensely polarized society. In Mali, Tuareg and Arab groups are racially and ethnically similar, but a pattern of cultural-political discrimination has imposed a divide between those groups, which have come to consider themselves as racially distinct.

Regional concentration of ethnicities matters more than the ethnic fragmentation of the entire country.[21] In Nigeria, despite having more than 200 ethnic groups and an ELF score of 87/100 (which places the country above the 95th percentile of fractionalization for all countries in the world), there is significant ethnic dominance in the regions where conflict has occurred. If we used the subnational region rather than the entire country as our unit of analysis, we would find a different relationship between ethnic fragmentation and violence. In Russia, the Chechens are only a small minority of the population, but they are a majority (73 percent) in Chechnya. In Indonesia, 90 percent of the population is Muslim, which might lead one to argue that religion is not a politically relevant cleavage. However, the distribution of Muslim population in various islands makes religious affiliation politically salient in some of the Indonesian conflicts. In Kenya, Kimenyi and Ndung'u (volume 1, chapter 5) find that of the 13 most ethnically diverse districts in Kenya, 12 have had violent conflicts of one type or another, whereas of the eight most ethnically homogenous districts, only Kisii experienced violence.

At the same time, the concept of ethnic dominance used by Collier and Hoeffler is shallow and focuses exclusively on the size of the largest group. This brings us back to an earlier point, on the need to recognize politically salient ethnic cleavages. The CH definition leads the authors to code Bosnia, United Kingdom (Northern Ireland), and Lebanon as not ethnically dominated, so the model predicts a low risk of civil war in these countries. But this coding rule does not capture the full potential for ethnic conflict that can be created with polarization. Knowing the size of the second largest group is critically important in understanding ethnic violence in each of the three cases above. Improper measurement of ethnic dominance contributed to a false-negative prediction in the case of the Biafran war in Nigeria. According to Zinn (volume 1, chapter 4), Collier and Hoeffler code Nigeria as not ethnically dominated, but in practice, each of the three semiautonomous regions is dominated by a single group. Northern dominance has been a constant source of conflict in Nigerian politics. We also have ethnic dominance in Mozambique, as the Macua-Lowme tribe is larger than most other sizable minority groups (Weinstein and Francisco, volume 1, chapter 6). This establishes a good fit with the CH model, although Weinstein and Francisco never focus on this aspect of Mozambican society to explain the war.

Finally, currently available measures of ethnic fragmentation do not tell us anything about the degree to which ethnic, religious, racial, or other identity cleavages are cross-cutting. How many of the 250 ethnic groups in the DRC share one or more cultural characteristics that might lead to them to forge alliances? We do not yet know the answer to this question for a large enough number of countries. Theorists of ethnic conflict have argued convincingly that conflict potential is maximized when ethnicity overlaps with class, resulting in so-called "ranked" systems

(Horowitz 1985). But we do not have the data necessary to classify systems into ranked and unranked cross-nationally; and perhaps this concept would be better at describing the power relationships between pairs of groups, rather than characterize entire societies. Several of our cases, however, highlight the explosive potential of ranked systems. Northern Ireland is one of them. The divide between Catholics and Protestants was reinforced by a pattern of socioeconomic stratification that over-lapped with religious cleavages (Woodwell, volume 2, chapter 6).

These insights from the case studies suggest ways in which the CH model must be respecified to test better the hypothesized relationship between ethnicity and civil war. We do not simply need better measures, but also measures that correspond better to our theories about the ways in which ethnic affiliation leads to political violence.

Neighborhood and Spillover Effects of Civil Wars

Another largely neglected dimension of civil wars in the quantitative literature is the regional dimension. If civil wars are caused by military, economic, or diplomatic interference by major powers or neighboring states, then the CH model must be respecified to capture that dimension. One promising direction for further research is to explore the contagion and diffusion effects of civil war.[22]

Demonstration (diffusion) effects were clear in several of the cases. A good example was the rebellion in Indonesia's Aceh province, where an independence move-ment had been simmering for decades, after the revocation of Aceh's "special region" status in 1968 by the Suharto government. A brief civil war in 1991 quieted down in the mid-1990s and re-ignited in 1999 when, in a climate of political instability and economic recession due to the East Asian financial crisis, East Timor's referen-dum on independence emboldened Acehnese resistance. Ross (volume 2, chapter 2) traces the onset of mass protest in favor of independence in Aceh in November 1999, following soon after the September 1999 referendum in East Timor. In Senegal, Humphreys and ag Mohamed (volume 1, chapter 9) argue that the Casamance movement was influenced by the ideology of the independence struggle in Guinea-Bissau. This influence became more tangible as war broke out in Casamance and Guinea-Bissau was used as a location for cross-border bases, a market for goods, and a source for arms.

Examples of regional contagion are even more common. Yugoslavia's wars, in Croatia in 1991, Bosnia in 1992–95, Croatia again in 1995, and Kosovo in 1998–99, all shared similar characteristics and were influenced by the ideology of greater Serbia and greater Croatia. In the former Soviet Republics, wars clustered in the Caucasus in the early 1990s, taking advantage of war-specific physical and human capital in the region (Zürcher et al., volume 2, chapter 9). Sierra Leone's civil war was sustained by international crime networks that were engaged in arms-for-diamonds trade and the Sierra Leone rebels received direct assistance and sanctuary from Liberia's Charles Taylor (Davies and Fofana 2002). The civil wars in the African Great Lakes region are perfect examples of contagion as recurrent wars in Burundi and Rwanda spilled over their borders and influenced each other as well as the DRC and involved Uganda and Zimbabwe in international military interventions in the Congo.

There is substantial cross-national evidence in quantitative studies that highlights these neighborhood effects, but these studies do not distinguish between diffusion and contagion mechanisms. Sambanis (2001) analyzed ethnic civil wars from 1945 until 1999 and found that living in "bad" neighborhoods (i.e., neighborhoods with undemocratic countries and countries experiencing ethnic wars of their own) increases a country's risk of having a civil war threefold. Recent empirical work at the dyadic level suggests that the presence of common ethnic groups across national borders influences the patterns of external involvement in civil war and the spread and internationalization of these wars. The risk of a violent conflict increases if two countries share an ethnic group and one of them has an ethnic majority composed of that group (Woodwell 2004). The presence of ethnic kin across the border may be one of the principal mechanisms that transmit civil war across borders. In Macedonia, Lund's study makes clear that the main risk of civil war in the 1990s came from ethnic Albanians who were actively supporting independence in neighboring Kosovo and moved across the border when their movement in Kosovo was blocked by the international intervention. Another possible mechanism of contagion occurs through the accumulation of war-specific capital (e.g., small arms) in regions experiencing wars, making it easier for other wars to start.

This argument has two implications. First, civil wars in neighboring countries may be regional phenomena. If the war in Burundi or Rwanda is really a war between Hutus and Tutsis in the Great Lakes region and not one specifically between Burundi Hutus and Burundi Tutsis or Rwandan Tutsis against Rwandan Hutus, then the country-year is not the appropriate unit of observation to analyze such civil wars. Instead, it would be more appropriate to focus on the ethnic group or we should analyze patterns of violence in a geographical region that does not necessarily correspond to predefined national boundaries. With current data limitations, however, it may not be feasible to adjust this unit of analysis problem.[23] Second, civil wars are affected significantly by wars in neighboring states or by nonstate actors in neighboring states. These influences must be modeled and properly analyzed. Gurr (2000, 92), for example, argues that the presence of politically mobilized ethnic kin across the border increases the opportunity for rebellion. This implies the need for the implementation of methods from spatial econometrics that control for the non-independence of cross-sections (countries) in our panel data sets (see Sanchez, Solimano, and Formisano, volume 2, chapter 5). For these relationships to be properly modeled, we must identify some of the diffusion and contagion mechanisms that underlie these trans-border influences.

Our case studies identify two contagion mechanisms: refugee movements and external intervention. First, refugee flows contribute to the risk of civil war by supporting cross-border movements by insurgents with access to refugee camps (see the chapter on Burundi); and by changing the demographic balance in conflict-prone neighboring regions (see Ndikumana and Emizet's discussion of the consequences of refugee inflows from Burundi and Rwanda to the Kivu region). Second, external military and economic intervention can increase the length of civil war by influencing the military balance between the state and rebels (Elbadawi and Sambanis 2000; Regan 2000, 2002) and may also be critical in helping potential insurgents organize their rebellion and start a civil war, as illustrated by the case studies on Mozambique, the DRC, Burundi, Georgia (Abkhazia), Bosnia, Sierra Leone, and Lebanon.

Questions that still need to be addressed include: Can negotiated settlements be achieved without external intervention and, if intervention prolongs civil war, how do we weigh the pros and cons of such interventions? If unilateral interventions are more effective in ending the violence and multilateral interventions are more effective in keeping the peace, how can the international community develop appropriate mechanisms to address the different challenges of war and peace?[24] The impact of refugees on civil war risk has also not been sufficiently studied in quantitative analyses. Analyzing the effects of refugee movements on political stability and economic growth can be a first cut at this question, since the effects of refugee problems on civil war risk may work through those two channels (instability and growth).

Civil War as Part of a Cycle of Violence

The CH model accounts for the temporal association between episodes of civil war in the same country over time by controlling for "peace time"—the number of years at peace since the last war. Several case studies have pointed to problems with this variable. One of the problems is that the temporal dependence of violence is complex and cannot be captured only by a variable measuring time since the last civil war. Rather, this measure should account for linkages across several forms of organized political violence over time. Additionally, temporal dependence should be considered together with spatial dependence (see the earlier discussion on regional effects).

There is currently no overarching theory of political violence that explains how societies transition from one form of violence to another (see Sambanis 2004a for an outline of such a theory; and Tilly 2003 for a related discussion). But such a theory may be necessary, particularly given the difficulty in clearly distinguishing civil war from other types of violence. The quantitative studies assume that civil war is a clearly defined and coded category of violence, but several case studies cast doubt on this assumption. Very bloody coups are often classified as civil wars (e.g., Costa Rica in 1948, Bolivia in 1952, Argentina in 1955), whereas genocides or politicides are not, given that a theoretical distinction is made in the literature between one-sided and reciprocal political violence. This distinction may well be valid, but which of the variables in the CH model can account for the conditions under which violence will be one-sided as opposed to reciprocal? Perhaps the "terrain" variable or variables currently outside the model (such as external intervention, or level of prewar political organization) could explain such differences. But, in its current formulation, the CH model and the related empirical tests assume—they do not explain—why violence will take the form of a civil war.

Civil wars can degenerate into organized crime, as in the case of Russia or Colombia. State weakness favors both insurgency and organized crime. Looting, which can sustain insurgency, is also the primary function of organized crime. Another function shared by rebel groups and criminal networks is the provision of security to local populations in areas beyond the control of the state. Crime and insurgency create production externalities for each other and work together to undermine state authority and capacity. Violence is the by-product of both crime and insurgency and the form that violence will take is determined by, among other factors, the type of available "loot" and the way that it can be appropriated.

Terrorism can also feed from civil war and vice versa. In Egypt, terrorism against Western tourists was the direct result of government suppression of and armed struggle against the Gamaat Islamiya, an insurgent group. The Israeli-Palestinian civil war (since the first Intifada of 1987) has been at the heart of international terrorism, certainly during the period of PLO's involvement in supporting such activities (before the Oslo accords of 1997). Kidnappings in Colombia are a direct consequence of the civil war and a means for the rebels to finance their insurgency (Sanchez et al., volume 2, chapter 5). Chechen terrorism in Russia today is the outgrowth of the Russo-Chechen war (Andrienko and Shelley, volume 2, chapter 4).

These interrelationships among various forms of violence (civil war, coups, terrorism, and organized crime) are outside the purview of the CH model and are also not considered by other prominent models of civil war (e.g., Fearon and Laitin 2003). A quick "fix" for the CH model would be to revise the definition and measurement of the peace-time variable so that it could account for time since the last incident of a broader set of violent events. But a fuller treatment of the organization of violence is needed before we can explain why some countries experience civil war as opposed to other forms of violence or crime.

Unit Heterogeneity: Ideology, Ethnicity, and Types of Civil War

This discussion of a taxonomy of violence suggests another question: should we distinguish between different categories of civil war and does the CH model explain each category equally well (or equally poorly)? Rich and poor countries seem to have very different structures of risk; indeed, the inclusion of highly industrialized countries in the data set might well account for the strong results on education and income variables in the CH model. Another possible source of heterogeneity in the data might be uncovered by looking at the organization of rebellion. In ethnically organized rebellions, the CH model's economic opportunity cost argument need not be as central as in loot-driven or class-based rebellions, where private or class-based economic interests are driving rebellion (Sambanis 2001). In pure "ethnic" conflicts, such as conflicts over self-determination—understood as conflicts between ethnic groups over issues that are at the core of ethnicity—ethnic solidarity and ideology may compensate for the lack of financial motives ("loot") and the causes of separatist war may be different than the causes of popular revolutions (Sambanis 2004c).

In most of our case studies, we saw that violence was "ethnicized." Some authors downplayed the ethnoreligious dimension of the violence (e.g., Lowi, volume 1, chapter 8). But it is an open question whether this ethnicization is unimportant for understanding the origins of the violence. In Algeria, Lowi argues that economic decline and demographic pressures led to the emergence of Islamist protest. But she also points to more than one period of serious economic decline in that country. Under Boumedienne (1965–78), Algerian society saw rapidly declining economic growth and increasing unemployment and corruption, yet there was no Islamist backlash. What was the impact of a "bankrupt" political system on Algerian society during successive periods of economic decline? Might an explanation for Islamist protest be found in political, not economic, failure in Algeria? And, if religion is not causally linked to civil war, why was protest organized along religious cleavages? The same question should be asked with reference to several of our case studies, where rebel groups were organized along ethnoreligious lines, as in Burundi, Lebanon, the DRC, or Georgia and Chechnya.

Some scholars argue that ethnicity is used as a cover for economic motives (Collier and Hoeffler 2001), personal animosities (Kalyvas 2003), criminality (Mueller 2001), or an assortment of other motives that are not truly ethnonationalist at their core (Brubaker and Laitin 1998). But, even if many conflicts can become "ethnicized" after they start for a variety of reasons, the empirical regularity that some wars are organized along ethnic lines while others are not cannot be explained away simply because of the presence of other competing motives for war. A large literature on nationalism has taught us that ethnic identities are not always salient and that they can change over time. Some social systems can encourage pathological patterns of identity evolution, leading to the outbreak of civil violence (Anderson 1983; Brubaker 1995). Given that the salience of ethnic identity is malleable, the focus of much research on civil violence has been on the role of elites in manipulating ethnic, religious, or class identity to pursue private goals (e.g., Brass 1985, 1997; Chandra 2000; Darden 2002; Kasfir 1979). But that literature cannot explain why groups define themselves along ethnic lines in the first place (as opposed to other identity categories) or why membership in such a group draws upon a set of perceived objective, ascriptive characteristics that resemble kinship ties. If there is something special about ethnic ties, then wars that are aimed to preserve those ties may be different from wars that are unrelated to ethnicity. (It should not be the case that ethnicity can always be relied on as a source of mass mobilization for violence.) To address properly the question of differences across war types, we must disaggregate the concept of civil war and systematically test for differences between ethnic wars (e.g., wars over secession) and nonethnic wars (e.g., revolutions), just as we should test for differences across various other forms of violence, such as coups, genocides, and riots.

Leadership and the Roots of Ethnic Violence

This discussion of social mobilization reveals that the CH model is silent on the role of political elites. Many case studies in this volume have pointed to the importance of political leadership in mobilizing support for violence (e.g., Indonesia, Nigeria, Burundi, Bosnia) or, less frequently, in reducing social tensions and helping prevent a war (e.g., Macedonia). The case studies have used terms such as "charismatic leadership," "cleptocracy," and government "legitimacy" to describe the ways in which leaders matter. These terms are hard to quantify, so it is not surprising that quantitative studies have been unable to test the effects of leadership, though few authors would argue that elites have no role in organizing and sustaining a rebellion.

But even where narratives of elite-driven mobilization seem entirely plausible, we still need to explain which groups are likely to be mobilized and why? What type of person chooses to commit violence and why? Bosnia has been a case to which authors have applied the mobilization explanation, blaming the war on Milosevic and other elites. A closer look at the pattern of violence reveals that most of the violence (particularly against civilians) was in fact perpetrated by organized militias, which were composed of criminal elements and paramilitaries (Kalyvas and Sambanis, volume 2, chapter 7). Those are groups that derive tangible benefits from their actions and we would not expect their motives for being mobilized to war to be the same as the motives of the general population. The mass mobilization perspective should not have to rely on cases where most of the killing is done by a few criminals.

There is a considerably large literature on the risks associated with elite manipulation of ethnicity. Such mobilization is easier when ethnocultural identity is already more salient than other socioeconomic identities, and when actual or expected group-level grievance increases groups' interest in political protest and forces groups to become more cohesive in the face of an external threat (Brass 1997; Gurr 2000; Hardin 1995). This literature, which has been influenced by constructivist theory on identity formation, differs from so-called primordial perspectives because it does not view ethnic identity as inherently conflictual and focuses on social interactions and patterns of identity evolution to explain violence (Anderson 1983; Brubaker 1995). However, the mobilization perspective (see De Figueiredo and Weingast 1999 for an application to Bosnia) must also explain why followers are not as strategic as leaders and why they allow themselves to be manipulated.

If people are prone to being manipulated, we must understand the root of their fear and distrust which allow them to be manipulated. If rebellion is "easy" to motivate, then the distinction between the leaders' influence and the people's proclivities becomes smaller and is, at best, a distinction between proximate and permissive causes of violence. Therefore, elite-driven explanations of wars such as the Bosnian war must be interpreted within the context of a history of ethnic violence and prior conflict. Without the historical memory of violent conflict between the Ustashe and Chetnicks during World War II, how would Serbs have been mobilized by their elites to preempt another round of victimization by the Croats? It is the mixture of a perception of ethnic difference, combined with memories of old group-level conflicts and new manipulation by elites, that best explains how groups can be mobilized to use violence.

Formation and Growth of the Rebel Organization

The question of who fights and why leads me to consider how rebel organizations grow. An important contribution of the case study project is that it provides us with systematically collected evidence on the formation and growth of insurgent groups in several countries. We see clearly that most insurgencies start small—very small—and grow into civil wars only under certain conditions. The CH model's focus on "opportunity cost" gives only part of the answer to the question of how do rebel groups grow. Frequently, insurgent groups grow if and when they receive external assistance (through alliances with foreign actors or financial support from diasporas) and this is consistent with the CH model. But they also grow through several other mechanisms. Ethnically based rebellions grow by tapping into ethnic networks, or as a result of anger, hatred, resentment, or fear of victimization at the hands of a hostile ethnic majority. Ideologues join rebellions as a result of their beliefs. Criminals may join to maximize their profits. Rebel leaders can coerce participation by threatening civilians or by abducting children and turning them into fighters. Secessionist parties can benefit from manipulating the administrative capacities of regional governments and they can utilize ethnic parties and preexisting political organizations to mobilize support for rebellion.

Thus, while Collier and Hoeffler are certainly correct in emphasizing the importance of opportunity structures in explaining civil war occurrence, the case studies have illustrated several mechanisms that influence the organization of rebellion that the CH model has not considered.

Inequality: Interpersonal vs. Interregional Inequality and War

Inequality is another variable that keeps coming up in the case studies, but it is dismissed as nonsignificant in most quantitative analyses of civil war. How can inequality be nonsignificant in the CH model and yet be so much a part of the narratives? There can be several explanations. The authors may have been misled by discourses of inequality by the rebels, whereas the true motives of the rebellion lay hidden. It could also be a selection problem: The cases in this book may not be representative of the population of cases, and inequality may not be significant in the population of cases.

Alternatively, the problem may lie with the quantitative studies. It could be that Collier and Hoeffler are looking at the wrong kind of inequality. Their focus is on economic interpersonal inequality, measured by the well-known Gini coefficient. This is known as "vertical" inequality in the literature. Some authors have argued that it is horizontal inequality that increases the risk of war.[25] Others distinguish between income and asset inequality and find disputes over land rights to be a salient cause of ethnic violence (Bates 1989; Humphreys and Mohamed, volume 1, chapter 9; Kimenyi and Ndung'u, volume 1, chapter 5).

Several case studies suggest that the Gini coefficient may be poorly measured and that it does not measure the sort of inequality that is relevant to civil war. This should not surprise us, because it is not clear how interpersonal inequality would influence the ability to organize a civil war. There may exist a relationship between inequality and popular revolutions or class conflict, which is another reason to consider disaggregating the cases of civil war. But ethnic or secessionist wars should, in theory, be driven more by group-based inequality (which I refer to here as horizontal inequality) than by interpersonal inequality. High levels of interpersonal inequality in all ethnic groups may actually reduce the ability to coordinate an ethnic rebellion as they can erode group solidarity. Thus, if group-level data on inequality are not available, a useful measure of inequality to consider should be regional inequality, measured in terms of the differences between mean levels of per capita income across subnational units (such as provinces or republics).[26] Several of our case studies point to the need to consider the regional concentration of resources as an explanation of war (see chapters on Burundi, Senegal, Lebanon, and the DRC, among others). Interregional inequality could motivate the demand for more autonomy, or even secession. Thus, a potentially useful modification of the CH model would be to incorporate such a measure of inequality and see if it can explain ethnopolitical rebellion in subnational units rather than in entire countries.

Conclusion

This book has demonstrated one way in which a comparative case study project can be combined with large-N quantitative analysis to produce better theory and better empirical results about an important social problem. The case studies have all applied the Collier-Hoeffler economic model of civil war as a way to structure their analyses and they have suggested several improvements to the model. One gain from reading these cases is a better understanding of the process leading to civil war. The cases help us understand the complex interactions among variables in the formal/quantitative model and illustrate several different ways in which the same variable can operate in different contexts. Case narratives also help establish if empirical proxies used in the quantitative analysis are measured accurately and if they are good operationalizations of the theoretically significant variables. Case studies illuminate the mechanisms that underlie the Collier-Hoeffler theory but are not always distinguishable in the quantitative analysis. Finally, case studies help us formulate hypotheses about the role of variables that are omitted from the theoretical model, but should perhaps be added to the model so as to obtain better predictions and reduce the risk of omitted variable bias.

Taken as a whole, the case studies in this book suggest that we need to refine the economic model of civil war and improve the basic measures used to test the model. Drawing on the case studies, I have argued that we need to define and measure civil war better; that the relationship between ethnicity and political violence is still not well-understood, despite many empirical results on this topic; that we must consider regional dimensions of civil war; that country-, region-, and period-specific effects must be further explored; that the unit heterogeneity assumption that underlies the Collier-Hoeffler model must be tested; and that the relationship between different forms of violence must be the subject of new theorizing and new empirical tests.

Although the case study project has helped improve our intuitions about civil war and could help improve the Collier-Hoeffler model, it is also clear that the research design that guided these case studies would not have been possible without Collier and Hoeffler's theory and empirical results. Their model has made a seminal contribution to the field and was used here to provide an analytical framework within which qualitative analysis could help theory building that could then feed back into more empirical testing. The case studies were thus a secondary line of inquiry designed to illuminate the pathways through which independent variables influence the dependent variable and to explore interactions among the independent variables.

The Collier-Hoeffler model fits most of our cases quite well. But the improved understanding of the causal mechanisms that underlie the model should help us take civil war theory further. After reading these complex narratives, it becomes harder to see "greed" and "grievance" as competitive explanations of rebellion. Greed and grievance are often alternative interpretations of the same phenomenon; they are shades of the same problem. Indeed, we often see more political greed and economic grievance than the other way around. If political institutions can reduce grievances and if economic variables can influence the stability of political institutions, then economic variables will indirectly affect "grievance" factors in the Collier-Hoeffler model. And if state failure or government illegitimacy turns domestic politics into a near-anarchic world, then what Collier and Hoeffler call "greed" is really synonymous to the pursuit of survival. Civil war may be a response to either greed or grievance, but most often it is the result of both. We must now move beyond the greed-grievance distinction to explain why civil war occurs. Moreover, if it is civil war that we want to explain, our theories must be able to explain not only which countries are more likely to experience violence in general, but more specifically why violence takes the form of a civil war as opposed to other forms, such as genocide, coups, riots, or organized crime.

Notes

1. "Quantitative indexes [sic] that do not relate closely to the concepts or events that we purport to measure can lead to serious measurement error and problems for causal inference" (King, Keohane, and Verba 1994, 44). These measurement errors do not introduce bias in the analysis, but they may decrease the efficiency of the results (King et al. 1994, 155).

2. For example, Fearon's (2001) and Licklider's (1995) coding of civil wars correlates only up to the range of 50–56 percent with civil war dates included in the Correlates of War 2 project (Sarkees and Singer 2001; see also Singer and Small 1994 for an earlier version of the COW list).

3. The coding of right-hand-side variables becomes more complicated in these cases, as the variables refer to entire empires.

4. This is one potential explanation. We cannot say with certainty that any single factor caused an outcome of war or peace in a single case, because within each case study, there is little variation on which to base such a claim. Yet, the narratives in the case studies take into account over-time variation in the explanatory variables, so there is a basis for Woodwell's (and others') causal arguments.

5. That death toll qualifies the cases as a civil war according to most criteria, but Collier and Hoeffler code no civil war in the United Kingdom.

6. Woodwell (volume 2, chapter 6) also notes the deterrent effect of the Royal Ulster Constabulary's strength of 13,500 members.

7. The same is true in quantitative tests of the CH model, because they include no controls for civil society or the government's degree of liberalism.

8. Here coding wars is an issue that complicates the analysis. The Shifta war in the 1960s against Somali secessionists probably qualifies as a civil war. And some data sets (e.g., Doyle and Sambanis 2005) code a civil war in Kenya in 1991–93 because of the extensive involvement of the state in organizing and financing the violence. For a discussion of these cases, see Sambanis (2004b).

9. Indeed, subsequent versions of the CH model have performed such a test.

10. This may explain the CH model's false-negative prediction for the Biafran war. Nigeria's primary commodity export share of GDP increased to 38 percent in 1990–94.

11. Esty et al. (1995) include a trade variable in their models of state failure; so does Gleditsch (2003).

12. See, for example, Mao Tse-Tung's (1954) own writing (he was more than a "scholar" of insurgency). See, also, Kocher (2003) for a quantitative analysis. Other cases, however, do not fit this mold. In the Algerian war of the 1990s, the violence has been concentrated in regions with the greatest population density and highest rate of urbanization.

13. A civil war broke out in the Côte d'Ivoire after the end of our analysis period (the CH data set goes up to 1999). The chapter on the Côte d'Ivoire is not included in the volume, but is available online.

14. I thank Keith Darden for pointing this out.

15. See Jones-Luong (2002) for an argument of the impact of constitutional design in preventing violent conflict in Central Asian Republics in the period of post-Soviet transition.

16. Horowitz 1985; Lake and Rothchild 1996; Lijphart 1977, 1984.

17. I develop each of these topics further in several papers (Sambanis 2002; 2003; 2004a, 2004b, 2004c) and Sambanis and Zinn (2004).

18. Theoretical works and large-N studies have also suggested this. An important paper is Lichbach (1987). See, also, White (1989) on the escalation of the Northern Irish conflict.

19. For a conceptual discussion of this point, see Laitin and Posner 2001.

20. Some authors do not consider race as part of ethnicity, because a racial group need not share a belief in common descent. Horowitz (1985) considers ethnic identity to derive from all ascriptive characteristics.

21. Sambanis and Milanovic (2004) have developed a theory of secession that focuses on, among other variables, the impact of ethnic difference across regions of a country. See, also, Fearon and Laitin (2002) and Toft (2003).

22. On contagion and diffusion, see Lake and Rothchild (1998).

23. The Minorities at Risk (MAR) data set is a good source of data at the group level. But it currently does not have sufficient data on groups not "at risk" so it cannot be used to predict war onset. The MAR is moving to expand its data collection to address this issue.

24. See Doyle and Sambanis (2005) for a book-length discussion of the impact of multilateral United Nations interventions on postwar peace building and the risk of civil war recurrence.

25. A comparative case study by Frances Stewart argues that complex humanitarian emergencies occur where group identity coincides with horizontal inequality that is widening, over a number of dimensions.

26. See Sambanis and Milanovic (2004) for such a measure.

References

Anderson, Benedict. 1983. *Imagined Communities: Reflections on the Origins and Spread of Nationalism.* London:Verso.

Azam, Jean-Paul, and Constant Koidou. 2003. "Rising Threats: Containing Political Violence in Côte d'Ivoire." World Bank-Yale University Case Study.

Bates, Robert H. 1989. *Beyond the Miracle of Markets: The Polictical Economy of Agrarian Development in Kenya.* Cambridge, UK: Cambridge University Press.

Brass, Paul R. 1985. *Ethnic Groups and the State.* London: Croom-Helm.

———. 1997. *Theft of an Idol: Text and Context in the Representation of Collective Violence.* Princeton, NJ: Princeton University Press.

Brubaker, R. 1995. "National Minorities, Nationalizing States, and External National Homelands in the New Europe." *Daedalus* 124 (2): 107–32.

Brubaker, Rogers, and David D. Laitin. 1998. "Ethnic and Nationalist Violence." *Annual Review of Sociology* 24: 423–52.

Chandra, Kanchan. 2000. "Why Ethnic Parties Succeed." Ph.D. Dissertation, Harvard University.

Collier, Paul, and Anke Hoeffler. 2001. "Greed and Grievance in Civil War," World Bank Policy Research Working Paper 2355, World Bank, Washington, DC.

Darden, Keith. 2002. "The Scholastic Revolution." Mimeo, Yale University.

Davies, Victor A. B., and Abie Fofana. 2002. "Diamonds, Crime and Civil War in Sierra Leone." Paper prepared for the Yale University-World Bank Case Study Project on the Political Economy of Civil Wars.

De Figueiredo, Rui, and Barry Weingast. 1999. "The Rationality of Fear: Political Opportunism and Ethnic Conflict." In *Civil Wars, Insecurity, and Intervention,* ed. Barbara Walter and Jack Snyder, 261–302. New York: Columbia University Press.

Doyle, Michael W. 1997. "Authority and Elections in Cambodia." In *Keeping the Peace,* ed. Michael W. Doyle, Ian Johnstone, and Robert Orr, 134–64. Cambridge, UK: Cambridge University Press.

Doyle, Michael W., and Nicholas Sambanis. 2005. *Making War and Building Peace: The United Nations in the 1990s.* Princeton, NJ: Princeton University Press.

Elbadawi, Ibrahim A., and Nicholas Sambanis. 2000. "External Intervention and the Duration of Civil Wars." Policy Research Working Paper 2433, World Bank, Washington, DC.

———. 2002. "How Much War Will We See? Explaining the Prevalence of Civil War." *Journal of Conflict Resolution* 46 (3): 307–34.

Esty, Daniel C., Jack Goldstone, Ted Robert Gurr, Pamela T. Surko, and Alan N. Unger. 1995. *Working Papers: State Failure Task Force Report.* McLean, VA: Science Applications International Corporation.

Fearon, James D. 2001. "Why Do Some Civil Wars Last Longer Than Others?" Paper presented at the World Bank Conference on "Civil Wars and Post-War Transitions," University of California, Irvine, May 18–20.

Fearon, James D., and David Laitin. 2002. "Group Concentration and War." Unpublished manuscript, Stanford University.

——. 2003. "Ethnicity, Insurgency, and Civil War." *American Political Science Review* 97 (1): 91–106.

Gleditsch, Kristian. 2003. "Transnational Dimensions of Civil War." Unpublished manuscript, University of California, San Diego.

Glenny, Misha. 1999. *The Balkans: Nationalism, War, and the Great Powers, 1804–1999.* Penguin Books.

Gurr, Ted Robert. 1970. *Why Men Rebel.* Princeton, NJ: Princeton University Press.

——. 1993. *Minorities at Risk.* Washington, DC: U.S. Institute of Peace.

——. 2000. Peoples Versus States: Minorities at Risk in the New Century. Washington, DC: U.S. Institute of Peace.

Hardin, Russell. 1995. *One for All: The Logic of Group Conflict.* Princeton, NJ: Princeton University Press.

Hechter, Michael. 2001. *Containing Nationalism.* Oxford: Oxford University Press.

Hegre, Håvard. 2003. "Disentangling Democracy and Development as Determinants of Armed Conflict." Paper presented at the Annual Meeting of International Studies Association, Portland, OR, February 27.

Hegre, Håvard, T. Ellingsen, S. Gates, and N.-P. Gleditsch. 2001. "Toward a Democratic Civil Peace? Democracy, Political Change, and Civil War, 1816–1992." *American Political Science Review* 95: 33–48.

Horowitz, Donald, L. 1985. *Ethnic Groups in Conflict.* Berkeley and Los Angeles: University of California Press.

——. 1991. "Self-Determination: Politics, Philosophy, and Law." In *NOMOS XXXIX,* ed. Ian Shapiro and Will Kymlicka. New York: NYU Press.

Iatrides, John O. 1993. "The Doomed Revolution: Communist Insurgency in Postwar Greece." In *Stopping the Killing: How Civil Wars End,* ed. Roy Licklider. New York: NYU Press.

Jones-Luong, Pauline. 2002. *Institutional Change and Political Continuity in Post-Soviet Central Asia: Power, Perceptions, and Pacts.* Cambridge, UK/New York: Cambridge University Press.

Kalyvas, Stathis N. 2003. "What Is Political Violence? On the Ontology of Civil War." *Perspectives on Politics* 1 (3): 475–94.

Kasfir, Nelson. 1979. "Explaining Ethnic Political Participation." *World Politics* 31 (3): 365–88.

King, Gary, Robert O. Keohane, and Sidney Verba. 1994. *Designing Social Inquiry: Scientific Inference in Qualitative Research.* Princeton, NJ: Princeton University Press.

Kocher, Matthew. 2003. "Human Ecology and Civil War." Ph.D. Dissertation, University of Chicago.

Laitin, David D., and Dan Posner. 2001. "The Implications of Constructivism for Constructing Ethnic Fractionalization Indices." Mimeo.

Lake, David A., and Donald Rothchild. 1996. "Containing Fear: The Origins and Management of Ethnic Conflict." *International Security* 21 (2): 41–75.

——. eds. 1998. *The International Spread of Ethnic Conflict: Fear, Diffusion, and Escalation.* Princeton, NJ: Princeton University Press.

Lichbach, M. I. 1987. "Deterrence or escalation? The puzzle of aggregate studies of repression and dissent." *Journal of Conflict Resolution* 31 (2): 266–97.

Licklider, Roy. 1995. "The Consequences of Negotiated Settlements in Civil Wars, 1945–1993." *American Political Science Review* 89 (3): 681–90.

Lijphart, Arend. 1977. *Democracy in Plural Societies.* New Haven, CT: Yale University Press.

——. 1984. *Democracies: Patterns of Majoritarian and Consensus Government in Twenty-One Countries.* New Haven, CT: Yale University Press.

Linz, Juan. 1996. "The Perils of Presidentialism." In *Global Resurgence of Democracy,* 2nd ed., ed. Larry Diamond and Marcg F. Plattner. Baltimore: Johns Hopkins University Press.

Mueller, John. 2001. "The Remnants of War: Thugs as Residual Combatants." Mimeo. Ohio State University.

Przeworski, A., M. E. Alvarez, J. A. Cheibub, and F. Limongi. 2000. *Democracy and Development: Political Institutions and Well-Being in the World, 1950–1990.* Cambridge, UK: Cambridge University Press.

Regan, Patrick M. 2000. *Civil Wars and Foreign Powers.* Ann Arbor, MI: Michigan University Press.

——. 2002. "Third Party Interventions and the Duration of Intrastate Conflicts." *Journal of Conflict Resolution* 46 (1): 55–73.

Reynal-Querol, Marta. 2002. "Ethnicity, Political Systems, and Civil War." *Journal of Conflict Resolution* 46 (1): 29–54.

Ross, Michael L. 2000. "Does Oil Hinder Democracy?" *World Politics* 53: 325–61.

Rothchild, Donald. 2002. "Settlement Terms and Post-agreement Stability." In *Ending Civil Wars,* ed. Stephen Stedman, Donald Rothchild, and Elizabeth Cousens. Boulder, CO: Lynne Rienner.

Sambanis, Nicholas. 1999. "United Nations Peacekeeping in Theory and in Cyprus." Ph.D. Dissertation, Princeton University.

——. 2001. "Do Ethnic and Non-Ethnic Civil Wars Have the Same Causes? A Theoretical and Empirical Inquiry" (Part 1). *Journal of Conflict Resolution.* 45 (3): 259–82.

——. 2002. "A Review of Recent Advances and Future Directions in the Literature on Civil War." *Defense and Peace Economics* 13 (2): 215–43.

——. 2003. "The Causes of Genocide and Civil War: Are They More Similar Than We Thought?" Unpublished manuscript, Yale University.

——. 2004a. "Expanding Economic Models of Civil War Using Case Studies." *Perspectives on Politics* 2 (2): 259–80.

——. 2004b. "What Is a Civil War? Conceptual and Empirical Complexities of an Operational Definition." *Journal of Conflict Resolution* 48 (6): 814–58.

——. 2004c. "What Is an 'Ethnic' War? Organization and Interests in Ethnic Insurgency." Unpublished manuscript, Yale University.

Sambanis, Nicholas, and Branko Milanovic. 2004. "Explaining the Demand for Sovereignty." Paper presented at the Carnegie Corporation-YCIAS Conference on Self-Determination, May 15–16.

Sambanis, Nicholas, and Annalisa Zinn. 2004. "The Escalation of Self-Determination Movements: From Protest to Violence." Paper presented at the Carnegie Corporation-YCIAS Conference on Self-Determination, May 15–16.

Sarkees, Meredith Reid, and J. David Singer. 2001. "The Correlates of War Data sets: The Totality of War." Paper prepared for the 42nd Annual Convention of the International Studies Association, Chicago, IL, February 20–24.

Singer, David J., and Melvin Small. 1994. *Correlates of War Project: International and Civil War Data, 1816–1992.* Inter-University Consortium for Political and Social Research, Ann Arbor, MI.

Sisk, Timothy. 1996. *Power Sharing and International Mediation in Ethnic Conflict.* Washington, DC: United States Institute of Peace.

Smith, M. L. R. 1999. "The Intellectual Internment of a Conflict: The Forgotten War in Northern Ireland." *International Affairs* 75 (1): 77–98.

Tilly, Charles. 2003. *The Politics of Collective Violence.* Cambridge, MA: Cambridge University Press.

Toft, Monica. 2003. *The Geography of Fear.* Princeton, NJ: Princeton University Press.

Tse-Tung, Mao. 1954. *The Chinese Revolution and the Chinese Communist Party.* Peking: Foreign Languages Press.

Walter, Barbara F. 2002. *Committing to Peace.* Princeton, NJ: Princeton University Press.

Wantchekon, Leonard, and Zviika Neeman. 2000. "A Theory of Post-Civil War Democratization." Mimeo, July 28.

White, Robert W. 1989. "From Peaceful Protest to Guerilla War: Micromobilization of the Provisional Irish Republican Army." *American Journal of Sociology* 94 (May): 1277–1302.

Woodward, Susan. 1995. *Balkan Tragedy: Chaos and Dissolution After the Cold War.* Washington, DC: The Brookings Institution.

Woodwell, Douglas. 2004. "Unwelcome Neighbors: Shared Ethnicity and International Conflict During the Cold War." *International Studies Quarterly* 48 (1): 197–223.

Contributors

HABAYE AG MOHAMED is a lawyer based in Nouakchott, Mauritania. A Malian national, he is presently working as a consultant with the EU, Oxfam, and Espoir on human rights intervention issues in the subregion. Recent work has focused on human rights training in Mauritania, Mali, Senegal, and Burkina Faso. Past research has also included studies of citizenship and development in West Africa, water politics, and anti-personnel mines.

ALI ABDEL GADIR ALI holds a Ph.D. in economics from the University of Essex in England (1974). He taught economics at the Universities of Khartoum and Gezira, Sudan and the University of Kuwait and was Professor of Economics at the University of Gezira. Currently, he is an Economic Advisor at the Arab Planning Institute (Kuwait). His research interests are in development economics, including issues of policy analysis, growth, inequality, poverty, and civil wars.

PAUL COLLIER is Professor of Economics and Director of the Centre for the Study of African Economies at Oxford University. During 1998–2003, he was on leave at the World Bank as Director of the Development Research Group. He has specialized on Africa, being a founding editor of the *Journal of African Economies,* and a coauthor of the *Journal of Economic Literature* survey article on African economic performance (1999). Much of his recent research has been on conflict, including coauthorship of "Greed and Grievance in Civil War" (*Oxford Economic Papers,* 2004) and *Breaking the Conflict Trap* (Oxford University Press, 2003). In 2004 he gave a keynote address on "conflict and development" to the General Assembly of the United Nations.

IBRAHIM A. ELBADAWI, a Sudanese national, holds a Ph.D. in economics and statistics from North Carolina State and Northwestern Universities. He is a Lead Economist at the Development Economic Research Group of the World Bank and a former Director of Research at the African Economic Research Consortium

(1993–98). In 2000 he coordinated a major collaborative study (sponsored by the World Bank and several African research and policy institutions) aimed at analyzing Africa's development prospects in the next century and produced a book, *Can Africa Claim the 21st Century?* More recently he codirected the World Bank project on the economics of civil wars. He has wide research interests, covering economics of civil wars, growth, and macroeconomic issues. His regional expertise covers Africa and the Middle East.

ATTA EL-BATAHANI is Associate Professor in Political Economy and head of the Department of Political Science, Faculty of Economics, University of Khartoum. He was educated in the Sudan and Britain and is a founding member of the Sudanese Civil Society Network for Poverty Alleviation (SCSNPA). He has been a consultant to numerous international organizations and agencies, including UNDP, IDRC, IGAD, and OXFAM on a number of development topics. His research and publications span a wide range of topics, including the development impact of ethnic and religious conflicts in African countries; governance and state institutional reform in Africa and the Middle East; gender politics; the politics of HIV/AIDS in Sudan; and peripheral capitalism and political Islam in Sub-Saharan Africa.

KISANGANI F. EMIZET is Associate Professor of Political Science at Kansas State University. He received his Ph.D. in political science at the University of Iowa. He is the author of several book chapters and a monograph titled *Zaire after Mobutu: A Case of Humanitarian Emergency* (Helsinki: UN University WIDER, 1997). His articles have appeared in *African Studies Review, Journal of Modern African Studies, Comparative Political Studies,* and other political science journals. He was a Fulbright Fellow at the University of Oregon and a Rockefeller Fellow at the University of Kinshasa-Congo.

LAUDEMIRO FRANCISCO is a Ph.D. candidate at the Department of African Studies, Howard University, Washington, DC. Between 1995 and 2001 he lectured in the departments of Economics and International Relations of the Higher Institute for International Relations (ISRI) based in Maputo, Mozambique.

ANKE HOEFFLER is a research economist at the Centre for the Study of African Economies at Oxford University and has worked as a consultant to the World Bank's Development Economics Research Group. Her research interests are focused on economic growth and the economics of conflict. She is the coauthor (with Paul Collier) of "Greed and Grievance in Civil Wars," published in *Oxford Economic Papers.*

MACARTAN HUMPHREYS is Assistant Professor of Political Science at Columbia University in New York. His work is motivated by concerns over the linkages between politics, conflict, and human development. He is a research scholar at the

Center for Globalization and Sustainable Development at the Earth Institute and a member of the Millennium Development goals project poverty task force where he works on conflict and development issues. Ongoing research includes experimental studies of ethnic politics, econometric work on natural resource conflicts, game theoretic work on political bargaining, and survey work of ex-combatants in Sierra Leone.

MWANGI S. KIMENYI holds a Ph.D. in economics from the Center for the Study of Public Choice, George Mason University. He is currently Associate Professor of Economics at the University of Connecticut. Previously he was Assistant Professor of Economics at the University of Mississippi. Between 1999 and 2004, he served as the founding Director of the Kenya Institute for Public Policy Research and Analysis (KIPPRA). He has published over 60 refereed journal articles and authored and edited seven books.

MIRIAM R. LOWI is Associate Professor of Political Science at The College of New Jersey. Her research interests concern the natural resource dimension of political behavior, with a concentration in the Middle East and North Africa. Her earlier publications treated transboundary water disputes and environmental security. Currently, she works on the political economy of development in oil-exporting states, and she is writing a comparative study of the politics of breakdown, with Algeria as the central case. She has also published on the political economy of violence in Algeria, including "Algérie 1992–2002: une nouvelle économie politique de la violence," *Maghreb-Machrek* (France, No. 175, spring 2003).

LÉONCE NDIKUMANA is Associate Professor of Economics at the University of Massachusetts, Amherst. His research is in applied macroeconomics and economic development. His main interest in macroeconomics is on the role of financial systems for investment and long-run economic growth. His research in economic development investigates the causes and effects of capital flight from African countries, and the economics and politics of conflict in the Great Lakes region of Africa.

NJUGUNA S. NDUNG'U is the Director of Training at the African Economic Research Consortium (AERC), Nairobi. He holds a Ph.D. in economics from the University of Gothenburg, Sweden and Masters and Bachelors degrees in economics from the University of Nairobi. He has lectured in advanced economic theory and econometrics at the University of Nairobi, where he now is Associate Professor of Economics. He has been a researcher with AERC network and has published in international journals as well as chapters in books on economic policy issues ranging from economic growth, poverty reduction, inflation, interest rate and exchange rate issues, macroeconomic performance in Sub-Saharan Africa, financial management, public sector growth, external debt, financial liberalization in Anglophone Africa, structural adjustment, employment, and labor market issues.

FLORIBERT NGARUKO is working with the World Bank's Operations Evaluation Department (OED) in Washington, DC and the Global Development Network (GDN). Since the 1990s, he has authored a number of studies on topics including gender, corruption, decentralization, industrial development, and interpersonal private transfers, with a focus on Sub-Saharan Africa. He holds a Ph.D. in economics, and his current research interests include the economics and politics of conflict and postconflict reconstruction in the Great Lakes region of Africa, and the politics and economics of inequality, institutions, development, and growth. He is currently affiliated with the Centre d'Etudes en Macroéconomie et Finance Internationale (CEMAFI), University of Nice, France.

JANVIER D. NKURUNZIZA works for the United Nations Economic Commission for Africa (UNECA). He holds a D. Phil. in economics from the University of Oxford where he was affiliated with the Centre for the Study of African Economies. He was a Post-doctoral Fellow at Harvard University and Coordinator of a Discussion Group on African Politics in the Institute of Politics. Before joining Oxford University in 1998, he worked for the United Nations Economic Commission for Africa after a two-year period as a researcher and lecturer at the University of Burundi. He is a research member of the African Economic Research Consortium (AERC) and the Global Development Network (GDN). He has authored a number of studies on Burundi and his research interests include economic growth, political economy of Africa, economics of civil wars, and applied industrial organization.

NICHOLAS SAMBANIS is Associate Professor of Political Science at Yale University. He received his Ph.D. from Princeton University's Woodrow Wilson School in June 1999. From 1999 to 2001, he held the position of economist at the World Bank's Development Economics Research Group, where he was part of the core research team for the project on "The Economics of Political and Criminal Violence." He has researched several topics on ethnic conflict and political violence. He is coauthor of *Making War and Building Peace: United Nations Peace Operations,* a book evaluating the effectiveness of UN peacekeeping and peacebuilding after civil wars.

JEREMY M. WEINSTEIN is Assistant Professor of Political Science at Stanford University. His current research focuses on the formation and internal organization of rebel groups. He draws on extensive fieldwork in Uganda, Mozambique, Sierra Leone, and Peru. Weinstein holds a Ph.D. in political economy and government from Harvard University.

ANNALISA ZINN is a Ph.D. candidate in the Department of Political Science at Yale University. She specializes in the political economy of political and ethnic violence. She received a B.A. in ethics, politics, and economics from Yale in 2001 and a M.A. in political science, also from Yale, in 2003.

Index

Note: Information presented in tables, figures, and notes is denoted by *t*, *f*, or n, respectively.

A

Abacha, Sani, 108
ABAKO. *see* Alliance de Bakongo
Action Group (Nigeria), 97. *see also* Nigeria
Adoula, Cyrile, 68, 69, 70, 71
AFDL. *see* Alliance of Democratic Liberation Forces
Afghanistan, 4*t*, 231
África Livre, 178–79
African National Congress (ANC), and Mozambique, 163, 180
AIS. *see* Armée Islamique du Salut
Algeria, 221–241
  area of, 223
  Berbers in, contribution of, 223
  causes of conflict in, 325
  in CH model, 226–27, 240–41, 304–05
  civilian killings in, 235
  counterinsurgency in, financing of, 236–37
  coup in, 221
  dates of civil war in, 4*t*
  diaspora of, 243n16
  economy of, 223–25
  elections in, 221
  exports of, 223
  financing of insurgency in, 232–33

food importation of, 224
geography of violence in, 237–38, 240
government responses to, 234
gross national product of, 224
industrialization in, 223–24
insurgency in, attraction to, 234
looting in, 238
and Mali, 255, 256, 285–86, 292n41
multi-party system in, 221
negotiations in, 236
objectives of insurgency in, 232–34
oil in, 223–25, 227, 238, 241
opposition in, emergence of, 225–26
population of, 222–23, 225
poverty in, 242n4
rebel organizations in, 227, 230, 231–32
recruitment in, 231–32
soldiers in, 234
terrain of, 223
unemployment in, 224
violence in, phases of, 239*t*, 243n25
vs. other countries, 228*t*, 229*t*
War of Independence in (1954-62), 276
Alliance de Bakongo (ABAKO), 66. *see also* Congo, Dem. Rep. of
Alliance of Democratic Liberation Forces (AFDL), 77, 78*t*, 86n11. *see also* Congo, Dem. Rep. of
America. *see* United States
Anas, Abdallah, 242n12
ANC. *see* African National Congress; Armée Nationale Congolaise

339

CPSIA information can be obtained at www.ICGtesting.com
Printed in the USA
LVOW11s1620150915

454264LV00003B/734/P

UNDERSTANDING CIVIL WAR